Refuse to Stand Silently By

For Ruth —
   Thanks for your
genuine concern!
   Eliot W. Sister

May 8, 1992

—

Doubleday
New York   London   Toronto   Sydney   Auckland

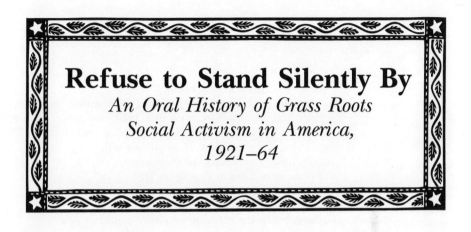

Refuse to Stand Silently By

*An Oral History of Grass Roots
Social Activism in America,
1921–64*

Edited and with an Introduction by
Eliot Wigginton

PUBLISHED BY DOUBLEDAY
a division of Bantam Doubleday Dell Publishing Group, Inc.
666 Fifth Avenue, New York, New York 10103

DOUBLEDAY and the portrayal of an anchor with
a dolphin are trademarks of Doubleday,
a division of Bantam Doubleday Dell
Publishing Group, Inc.

The interviews with Julian Bond herein originally appeared in a
different form in *Southern Exposure*, Volume III, Number 4
(Winter 1976). Used by permission.

BOOK DESIGN BY ANNE LING

Library of Congress Cataloging-in-Publication Data

Refuse to stand silently by : an oral history of grass roots social
activism in America, 1921–1964 / edited with an introduction by
Eliot Wigginton.—1st ed.
    p.   cm.
"A Greene communications book."
Includes bibliographical references and index.
    1. Social movements—United States—History—20th century.
2. United States—Social conditions. 3. Highlander Research
and Education Center (Knoxville, Tenn.) I. Wigginton, Eliot.
HN57.R38 1991
303.48′4′0973—dc20   91-31101
                                    CIP

A GREENE *Communications*® Book
ISBN 0-385-17572-8
Copyright © 1991 by Highlander Center
All Rights Reserved
Printed in the United States of America
May 1992
1 3 5 7 9 10 8 6 4 2
FIRST EDITION

This book is dedicated to Myles Horton and to all those who carry his spirit forward.

What's it going to take? That's the question. We know we need some big changes, but how are we going to get them? I think it's going to take the courage of people who refuse to stand silently by.

—Pete Seeger

Contents

Introduction

This book is about people who finally said, "That's it. Enough. That's all I can stand," and then, instead of quitting, moved into action.

It is also about an institution named Highlander, but that too is largely about a man who said, "Enough."

Each of the men and women interviewed for this book played a critical role in the early days of some of the most painful struggles for social justice our nation has experienced in this century. Some, like Rosa Parks, blazed into prominence for one brief moment and then backed gracefully out of public view, having made a contribution dramatic enough for any single lifetime.

Others, like Andrew Young and Pete Seeger, turned headfirst into the winds of public opinion early in their lives and have struggled eloquently, publicly, and unceasingly ever since for equal rights for all our citizens.

The roles these individuals played have been widely documented. Most of the readers of this book will know, for example, what it is that Rosa Parks was finally moved to do. Less well documented, however, are the backgrounds of these individuals. Who were their parents? Where and how were they raised? What were the formative influences in their lives?

In part, this book tries to answer questions like those. The reason, though, is only partially about supplementing the historical record. At the core of this book there is a large question that has to do with courage. When people are assured that if they take certain stands, they will be vilified, ostracized, fired, jailed, or shot at and perhaps even killed, then where does the courage come from to take those stands? What is the source of the values that ultimately lead to that very private, personal, and frightening decision to act instead of withdrawing into the passive role of spectator? Or is the act less a question of values than circumstance?

Because I am a public school teacher, I especially wanted to explore the possible influence of elementary or secondary school experiences on the values, the determination, or even the shape of the actions those interviewed took as adults. Were any of them ever led by a concerned teacher to take an Emperor's New Clothes look at some of what was happening in the larger society around them? Did they ever look at the specific causes, for example, of our labor problems or the laws of segregation? Did they study civil disobedience, or the inalienable rights that come with citizenship and were born in the fact that this country itself was founded through protest? Did they ever talk in class about the fact that they might someday not only have a chance, but an obligation, to participate in the righting of certain wrongs?

I knew that such discussions were not common public school fare, but I did start this project believing that with this group of individuals at least, something in their educational backgrounds must have been formative. I was not prepared for how completely wrong I was.

Much more influential were parents, family, the church. And all were affected to varying degrees by the fact of Highlander. Even Studs Terkel, though he has never been to the school itself and never participated in a workshop there, feels the energy that has radiated from the place for sixty years.

As related in the interview with May Justus, who was there, the school was founded in 1932 near Monteagle, Tennessee, by Myles Horton and Don West, and then directed through nearly forty years of its existence by Myles. Later led by Mike Clark, then Hubert Sapp, and now John Gaventa, the style of education that has been the school's hallmark has remained consistent—and virtually unique:

On a Friday afternoon, cars begin to arrive at Highlander's graveled parking lot. They bear license plates from Kentucky, Vir-

ginia, and Tennessee. From the cars emerge adults, in groups of
two and three, carrying suitcases. Many have never met each other
before. They straggle toward a long, two-story, cement-block building where they are directed by a staff member toward sleeping
quarters: two separate, nearly bare rooms filled, barracks-style,
with metal bunk beds—men on one side, women on the other,
separated by a central core of showers and toilets. A bit bewildered
and concerned by the nearly complete lack of privacy, they nevertheless stake out their claims to beds with their suitcases and then
drift back outdoors, joking somewhat nervously, to reconnoiter. As
they talk, still clustered in groups of two and three, they inevitably
stand facing the panorama of the ridges of the Great Smoky
Mountains spread out before them like a giant mural.

At 6 P.M., a dinner bell rings and the groups move instinctively
toward the sound, merging together into two lines that move
down either side of a table on which have been placed serving
bowls filled with beef stew, fried okra, corn on the cob, salad, and
cornbread. Joined by the residential staff, including Nina, the
cook, and Myles, who is just back from a trip to Central America,
the thirty-five or forty adults gather around wooden tables, each of
which seats ten, and begin to meet each other. When the meal is
finished, a staff member requests volunteers to help with the clear-
ing and washing of dishes, and almost automatically, several stand
to help. The request does not have to be made again.

By 8 P.M., the visitors and those staff assigned to the workshop
have gathered in a circle of rocking chairs in the circular meeting
room above the dining area. The meeting begins, as always, with
music. Guy and Candie Carawan lead the group in singing spirituals and anthems of protest: "This Little Light of Mine," "Will the
Circle Be Unbroken," "Down By the Riverside," "We Shall Overcome." Though many of these people may not yet know each
other, they know these songs, and the room is filled with harmony
and rhythmic clapping and smiles of recognition and gratitude for
songs that have given strength and sustenance to battered spirits.

In the silence that follows the last song, a staff member asks
the visitors to introduce themselves and tell the group something
about their communities and the specific concern that has
brought them here this evening. As each tells his or her story, it
becomes clear to an outside observer that the workshop that has

just begun has a central theme. In each of the communities represented, toxic chemicals from nearby factories are being dumped in convenient mountain hollows into improperly constructed landfills by truckers hired by the plants to pick up their waste and "get rid of it." The water supplies for the communities downstream have been poisoned. The streams run red and yellow. Water from some residents' wells is undrinkable. Children have developed cancer.

The visitors in this room, some of whom did not finish high school, and none of whom has attended college, simply do not know what to do. All their lives, people more powerful and better connected have controlled their destinies—have dictated their occupations and their working conditions and their salaries and have constricted their options—and now these same people are killing them. They don't know what to do, but they are ready to do something.

It is with a shout of frustration into the Tennessee night, then, that this workshop, and hundreds that have preceded it, begins.

By Sunday, one has the beginnings of an appreciation for the wisdom of the rather contrary assumption that is the bedrock of Highlander's educational philosophy. Saturday was characterized by twelve hours of wide-ranging, heated, emotional, and sometimes wearingly repetitious discussions punctuated and refocused by the insertion from Highlander staff of factual information that these people did not have, such as names of parent companies, subsidiaries, previous court cases and their dispositions, pending litigation, and sources of other facts and figures. Today, in marked contrast to the day before, the participants, again gathered in the circle of rocking chairs, again in turn, relate precisely what they intend to do about the problem upon returning home. A sense of forward momentum begins to emerge, a sense of hope, a sense that something *can* be done—and that it will work. And if an academic schooled in the study of the history of people's struggles were to find the plans expressed here less ambitious than he might have hoped, and less sophisticated, he would miss the whole point. For the point is the truth of this assumption: If people who share a common problem come together, without solutions but with a reservoir of personal experience, when provided with accurate information, those people have the wisdom and intelligence and insight among themselves, collectively, to find the answers to their problems. In fact, they *are* the answers to their problems.

And their realization and acceptance of this simple but deeply profound fact is, at this moment, on this Sunday, a more important result than any of the specific solutions that they have forged. And had that visiting academic (or a staff member) said, "Now listen to me. I know what I'm talking about. This is exactly what you must do next," he would have subverted the workshop's most important goal.

A noon meal, a few last songs, and the workshop ends. Addresses and phone numbers have been exchanged. People eat slowly and hang around for several hours afterward, savoring new friendships, new connections, and tying down final plans for action that may now involve several communities working in concert.

And when they get home, Highlander staff will stay in touch, encouraging them, nourishing their work, providing them with new contacts and sources of information, sending them materials and supplies as they are needed, cheering as their sometimes relatively unsophisticated early moves evolve into more grounded and self-assured and politically astute and effective tactics; and those who begin to emerge as leaders in the fight will be urged to return to Highlander to share their experiences with new workshops while simultaneously becoming both reenergized themselves and introduced to other causes.

Of all the various elements that characterize the Highlander approach—music, the residential and family-style dining components of every workshop, the gentle, affirming, sensitive hand of staff, the exclusion of self-professed "experts"—the one that hits hardest is the unvarying respect those associated with the school have for working people, their experiences, and the ability they have when working collectively to find unique solutions to the problems that beset their lives.

And because the solutions they find are often elegantly tailored to their particular circumstances (and therefore workable), and because the solutions are, from the outset, *theirs*, an almost fatalistic acceptance of their status as victims slowly gives way to a growing sense of strength, of power, of control over their futures.

Inevitably, the actions of these people over the years challenged the status quo and battered at the gates of societal, educational, political, and/or corporate institutions. Thus Highlander found itself under constant scrutiny by the FBI, which suspected that the school was run by Communists, and by various state agencies, convinced that the school was wantonly breaking state laws. The suspicions of the state agencies, at least, were undeniably accurate. Convinced, for example, that the laws of segregation were unconstitutional in a country that reveres a document that begins, "We hold these truths to be self-evident," Myles Horton and his staff held numerous residential workshops during the days of the civil rights movement that were attended by blacks and whites together. In return, local law officers not only raided the school and jailed some of the participants of one workshop, but assisted the state of Tennessee in later confiscating the Monteagle property, with all its buildings and furnishings and all the farm's equipment, and selling the whole lot at public auction. In these attempts to stamp out activities they regarded as un-American and unpatriotic, they had engaged, paradoxically, in a conflict with people who were arguably far more American than they.

In any event, rather than quitting, Myles simply moved to downtown Knoxville, reorganized the old Highlander Folk School as the Highlander Research and Education Center, and continued operating. Today, the Highlander Center is located outside New Market, Tennessee, on a 110-acre farm that the board of directors is still struggling to pay for.

In retrospect, it is almost hard to imagine what all the fuss was about: hard to imagine a time within the memories of still-living men and women when adults and children labored together, driven like mules through endless days of mind-numbing, back-breaking routine in the Dickensian environments of mines and mills; hard to imagine a time—Lord, in *my* lifetime—when blacks were regarded as so inferior that they were separated from whites by *law* except as servants. Hard to imagine. Undeniably a measure of how far we've come. And yet there are many wars yet to wage, several of which, right now, if not won, can end all life on the only planet that can sustain us.

All of which brings up an issue worth considering: To what extent should it be not only permissible, but even imperative, for public school teachers to help their students understand both the great human and environmental issues of this world's societies, and the processes by which those issues have been and still must be addressed? To say that the discussion of such issues in public schools is inappropriate is, in my opinion, irresponsible and indefensible. Though certain site-specific community tensions may be "too hot," and thrusting a community's children into the midst of them could only be destructive and counterproductive, still, in every community there are generous opportunities for sensitive discussion—and action.

I teach in a public high school in an Appalachian mountain community so conservative that a teacher can be fired simply for having a beer with dinner in a public restaurant. Every semester, however, the twenty-five seniors in my college-level research class prepare publishable papers in MLA format which explore issues that range across the spectrum of their interests, from teenage pregnancy and sex education to corporal punishment and acid rain. In every instance, they must "bring the topic home" and relate it specifically to its implications for our county. Recently, a student project was partially responsible for the implementation of our school system's first AIDS policy. Another student project was consulted by the producer of an ABC Barbara Walters special about the dropout problem in rural America, and with the student as entrée, the producer was able to interview the same dropouts my student had interviewed.

During the summer, I also teach graduate-level classes for practicing teachers at several colleges and universities, and teachers from those courses have found that they can involve their students in responsible activities that the community not only does not condemn, but applauds. In Harlan, Kentucky, for example, one teacher's second graders produced a half-hour videotape about garbage and pollution in their county that won a Take Pride in America award. In Gainesville, Georgia, as the result of a classmate's abduction and murder, another teacher's fifth graders wrote and published a twenty-four-page booklet about child safety that they distributed, free, to every student in their elementary school. In Winder, Georgia, high school students mounted a successful campaign to save and restore an endangered covered bridge that spanned a river between their county and its neighbor and thus involved two separate groups of local politicians. Middle school students in the classroom of another Kentucky teacher tracked a trainload of coal mined in their community from its source to its final disposition, studying, at the same time, the extent to which its final use contributed to air pollution.

Around the country, other students have adopted and cleaned streams, and they monitor their conditions regularly. Others have raised the awareness of the danger of aerosol sprays to such an extent that their communities now point with pride to highway signs proclaiming their town as aerosol-free. McDonald's no longer uses Styrofoam containers, partially as a result of student action.

None of these activities is as dramatic, perhaps, as those recounted by the individuals interviewed for this book, and none is going to result in the kinds of changes documented here, but all are blood relations. None of the teachers has been fired. No children have been angrily withdrawn from school. And, most important, the students involved now have some understanding of a *process* not unlike Highlander's by which problems are identified, solutions are shaped to fit the local situation, and action is taken. And if these students are interviewed years from now, most will identify such projects as being among the most memorable events of their public school careers. And one holds to the hope that because the process has been demystified, some of these students as adults will continue the energy this book represents, leading— or at least participating in—positive change rather than retreating into negativism of self-centered preening. One hopes.

And Highlander, traditionally a gathering place for adults, began to conduct workshops for teenagers shortly before Myles' death in 1990.

As a Highlander board member, I offered to put this book together partly as a way of expressing my gratitude for all that the institution has taught me. (Royalties generated will support that work, perhaps helping, finally, to pay off the debt on the new farm and center.) Primarily, though, it is a celebration: of foundations like the Field Foundation and the Emil Schwarzhaupt Foundation, and of the numerous individual donors who supported the school's work despite the controversies that swirled around it; of an educational process that empowers rather than indoctrinates or belittles; and of people—once ordinary people like you and me— who are now regarded as extraordinary because they had the courage to do what all of us could do if we would: stand in the face of clear wrong and injustice and declare, "This has to stop."

And as we dare to continue to dream about an America that matches its description of itself, and a planet free of conflict and human and environmental tragedy, and as we summon up the courage and the honesty to confront the obstacles that now prevent that dream from coming true, we have, in these pages, some patterns to go by.

Eliot Wigginton

Acknowledgments

Originally intended to be published on Highlander's fiftieth birthday, this book is nearly ten years late. I accept the blame for that. It has been a long process.

Initially, I negotiated a contract with Doubleday. The advance was turned over to Highlander to pay staff members like Linda Selfridge to transcribe the tapes and type the final, edited chapters.

Next, I drafted a letter to potential interviewees and a list of criteria for the interviews and invited Highlander friends and staff and board members to help conduct them. Many responded. John Egerton, for example, interviewed Cecil Branstetter, Peter Wood conducted one of the interviews with Septima Clark, and Sue Thrasher interviewed Don West. Sue, who was on the Highlander staff at the time, soon became my primary collaborator and associate. She interviewed Ralph Tefferteller herself, but she and I also did a number of interviews together, taking advantage of the presence of subjects like Dorothy Cotton, Rosa Parks, Septima Clark, and Bernice Robinson at Highlander when they visited the school for various events.

Other interviews I conducted alone, or in the company of Rabun County High School students who happened to be traveling with me. It was all coordinated so that when I was in a city on business, and one of the subjects happened to live nearby, I'd grab the opportunity. Some of the memories are indelible. There was the day in Chicago, for example, when Studs Terkel and I went out for lunch together and then returned to his radio station where I interviewed him. Toward the end of our visit, he suddenly decided that I should also catch Ralph Helstein, the retired labor leader for the Packinghouse Workers union. Grabbing a phone, he called Ralph, set up an appointment on the spot, put me in a cab, and shot me across town to the home of a man who provided one of the most remarkable chapters in this book. As I talked with Ralph in his studio, his wife prepared dinner, and when it was ready, we were still so deeply engrossed that I got permission to bring the recorder to the table, where we continued talking until the moment I had to leave to catch my evening flight home.

Or the interview with Pete Seeger. A friend from Cornell, Jeff Sanders, had become a high school biology teacher. For the trip to Pete and Toshi's, since I had none of my students along, Jeff selected several of his, and all of us drove to Beacon together for a six-hour session. Their home overlooks the Hudson River. Through the sloop *Clearwater* and the Clearwater festivals, Pete and Toshi have been instrumental in raising public consciousness about, and subsequently cleaning the river of, pollutants which, until recently, had made the fish caught from the river inedible. That day for lunch, Toshi served shad pulled the day before from the Hudson.

As the interviews, many of them four and five hours in length, were completed, the tapes were delivered to Linda for transcribing. Copies of the transcripts were sent to me to be edited down to manageable proportions. The final edited pages, then, were sent back to Linda to be retyped.

The editing of interview material for publication is frowned upon by many oral historians who believe that the cutting/pasting/combining and eliminating of the give and take between informant and interviewer destroys the integrity of the document and the experience. I agree. In order to present the interviews intact, however, this book would have to have been over four thousand pages in length, and the reader would quickly become lost in the circuitous conversations with their false starts and their repetition. Even lightly edited, the book would have been over twice its present length, and for most readers, I believe the interviewers' questions would remain a distraction and a nuisance.

Trying to be sensitive to the needs of historians, however, I made sure that all tapes, complete transcripts, all my original pages of editing, as well as all the interviews that were not selected for publication, were deposited in the Highlander archives to be made accessible to any scholars who might wish to use them. A copy of the edited interview was sent to each informant with a self-addressed, stamped envelope so that each could make any changes and corrections he or she wished. Each then signed a permission slip.

Even after all that, however, the manuscript delivered to Doubleday was still several hundred pages too long. At this point, I ran out of steam. Over several years, I would return to the project occasionally, determined to finish it and then stalling in frustration. One Christmas I spent the entire vacation working with the material, and despite ten days of work, I was able to cut only about sixty pages. With Sue Thrasher's help, I eliminated some interviews entirely. Still too long.

The impending publication of *The Long Haul,* a book about Highlander's educational philosophy by Myles Horton and Herb Kohl, also from Doubleday, provided the impetus required to conclude this project once and for all.

Finally, through John Egerton, I found and hired Randy Greene, a former editor at Doubleday who now owns Greene Communications in Cynthiana, Kentucky, and specializes in getting people like me out of fixes like this. Randy did the additional cutting and summarizing and reorganizing that I couldn't do myself.

John Gaventa, the Highlander director, provided the Afterword and Highlander staffer Candie Carawan prepared the Biographical Profiles.

Many people pitched in, in other words, to bring this volume to you, and without their help, it is absolutely true that this book would not exist.

Eliot Wigginton

Refuse to Stand Silently By

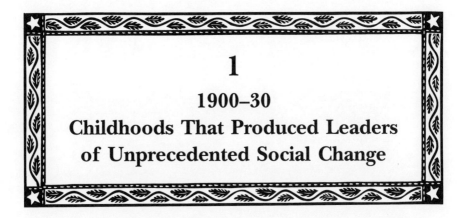

1
1900–30
Childhoods That Produced Leaders
of Unprecedented Social Change

The only people who ever are known in terms of any kind of social change . . . , and democratic ideas, are people who have been imaginative and courageous enough to do what's unpopular. It's true of the Founding Fathers and it's true today. . . .

People who set out to be respected and to be famous, however, seldom get beyond mediocrity. I think anybody that wanted to be recognized and get accepted, and tried to design their life to do it, would be doomed to be recognized only in a very small circle which had no real social significance.

Most of the people in this book, on the other hand, just didn't give a damn about fame and were going to do what they thought was the right thing, and wanted to be useful, and didn't want to serve their own interests, but had a vision of being part of a larger society, and decided to act because they wanted to do it, because they believed in it. . . .

—*MYLES HORTON*

★

"Little Ma" From the Promise Land School
Septima Clark

A black woman gathered evidence. Then the National Association for the Advancement of Colored People agreed to use that evidence in a South Carolina lawsuit. In 1936—the year that Jesse Owens garnered four gold medals at the Berlin Olympics—the state court ordered that black teachers in Columbia's public schools be put on the same pay scale as white teachers.

Nineteen years after her victory, however, this same black woman was dismissed as a public school teacher in Charleston. Her only "offense" was that she refused to deny her membership in the NAACP. But even this dismissal in 1955 did not end Septima Clark's contributions as a teacher. Within two years, she helped establish what became known as "Citizenship Schools."

This program—which the Southern Christian Leadership Conference expanded in the early sixties—taught thousands of blacks in the South how to read and write. And equipped with such skills, these blacks overcame discriminatory barriers that had prevented them from registering to vote since the Civil War. One wonders: Was an entire political revolution rooted, in part, within a solitary black teacher's determination? If so, then where did she get such foresight and wisdom and courage?

My father's name was Peter Porcher Poinsette. His background has always been confusing to me. His mother must have been brought to the Bahamas, and then brought from there to some part of Georgia. I understand that a ship named the

Wanderer was involved in that trip from the Bahamas, but the story is confused. At any rate, he was raised as a slave on the Joel Poinsett plantation on the Waccamaw River near Georgetown, South Carolina, and his mother, whose name was Maggie Shine, must have been there too because she died on that same plantation. His brothers were all scattered to other locations, so although they knew each other, they weren't reared together; and I never heard him speak of a father at all.

He did tell me about his mother dying, though. He said the body stayed in a little shack all night long until they could get somebody to make a coffin. Then at work the next day, they would sing something like "Way Down Yonder by the Cornfield," and that would let all the people know that there was going to be a funeral that night in the woods by the cornfield. That night, they lighted flambeaux and went through the woods singing. They had to bury her by night because they didn't have time in the day. Then they got back before sunrise and went right back to work. He didn't tell the story in a violent tone [as though he were angry about it], but this is what they did. I can remember him talking about that.

And he told me about his owner, also. Poinsett is the man who gave the poinsettia its name, and he was a unionist. Apparently, although he kept slaves, he was a very nonviolent man and had wonderful ways of working with them. My father never found any fault with him whatsoever. In fact, he didn't find any fault with any white people at that time; he was just that way. The reading and writing that he didn't get didn't bother him. He just talked about taking these Poinsett kids to school and not ever being able to go in and learn to write his name. But he didn't feel worried about that. Taking the kids to school was his main job, and he was just proud to be one of the "house natives"—or house servants— and not have to work in the fields. The children were ones Poinsett's wife had by a previous marriage to a Mr. McGuire, and my father would take them to school every morning, take their books into the classroom, and then go back outside and tie the horses up and stay there on the doorstep or under a tree regardless of the weather until they were ready to go back home. He never resented the fact that he wasn't allowed to learn himself.

He didn't even find fault when some of the slaves had to get whippings. He said they got that because they would steal. He said the cook would sometimes leave a key out on the outside, and they would get this key and go into a smokehouse or one of the houses where the food was stored and steal some. When they were caught, they got a whipping. I guess he thought they deserved it.

Then when the Civil War came, he took water to the Southern soldiers who were fighting to keep him a slave. The Yankees were in the harbor coming to free him, but he helped carry supplies for the cannons the Southern soldiers were using. The thought of being freed frightened many of the slaves because they didn't know what was going to happen to them. Some of them were afraid they wouldn't be able to eat. They only thought of that paternalistic life that they had, where they were furnished food and that one piece of cloth that covered their body. This is what he told me. I can't remember the name of that thing that they used to make to cover them, but that's all they had. A man would bring up some cloth, and each one would get a piece, and that little shirt thing that they made to wear was all that they had, and a number of them felt that they wouldn't even have this anymore, and so he said they really cried. There were some people on the plantation who had a different way of thinking, but he never sided with any of them.

He just grew up not knowing it was wrong for him to have to do things like stand back until every white person was served. He didn't even learn how to write his name until after the First World War when Joel Poinsett's wife's sister helped him get a job as a custodian at the first USO that was opened here on King Street. They paid him in checks, and he had to sign his name to cash them. By this time, he had eight children, and one of them—my youngest brother—sat down on the floor with him and taught him to write his name.

He met my mother in Haiti. Her name was Victoria Warren Anderson Poinsette. She was born in Charleston, and her mother was part Santee Indian, but as a little girl, her mother died, and her two married brothers who were working in Haiti inspecting cigars in a factory there came and got her and her two sisters and raised them in Haiti. After slavery, my father found a job working on a Clyde Line steamer out of Charleston harbor, and when the ship went to Haiti, he met her, brought her to Jacksonville to marry her, and then brought her back to Charleston to live.

My mother had learned to read and write quite well. Apparently the English in Haiti did a much better job of education than was done for the slaves in South Carolina. Whatever school it was she went to, she boasted that she was never a slave. She was a free issue, and so she never had to go through the regulations of a slave. She never worked in the field at all, so evidently they had a different life from that of my father.

My mother and father had very different personalities. She used to get angry at him because he refused to condemn the whites who mistreated him. He refused to take sides on anything. I never will forget his saying, "You don't exalt yourself. You always see other people and let them feel they have some good in them." He felt that all the time, and that was really driven into me. The one place they did agree was on education. Every school night after our supper at six o'clock, we had an hour for study, and Mother would sit with us and make sure we got our lessons.

The only thing I remember that my father would whip you for was if you didn't want to go to school. And there were times we didn't want to go. That's the only time I can remember getting a whipping from him. I cried one morning because I didn't want to go to school, and he whipped me with a strap and then took me down there. Even then, though, he wasn't angry. I don't remember him ever getting angry. He was completely nonviolent.

My mother, on the other hand, would get angry and would hit very quickly. She was always ready to fight. One time our dog scratched a little boy's face and the mother called a policeman. My mother hid the dog up in the attic and when he came and wanted to come in the house to look for it, she refused to let him. She said, "Don't you put your feet across the sill of my door." She had a little saying. She'd say, "I'm a little piece of leather, but I'm well put together. And if you come through here, something's going to happen to you." She meant that, too. She would fight if she had to.

Our neighborhood was very mixed racially. We had Italians and Irish Catholics and Germans all on my street. Some of them were white men who were living with black women, and the women didn't work and stayed behind closed doors and windows most of the time—never married, but had beautiful children and were kept on a high pedestal. At any rate, there was a group of either Germans or Irish living right across from us, and they had a car out in the street and they sold bootleg liquor, and they would come and sit on our step, you know, and people'd come up and buy the bootleg liquor from that car. I really didn't know what they were doing at that time, but my mother didn't want them to sit on her step. I guess she understood what they were doing. She would lock the door and then take some water and run it under the door to run them off. They'd be getting up and looking, wondering where this water was coming from. That's the way she did. She wouldn't put up with it.

The thing that hurt my mother worst of all—and contributed greatly to her anger—was the kind of conditions we had to live under. The best job my father ever had was as custodian at that USO, and he brought home hardly any money at all. His pension from the Civil War was only eight dollars a year, and whenever he received it, she'd say, "Don't bring any of it here. Just go and buy you a little pinch of something. That's all it's good for." She was really bitter about that. I'd hear her say, "The clothes that I put over my head, I'll never put over again." That was her way of saying her status in life had changed by marrying and she couldn't buy the kinds of things she used to buy. I remember she lost a baby—it must have been eight or nine months old—and there was no money to pay for the digging of the grave. She had to get four dollars from a sister of hers to pay for the digging of this baby's grave, and she cried bitterly. She hated to have to do that.

But despite that, she was very haughty and proud. She was against slavery—terribly so—and she just actually hated the name of it. She always claimed that she never was a servant, and she wasn't going to be one. The sad part was that she had to take in other people's washing and ironing to bring in the extra income we had to have—she was really a washerwoman all her married life —but she used to boast that she "never gave a white woman a cup of coffee." She felt that would make her a servant.

All of us had to work to help out. My brothers used to carry the papers as little boys in the morning and in the afternoon, and my sisters and I helped with the wash. When we got home from school, she had our work set out for us. On Mondays, Tuesdays,

and Wednesdays, she'd have a tub of clothes set out ready for us to
wash, and on Thursdays and Fridays she'd have the ironing board
and iron set out ready for us to iron. We had to heat the irons in
the chimney winter and summer. After I got up about eleven or
twelve, she let me take care of a lady's two children that lived
across the street, and the dollar and a half a month I made from
that is what paid my tuition to Avery Institute, the private school I
went to. I received the Licentiate of Instruction from that school
in 1916 and went to the country to teach.

She was determined that we be highly cultured ladies. She
never could get me to be one, but she tried. "Being a lady" meant
that we could almost never play with the other children in the
neighborhood. She felt they were beneath us. She hated that
neighborhood. On the street where we lived were a number of
alleys. Common-law couples lived in those little alleys, and they
would comb their hair on the steps, and come out and use a
dishcloth and wash the top of their bodies on the porch. And it
was real hard for her to see them do that. And lots of the children
had mothers who weren't married, so my mother wouldn't associate with the neighbors at all, and she didn't want us to. Once in a
while she made exceptions. A German lady down the street took
sick with throat cancer, and she went to the hospital and came
back home. I was in the fourth grade in school, and every afternoon I went over to her house and read the Bible to her. I read
the whole of the first part of the Bible and started on the second,
the New Testament, before she died. I could go over there and
read the Bible to her—she wanted it done, and my mother con-
sented for me to go and do it—but we couldn't play with her
children.

Being a lady also meant that you could almost never go to the
store. My mother brought from Haiti the fact that women didn't
go to the stores because there was so much beer and things being
sold in the stores at that time. We weren't supposed to go. She
wouldn't go to the store. Right on my corner there was a German,
and there was an open bar in his store, and we couldn't go around
there at all. Sometimes on Saturdays, my mother and father took a
basket and went shopping for things we had to have, but my father
did most of the buying. For produce, we had a garden in the
summer for our fresh vegetables like okra and corn and tomatoes

and string beans. At other times, we had vendors that came
through with those baskets of vegetables on their heads. That was
another thing my mother wouldn't do—she wouldn't come out on
her porch. She wouldn't come out to those vendors. That was not
the way ladies did. They brought their produce and put it down on
the steps and she looked it over and let them know what she
wanted and they'd bring it to her and get their money. Same thing
with the shrimp man. Every Saturday we bought shrimp. You
could get three pounds for a quarter. And three strings of fish—
the fish were on palmetto string—and you could get three strings
of fish for about a quarter. They would come to you. They had a
pushcart and they'd be singing their thing:

> *Shrimpee—Roe, Roe, Roe, Roe.*
> *Oh, Shrimpee Roe*

and then,

> *Shark steak don't need no gravy.*

I can't forget that. [*Laughs*]
    Put shark in the pan and it makes its own gravy. We'd clean
and cook those fish on Saturday nights since we weren't allowed to
do any cooking on Sunday as a rule. You made your salad and you
cooked your rice and you roasted your meat all on Saturday night.
Then you had those wood and coal stoves, and so you could just
put the food all in the oven and keep it warm. Grits and tomato
sauce and fish was the big Sunday breakfast, and then we'd go to
Sunday school, and when we came back, we'd have dinner. For as
long as I can remember, she'd have the minister over for dinner,
and the children couldn't eat at that table. I can tell you, I used to
stand back there and see him eating up that food! [Laughs] But
you dared not say a word; she'd have your head!
    And on Sunday we dared not play. We only could sit on that
porch. We had an organ, and we could stand around the organ
and one could play and sing, but those were the only things we
could do. The other children could be out playing ball or things
like that, but we couldn't.
    Being a lady meant, as well, that she was always wanting peo-

ple to say "Miss" or "Mrs." In speaking to us about my father, she just said, "Your father" or "Mr. Poinsette." She had been trained that way. It also meant to never go out without your gloves on, and never to let anybody know what you are going for. She said, "If you're going downtown for a common pin, it's nobody's business." And you dare not holler across the street. You're not supposed to yell across and say, "Hey, Sally!" or "Hey, Sue!" That's not the sign of a lady. And you never ate on the street. You could buy a lot of peanuts for a penny, and there was a baker nearby where you could get a big bag of cookies for a nickel, but if you ate any of that in the street and somebody told her, you got whipped. You shouldn't eat in the street; that wasn't the sign of a lady.

Sometimes she would take us for a walk on a Sunday afternoon and once when I was little, I saw a little white girl drop a bag of candy, and I started to pick some up. Boy, did she give me a spanking on the street. The little girl's mother was not going to let her have it since it had fallen on the ground, and so I was going to take it, but my mother felt that that would be a sign of inferiority and she whipped me good.

She never whipped me too much, though, because I was very cautious of the things that I knew she disliked. She didn't want you to say "Well" or "What?" to her, for example, so I had to be very particular about that. I tried to correct her one Sunday morning when she was telling her sister something, and she slapped the teeth out of the front of my mouth and made me wash it out with some salt and water and go right on to Sunday school. I knew from then on how she was going to do. That same night she wanted me to say, "God bless Mama," and I wouldn't do it, so she whipped me again and put me into bed. She couldn't get me to say it. I just wouldn't say it. I quarreled with her, and I wouldn't say it. But I learned from that that it was best not to antagonize her!

Another thing that she was really strict about was our seeing boys. She had a feeling, and this was her way of saying it, that, "You'll be attractive to men. Men are here to ask, and women to refuse, until the proper time. And if you accept favors from men, men are going to mark you, and then you will be no good." She always said that. Even when we were very young, she told us that. Once in a while she'd allow my brothers to have friends over—

even though she wouldn't allow us to—and when their friends were around, we'd have something we had to do in the house.

When we were older and going to high school, I had a sister who really liked the boys. Sometimes the boys would walk her home from school and leave her at the corner to go on home alone, but if this woman down the street saw her letting a boy bring her to the corner and told my mother, she would whip her every time. She didn't want this. She was very strict when it came to things like that.

Even when I got up and I finished high school, she watched us. When the USO was here, I went there one night to work as a volunteer, and I met a sailor that I liked very much. I was afraid to ask him to come home, but I invited him to church. He came to church that Sunday, and he brought about six others with him. I was then a grown woman teaching school, but I still knew what was coming. After church I couldn't invite him to dinner, and I couldn't go anywhere with him, so I had to just make an excuse, and they had to go back to the ship. When I got home, why, she told me that all these sailors were considered terrible people, you know. The fact that they were sitting in our church and I was sitting with them was an awful thing to her. She didn't whip me because I was getting too large then, but she gave me quite a tongue-lashing about that.

[And] you know what [my father] would say? "Whatever your ma says . . ." He never took sides. That's what he always said. [*Laughs*] No. He wasn't going to talk against her. He never did.

[But] when she would say things [about him being unable to support her], most of the time he would say, "Vicky, a hundred years from today you'll never know the difference, and none of those things will make any sense." And he was so right.

I really think it bothered him, though, that he couldn't get the kind of money that would have helped him support her better. I understand that in the early days, they used to go out and go to parties and things, and she was a great dancer and that they had good times. Then after all these children came, she never did go anywhere. For a long time she didn't even want to go to church, because she didn't have the kind of clothes that she wanted to wear. . . .

I can remember her singing those blues so well, talking about the things that she had that she'd never have anymore. She hated it. But she did finally get to the place where she could have just about everything she wanted. My brother got up and was working, and I was working, and there were two others teaching, so money was coming in. I bought a house for her in 1948 and I had it repaired, and the night that we had the opening we surprised her with it. A lady came and took her out to a movie, and when she came back, all these people were there. It was her birthday, October 25. I never will forget it. She was jubilant. She just threw her arms around me and said, "Nice, nice to do this." [*Laughter*] I was happy too. I wish my father could have been alive, but he was gone by then.

I felt both of my parents had a great influence over me, though, even though we had our hard times. From my father I got my belief in nonviolence, and in patience. Whenever I had hard times getting people to take some kind of action, his influence would give me the patience to work with them anyway and wait for them to change within themselves to the point where they were ready to act. I knew that I should not feel angry or impatient with them, but continue to work with them until they were confident.

And from my mother I got courage. In the days when segregation was great, she had courage enough to speak to us against it. She wasn't afraid of anyone, and so when I had to face the Klan, I never felt afraid. Her courage helped me to do that, and to stay when others were running away. . . .

In 1904, I can remember, we moved to 17 Henrietta Street from Wentworth Street. I must have been about six years of age at that time, and I started going to school. I went to what they called the Mary Street School, and at that school they had what they called an "ABC gallery" where the children six years old were placed. There must have been a hundred children on that gallery. It was like a baseball stadium with bleachers and you sat up on those bleachers. About the only thing I could see that the teacher had time to do was to take you to the bathroom and back. By the time she got us all to the bathroom and back, it was about time to go home.

We didn't learn too much, and my mother was aware of that, so she took me out of that public school. There were numbers of elderly black women in Charleston who kept little schools in their homes, and so I went to one on Logan Street, where the Fielding Funeral Home is today. At that school, run by a Mrs. Knuckles, I learned to read and write. She taught us a very hard way. If you couldn't spell a word that she asked you, she whipped every letter into your hands. That was the way we learned to spell!

I went back to public school for the fourth, fifth, and sixth grades. There wasn't any public school in Charleston for black children beyond that, but then they opened the Burke Industrial School so that black children could go through the eighth grade. In fact, President Taft came down to the dedication of that school. So I went there.

When I was ready for ninth grade, I took a test and got into Avery. That was a private school for black children that was founded by a group of white missionary women out of Massachusetts who came down right after the Civil War. Since you had to pay a dollar-and-a-half-per-month tuition, there weren't many children of my class going there, but I told you how I paid mine. I was considered beneath a lot of the students there since my mother was a washerwoman and my father had been a slave, and so I couldn't go to any of the parties that were given by the parents of my classmates, but my mother was determined that I go. In fact, after I finished the tenth grade there, I could have taken a state department examination and started teaching if I passed, but my mother didn't want me to stop. At that time, if you went two more years, Avery gave something called a Licentiate of Instruction, which is equal to two years of college today, and I went on and got that, and graduated in 1916 at the age of eighteen.

That was quite an education. All the teachers were unmarried women who lived in a dormitory. They all lived there together. When they'd take us to a theater downtown, they couldn't sit down on the main floor with the other whites. They had to sit up on the third floor with us. Those who went to church went to black churches, but most of the time they never went to anything. Since we were segregated against, they felt that they couldn't go either.

We had to wear uniforms. Anytime you wore a blouse you could see your arm through, they would ask you did you want to have your person showing through your clothes? That was a sin! [*Laughter*] We wore a blue or black skirt in the ninth and tenth grades with a colored shirtwaist that could be in blocks, plaids, or stripes. When you got to be a junior or senior, you wore a white shirtwaist with those black or blue skirts. And when you got ready to have your prom, you had to buy material that didn't cost over a dollar. I don't mean a yard, but the whole dress. That was so nobody would spend too much money on something like a dress. If you wore one that cost more than a dollar, they would put you out of the prom. They couldn't have a whole lot of lace or embroidery.

And there was a lot of religious training. Every spring a man would come down to give that instruction. Every time the trustees came from the North, we had to sing the spirituals. I didn't know the history of the spirituals and I disliked them greatly, so I'd stand to the back and just move my mouth and wouldn't sing. Later I found out from people like Zilphia Horton the two great lessons from the spirituals: how they carried a message, and how they told of the sufferings of people. When I found those things out, then I felt better about singing them.

The teachers there were wonderful, though. They came to your home, regardless of what kind of a house you had, and talked with your parents. They wanted me to go to Fisk when I finished, and my mother was willing, but I just couldn't see her doing it. She would have washed herself to death trying to get up that much money. The board alone at that time was about nineteen dollars a month, plus the clothes to go and the transportation and all. I just didn't feel I could go. So I went over to Johns Island to teach after my graduation in 1916. I had been interested in teaching for a long time anyway. When I was a teenager, the children in the neighborhood would call me "Little Ma" because I took so many of them out of the neighborhood to church or down to The Citadel to watch the soldiers march on Friday afternoons. When I was around sixteen, I was head of the youth group in my church and was teaching Sunday school. I taught Vacation Bible School in the summers, too. I remember I had a children's choir, and we were invited to come across the street to the white Bethel Church to sing for the white people. There was a lady there whose brother was the minister of that church and she told my children, she said, "Now, I want you to know that you are different from us. You can look at yourself and see that you're different." She was a missionary to Africa, but she still wanted those little black children to know they were different from her and from her children. [*Laughing*] Well, that was a long time ago, [but] that wasn't unusual. [*Laughing*]

[In 1916, as I said], I taught at the Promise Land School. I had to go to the islands to teach because blacks weren't allowed to teach in the public schools in Charleston. I never will forget the very first night I went over. There was no bridge to the island then, so I had to go down to the Battery and take one of those little gasoline-powered boats over. Something happened that night to the boat and we had to stay in the creek all night. It took us nine hours to get from Charleston to the school.

There wasn't even a bridge over to the island from Charleston until about 1945, so those people just stayed right in their little shells, isolated, accepting whatever was there. And they really suffered. The children got sores. You know, coming from the edge of the water up to the school, there were some bushes that the dew would fall on, and when they cut their legs it would make sores, and those sores would keep right on running. We didn't have a doctor over there, you know. There was a Dr. Barnwell on Wadmalaw Island, but he had to do everything for five islands, so he was hard to get.

The people there were virtual slaves. They had no choice but to work in the fields for the white people. That's one of the reasons we had so many babies to die. A mother was only allowed to stay two or three days in the house after giving birth, and then she had to be back in the fields. She'd put her new baby in a box and put a "sugar tit" in its mouth—you know, lard and sugar in a cloth—and leave, and the mosquitoes and the flies had a good time on those babies. Very few of them lived to reach their second year.

When I first moved there, I lived with a man and his wife. She didn't have pots. She cooked soup right in the tin can. I was living up in an upstairs attic room, and I had a lantern for a light; that was all I had. On Saturday nights I had to wait till they all went to bed so I could bathe before that one chimney. We had to get water from a surface well, and when it rained, everything went into that well. You'd draw buckets of water and whatever else was in it, and you'd bathe yourself in it, and then you'd wash your clothes in that same water. My mother came over there and spent a weekend [*laughing*] and that was a terrible experience for her. She was really angry about it. [*Laughs again*] She didn't say anything to the people, though, and I was glad she didn't!

The Promise Land School had 132 children in it, and the older ones didn't get to come to school until after harvest was over. They came the last of November to the last of February. When it was time to put cotton in the field again, they had to go. But I taught them. I made twenty-five dollars a month, too, and I thought that was a great deal of money. That's when I started trying to save up to buy my mother that house I was talking about. You know what made me determined to do that someday? When we moved from Wentworth Street to Henrietta Street, we rented a house that was owned by a white man who owned a grits mill in Charleston. The rent was only five dollars a week, but there were times when she just didn't have that five dollars. Every Monday he would come to get that rent, and when she didn't have it, he was really ugly. [*Laughs*] He would say some of the worst things. Once my brother was going down the street with an old secondhand violin to take violin lessons after school, and he said, "Put that boy to work. Instead of him walking round here with a violin, let *him* help you get this money." I was sitting on the step listening to him, and I really felt real bad about that. But you know what it made me want to do? To buy a house. I wanted to get my mother away from there.

So when I started making that twenty-five dollars a month, I saved a hundred dollars and sent it to the real estate office on Broad Street to put down on a house I had seen for sale on Henrietta Street. He sent me that money back because that hundred dollars would hardly start paying for it, and he knew that with my salary, I'd never be able to pay for it. There wasn't anything I could do about it. It took me another thirty years to finally get that house!

But while I was on the island, I had my first experience with the NAACP. It hadn't been too long since their knowledge of lynching in Springfield, Illinois, in 1909, and a group of preachers came over to the island to tell about NAACP and what it was doing, trying to get chapters organized. The supervisor of Negro schools, a Mrs. Lesesne, was so enthused, and so were a lot of us. We had to go over to Charleston to cash our checks at the courthouse, and as we came out the door with our money, she was standing right there holding a nearly closed parasol upside down, and we slipped our dollar membership dues into that parasol as we walked past her. We didn't want anybody to see us putting it in because we knew the trouble it would cause.

I joined, though. Later the state passed a formal law that no city or state employee could belong to the NAACP, and I'm sure that's partly what killed Mrs. Lesesne. It grieved her. She was one person who was a big member of the organization, and she couldn't take it. She just withered away and died. I lost my job over that, of course, and she would have too.

[Back to 1919, however.] In the fall, I was able to get a job teaching at Avery. They had finally gotten to where they had a few black teachers there. There weren't any in the public schools, but Avery was private and could get away with it. They even had a black principal there named Mr. Cox. So I taught sixth grade there and made thirty dollars a month.

That's when I had my first experience with any sort of political action. An artist named Edwin Harleston called a group of us together to form an NAACP chapter in Charleston. Our first order of business concerned a black boy who had been accused of theft. People didn't have Frigidaires then; there were iceboxes. This black boy delivered ice on King Street, and he had carried some to a woman who lived upstairs over a meat market. She lost her watch, and she thought that this boy who brought the ice up took her watch, and so she had this boy arrested. When her clothes came back from the laundry she found out her watch had gone to the laundry in her apron. She was honest enough to tell it, and he was released. When that happened, Edwin Harleston got a group of people together and asked her to make restitution to this boy and pay for the time he had spent in jail and make a public statement, because he felt that when this fellow went to school, if she didn't make a statement, children would be teasing him about being arrested and call him a "jailbird" and just make things worse. That became a big thing, and the newspaper carried an account of it.

After that was over, we started thinking then about what we needed to do, and we got to the place where we felt we just had to have black teachers teaching in the public schools. Otherwise these students were just at the mercy of the white teachers, who often didn't care anything about them.

The excuse the lawmakers gave for not having black teachers was that they were sure the domestic workers and the chauffeurs and the garbage people and the longshoremen didn't want black teachers at all, but *wanted* white teachers to teach their children. Actually, the reason was that because of segregation, black teachers and white teachers could not work together, and if they had black teachers, they'd have to fire the whites to maintain segregation.

We talked to Tom Miller, the president of South Carolina State College, and he said we'd have to get signatures from the domestic workers and draymen and so forth saying that they *did* want black teachers. Well, Mr. Cox didn't want any of us involved. It was too controversial. And the older teachers at Avery didn't want to be involved anyway. But I didn't have many friends, and I didn't care, so I took my students along with me and we went door to door, up and down the streets. Some would take one side and some another. I did Cannon Street from King to the river, and by the end of the first day, we had ten thousand signatures. By the time we quit, we had twenty-two thousand signatures. We gave them to Tommy Miller, and he presented them to the legislature, and in 1920 we got some black teachers in the city of Charleston.

After two years at Avery, I went to McClellanville, South Carolina, to teach. By then we were making sixty dollars a month. It was while I was at McClellanville that I got married, in 1922. His name was Nerie David Clark. I met him while I was at Avery, when he was a wardroom cook in the Navy during World War I. He was on one of those submarines. When he was in town, we'd visit, but we'd have to sit on the porch of my house. Even though I was grown, my mother still had her ways! [*Laughing*] In fact, when I decided to marry him, she was very angry about it because he was from North Carolina and anybody from out of South Carolina was suspect. She considered him a real stranger, but I always say that there's a time in your life when you're just moved to say no, and this was the time. My father felt really different about it, but he dared not speak out because she would have jumped down his throat if he had. So even though she didn't want me to, I married him anyway.

It was a hard adjustment, because his folks were so different from what I was used to. They lived in Hickory, North Carolina, and their cultural ideas, being from the mountains, were so different from the ideas of the low country. It was a different life. I had never washed out in the yard in the snow before, and they did it all the time. And my feet got so frostbitten. Oh, I had a hard time.

But some of it was good. Since all the black women there were either household servants or washerwomen, they didn't have the class thing that my mother had. And in Charleston, we were members of the United Methodist Church, and to be a Christian in Charleston, there were so many different rules you adhered to. You hid so many things. Handicapped children were hidden. Girls who had babies were tabooed. In the mountains, they were all together. They were members of the African Methodist Episcopal Church, and it was much healthier. In fact, I changed my membership and joined my in-laws' church.

My husband and I had two children. We were back in Charleston when the youngest one died. For a long time, I felt that I was being punished for having disobeyed my mother and married a man from out of state. I really had that feeling. And I thought what I had done was against the will of God, according to the religious laws that I learned, and I felt very strongly about that. I even went down on the Battery one day and sat down and thought strongly about trying to commit suicide, but a brother found me on the pier and got rid of that feeling.

When the baby died, my husband was on board ship. He came down from the ship and found out that this baby had died, and then he went back on the ship and never came back. He left me to find a way to bury him. I know he was afraid of my mother. He knew what she was going to say to him. She never forgave me. She was strict like that. Very strict.

[So during that hard time], I took a job. There was an invalid woman here, a white woman, and she wanted somebody to go with her to the mountains to Hendersonville, North Carolina. I went with her to Hendersonville and stayed with her that whole summer. And her helplessness helped me to feel a different way.

Then her son got married and had a baby, and they brought it up to the mountains. They asked me would I do the diapers, and I couldn't. It made me think too much of my own child. I just sat and cried. And she was real sorry for me, too. And very soon after that I left and went to Hickory, North Carolina, to my husband's people. But that was a real hard time. Night after night I could sit and think about what had happened. I had to pray to get over that.

In 1926, I got homesick for Charleston and came back here to teach on Johns Island again. I tried taking my son with me on the islands for a while, but it was too hard living. Rainy weather and cold weather. It was just very, very hard. He'd get to be tired over nothing. I experienced it for one year, and he got right sick with the whooping cough and all, so then I decided that it would be better if his grandmother took him in the mountains. It was a real heartache, but I did know that she would take care of him. I sent money as I could, and she pretty much raised him. Now, with his children, the thing I missed in raising him, I'm getting plenty of with them! [*Laughing*]

I never married again. Never had the feeling that I wanted to.

During the 1929–30 school year I went to Columbia [South Carolina] for the first time. I taught third grade there. I got the job through Mr. C. A. Johnson, who was supervisor of black schools. I met him in a summer school I attended.

In Columbia, segregation caused us to have double sessions, so I taught from twelve o'clock in the day till five in the afternoon. In the mornings I could take two or three classes at one college, because I was in a college town, and at night I could take two or three more. And this was how I was able to take my degree, taking six hours. . . .

I also joined the NAACP in Columbia. It was a big chapter. They must have had eight hundred or more members. That's when I began to get active again politically. Dr. Robert Mance was president, and our big push under his leadership was to equalize the black and white teachers' salaries. In the Columbia system, I was receiving sixty dollars a month, and the white teacher right across from me with the same qualifications would be getting eighty-five. I was able to get affidavits from both white and black teachers about salary discrepancies, and get copies of their checks to verify that. Finally the NAACP sponsored a suit in court which we won in 1936. Thurgood Marshall was part of that decision.

Another good thing that happened to me in Columbia was that I learned some valuable methods of adult literacy training from Miss Wil Lou Gray. She had a big influence on me in teaching me to have enough patience to work with people who could not read and write. . . .

While in Columbia, Septima Clark earned her bachelor's degree in 1942 from Benedict College. In 1946, she was awarded a master's degree from Hampton Institute in Hampton, Virginia; by then, she was forty-eight years old. The following year her mother had a stroke, and Septima returned to Charleston. It was the daughter's turn to care for the mother. A decade later, however—in the fifties—Septima would do her most famous work.

For the continuation of Septima Clark's interview, see Chapter Four (page 236).

★

When Montgomery Was Not Like St. Louis
Edgar Daniel Nixon

"Porter, would you please . . ."

In 1925, when A. Philip Randolph organized one of this century's most important black labor unions—the Brotherhood of Sleeping Car Porters—his vision and strategies inspired a young Pullman porter from Montgomery, Alabama.

"Porter, would you please . . ."

Thirty years later, that same Alabamian would be inspired once again —this time by Brown v. Board of Education. *He would escort black children into an all-white school, but be turned away. The following year, he would encourage Martin Luther King, Jr., then a twenty-six-year-old Baptist preacher, to host a rally.*

That 1955 rally would make history. But the earliest decades in this century, as E. D. Nixon recalls, made history of a different sort: a chronicle of segregation.

"Porter, would you please . . ."

. . . I was born on July 12, 1899, on King Street in Montgomery, Alabama. My daddy had two wives, and he had bad luck with all the children. He was only able to raise seventeen of us! [*Laughing*] I was the fifth child by his first wife, and I was born at home is what I understand. Very few black *or* white folks was born in hospitals in them days.

My father was named Wesley Nixon and my mother was Sue

Ann Nixon. She died when I was quite young. He was a Baptist minister. He started preaching when I was quite a kid, and at that time he and my auntie, who was his sister, was living there together and his sister named me. Then my father left town running away from preaching and went down in the country and my auntie kept me. She always said that I was her boy and she kept me.

After I was eight years old, he came back and got me and carried me to the country. I didn't like it then, and I still don't like it, so in a couple of years then, I came back and then I hung around here for a couple of years, which made me a little over twelve. Ever since I was fourteen years old I fought and earned it for myself, and I had no help and very little schooling, but I refused to be handicapped for lack of formal school training.

My aunt was the big influence on my early life. It wasn't my parents. She planned everything. She was a Seventh-Day Adventist. I'll tell you this. You'll laugh about it. [*Laughing*] There was a slaughterhouse about ten blocks from the house. You could buy a cow head there for a dime. . . . She'd clean it and cook it down with onions and everything and if you'd tell me I didn't have something good to eat, I'd fight you!

But to show you the way she raised us when I was little, she'd give me a dime and put it in my pocket and then take a safety pin and pin it shut. Then she'd give me a bag with two handles, and another boy went with me, and I'd have one handle and he'd have the other one. She'd say, "Go get a cow head and don't take this pin out until you get to the man where he bring you the cow head. Then you unpin that and take the dime out and give it to him." He'd put that cow head down in that bag and I'd give him the dime and we'd carry that head home. All right. Nobody could have made me take that dime out until I got there. But today a child will tell you right to your face that he's going to take it out. It might be done spent when he gets where he's going. But she taught me how to be honest and be respectful to people. But she said, on the other hand, that I like to see you be man enough to stand up for what you think is right. And I've done that.

If she had any views about civil rights back in those days I didn't understand it because I was over twenty years old before I knew that the whole world wasn't like Montgomery. Well, you see, I hadn't read nothing too much, and I didn't know what was right or wrong with reference to the civil rights until I made my first trip as a porter on the Pullman cars and I saw that that was different in St. Louis, Missouri, than it was at home. I was dumbfounded when I got up there and found black and white sitting down at the same table eating in the station. It had a heck of an impact on me. Here you have been conditioned traditionally to, "This is the way of life," and all your life that's all you have known, and you get twenty and twenty-five years old and begin to think the whole world is like that, and then all at once you see something like black and white eating together and it's just like water that's been backed up in a dam, and it breaks out and flows over. [By the time I got back to Montgomery at the end of that first four-day run,] I had started to think, "What can I do to help eliminate some of this?" I decided not to be a coward and move up North where things were different—not be scared to fight—but to keep my home in Montgomery and start fighting for what I thought was right. . . .

Before I was a porter I used to work at the baggage room. The manager of the Pullman Company came by one day and said, "We got an opening for a Pullman porter. If any of you boys want it, you can take a trial at it." Said, "If you don't like it, you can leave and come back and get your job. We won't hire nobody in your place till we are sure that you made good."

Well, I had been seeing these porters come through there on the train all dressed with white coats on, and I had wished many times I had one of them jobs, and when he come and told me that, I fell for it. And it was the best thing in the world that ever happened to me. All right, I was underlearned, and I discovered that I was underlearned. And I decided then that there was two things I was going to do. I was going to make every effort to learn how to read and write the best I could with what I had. And I went out and said I was going to prepare myself to live with other people and be able to conduct myself so that people would respect me for what I did. And I did that. You'd be surprised. If you got on a train with a newspaper or with a book or something, and you left it in your room and went to the dining car, by the time you come back I'd be done read it almost. And I made a memorandum of words that I couldn't understand. Kept this memorandum book and wrote them down, and when I'd get back to my room, I had a little dictionary, and I would look them up and see what they were.

[But the most important part of my education came in 1928, in St. Louis, when I met A. Philip Randolph.] See, I was on the St. Louis-to-Jacksonville run. Stay at St. Louis overnight, then go all the way to Jacksonville, stay down there all day, and then come back as far as Montgomery. Then I could get off there and stay home four days, and then get back on the train when it came through and go on to St. Louis—like that. Four days on and four days off.

Well, when we would get into a city like St. Louis, the company always had a place for porters to sleep—had rooms set aside in the YMCA there for the Pullman porters. We got in that day and the word was all up and down the line to the porters that Randolph was going to speak that night at the YMCA, and I went in to hear the meeting myself. We must have had a hundred fifty to two hundred people there. We had a whole lot of porters who came in that day, and there were all the porters who lived in St. Louis, and their wives. We just had a crowd of them.

What he was doing was organizing the Brotherhood of Sleeping Car Porters. See, the railroad had a union, but your job as a Pullman porter was not tied to the railroad there. The only thing the railroad did was lease the cars from the Pullman Company, but the Pullman Company was a different organization that was responsible to the railroad for that type of service, and we didn't have no bona fide union ourselves. At that time we were making about sixty-eight dollars a month, and the conductor was paid, I think, a hundred fifty a month. All right. We knew the difference in pay was largely because of color—any youngster could see the difference—and Randolph was talking about how we could get organized and get ourselves together and then use mass pressure to bring about some of the changes we wanted. And he showed us all these things and it was just as clear as it could be to me. So I said to myself, "If these things can happen, I'll take a chance. [If I lose my job here,] I can probably find one at home that will pay fifty or sixty dollars a month at least and let me stay home at night!" [*Laughing*] So I decided to take a chance with it.

After the meeting, I put a dollar in the collection plate and when I got ready to go out, shook hands with him, and he said,

"Where you from, young man?" I told him, "Montgomery, Alabama." He said, "We need a good man down there." So I joined the Brotherhood.

Lots of people were against our union. Even blacks. Even the black bishop of the Methodist people took a stand against unions in favor of the company and sent out a memorandum to all their ministers throughout the country to preach against interfering with the Pullman Company because they were scared that there would be fighting hand and fist. And all your black papers, except the Pittsburgh *Courier* and *Afro,* sold out to the Pullman Company. They printed only what the Pullman Company wanted them to print about the porters.

But I joined up anyway. When I got home the next evening, my boss man met me at the station and said, "I understand you was out to the Brotherhood meeting yesterday."

I said, "Yes, I was."

"Well, I'm gonna tell you right now, we ain't gonna have none of our porters attending them Brotherhood meetings."

I said, "Well, I know you got the message right, because I *was* there." And I said, "I just want to tell you not only did I attend the meeting, I joined the Brotherhood." I said, "And I made up my mind that anybody who messes with my job, I'm going to carry them to court." I didn't even know a lawyer at that time, but that thought just came up all at once. Just came up. And you know, they never bothered me. I had one Montgomery man join right after that—E. L. Catney—and for a long time there wasn't nobody but me and him. And then finally it come down to where there must have been twenty-five to thirty. Then finally we got a check-off system where a man from our area would *have* to join the Brotherhood. Then we had about eighty-some-odd in our area with about eighteen thousand members nationally. Then the dining-car waiters and train porters and all such parties like that joined in with us, and that added another three or four thousand. And where the other unions at first just saw Randolph as some little hotheaded guy trying to do something for publicity sake, they began then to see him kind of different. "Here's a guy that knows something."

But taking a chance on joining the Brotherhood is the best chance I ever took, 'cause I'm gon' tell you one thing. We were able to fight and create a union that made men out of people who worked on Pullman cars who were used like you use a piece of furniture. Nobody had no respect for you. I never will forget there was a man who used to get on my train at Decatur, Alabama. He'd drop his bag way down there when he come out from the ticket office and walk all the way down the side of the train and tell me, "Go get that bag, boy!" And that didn't happen just one time. It happened a dozen times or more.

We finally got a clause put in our contract where if a passenger wanted to accuse us of doing something, he had to have a witness to whatever you were supposed to have done or said before he could do anything about it. When we got that clause, that was the time for us!

He got on the train one evening and told me, "Go get that bag, boy!" just like that. So I went on and got the bag and come back and he followed me in the car and I carried the bag to his room, and when I got there, I slammed the door and I cussed him with everything I could think of. I told him if he ever called me "boy" again I would break his neck. He didn't have no witness and I took advantage of it. After that, when he got on the train, he would say, "Porter, would you please get my bag?" But I had to teach him a lesson. And it took him by surprise because he just didn't expect a black man to say that to him. I taught him a lesson and after that he respected me.

You'd be surprised at the things that the Brotherhood of Sleeping Car Porters have done in this town. One time we got a white man, who was a platform man, fired. He had done everything in the world to the porters he could think of doing and got away with it, until we got him fired. Then he got a job right up the street at a furniture store. We had about twenty porters who had an account in that store, and we got together and went and borrowed enough money from the bank to pay off our accounts there. Went in there and told the owner, "You got a man working here that kicked our porters around for a long time, so we came down here this morning to close our accounts."

He said, "Do what?"

I said, "We're going to close these accounts with cash money."

He said, "Why don't you let them run on until Saturday?"

I said, "No, this ain't no Saturday deal." I said, "This is to-day's deal." I said, "You either get rid of him today or we're gonna close our accounts." He called that man in and fired him.

When people mistreat you, you've got to stand up. Another time, I got home one morning and a man came running toward me and said, "Brother Nixon, they building a little booth down there for black folks to go around on the outside out there and buy their tickets so they won't have to go in the white waiting room."

I went on down and looked at it and I said, "What's this you building here?"

He said, "Damned if I know, they just told me to build it."

So I looked at him and said, "I don't know how I'm gonna do it, mister," I said, "but I give you my word, in the name of God, they'll never open it." Do you know what happened? They didn't open it. Because that night I got on the train and went to Mobile to talk with the superintendent in his office. I told him what had happened and I said, "I know that you ain't going along with the railroad treating colored patrons like this!"

He went into his private office to use the telephone. I couldn't hear what he said. He came back out and he said, "Porter," he said, "go on back to Montgomery. When you get there that thing will be torn down." When I got back to Montgomery that evening, they done tore all that stuff down and moved it away.

I can name you several other instances. But if you learn to be a part of a movement that's doing something and that's honest—and God knows A. Philip Randolph was an honest man—and you are sincere, you find ways to do things.

For the continuation of Edgar Daniel Nixon's interview, see Chapter Four (page 219).

★

Drinking the Same Water, Using the Same Dipper

May Justus

Most widely known as author of Other Side of the Mountain, *a novel first published in the thirties, this Tennessee writer did not merely "observe" her neighbors. May Justus also fulfilled practical functions within the Appalachian communities about which she wrote. She taught mission-school children, and served as a nurse to the sick and as an instructor during "moonlight" classes for adults. This storyteller was, indeed, a coworker at the tasks of everyday life in the hills.*

She recalls, as a child, that "evil never triumphed" in books she read aloud to her family. Later, as an adult, she settled west of her native hills in a county named Grundy. There, she and Vera McCampbell staffed another mission school and served for decades as teachers in the area. There, too, they would witness a triumph of civil injustices—at least for a season—when segregationists clashed in 1959 with proponents of integration at Highlander, then located at Monteagle, Tennessee.

As a result, Vera's job would be threatened, and at state hearings, May would be criticized for testifying on Highlander's behalf. But the women persisted. During the sixties, May wrote a series of novels that championed the cause of integration.

Here, however, her childhood memories recount how a wintertime storyteller was, unwittingly, preparing for seasons of injustice ahead.

I was raised in a small mountain community in Cocke County, Tennessee. We had very few material things. Now I realize that we were very rich and we were privileged in many ways that children nowadays are not. But we had to be careful of what we had. There was very little cash money. We sold eggs at the store and picked berries to buy the things that we needed. We didn't feel there was any hardship. We were glad when we had the berries and eggs to sell. I remember that my mother always felt that as long as a dozen eggs would buy a yard of cloth, she ought to sell them. (Eggs sold for five cents a dozen, and that would buy a yard of cloth!) So we traded. It was a process of barter, and it was a very good way. And we had what we needed.

My parents were not permissive with us and we didn't expect them to be. We felt that our parents were better and wiser than we and knew what was right and wrong, and when they said not to do something, we knew that the thing was wrong. I don't mean that we didn't go ahead and *do* things! We were perfectly normal children, capable of disobedience and of neglecting to do the things that we should do sometimes. I don't think that was our parents' fault. It was our fault and we knew it. . . .

In those days the discipline was much stricter and proper punishment wasn't considered child abuse. Switching children was accepted as the thing to do. People didn't think that was cruel. My parents were never *cruel.* They really felt that every child who came into the family was a gift God had sent them. That child was not accidental; that child was loved and wanted. It was really God's gift. "Train up your children in the way they should go" was the injunction parents felt they should follow. I can remember so many things my parents would tell us. They would always impress upon us that they were laying down the pattern for our lives. I remember my father saying, "Good girls usually make good women, and good boys usually make good men." He knew that it isn't always true. Children do depart from their upbringing sometimes, but I think in general he was right.

And they certainly were a great influence on what I became. My father was a teacher, and I became a teacher. My mother was a great reader and storyteller, and I also became a great reader and later wrote stories. In fact, when I was very young, the greatest pleasure that we had during the wintertime was sitting around an open fire and hearing stories. My mother read to us out of magazines, and even before I learned to read, I remember a Christmas present my father gave me was a storybook. I would take the book to my mother and ask her to read to me, and she would if she wasn't too busy. At other times she made up stories about animals in the forest like the possums and the foxes that would come in and steal our chickens. When we would say, "Mama, tell us a story," she'd say, "Aren't you tired of hearing about the possums and the chickens?"

And we'd say, "No." And I can remember that we were torn between sympathy with the family that was losing chickens, and the fox and the possum that were coming in and stealing chickens for the hungry little foxes and possums back home!

And then Mother told us so many stories she remembered from her childhood which sounded like made-up stories to us, going back to the days when their clothes were woven and everything was so primitive. She told how Grandmother knitted the socks and stockings they used, and how they made coverlets and quilts and did all those things. That was vastly interesting to us because we had graduated to store-bought goods. It was all like a storybook. And when the neighbors would come to visit, they would talk about old times too. So you see, I was brought up in a storytelling atmosphere from the beginning. And, unknown to the little girl who listened at that time, it was all stored away in her mind!

The first story that I remember reading myself was a Bible story. Mother would read to us on Sunday, and teach us catechism too, because for a while there was no Sunday school for us to go to. My favorite story was the one about Joseph. My little brother and I never tired of hearing it, and she never tired of reading it to us. One Sunday some company came over about Bible-reading time and she didn't have time to read, so she said she would read to us after the company left. They stayed and stayed, and there was no time left. So I slipped in by myself and found the story of Joseph and read it by myself. I had heard it so often that I almost knew it by heart, and it wasn't too hard for me to make out the words.

Finally I was old enough to go to school, and some of my happiest recollections go back to the Bat Harbor school in the Smoky Mountains in Cocke County, Tennessee. It was built so long ago that my grandfather taught there right after the Civil War. He taught my mother in that building. Then my father later taught there and I went to school under him. When I was sixteen years old, I did *my* first schoolteaching there.

The schoolhouse was built in 1862 and was used for church as well as school. Because there were no sawmills in that part of the country, the poplar logs used to build the school were cut from the slopes of a nearby mountain and hauled by ox team. The logs were forty feet long and fourteen inches wide. The roof was made of hand-riven boards. Most of the work in erecting this building was done in three days.

There were no desks in it. You held your books in your lap or put them on the floor beside you. Water was carried in a bucket from a stream close by. We all drank from the same dipper. We children always went on those trips to the stream [to get water], two boys or two girls, but never a girl and a boy. That would have been unseemly. In fact, in those days, we didn't even sit together. The girls sat on one side and the boys on the other side of the room, as the men and women did in church.

I couldn't understand when I grew up and would hear children talking about hating for school to begin and being glad when it was out, and playing pranks on their teachers, because where I went to school, it was a place where you got to play and be with your schoolmates, and it was a social thing. It was a place where you were with your friends and your neighbors, and your family's friends. I remember very little of lessons, but I remember I loved walking to school through the woods and gathering wild grapes along the way. And I remember with great pleasure the games we played in the big yard at recess. My father, who was the teacher there, would pitch horseshoes or play ball with the boys on one side of the schoolhouse, and we girls would play singing games like "Skip to My Lou." In the afternoon as we walked home I did not lag behind my father. It was all he could do to keep up with me as I skipped along singing: "Gone again, skip to my Lou, Gone again, skip to my Lou, Skip to my Lou, my darling."

And I remember the lunches we would have at the noon recess. Father and I would walk down to the creek together until we came to a pretty place under a giant sycamore tree. We had sandwiches made of blackberry jam and Mother's good homemade bread, and fried chicken and ripe red tomatoes. And we finished up with a large sugar cookie which we called a "teacake." This was the only kind of cookie that I ate as a child. Teacakes were always flavored with nutmeg and smelled as good as they tasted. When we got home, my little brother would run out to meet us and would grab the lunch basket because he wanted to explore what was left in it.

When it was time to pull fodder, Father would announce to the children that school was closing for two weeks. The older boys would already be busy in the cornfields. It was customary to have this time out of school about the middle of September. Then the blades of corn fodder were turning gold and brown, ready to pull and tie into great bundles and store in barn lofts for winter feed for the horses and cows. Peas and beans were ripening, too, and any child who could toddle was given a basket and sent to harvest on the hillside roads. The peas and beans not needed for food during the long winter were sold two miles away at the nearest store. That was the way we bought our winter shoes. And when the soles grew thin they were mended and made to wear a few months more because they *had* to last all winter. Our cobbler was a neighbor woman whose father had been a shoemaker in the days just after the Civil War. . . . I liked to see her cut the leather apart from the worn-out shoe and tack new leather neatly into place. In sewing rips in the shoe, she used an awl to punch the holes for stitches and a large needle with a length of beeswax thread. Mrs. Click took pride in her work and we were proud to wear the shoes that she remade as good as new. My mother would finish the job with a good rub of mutton tallow which left our shoes soft and shiny, and also weatherproof. But one pair of shoes did very well to last from October until spring on our rough mountain trails and wagon roads—even with two or three good mending jobs.

After public school closed in early December, a subscription school might be opened in the winter. I never went to one of those, but I know tuition was one dollar a month. Even this sum was hard for some parents to pay in cash, but they could be counted on to pay in meat, meal, potatoes, molasses—just whatever they had.

But the way our family would do in the wintertime [while school was closed] was to go over our schoolbooks ourselves. My father had ten children. He had six by his first wife, and my mother was his second wife, and they had two boys and two girls. I am the eldest of the second set of children. (One of my brothers died when he was quite young.) And when I was born, my oldest half-sister was already old enough to teach school. So the way we would do was to study at home a great deal. The older ones would often help the younger ones.

When I was older, for example, I would read while my mother sewed and my brother, Hal, would be whittling and my little sister curled up with her dog or a kitty around the fireplace. We would roast chestnuts and apples, and we enjoyed these times. We read the Bible and *Pilgrim's Progress*. In fact, we read all the books we had. Sometimes we read history. That was interesting to us. And we read books that we borrowed. There was a family named Huff down the French Broad River. Major Huff had been an officer during the Civil War, and he had a very fine library. I was always welcome to come down and get books from it. He had two daughters, Miss Elizabeth and Miss Josephine (we always called her Miss Jo). I would go and bring books home from there all through my childhood, and they were delightful. Miss Jo had had a copy of *Alice in Wonderland* when she was a little girl and she let me have that.

In John Ruskin's *Sesame and Lilies*, he advised parents to let their children, especially their girl children, have freedom in their choice of reading and when they came to the weeds, he said, they would discard the weeds, and the flowers would give them a great deal of pleasure. It certainly was that way with me because even when I was about twelve or thirteen, I was borrowing from Miss Jo, who had a complete set of Shakespeare. She never said I was too young to read things she had—even Tolstoy and Schopenhauer and Nietzsche. (I was in my teens by that time, of course.) She let me take home Emerson's essays when I was sixteen years old, and you can imagine how a little sixteen-year-old girl would appreciate reading about the oversoul and things of that kind! I knew who Emerson was because of some of his poems. I remember the one "The Mountain and the Squirrel." Years later my brother asked me if I remembered that one, and I said it aloud and never missed a word of it. I can say it even now. I remember that it ended: "If I cannot carry forests on my back, neither can you crack a nut!"

. . . That was one of the great blessings of my life—reading good literature.

Most of those books were in fine print and it's a wonder I didn't destroy my eyes reading them. We read by a kerosene lamp and when the lamp went out, my brother would throw a pine knot on the fire from the supply of kindling we kept in a corner. It was impossible to stop at a very exciting place!

I remember one night we read *Uncle Tom's Cabin.* We were so interested in reading that story that we sat up till midnight or after, that night, and I finished it with tears streaming down my face and I think everybody else was crying too. That was a most memorable reading experience! And it caused my first sympathy with the Negro people.

When I look back over my childhood, I can remember not only being interested in the great and good authors like Hawthorne, but in fine works of art that were reproduced in our school readers. We read a series of books called the Lee Readers. I don't suppose they were published out of the South. All the stories in these books were taken out of things like *Bulfinch's Mythology,* and other excerpts from the great authors. And I can remember a [picture] about *The Angelus*—this man and woman out in the field at sunset—and when the church bell sounded, everybody was supposed to stop their work and bow their heads in prayer. And there they were with bowed heads. I was a little girl, but that impressed me very much that those people would stop their work for a moment of silent prayer. And then it had the story of *The Angelus* and told us about Millet and what a hard time he had and that he sold his pictures for less than a hundred dollars, and that now they were in the great picture galleries of Europe and were sold for as high as a hundred thousand dollars. That impressed me, even though I was just in the third grade, and all of my life since then, though I've never been over there to see the originals. Some of my family and friends have been and they have told me how beautiful they were. They said, "Do you remember that picture of *The Angelus* in our third reader?"

And I said, "Yes, I remember that."

That's what our schoolbooks were made up of—things that would inspire a child to see a bigger and a better life, and to meet people who had had lofty ideals. And I was never satisfied till I got

hold of more of Hawthorne's books, and read those to our family
—*Tanglewood Tales* and *Twice-Told Tales* and *Mosses from an Old
Manse.* I read them and we were all very excited over them. My
brother and I counted one time and figured that I had read aloud
to them a hundred and fifty books between the time I was twelve
and fifteen years old. He said that when he went to college, there
was hardly a book that he had to have in his English courses that
we hadn't read at home. . . .

Of course, we didn't have television and radio, and we didn't
have so much of the entertainment that children do now. So those
books were a blessing to us. My brother has asked, ''Why were we
so different?'' We didn't realize that we were so different, but we
were. When I went out into the world, I realized that our standards
of conduct were different from those of the people around me,
and now I realize that from books we knew a world that no longer
existed. He said, ''It was like stepping into a new civilization, but
they helped form our characters. And in those books, evil never
triumphed.''

It was during that time that I began to want to write myself. It
grew partly out of reading *Little Women.* You remember that Jo
March wrote stories and supported her family. I thought that it
would be wonderful if I could write a story [and sell it] and help
Mama with the children's expenses. It didn't seem too farfetched
to me for a little girl to do that. . . . So that was when I began to
write, dreaming of the day when I could write a story good enough
to sell. I thought I could be an author. The letters that people
would write Mother sometimes were written on one side leaving
the other side blank. Instead of throwing these away, my mother
would give them to me, and I wrote on the blank sides. I remembered in our Tennessee history how people in pioneer days made
pens out of goose quills and made their ink out of pokeberries.
Well, pokeberries grew in abundance around our house, and I
thought what the pioneer girls could do, I could do too. So I made
the pokeberry ink. We didn't have geese but a neighbor did, so
they told me how to make a goose quill pen. I took a sharp knife,
pointed the quill, and made a little split from the point back so
that it would hold the ink. (That was the way the steel pens of that
day were made.) And I wrote my stories that way!

Then when I was twelve years old, I won a spelling bee at

school. The prize was the complete works of Elizabeth Browning. I remember that I ran all the way home to show the book to my mother. To think, the teacher might have brought *Alice in Wonderland* or *Twice-Told Tales* or something more suitable for a child. But she gave me Mrs. Browning! I felt highly honored. Mama was so proud. So then I began to write little poems too. I wrote these stories and little poems for myself at first, and then when I was fourteen or fifteen, I began to send some of them to the children's page of the *Sunday School Press*. I wrote an Easter poem and the editor published it on the front page of the magazine and put a little border around it. I was very proud of that border! In fact, I had many things published there. I was never paid, but the editor took practically everything I sent. Those were the first things I actually had published. Later, when I was twenty-one, I began to receive two dollars and a half for each poem of mine that was published, and even though it wasn't much, it was very exciting to be paid. From that point on, I wrote constantly.

By that time, my father had been dead several years, and I had already become a teacher. Even when I was very young, he wasn't well. I remember, for example, the time when his health really began to fail. One night [when I was about six or seven years old], I got to go home with some friends for an all-night visit, which was always a special treat. When I got home the next day, there was a great surprise waiting for me. A beautiful baby sister was lying in bed with my mother. She seemed like a live dolly and I begged to hold her. My mother said, "Not right now. She's asleep. Before long you'll be rocking her to sleep and saying 'hushabye.' "

This put a notion in my father's head. He took down his old fiddle and raised up the bow. Winking in my direction, he said, "We might as well start practicing, I guess."

"Not now! You'll wake the baby," my mother cried.

My father nodded and slipped out the door, motioning for me to follow. We went a little way from the house and sat under an apple tree where my brother Hal was playing with the grasshoppers. My father began to play "What'll We Do With the Baby'O?" which I knew by heart from hearing Mother sing. It was a happy time for us.

But that very morning my father came down with a heavy cold which settled in his lungs, bringing back the affliction which he thought he had recovered from—consumption, they called it then. Tuberculosis now. From that time on, he coughed his life away by spells which left him weaker and weaker as the long winter passed. The spring brought hope and he played his fiddle in the sun and made plans to teach again that fall. Mother told me later that she had no hope then of Father's ever being better but she listened and planned along with him. It was a sad time, but a happy time too, because my baby sister, Helen, had been born and was one of us.

Some years after my father died, and my brother and I were old enough to go to high school, they built a dormitory out at Edwina at the high school there, and we boarded there so that we could go to school through the winter months. Then when spring opened up, we had to go back on our little farm to do the work, and my brother and I would walk that four miles every day to school so that we wouldn't miss out on our classes.

When I was about fifteen years old, after all the schools had closed around there for the winter, I got my youngest sister, Helen, and some of the neighbors' children, and had a little school for all of them—just a girl teacher like I was. And now when you read *The House of No End Hollow,* you'll read about a school like that with Becky, who gets the neighborhood children together and she has a little school.

Then when I was sixteen, a very well-educated young woman, Miss Clara Wardroup, came to teach at our same old Bat Harbor schoolhouse. She had so many children that year—oh, she had so many!—and she was the only teacher for all those children. There were forty or fifty, I guess. I had to stay home that year. I didn't get to go to school anywhere, so she told me that if I would come and help her teach the little children, that she would teach me my Latin and mathematics. In those days, everybody learned Latin, you know. So that's what we did. That was my first public school teaching (besides that time teaching the neighbors' children). And there I was teaching in this very same old building where Grandpa and Papa had taught. That was a very unusual experience for me, and I used it over and over again in stories and books I've written.

*   *   *

When May Justus was seventeen years old, Elizabeth Huff, the neighbor who had loaned her so many books, tutored her in geometry and Latin. She received her high school diploma from Haywood Institute a year later and took the examinations to qualify as a teacher. She taught in Cocke County for the next three years. When she was twenty-one, she moved to Scott County and taught there three years. All during this time, she also took correspondence courses and attended summer school to get her college degree.

[To help pay for my sister, Helen, to go to college,] I took a summer job in Louisville, Kentucky, as a playground director at Neighborhood House when I was twenty-four. That was in the early 1920s.

One Sunday morning I went to hear Dr. John Tyler speak. He was head of the Guerrant Inland Mission located in the Kentucky mountains. The mission was founded by a Georgian, Dr. E. O. Guerrant, who had served in that area during the Civil War. He found that there was an area up in there that had no schools or churches. And he promised God that if He would get him through the war alive, he would devote the rest of his life and all his money to founding and building churches and schools up in Kentucky.

He'd build a little house for the teachers who were the mission workers and he'd build a building that could be used as a school and church. Dr. Guerrant found that the mountain people were a little suspicious when he sent just men there as mission workers. That was the time when strangers were very suspect. [They might be revenuers.] Well, he found that if he sent a man and his wife and their children there to the mission that the people would accept them. Otherwise, he would send two ladies interested in mission work, preferably people who had chosen teaching as their profession.

That began a new life for me. Dr. Tyler told about the great need there was for workers in his mission. He said it was a hard life and that two years was the longest they ought to keep people there. They then had a lady who was working alone there and she was leaving soon. They needed someone to come and carry on the work there.

As I listened to him, I thought, "What am I doing here? A mountain girl working with city children, when there are people in our mountains who need me much more?" So I went to him after the service and introduced myself. I told him I was a mountain girl, born and bred, and I had done my teaching in mountain communities until I had come to Louisville. I told him something about myself and said I was very much touched by his appeal for workers. "Dr. Tyler," I said, "do you think I would do?"

He put his hand on my shoulder and said, "My child, I think you're an answer to my prayer!"

And so I went to the mission school in Lee County, Kentucky. Conditions were pretty primitive there. Our mail came in a covered mail wagon, from eight miles away, drawn by two mules in good weather and four mules in bad weather. And the church could only afford to pay fifty dollars a month. But it was good work. In fact, a friend of mine from Knoxville named Vera Mc-Campbell got so interested [in what I was doing] that she felt her life would be more worthwhile to come up there and join me. I needed somebody to help me, and Dr. Tyler hired her. From that time on we lived together, and she worked there with me. She was one of the best people I ever knew.

The county schools, where there were any, only lasted three to four months a year. When they closed, the children interested in getting more education would come and join our mission school.

Vera and I taught all day and then would visit the people in the communities to invite them to our Sunday school and church services on Sundays. We'd take medicine to them if they needed it. We had the only drug supply in the county. There was one doctor and he lived over the line in another county. When you sent for him, he was liable to be two or three counties away. When any of the people in the coal mines had accidents, we could give them first aid. We had had first aid training and could handle simple emergencies.

Dr. Guerrant's son was the head of the Winchester hospital about forty miles away and once a year he would come up to the mission and we would turn the schoolhouse into a hospital. He would perform operations up there and take care of people that could be cared for under those circumstances. He would have the others [needing extensive care] come down to Winchester on the train.

That was about the extent of the health care available, though. Sometimes when we were almost ready for bed, someone would come and want us to go where someone was hurt, or sick. We had boots that came over our knees and we would wade the creeks to the place and then someone would walk back home with us. They were very good to us. We were treated with great kindness, although it never occurred to us that we should be afraid. If the call were nearby, we would come back alone maybe, and didn't feel afraid. We never had to lock our doors.

We didn't even have to raise our own garden or chickens. Those people shared whatever they had.

If anyone died during a time when the circuit preacher wasn't around, we also held funeral services. When the minister came through, he would hold formal services for the dead we had buried.

And Vera's mother, Mrs. McCampbell, came from Knoxville to live with us shortly after we got settled. She worked with the community women. When we had quiltings for our orphanage, she would help with them. She did our cooking so we wouldn't have to cook when we came home in the evening. And although she had been very gently reared herself—she went to a fashionable finishing school when she was young—she never made us feel that we were living a life of hardship. She was a person who was young at heart, and she shared everything with us.

But after a while, Mother McCampbell developed cancer. Young Dr. Guerrant came up to see her from Winchester. He said it would be too hard for us to get her back and forth to the hospital there for treatment. So it looked to us as if we would have to leave the mission for a while [because I planned to go with Vera to care for her mother].

That was when I remembered Dr. Lillian Johnson. She had written me several years earlier about a school she had established in Summerfield, Tennessee. When Dr. Johnson first came to Grundy County in 1915, she had the idea of building a school here that would be considered a model mountain school. She built a summer home and she lived there and began at once to help the community. First, she remodeled the little public school building there that has long since become part of the consolidated system. A room was added on to the original building; she built a cloakroom, and put a furnace in the basement. That little school became the center of life for the community, and she taught there herself for a while.

She had one assistant which the county gave her, but in those days the school went only until Thanksgiving or Christmas. So she would then go back to Memphis, Tennessee, and go among her friends and solicit money to pay teachers and help the school to last longer.

She wanted to get teachers who would come and live in the community and become a part of the community, but her great difficulty was in getting teachers who would stay. They would stay for just a year and then they'd go somewhere else, you see. So she asked me if I'd be interested in coming and said she especially wanted a teacher who would help the children with reading. Well, it all sounded exciting to me because I had heard so much about Dr. Lillian's work, but I couldn't leave my school and go to this new place. Then Vera's mother got sick. That was when Vera and I made the decision to come here to Summerfield, Tennessee. Mother McCampbell would be close to a hospital, and we could teach here. When we moved here, we decided to stay in Summerfield for about a year, so that Mother McCampbell could get medical treatment nearby. She died during that year, but we decided to stay on rather than go back to the Kentucky mission. We had both fallen in love with the community, and Dr. Lillian was very persuasive. She said, "I don't see why you two don't feel like you could do as much to serve the Lord, humanity in general, and me in particular by staying on here." So here we stayed. Vera has since died, but I've been here ever since.

Vera and I lived for the first three years in two rooms—this living room here and the kitchen, and that tiny attic bedroom that I later converted into our "library." We added on to the house later, but we always stayed right here. After we moved here, we never moved again.

At the school, Mary B. Thompson, a girl from Memphis, Tennessee, taught the first four grades and was playground director. She was a very fine teacher. I taught the fifth, sixth, seventh, and eighth grades, and Vera taught cooking and sewing. It was a rather unusual mountain school, especially for that time. The county paid my salary and half of Vera's. Dr. Johnson raised the other half. She had the idea of developing a school that would go much farther than the ordinary public school, so we began to put this new teaching plan into effect in 1925, the first year we came here. She wanted the girls to be taught cooking and sewing, and the boys to be taught agriculture and other extra things.

One of the things you might be interested in hearing about was the "soup pot" we had. One of the things we taught in school was arts and crafts. The girls made rag and hook rugs and honeysuckle baskets, and the boys made toys, bookends, book racks, anything they could make with a coping saw. We sold our crafts, some locally, and some of them we sold through my publishers. By the time I retired from teaching, we had markets in five different cities. With half of the money we made from the sales of the handcrafts, we bought food for our soup pot. We were running our soup pot before there was anything like lunchrooms in this part of the state. The mothers would send me canned tomatoes and green beans, anything like that. And the children brought all sorts of vegetables from home. We had a seven-gallon lard bucket and a great old big potbellied stove to cook on. I would buy rice, and the various things they couldn't bring from home. And later on, another teacher would bring meat down from Tracy City where she lived. We'd peel our own vegetables and prepare everything for the soup. So many of the children have said, "We were just like a family." And school *ought* to be an extended family. It can't be that way, though, when it's so big.

Dr. Johnson also got a purebred bull from a farm outside Memphis. They lent him to her. She didn't buy him, but for years and years, he stayed over in a pasture that was next to the schoolhouse there. He was useful in bringing new stock to the community. Then she got a Smith-Highes man here. [These were agriculture teachers funded by a provision made in the Tennessee legislature.] He also taught biology to my boys. I would excuse them from the regular classroom and they would go over to the agriculture house. All these were very far-out ideas in a little country school at that time. You just didn't think about animal husbandry being taught in a high school then. She would get people from the University of Tennessee and other places to come and lecture to the people. She enlarged their horizons.

Some people of the community did think all this activity

strange and did not understand why she wanted to change their ways of thinking. It was such a new thing and people are very wary about new things and new people. Someone has said that you must teach man as though you taught him not. They resent the encroachment of new ideas sometimes. Dr. Johnson showed me a letter one time, an anonymous letter, that she got right after she came here. It was very resentful of her—implying that this community would be better off without her newfangled ideas. I don't think that she showed that letter to anybody else.

We got along well with Dr. Johnson. I felt that with the experience she had in educational matters, it was natural that she would be the leading spirit. The thing about me was that I was a mountain woman myself and I felt that I knew the mountains and that I was one of the people, and sometimes that I had a little more insight into mountain attitudes than she did. I think that was the reason she wanted to keep me. I could be a go-between [with the people of the community]. She was of a different culture. You can't imagine two women of more widely diverse cultures than Dr. Lillian Johnson and May Justus.

I believe it was during our first winter here that we also started a school for adults. We were up at the church one Sunday and after the service was over, the parents and the teachers were standing around talking. One of the fathers said he had been telling his children how little chance he had had to get an education. He was telling them how proud they ought to be to have the chance that they were having to learn the things he wished he'd had the opportunity to learn. I told them about the moonlight schools of Kentucky and somebody said, "Wouldn't it be wonderful if we could have a school like that here?"

I said that we could. And that was the nucleus of the idea. We started it in our kitchen where my bedroom is now. I didn't think folks would come. I thought they were just being nice to us, but that night there were about half a dozen. That was the first night, and we started. We sat around our great big kitchen table and we taught reading, spelling, writing, and simple figures. That was the curriculum. Mary B. Thompson taught writing because she had beautiful handwriting herself.

They kept coming. One man said that he wanted to learn his figures so well that he could figure out how much wood was in a cord of wood. He had suspected many times that he was being cheated. And another man sold wood, and he wanted to know about measuring cords of wood, too. They would come here and get me to figure things out for them. . . .

All this time, I was also writing books for children. Finally my first book was published in 1927 when I was twenty-nine years old. It was called *Peter Pocket.* I had sent the manuscript to Doubleday and they kept it and kept it. I wrote them a letter in the form of a poem. I said that I was afraid that Peter Pocket, the little mountain boy, had wandered from the Cumberland Mountains and had gotten lost in great New York City. So the editor sent me a telegram and said they were happy to have Peter. They brought it out the next August.

I kept writing Peter Pocket stories because the children loved him and they kept asking what would happen next. (He was a little orphan. His father was a poet, and they called him the "songmaker." When he died, he left his poems to this little boy.) The stories go on and on. Holt brought out two books called *Peter Pocket's Surprise* and *Peter Pocket and His Pickle Pup.* Then Doubleday brought out one big book called *Peter Pocket's Book.* I continued writing these mountain stories published by Doubleday. The next book was *Other Side of the Mountain.* Then I did *Honey Jane.* It was a story about a little girl whose childhood was much like mine. Honey Jane, as I had, kept writing poems and sending them in to a publisher of children's literature hoping to get paid some money to help with the family's expenses. So finally I was a published author. . . .

For the continuation of May Justus' interview, see Chapter Two (page 75).

★

Callie Didn't Let Us Forget She Was Black

Ralph Tefferteller

Back when a boy's entertainment came from Tom Mix movies and his snacks from American chestnut trees, a maverick-to-be was also absorbing stories and songs and values in the Great Smoky Mountains. Over the years, he would find use for them all.

In 1937, he served as an instructor for Local 95 of the Amalgamated Clothing Workers of America during an historic labor course. It rallied four thousand people to parade through La Follette, Tennessee, and their unity demonstration inspired the film The People of the Cumberlands, *which premiered the following year. Later, in New York City, he and his wife, Ruth, began a twenty-one-year career at the Henry Street Settlement, where he compiled the book* The Addict in the Street. *During the Vietnam War, the couple also established a training center for the Ministry of Social Welfare in Saigon.*

Their careers demonstrate one definition of an activist: one who goes when, and to where, social change is needed most.

I came from a fairly long line of pioneers. I've discovered that I represent the tenth generation in my family in America. Among those that preceded us, the earliest were Jacob and Joseph Tefferteller, who set sail from a port in Holland around 1666. Now, I'm not sure whether they set sail voluntarily or whether they were just two steps ahead of those who wanted to dispose of them, or restrict their freedoms.

At any rate, I arrived on the scene on a little family farm of about a hundred sixty acres near the village of Armona, which is in Blount County, Tennessee, about three miles from Maryville, the county seat. Our farmhouse had been built about 1900, and I was born there in 1910 with what was to be a family of eight children. Now, you know 1910 was a famous year both here on the face of the earth and out in space because Haley's comet appeared in 1910. One of my hopes is that I will live in good health until Haley's comet reappears some six years or so from now.

Well, anyway, there we lived in a completely rural setting extending into the foothills of the Great Smoky Mountains. Beautiful, scenic, but losing a lot of topsoil because the farmers were interested in tending as much acreage as possible, and the heavy rains at certain times of the year, with the topsoil loosened and plowed, just washed it down into the hollows and into the low places. And so, in the hills, ofttimes it was the low places only where you could grow anything.

We were surrounded by family. My mother's family were Sterlings and Wallaces and were part of that early Scottish-Irish migration into the mountains. They settled in Blount County, where her father, John, died in a wheatfield of a heart attack. He was only a young man—beautiful, wonderful human being—but there it was. His wife, though—my grandmother Sterling—was still alive, living by turns with her two daughters and a son. This was the way you took care of older people then. They lived about from one family to the other. As youngsters, we sat at her knee, in the old farmhouse when she came to stay with us; and she'd read us the Bible and get quilting parties together on our porch to make quilts to raise some little monies for the church.

Then there was Uncle Steve and Aunt Lizzie. Uncle Steve was actually Grandpa Tefferteller's brother. They lived in a log cabin just seven miles from our farm back in the real hill country in a hollow so deep the sun didn't get in there until way late in the morning. They had thirteen children, and the last two were twins born when Aunt Lizzie was way up into her forties. As the family grew, they just added rooms—you might have called it a modular log cabin! We'd go visit them often. Uncle Steve was a scrawny little man who always grew his supply of broadleaf tobacco every year, and we'd often find him sitting in the corner near the open fireplace making twists out of his tobacco. He was just pioneer stock from head to toe.

He and Aunt Lizzie developed great big sons, and I used to go there to go catfishing with them. We'd go out to the nearest river in a wagon filled with straw and we'd set out our lines at night across the river and then sleep in the bed of the wagon. In the early hours of the morning we'd tend our lines to get the catfish and go back. I would also go there in the fall to gather nuts. Those were the days when the great American chestnut was in its prime. I can remember going there and we would rake the leaves aside and then scoop up chestnuts in double handfuls, there were so many chestnuts on the ground.

Grandfather Tefferteller, who died when I was six, had been as poor as Job's turkey. He actually sliced his way out of the wilderness with an ax and a crosscut saw, adding acre to acre there in Blount County when acres only cost fifty cents apiece. He was a big man, and he came to be a leader and much respected. He wanted to be sure each of his sons and daughters got a good start in life, and one thing he did [toward that end] was build a log house on his farm that he put the newlyweds into. It was called a weaning house—weaning the boy and girl away from their families—and that was the beginning house. My father and mother got their start there. After their first year, my oldest brother was born, and that's when they built the farmhouse that I was born into on land that was part of my father's inheritance.

Being born in 1910 in that part of the world, I'm old enough to have gone back pretty much to the handicraft age where people were self-reliant and made most of what they needed themselves. On our farm, for example, we had a blacksmith shop and my father made the horseshoes and shod all our workhorses and rebuilt wagon wheels when the rims had broken. I was the bellows pumper. I'd get the coals red-hot and he'd snatch that red-hot metal out of the forge onto the anvil and hammer it into shape. That was hard, basic work on the farm, and the kinds of skills that were handed down by fathers to their sons.

We also, of course, tried to grow a number of cash crops. Armona at one time was a stop on the Louisville and Nashville Railroad. The line ran across Grandpa's farm and right at the edge of our farm. That was a big strawberry-producing area then, and L and N boxcars would pick up the strawberries and take them out. The trains still ply those rails going through Armona, but they don't stop there anymore.

But believe you me, strawberries were one of the first cash crops that I became aware of as a youngster growing up because my barefooted brothers and I had to cultivate the strawberries on our farm and get down on our knees and pick out the crabgrass. We never got paid for picking our family's strawberries, but after ours were picked, we could go to the Sutton farm nearby and pick for him for three cents a quart. Those were some of the first nickels I earned as an eight-year-old. . . .

Pork was the principal diet, of course, with chicken and turkey. Those turkeys! That's one of the vivid memories of my childhood. Every child was moved from one set of chores to another as he grew older and the older person taught him how to perform the next set of chores. You started with such things as stalking the turkey hen. Now, if you've never stalked a turkey hen who's going to her nest, then you've missed one of the pleasures of childhood. You are assigned. It's your job to find the turkey's nest. You've got to get the eggs before a skunk or some other animal finds the nest and sucks those eggs and we've lost a turkey. You've got to get the turkey eggs and bring them in and get them under an old setting hen who's going to keep those eggs warm and hatch them so you can raise the little turkeys to adulthood and into your meat supply. Well, a turkey hen is one of the wiliest of the two-legged animals. *Smart,* oh, so smart, and so knowledgeable about the ways of human beings and little barefooted boys of eight, nine, ten years of age. She knows that she's being stalked, and so she has all of these natural hiding places: She will go down the old cedar lane toward the lower field, and she'll go through into the oat field.

Then she'll cross through the rail fence, and on the other side, in the crook of the fence, she's going to sit down for a while and she's going to try and convince you that that is her nest. By now you're short on patience, so you turn and head back toward the house. You're going to tell the folks that you know where it is.

At the end of the day, you take one of the older members of the clan to show him or her the nest. You go down to that crook in the rail fence and you say, "It's just over there," and the two or three of you lean over and there's the place kind of pressed down a little where the old turkey hen had squatted to throw you off the track. And boy, do they razz you. [*Laughter*] They say, "Tomorrow, tomorrow, you stick with that old hen, we've got to get those eggs!"

And so tomorrow comes and you single her out, and she slyly begins to edge through the barnlot and through an opening and out she goes again. She goes a different way this time than she went the day before. Once she gets to the wheat field, there are larger clumps of new growth of winter wheat where there was horse manure or cow manure, and there the stalks are higher, greener, more inviting places for a turkey hen to make her nest in, you see? And so she goes from one clump to the other and finally secrets herself in one trying to throw you off; but you, oh, you're wary this time and you're wiser. And so you stick with the old hen until she goes through that wheat field.

This time she eases over toward Uncle Will's property and goes down a little hollow and she's out of sight. During this time, she runs, low, close to the ground, and she gets into the crook of another rail fence and she hides from you. Well, it takes you quite a while to determine that it's the old turkey hen you're seeing and not just leaves and things. Finally, you know you have found her nest; you know that that's the place where she laid her eggs. This time, the confirmation is had when you take a member of the clan and show them. The eggs have been carefully covered by the old turkey hen and don't show at all. She has covered them and there are three eggs in there. We take a false egg and put it in the nest, take the three eggs out, and we carry these back to the house so we can get them under an old setting hen. And about that time, you're crossing the barnyard and you see the old gobbler in all his regalia gobbling out his message to the world! Well, life was not always that easy on the farm. . . .

We grew oats and barley and wheat, and we threshed the wheat right there on the farm, and I tell you, the occasions like the threshing of the wheat were very very special occasions on any farm. We did our own cutting and shocking of the wheat. Putting up a shock of wheat is an art, because if it isn't put up properly, the first gust of wind that comes along takes off the cap. Then when it came time to thresh, the Jeffrey brothers came to your farm with their thresher. They were itinerants who moved from farm to farm and were paid in kind, in bushels of wheat, depending on how much they threshed out.

I can see them coming now across the lower field and under the railroad culvert from Uncle Will's place—coming in that old wood-fired steam thresher. We always laid a section of rail fence down so they could come through the opening, and if you didn't watch out, they'd burn up your rail fence, because there's nothing they liked better than to get rails and cut them up in four-foot lengths and chuck them into the engine's firebox. That's how the first power came onto the farm.

Meanwhile, the wagons have been sent into the field to gather the shocks of wheat. You have men on the ground with pitchforks, forking up, and a man on the wagon packing, and he has to pack carefully or he'll lose his load going up the side of a hill. And once he gets to the threshing machine, he moves in on one side of the machine and another teamster comes in on the other side and there's a man standing there in the middle. This man is the feeder, and oh, is he skillful! Then you have two juveniles flanking the feeder, and each one of them has a sharp knife, and as the packer throws a bundle off the wagon, one juvenile makes a slashing movement and cuts the tying string. By that time the feeder is ready to reach with one hand and feed that bundle in at the same time the boy on the other side has another bundle ready for his other hand, and this is the way he goes, rolling with his right arm and hand and rolling with the left arm and hand and feeding those bundles in. And these juveniles have to be damn sure that they don't cut his fingers off, because they've got sharp knives and they are slashing with them.

Usually my father and the elders were the ones who handled the sacks at the end of the chute. The wheat came down into a sack and when it filled, then you had a sewer who had a needle about as long as your finger, and he had the twine already threaded in it, and he held the corner of the sack with one hand and he ran that needle through and did a knot. Then he quickly wound it around and that became one of the ears. Then he began the sewing all the way across; and then around and around and he had another ear. Then he did another couple of turns and flipped that sack over and there it was. It was ready to be toted.

Any surplus wheat we had left out of that crop was another

cash crop for the year, but we ate so many wheat biscuits that sometimes there wasn't much left. My father was just a scrawny little man, a hard-working dirt farmer, and he used up so much energy that he ate tremendous amounts of food. Molasses, butter, and biscuits was his favorite food, and sometimes he'd eat as many as twenty biscuits for breakfast. He'd eat his other food first and then start in on those biscuits my mother cooked every day in the wood-burning oven. If it hadn't been for sorghum molasses and biscuits and cornbread and sourbelly and chickens, believe you me our family would have had a hard time making it through many a winter. There's nothing better, though, for a little boy coming home from a rural school in the afternoon than coming home to a corn dodger that's just been prepared on the coals of an open fire in a black iron skillet. To take that and some sweet milk or buttermilk and crumble the cornbread with its thick crust up into it and stir it around and then take a spoon and eat it was the most delicious kind of snack which a youngster could have. Well, we've gotten away from that unfortunately.

So we raised and consumed a lot of corn ourselves. We'd haul it in from the fields and put it up in log corn cribs and use some of it to feed enough hogs so we could have meat the year round. And there was another chore for a boy like myself—to go out there every evening and throw corn out onto the hard ground for the hogs. It's one chore I especially enjoyed—being there with the animals and hearing this wonderful crunching sound as they opened up the husks and ate from the ears.

When it came time to sell the hogs we weren't going to eat ourselves, we would have a hog drive, and drive these fat hogs on their spindly legs the three and a half miles to Maryville to market. If you've never driven hogs, then you are not aware of the fact that as you go along the road, if there has been a recent rain and there are puddles along the side, there is nothing more inviting to those three-hundred-pound hogs than those puddles. Especially when they are hot and their feet are tender after being driven several miles over a gravel pike. I can hear those hogs now enjoying the relief of those puddles. [*Laughing*] But the problem was to get them up on their feet again and drive them on into town!

And remember, now, this was at the time when Tom Mix was in his glory. If you got into Maryville on time on a Saturday, you could catch the silent movie of Tom Mix and his great horse. They'd show cattle drives that were just the thing to catch a child's imagination, and for days after, back home, as you rode the work-horses on the farm, you'd imagine yourself on a cattle drive!

And then, of course, there was church. That was another of the diversions for people in rural parts. I'd say it was the prime social center, in fact. Our family was split over church. My mother and her people were strong Presbyterians, and my father and his side were strong Southern Baptists, so we kids got equal doses of each. We'd go to the Armona Baptist Church in the mornings, which was located on a little corner of property given to the church by Grandpa Jim. Then in the afternoons we had to go to the Mount Taber Presbyterian Church—a little white one-room rural church with its little spire.

They were very different churches. The Baptist church is where we got all of our hellfire-and-brimstone training. If Reverend Burns was available and wasn't suffering from the gout, he preached after Sunday school and tried to save us all. He always assumed that everyone had backslid since last time he spoke, so he came down hard on each one of us to make each feel like he was a poor and sodden unforgiven sinner. And then if he didn't do the job during the year, when crops were laid by the latter part of August, then came the protracted meeting. And this one ran for ten nights or two weeks. And *that was a time,* believe you me! And if you weren't saved by the end of that time, there was something wrong with you, because all of your friends and neighbors ganged up on you, and they would come while hymns were being sung about the poor sinners of this world and they would beseech you to come forward and declare yourself as a converted Christian and a follower of Jesus, and to atone for your sins during the course of the year.

And if *that* didn't get you, there was a Holiness tabernacle up on a ridge just three farms from ours. The tabernacle had sawdust on the floor and long benches and open-slatted sides so you could look in from the outside and watch while people were overcome with emotion and would get up and start shouting. There was a lot of soul-saving that went on there. They'd preach all morning; then everyone would go outside and spread dinner out under a chest-nut tree and eat, and then they'd go back inside and start up again. If you were young, you skedaddled and let the adults go on in while you went down, down, down the hill to a little man-made lake that had a little flat-bottomed boat, and you'd get out in it. Or you looked across the slope on the far side at Uncle Will Hick's watermelons. He led the singing and taught shaped-note music in the church. While he was unaware, you can imagine the watermelon splitting that took place there near the tabernacle!

Mount Taber had a very different atmosphere. There was none of the shouting and none of the emotion. It was very dignified. The preacher was an itinerant preacher with three churches. He was a professor at Maryville College—Professor Hall—and he was very erudite. He was also a marvelous person because he gave the young people real responsibility. I was a deacon of that church at the age of seventeen, and the treasurer at eighteen, collecting the monies and paying Professor Hall. What a responsibility that was for a young person!

He had real skills in developing leadership, and I lay some of my earliest leadership training to this man's hand and fine example. He was perhaps the first who got me interested in going on to college.

So those were some of the early formulations of my character. Many of them came through close association with adults. I'll never forget one lesson I learned at the hand of Oscar and Callie Wallace, a black couple that lived on Uncle Will Tefferteller's farm. I was about twelve, and my cousin—Uncle Will's son—and I liked to be together, and we were down at Oscar and Callie's home. There were times when we'd forget they were black, and we'd be having a meal with them, chattering along; and as youngsters do in thoughtless moments, we'd say things within the context of the culture which taught us, and all of a sudden a derogatory term would slip out in referring to a black person. And at that moment, teaching took place. Callie would never let it go unremarked. Oscar Wallace wouldn't say anything. He knew she'd take care of it. She was very sensitive to the black man's sufferings at the hands of the whites, and she would be furious with us and would give us tongue-lashings. I've never forgotten those experiences. She really taught us to respect our fellow black citizens. She wasn't about to let two young punks low-rate her and her man and her race. And I've often thought, if only this could occur in the

lives of more white children. The best teaching comes from the
persecuted—from the person who can speak up for himself. Not
what you *ought* to do in relations with your fellow man, but how I,
the persecuted, feel about it and how I'm not going to allow you to
get away with it. That's good education, and it really leads to
changes in attitudes, and it leads to learning. . . .

Even as I was a child, though, that old way of living was changing as we moved out of the handicraft age into the industrial age.
Before the First World War, most fathers on farms like ours expected that their sons would carry on in their footsteps, work on
the farm, maybe add some acreage, raise their children, and so on.
That wasn't to be in most cases, however, because America was
changing. Shortly before World War I, for example, because of the
abundance of water power, the Aluminum Company of America
began buying up the farms near us to put in a plant to smelt
bauxite to get aluminum. It was phenomenal. Here we were in a
rural county where the biggest industry had been Maryville College, and here came the aluminum company and set up their pot
rooms and began smelting, and what a sight that was! In building
it, it meant some jobs locally then, as well as after the plant was
completed, and so the lives of the people began to change. In
addition, they brought in imported labor which they housed first
in tents. Then those tents were gradually converted into small
houses and suddenly there was a company town that they named
Alcoa that became kind of a twin town to Maryville. Here they
were, sitting side by side.

[We lived in sort of an uneasy truce with the new plant.] The
company houses in the middle of the town near the pot rooms
were reserved for the black laborers they brought into the area—
an area where until then there had been very few blacks. Well,
another cash crop which we tried earnestly to come up with was
wood. We were always trying to clear another acre of land anyway
so that we could put it under cultivation. When we had cleared
close to twelve acres, the sawmill people came and the workmen
brought their mules and set up a sawmill and they lived there near
our farmhouse, and this was some *experience* for a boy my age to
have a mobile sawmill crew come and live on the place while saw-
ing the timber. Most of the lumber then had to be cured for
building the new barn at our farm. As a youngster I can remember

so well that as the carpenters worked up on the structure of the new barn, they'd hit a nail the wrong way and *ping*, that nail would come down. Sometimes tenpennies, sixteenpennies, twentypennies, great big nails. And you'd go after these nails, and you had secret places where you put your treasures where those carpenters would never find them. Those were your nails from then on.

At any rate, the wood that came from the tops of the trees we cut into stovewood and ricked into half cords and cords of wood, and then after that wood cured out, we sold it. Well, those black laborers who worked in the pot rooms had no access to wood, so they had to buy it from the farms. We were one of the suppliers to that little section of Alcoa that became known as Blackbottom. Coming home from the little rural school in the afternoon, one of my tasks was to hitch a team of mules to a wagon and get that wagon to one of these cords of wood and fill that wagon bed up full of wood. Then I had an address in Blackbottom and I headed off toward Alcoa through the woods. This was all still uncleared. When I came to the town line, I'd go on to those little houses and ferret out these dirt streets and find the little house on my address. In the basement of that little house, that's where the wood had to go. Couldn't just throw that wood beside the house and let it go at that. So I became an expert in backing the wagon up and getting close to this opening that had a chute that led into the basement and then throwing that wood from up on the wagon down into that hole and into the basement. Then at the end of that operation, the Missus came out with pay. It was a dollar and a quarter for that wagon load of wood. And I stuck that well-used dollar and quarter down in my jeans and headed back toward the farm and through the woods. That was my afternoon's work and contribution to the family larder—so to speak—to the family exchequer and one of several ways that we, too, were affected by Alcoa.

Then, following the example of Alcoa, electricity came in. They had to have some right-of-way across our farm for the new power line, and I can still hear those wires zinging and see the bolts of lightning that would bounce off the wires in electrical storms. It's quite a sight to see. Scary. Sometimes those bolts would run the lines and jump off on a shock of wheat and set it afire.

Next the little gas line coming out of Texas came across our strip of farm. And then, sure enough, when the Knoxville airport was built, they had to have part of our farm to build it. And the Aluminum Company on the other side. Isn't that something? One little patch of land getting hit like that. It's amazing. Industrialization and change coming to the mountains.

Uncle Steve and Aunt Lizzie never got used to that. They died back there in their log cabin. Their sons and daughters moved out of there to seek a new way of life.

It was the same with Ella and Jim. They were tenant farmers who lived in a little farm building on our land. And what a hard life they had. Ella took in washing from our large family to earn some extra money while Jim was in the fields. She boiled those farm clothes in a black pot and ironed them. What a worker she was.

And Jim was literally my earth teacher. Working with Jim down the long rows of corn, chopping out weeds in the early summer and springtime, you talked about many things. You talked about the natural world around you, and you learned how to predict the weather. We worked from sunup to sundown. And when you came in and you got the stock into their stables and fed, then you headed for the gate around the barn lot, and when that gate chain was dropped over the nail that held it, then you turned and your day was finished. Then Jim would lift his hat back and scratch his head and he'd look. By this time it was dusky, and there would be some indication, you see, of what was coming for the morrow. He was always reading the signs to see what kind of weather we'd have on the next day. . . .

Recently I reestablished contact with . . . one of Jim and Ella's sons . . . and he was telling me that his little farm, which he has acquired through the years, has a little livestock that furnishes him meat and so on. But for most of his manhood, he's been working at the plant. His story is repeated over and over again by farmers who lived nearby and whose cash crop became their work in the plant.

Suddenly rural folk had become industrial workers, and this is the way it was all through the Southeastern part of the country.

And so it was there, in the midst of new influences that came into our placid community and county, that I finished the eighth grade in 1923. That was in a two-room schoolhouse built on land given by Uncle Will. The "roaring twenties" roared right past us and didn't affect us much. The boys came home from France and marched right down the main street in their khakis. I marked my entry into the world of adulthood with my first suit of clothing with britches that went below the knee.

My mother wanted to be sure that her children got at least a high school education. The company town, Alcoa, had built a high school named Springbrook, and so a chap who graduated from the little two-room school at Armona with me and I each saddled up his horse and rode over there. You had to get special permission to go from a county school into that high school, but we had it. . . . I became very active in sports, and began to become known in the community as a leader. Though there were only six or seven of us in the graduating class, I was the valedictorian. The last major paper I researched and delivered at graduation was on the hydroelectric possibilities in East Tennessee. I didn't realize at the time how much that subject had bearing on our future in East Tennessee!

After I graduated from high school in 1928, there was the question of returning to the farm or going on to Maryville to college. Professor Hall, the itinerant Presbyterian preacher, was one of the strongest influences on my decision to try college, along with one of the local farmers who had gone himself. My mother was very much in favor of it. My father wasn't. He was a very practical man for whom education was useful only insofar as it helped you deal with your animals and the elements and the demands made on the farm by the increasing number of mechanical things. Even the threshing machine was becoming a little more complex each year, and people were changing from horses and mules to tractors. That added a lot of complications. But basically, for him, losing me to college meant losing a farmhand.

I entered Maryville in the fall of 1928. Maryville was known for sending out ministerial candidates by the carload, and so I began drifting in that direction. I majored in religious education and began to understand a little about the old prophets and some of the really revolutionary ideas of the Great Galilean, Jesus. I spent a good deal of time looking a little more deeply into the meanings of His teachings. I was also very active in sports, and lettered in football, baseball, and wrestling. And I became active in the YMCA.

During my junior year, I was elected president of the YMCA. That meant a very special privilege because it meant that during my senior year I had a free room in the YMCA building. It also meant that during the summer before my senior year, I was entitled to go to the Southeastern Student Conference at Blue Ridge, North Carolina. And *that,* my friend, was a *real* privilege. It was like leaving the wheat fields and entering another world. Physically it was spectacular—looking across the valley toward the Seven Sisters marching up toward Mount Le Conte on the other side. And the experiences I had there. . . .

I went that June of 1931 to attend the ten-day conference. Other students were selected to work there for the whole summer. I wasn't one of those, but I was so taken with it that I put in an application while I was there hoping against hope that I might receive a summons to come back, and I went home and right back into the wheat fields that first day. It was already time to cut the wheat and start the threshing. We were threshing wheat on the neighboring farm and I saw one of my younger brothers coming across the wheat field—this barefoot boy coming through the stubble—and here the threshing machine was grinding away and it was noisy, and my father was there. My brother came up bringing a telegram saying, "Report to Blue Ridge, North Carolina." There I was. My father wasn't a bit interested because it meant taking a hand away from the field, but I turned to my friend, the farmer, who had gone to college, and he was so pleased. So was my mother. They encouraged me. They said, "By all means, go. You must go." I walked out on my father, caught the bus, and headed in toward Asheville. I couldn't wait to get there.

For part of the time, I was one of the workers. That meant we did all the chores from making beds, to sweeping, to teaching tennis, to teaching swimming, to serving in the dining room and running the little soda fountain—all of these jobs were done by students and they came to be known as PWBs and PWGs. That stands for "Poor Working Boys" and "Poor Working Girls." This came from an old lady who was there for a conference some years ago, and she looked about her and saw all the work being done by these poor mountain people, young people, and she was noted to observe at one point, "Oh, my, I do wish that these poor working boys and poor working girls could go on to school and get a college education." She didn't realize that every one of them was finishing college and some of them had already amassed a number of credits toward their master's!

But more importantly, I began to meet people from outside the South. It was there, for example, that I had my first contact with someone from Union Theological Seminary in New York. I also began to become more interested in boys' work—or social work—than the ministry. This happened because Dr. W. D. Weatherford—whose son, Willis, [became] president of Berea College—ran the YMCA school on the campus of Vanderbilt during the school year, but during the summers he moved it to Blue Ridge and set up shop there and ran a school. There, you could gain credits toward your master's in boys' work at Vanderbilt.

In May of 1932, I graduated from Maryville, and right back to Blue Ridge I went for my second summer. Couldn't wait to get back. I was a PWB again, but I also continued to take the classes that would build credits toward my graduate work at Vanderbilt. We had courses in philosophy and physical education and recreation and lifesaving and boating. One of my favorite courses had to do with the folk arts and folkways of rural people. That was a natural for me because of my background. I had grown up where people did square dancing in their homes—just move the furniture aside and dance—and so I especially enjoyed it when we concentrated on the dances of the region. That had always been a real love of mine anyway.

So here we were, leaving college in the depths of the Depression. Everything had fallen to pieces, but we were happy as larks in this idyllic setting in the mountains as though nothing was wrong at all.

Traditionally, the young people from our area who came out of Maryville and were going into the ministry went on to schools in the region like Vanderbilt and McCormick and Louisville—all more conservative schools. And that's what I would have done, I suppose, had it not been for the fact that two upperclassmen who graduated a year before me—and who were outsiders who had come into the region to study at Maryville—decided to study at Union Theological Seminary in New York. Since we had been friends, we had stayed in touch. Going to a place like Union was an unheard-of step for a Blount County type from the middle of the Bible Belt. Union was considered very modernist—Riverside Church had been built by them and Harry Emerson Fosdick was preaching on the radio and all—and it just wasn't the kind of place that one of us would ever go. It was viewed as a very radical seminary.

But a parallel force pulling me toward Union was that I had met Charlie Webber at Blue Ridge. He was on the staff at Union and I was very impressed with him. So I began to have doubts about going on to Vanderbilt and limiting myself to boys' work.

During the second summer, Dr. Mitchell and his wife—the parents of George and Broadus—came to Blue Ridge again where he served as sort of a professor in residence lecturing on international affairs. He was so stimulating we just idolized him. One day I mentioned to him the possibility that I might be able to get a scholarship to study at Union, and he said, "Young man, if you have any opportunity to do postgraduate study outside your region, by all means, do so!" This was like one of the prophets speaking to me. It was the word! I never gave it a thought after that, because Dr. Mitchell had spoken, and I admired him so much.

I got in touch with Union and it was arranged that I could work out most of my tuition and I could get another four hundred and fifty dollars or something like that, and they would find a fieldwork assignment for me through Charlie Webber's department. And so I was drawing away from my rural past, drawing further away and out into the world. Here I was a nice, upright product of a well-respected, hardworking Blount County family, going to New York City. I remember one of the last entreaties made to me personally before boarding the bus in Maryville was by an older man who took me aside and told me, "Beware, beware of them Jews in New York. You're going where the Jews are. They'll get you. Beware."

For the continuation of Ralph Tefferteller's interview, see Chapter Two (page 102).

Great Numbers of People Went Down to the Mills

Don West

*Persons as different in backgrounds and interests as Septima Clark, Edgar
Daniel Nixon, May Justus, and Ralph Tefferteller might never have en-
listed in larger, common causes of historic value had they not been influenced by mentors. A. Philip Randolph, for example, inspired Nixon.*

*But social activists also need enablers. Causes rarely fade from public
view because there are too few supporters; more frequently, it's the zeal that
vanishes first from the ranks. So just as history may conclude that Myles
Horton became such an enabler, so, too, did Don West.*

 I was born in 1906 on the Cartekay River in the little Cartekay
community in Gilmer County, Georgia, not far from Ellijay. I was
the oldest of nine children. It was strictly a farming community—
very poor. We had to work very hard. A lot of the winter months
we wouldn't be going to school at all, so we would go out and track
possums and rabbits in the snow. It was always an exciting thing
because this was a way, of course, that we had of supplementing
our food on the table. Today I can't shoot a rabbit or a deer or
anything like that—I can't even eat that kind of meat—but back
then it was exciting. Just like hunting ginseng in the fall. We could
dig a little poke of ginseng roots and take it to the store and swap
it for a great big poke of flour, which was something of a delicacy
because our land was too rough to raise wheat, so we normally ate
cornbread instead—three times a day. To sit a visitor down to

breakfast with cornbread was not thought to be very good hospitality, so if someone like the Jewish peddler would come in, my mother would call me aside and say, "Run down to Roxie's and see if she's got a little bit of flour," and maybe Roxie would have a little and maybe she wouldn't.

So mostly we used cornmeal. I've gone to John Bunyan William's corn mill on Turkey Creek many times on a mule with a sack of corn we raised behind me to be ground. I went to the mill that way when I was so little that one time the sack fell off the mule and I was too little to reach up and put it back on. There were some big hogs, and they came around and smelled that meal and I was having a time keeping them off of it until finally along the way came one of our neighbors who was a grown man and he put my meal back on for me. I was in a real critical situation there for a spell.

They all made their living farming and things related to farming, and everybody looked upon each other as just being equal, and we shared in what we had. If some one of our neighbors should get sick in the summertime when his crops had to be worked, the neighbors would get together and go in and hoe out his crop. We farmed hillsides so steep that we couldn't drive a wagon over them to collect our corn. We had to carry it off the hills on our backs in sacks. Plowed with mules. It was subsistence farming, raising everything that we used in the home and supplementing this farming by selling various things to get a little cash money. In the fall, for example, we would take beans and corn and apples and potatoes and cabbage—whatever we had raised—and pack some of them in wooden barrels with two sacks fastened over the top and haul them to Ellijay and put them on the train and ship them to Atlanta. Then we'd load the rest into a covered wagon and hitch two mules to it and drive down through Tate and Canton and Marietta to Atlanta with that load of produce we were bringing out of the mountains. Frequently there would be three or four wagons. Three or four families would go together and that was pretty nice because we had a good time talking and visiting along the way and if somebody broke down or stalled or something, there was always somebody else to help him out. We'd camp along the way. I remember the first place we always camped was called Double Branches. It was between Jasper and Tate. We'd tie the mules up and feed them and we'd cook something in a skillet over a fire we'd build and then we'd sleep under the wagon on quilts we'd brought along. I was always very happy when I could get to go with my dad on one of those trips because we saw so many things that we never saw up in the mountains. Atlanta was a big town of course. When we got to Atlanta, we'd peddle out the load we'd brought on the wagon. Then we'd go to the depot and get the produce we'd shipped and peddle it out. Sometimes it'd take us two or three or maybe four days in Atlanta, and we would stay in the livery stables where they kept the horses and mules. You could put up overnight there and we could sleep in our wagon right in the livery stable with the mules.

We also supplemented the farming by hewing crossties for the railroads and peeling tanbark from the chestnut oak trees for the tanneries. As I walk through the woods around here now, there's not a tree anywhere here that I don't know, and that comes from away back in the early period when I had to know the trees and what they were good for. I knew what made a crosstie, what made the best tanbark, what made the best white-oak splits for bottoming chairs. As I say to some of the kids, I have a lot of information that's no good anymore because that's all out of style. But we once did all those kinds of things to get a little cash money.

[About the only break we had from work was Sundays when we'd go up] on Burnt Mountain to a little foot-washing church there. It was about three miles up there to the top of the mountain [where the church was] and I remember once we'd gotten halfway up the mountain and my dad was driving the mules along and he said, "Oh my goodness, I forgot the washpan." He said, "You all just drive on and I'll walk back and get it." And he went back and got our washpan because it was going to be a foot-washing service that day and we needed it to participate. A few years ago, much of that mountain was bought by a bunch of people from Atlanta— Ralph McGill had a summer home up there, among others. They changed the name of it to Tate Mountain, but, of course, to people like myself, it will always be Burnt Mountain. They bought everything up there except the little Burnt Mountain Church and the graveyard and a little bit of a lot around the church. The people refused to sell that piece of ground.

Both of my grandfathers were alive while I was growing up.

One of them was old man Bud West. He was a very gentle person and he influenced me a great deal because he was so gentle and kind. His wife, my grandma, was pretty sharp and brittle as far as her talking to my grandpa. She would sometimes bawl him out and Grandpa would take it in a very philosophical way. I remember how nice it was to go visit them. But they left the mountains about 1913. You see, in the early 1900s great numbers of mountain people went down toward Atlanta to get jobs working in the cotton mills that had come in and were paying about three to four dollars a week. Grandpa Bud died working in a cotton mill near Cartersville making five dollars a week. My aunt Mae and aunt Mattie worked there, too. Aunt Mattie taught me a song about it that goes, "Worked in the cotton mill all my life; / ain't got nothing but a Barlow knife." I've heard that song since, and I've wondered if the people who were singing it knew what they were singing about, or knew what it was to go hungry or not know where the next meal was coming from or what it meant to work in a cotton mill and not have anything for it. You know, the Barlow was the poor man's knife. You could buy one for ten cents.

Grandma West didn't work in the cotton mill but she was very good at making moonshine liquor and peddling it. She had a big gray horse and she had a good buggy, and she would take her liquor and put it under her lap robe in the bed of the buggy and take it to Cartersville to peddle it. Several times Grandma got caught selling this bootleg stuff, and Grandpa would have to go pay a fine for her, and he'd say, "Ann, you ought not to do that. You ought to cut out bootleggin'." And Grandma would say, "Well, you know, I thought if I could do a little bit more I could buy that bed that we need," or something like that. And she'd go back after the fine was paid and try it again. She did that a great deal. She was, in some ways, a close personal friend of Mrs. Rebecca Felton of Cartersville, the wife of William H. Felton, who had been a congressman from this Seventh District of Georgia a couple of times on an independent ticket. He bolted the Democratic Party and ran as an independent and was elected. He was—incidentally—a very progressive guy. Somebody ought to do a biography of William H. Felton because he was a mountain man who was hard-hitting, a straight-shooter, and very liberal. I guess he was in many ways a radical man, as many mountain people have

been. He for example was one of those—along with the coal miners of Coal Creek, Tennessee—who fought so hard against the
convict lease system in the early 1890s. Back in those days, before
it was finally abolished, a corporation or a landlord could lease
prisoners from the state. They paid maybe sixty dollars a year
apiece for these men and then they were their men. The L and N
railroad that came from Atlanta up through the north Georgia
mountains and then on into Copperhill and Ducktown, Tennessee, was partially built with convict labor. There's a graveyard
north of Ellijay, up at a community we used to call Whitepath until
somebody changed the name. Whitepath had been a principal war
chief of the Cherokee at one time, so this graveyard is in that
community. It used to also be a gold-mining community. But these
graves now are grown over with bushes and trees. I was walking
through that area a few years ago with a distant cousin of mine
who happens to be the official county historian of Gilmer County
and he was pointing out to me these gravestones—they were just
rocks—and he said, "Now these were people who died or were
killed building the railroad through Georgia, and they were con-
victs who had been leased from the state." And since he was then
working on the history of Gilmer County, I said, "Are you going to
put this in your history book?" And he said, "No, this is too negative to put in." I think that's indicative of how a lot of history has
been written.

    My other grandfather was Kim Mulkey. He was a great tall
fellow who had a big beard that came down on his chest. He went
to Texas in a covered wagon with all of his family once. They got
out to Texas, spent the night and looked around, and the next
morning he hitched up his mules and drove back to Gilmer
County. [*Laughter*] Actually, he is the one that did more than any
other person to begin to quicken my conscience and to get me
concerned in a social way. He was not religious in the pious sense
certainly, but he was concerned about human welfare, and I was
influenced greatly by him. As a matter of fact, as I look back on my
childhood remembrances, I remember how I considered my
grandfather to be just almost infallible. In those days, when I
thought in my imagination of what God was like, God and my
granddaddy always looked just alike, you know. [*Laughter*]

    I remember he used to call the hogs home every evening

about dusk. Back in those days we had free range where you didn't have to fence the stock and they could ramble anywhere. To keep them from going too far, the farmers would go out about dusk and call their hogs home. We lived down Turkey Creek about a mile from my grandfather's, and I could hear his voice coming down the creek, down between the mountains, down that very narrow valley there, and I would think, "My gracious, what a voice he has."

He had a great influence on my early attitudes. He used to teach us that we should regard all people as human beings, regardless of their color, their race, or their national background. He had only a second-grade education, which is typical of what happened in the mountains. His grandfather had been a medical doctor. When I say typical—the people who originally settled in Appalachia were not an illiterate people. They had been as well educated as the ordinary people of the times. But there was sort of a recession or a backward swing. We stagnated in the mountains for lack of schools and educational opportunities. My dad had only had a third-grade education. My mother maybe went through the fifth grade. She read a great deal, though. She used to read whole books to us when I was a kid. That was something unusual because most homes when I was growing up did not have many books other than the Bible. I remember the Sears, Roebuck catalog had six classics like *Treasure Island* they advertised once at ten cents apiece and my mother ordered them and she read every one of them aloud to us. I remember one of our neighbor kids who had been to spend the night with us telling his mother, "You know, Don West's mother read a whole book to him." It was unusual because mountain families had just been denied books. Just didn't have them. And there was no daily newspaper. The first radio I ever saw was after we moved out of the mountains. We had no way of getting information from the outside world except just rumors here and there. This is one of the reasons why we always welcomed strangers coming in who had information from outside areas. I remember the pack peddler who came every year and stayed with us. He'd give my mother a bright scarf or something and he'd undo his package and show all the bright prints that he had packed in there, you know, and it looked like something marvelous to a kid. Then, of course, he'd tell us what was happening out in the world and talk until late in the night.

Anyway, I did manage to go to college. I went to school through the sixth grade in a little one-room school called the Kennimer School where my aunt Alice taught. It was one of those schools that only went four months a year so we wouldn't be taken out of the fields during the times we were needed to work. Dad wanted us to get a better education, so we left the mountains and moved down into the cotton country in Cobb County, Georgia, and sharecropped when I was fifteen. If a man from the mountains wrote a South Georgia landlord and told him that he'd like to be a sharecropper, man, they'd take him right on, because they said, "These mountain people have the reputation for being willing to work. They go out and get it. They're not afraid to work." So that's what we did. We raised cotton and vegetables and corn and kept a cow and that kind of thing. We could only keep a portion of what we made since we were sharecropping, but we made out. Dad would chop up wood with an ax and peddle stove wood in Marietta. Our next-door neighbors there were black people, which was unusual for me because I was past fifteen years old before I ever saw a black man. There just weren't any blacks in the mountains to amount to anything. But these black neighbors came to our house just like we went to their house and they would eat at our table if they came at dinnertime, just like white neighbors had always done. I remember once a local white person from Cobb County said, "You're not supposed to have niggers eat at the table with you." And my mother said, "Why?" She said, "They're our neighbors." They said, "Well, you know, it's not the custom." But my mother always invited them just like anybody else. This is the way she had been brought up. Her father had taught her that as well as the grandkids. That was indicative of the sentiment of many people in the Appalachian South. Up there at Jasper, Georgia, about seventy-five miles north of Atlanta, throughout the four years of the Civil War, they put the Union flag on the courthouse every single day. I spoke there at the Jasper High School a few years ago and there wasn't a single student that knew this about their own courthouse which was just a block or two away. They had all been taught that they were part of the old slaveholding tradition, but it wasn't usually true in the mountains.

At any rate, I went to high school at Douglasville—walked the six miles there and back every day. The only clothes I had to wear were these bib-type overalls, and these little Southern towns could be very, very cruel to the poor kids. But I never did let it get me down. I never have let any kind of criticism do that. In fact, it was during this time that I realized I was proud to be from the mountains, and that being a mountaineer was something I didn't need to be ashamed of. I've had this identity all of my life as a mountaineer and I've always been very much concerned about it.

So I went to school, and worked in the fields every day when I got home, and when I was sixteen, my father decided to let me leave home and go to a boarding school. The old custom was that a boy was supposed to stay home and work for his daddy until he was twenty-one years old. Then he was a free man. Dad said, "If you can get into a boarding school where you can work your way through, I'd be willing to let you go." So I corresponded with Berry School in Rome, Georgia, and made arrangements to get into the high school there. My uncle Horace loaned me seventy-five dollars to start on. And then after I got started, I worked. Berry had a work program where you had to work two days a week or two hours a day—one or the other. And then if you stayed in the summertime, you could work all summer and pay for your tuition and board for the whole year.

I stayed there until I was expelled when I was a senior. Back in my early period, I guess I was a rebel, because I resented certain things. They had a very excellent chaplain there by the name of Gurley, and he was very friendly with the students. Many of the faculty there had this idea that you couldn't associate with the students because that would be fraternizing, but this chaplain would invite us to his apartment where he had a record player and a lot of Vernon Dalhart and old folk-type records. That was something we never had a chance to hear, so we would just delight in getting to go to his apartment in the evenings and listen to the music. But he was accused of fraternizing with the students and he was fired right in the middle of the term. There were three of us who took up for him, and of course we were let out, too. I'd been there long enough to have seventeen units, though, so I had enough credit to get into college without a diploma, which I did.

Between leaving Berry and going to college, I worked with the

Southern Bell Telephone Company up around Tallulah Falls, Georgia, stringing wires. They gave us our room and board and ten dollars a week, but since I sent all the money I made to my dad, when I enrolled at LMU—Lincoln Memorial University in Cumberland Gap, Tennessee—I only had $1.65 in my pocket. I went in to see the dean and told him I would like to go to college but I didn't have any money. He said, "Are you willing to work?" "Well," I said, "that's all I've ever done." And I did everything from milking cows to hoeing corn to digging ditches to carrying laundry. That was an interesting school. [Two of the best-known Appalachian writers,] Jesse Stuart and James Still, went there. Like Berea, it specialized in education for mountain kids. It was a little more liberal than Berea, though. But it was there that I was just beginning to feel the effects of a little bit broader education and deeper reading and contacts [with what was going on in other parts of the mountains]. That was the period in the early thirties when the National Miners' Union was trying to organize coal miners in Harlan and Bell counties, Kentucky, and was beaten out with violence and terror. At the same time the cotton mill workers in places like Gastonia and Marion, North Carolina, and Elizabethton, Tennessee, were trying to get organized. As students, on weekends we would hitchhike over to Harlan or over to Elizabethton where there was a cotton mill strike going on and talk to the workers and learn from them, and then we'd come back to the college and discuss these things in bull sessions. And some of us became very concerned about it. It was a violent period. At Gastonia, it was the National Textile Workers' Union that was organizing, and that's where there was the very famous case of Ella May Wiggins, the girl who wrote so many songs about the sufferings of the working people there in the cotton mill. She was shot one Sunday as a truckload of union people were riding along the public road. The gun thugs peppered them with bullets from the bushes and Ella May was killed. They sang one of her songs at her funeral and put up a marker to her several years later. At Marion, it was the same kind of violence against the United Textile Workers. There the sheriff and his deputies shot into a mass of workers and six people were killed—just shot down in cold blood.

It was at LMU that I met Connie and we married. Jesse Stuart was best man. We had to marry secretly because we would have

been penalized if the school had found out. In fact, they did find
out in my senior year and took Connie's scholarship away from
her. At the same time I was expelled for participating in a student
strike that closed the campus down for a couple of weeks. We
didn't think the administration was giving us enough voice in campus affairs and we were just sort of out of harmony with the spirit
and policy of the administration. So that was a pretty rough time.

Connie stayed on at LMU and worked her way through to
finish, and I hitchhiked to Nashville to see if I could get into
Vanderbilt as a divinity student. I told the dean of the school of
religion that I had absolutely no money but I would like to go to
school, so he turned me over to one of the men in charge of
student work, who got me a job coaching basketball at the Martha
O'Brien Settlement House, which was right near Fisk University in
the black ghetto. I got my room and meals there and forty-five
dollars a month, so I was set up pretty well at Vanderbilt. Dr. Alva
W. Taylor was my major professor, and he was a tremendously
dedicated, able person, and completely dedicated to human welfare. He influenced many students. Claud Williams was one of my
classmates during that period—the Reverend Claud Williams?—
and Howard "Buck" Kester, and Ward Rogers. So many of Alva
Taylor's students went out into sharecroppers' or coal miners'
struggles or things of this kind. He had the knack for challenging
and stimulating students to get into the things that really mattered. For example, during that period at Vanderbilt, there was a
miners' strike over at Wilder, Tennessee—one of the pioneering
efforts of the Appalachian miners to get organized. There was a
long drawn-out struggle around the right to organize, and there
was much violence. But as students at Vanderbilt, Dr. Alva Taylor's
class through the week would see if we could collect some food or
maybe a little money—anything we could get that might help the
strikers. Then on the weekends, we would go out and take it to
them.

One weekend we got there and Barney Graham, the president of the local union, had been shot down by a couple of company gunmen. The company domination was so strong that there
wasn't a church that would let this dead union man's body be
there for a funeral. . . . That is indicative of how complete the
domination of the coal corporations was at that point in so many

places in the coalfields. Kill a union leader, and then the churches wouldn't even have his funeral. That was a bitter struggle. Barney's twelve-year-old daughter, Della Mae, wrote a poem about her father which was made into the song "The Ballad of Barney Graham."

So you accumulated experiences in that way that just increased the determination and desire to do whatever was possible to help. That's when I began to get more and more interested in the folk schools in Denmark. Olive Campbell had written about them, and I had read her work, and I felt it offered some hope for Appalachia. When Connie graduated from LMU and rejoined me, we spent a year teaching at the Hindman Settlement School in Kentucky. Some students there at that time became rather well known—students like Jean Ritchie, the folk singer, and Carl Perkins, the congressman from East Kentucky. Then Connie stayed there and I was able to go to Denmark for a year to study the folk schools firsthand through a Vanderbilt scholarship I won to study in Europe.

It was shortly after I got back from Europe, and finished at Vanderbilt, that Connie and I began to look for a place to start a folk school. . . .

For the continuation of Don West's interview, see Chapter Two (page 76).

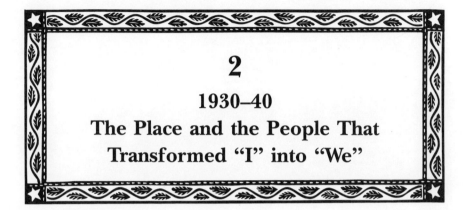

2
1930–40
The Place and the People That
Transformed "I" into "We"

Using the hysteria left over from World War I, American industry
—after it successfully defeated the steel strike of 1919—mounted
its battle plan and named it the "American Plan." Its purpose was
to destroy unions and to convince the country that they were un-
American. Through this plan they were successful in introducing
the "yellow dog" contract, industrial espionage, and armed hoods
that served as scabs and attacked picket lines. [It also] opened the
way for industrial racketeering, which became so lucrative as to
attract such leaders of "enterprise" as Arnold Rothstein and Al
Capone.

Out of the American Plan with its history of class violence
came years so ugly that men walked with their heads down, their
self-respect destroyed, their families hungry. . . . Jobs were not
to be had, and the government was unresponsive. . . .

It was in these lean years and turbulent times that Myles Horton—understanding the need for information and knowledge
and, above all, the importance of unity—established on top of the
Cumberlands in Tennessee a residential school . . . Highlander.
To this place came people, without regard to their race or color,
their religion or politics. For many years, until well into the fifties,
it was one of the few places in the South where black and white
could meet together, learn together, eat together, relax and laugh
together.

—RALPH HELSTEIN

★

The "One Year" Experiment
May Justus and Don West

Though Highlander would play major roles in such democratic causes as union organizing, integration, civil liberties—to name a few of the institution's contributions during this century—its launching in Tennessee in 1932 was quiet. Grundy Countians could add "and without ceremony," except that May Justus vividly recalls how she met Don West.

She was playing in a ball game with her students when the school's property owner, Dr. Lillian Johnson, brought the young man onto the field and promptly halted the game. During Dr. Johnson's introductions, she explained that West would be experimenting elsewhere on her property for one year with a labor school. Meanwhile, however, the students on the diamond were growing impatient. With or without a new school, they needed their teacher back on first base. So the adults agreed to meet that evening at Dr. Johnson's house. The time-out ended. And the friendships at Highlander began.

Recalling those first months, when she and Vera McCampbell began working as volunteers at Highlander, May Justus said:

After Myles and Don came, we had a group that met in the public school and they organized a garden co-op. I don't know how many people were there, but they were to can things. Highlander got a lot of tin cans. I don't know how they got them or anything about that, but it was a county co-op. We had a well there at the schoolhouse. They built a furnace right there, just an open furnace where the canning could be done. They canned a great deal of food and that was a great help. Then Mom Horton, Myles' mother, who was my next-door neighbor for many years, had a sewing co-op and they made square-dance skirts and all sorts of things. They marketed these things in cities. Friends of Highlander sold them.

Then there was folk music, and that was entirely Highlander. Zilphia Horton, Myles' wife, was an accomplished musician and played the accordion beautifully. After she came, the interest in music grew. Myles and Don invited us over to some play parties in those days. They were the only people living in Dr. Johnson's house. We didn't have any dancing then, just played games.

Then they began to have square dances over there. The people of the community rushed to me as they usually did. Dancing was very much frowned upon in this community, so they thought it was shocking and they would say to me, "How could Dr. Johnson, a good Christian woman, allow that sort of thing?" The church groups back in those days were very much against it and certain groups are that way yet.

The interesting thing was that in spite of that resentment, the dances were successful, and the young people and even the young married couples were going to them. It seemed that there were enough that accepted it, so that it entered into the scheme of things. That was along about 1933 or 1934.

Don West's memories about coming to Grundy County, Tennessee, begin a few months before May Justus'—right after he graduated from Vanderbilt and, with his wife, Connie, began seeking a location for launching the type of folk school he had studied in Europe:

The Southern Superintendent of the Congregational Church, Dr. Fred P. Enslinger, knew about this lady, Dr. Lillian Johnson, up on the mountain there near Monteagle who had some land. She had been trying to do a community program, and he thought she might be able to turn her farm over to me for a folk school, so he took me up there and we talked with her and she agreed. That summer I was in a YMCA Student Conference over at Blue Ridge, North Carolina, and I had a call from a man who said his name was Myles Horton and he was looking for a place to start a folk school also. He had heard I was starting one in Tennessee and he'd like to meet me. So he came over and we talked. Turned out we had both been in Denmark at the same time but hadn't run into each other. So we spent several days together after the conference looking around for suitable sites in North Carolina and Kentucky for Horton and didn't find anything that looked promising, so I invited him to come over to Monteagle. He liked the looks of the place and asked if he might come in as my partner, and that's the way the school got started. Connie suggested the name "Highlander" because we were up on a plateau of high land, and she made the first sign to go over the door gateway. Then we drew up the stationery and so on. The stationery said our purpose was "to educate rural and industrial leaders for a new social order" because we were looking for students from the industrial and rural areas who would be potential leaders in this kind of struggle. Since I had majored in social ethics at Vanderbilt under Dr. Taylor, I had some ideas along those lines. At the same time there was the cultural aspect that the Danish folk schools did so well, where the content of the curriculum was largely built on the cultural heritage of the Danish people—the myths and the stories and the folklore and the history. It helped to restore to the Danish people a feeling of self-assurance and human dignity. Here in Appalachia, I've always felt that we needed that. We need that restoration. We still need it as badly as we've ever needed it. We have had our heritage destroyed in many ways and so many of our people have no knowledge of it at all. They became ashamed in the mountains here of being mountain people. Our music suffered. Much of our folk music was considered inferior and not fit to be played, and mountain people in general were—and still are—ridiculed and caricatured. All that caused many mountain people to lose confidence in themselves as a people. The folk school movement in Denmark helped restore an awareness and understanding of the culture and heritage in a wonderful way.

So that was the kind of thing Highlander was set up to address. There were five of us as staff members that first year: myself, Connie, Myles, and two friends of Myles's, John Thompson and his sister, Dorothy. Jim Dombrowski came the next year. We lived together in Dr. Johnson's big house, and for food we bought a hundred-pound bag of beans and a hundred-pound bag of wheat and we'd boil the wheat and have it for cereal for breakfast with a little milk. And we would have the beans. We just about lived on beans and wheat. It was slim pickin's.

And at first it was rather difficult to find students. The idea of a school for students eighteen years old or older being operated with no credits or diploma or anything was a bit new. I can remember Myles and I went over to East Kentucky and I remember we walked down Cutshin by Mary Breckinridge's Pioneer Nursing Service there in Leslie County, Kentucky, just looking for students. We'd meet somebody and we'd talk to them and we'd say, "Would you be interested in going to school?" and so on. We were just beating the bushes around like that at first, you know. It was hard.

So I used to go out into the community and have educational meetings with community people in their homes. I'd go out around Grutlie and Palmer and Tracy City and get people together and we'd talk about our problems and have evening classes. Grundy County, of course, was one of the poorest counties around. There had been a tradition there in the past of having had a pretty considerable amount of union sentiment. From 1891 to '93, Tracy City had been a place where they had tried to break the miners' union with this convict labor and there had been a tremendous amount of militancy on the part of not only the miners, but also the common, ordinary farming people who had supported the miners in their opposition to the use of convict labor. But now it was the Depression and there was really a lot of hardship there, a lot of hunger, and a lot of just plain poverty, and there weren't any unions around that area then. It was later that the CIO got under way. And so when we talked about unions, it caused some controversy. We had been holding meetings in public schoolhouses at night and some of the people got excited about that and the county board of education decided to bar Myles and myself from the public schools. I can understand why, in the absence of an organization that's really viable and strong, people are afraid to stick their necks out and get cut off from what little bit they have.

But we did make some friends. The newspaper editor at Tracy City wrote two or three articles that were friendly. And we had wonderful friends like May Justus—people like that. My approach always was to go out to the people in the community and just talk with them man to man, you know, about problems that they were concerned about and interested in, and we had a considerable amount of good friends there among just the plain ordinary poor people who didn't have much power.

So we made some progress. Later, when the CIO got under way, Highlander became an educational center to some extent for their training courses. But by then Connie and I had left. . . .

Although the Wests departed Highlander in April 1933, they continued to pursue interests elsewhere in the South that often paralleled Highlander's concerns. Thus, while Don's memories veer momentarily from the Monteagle story, the incidents he recounts are illuminating. An atmosphere was developing in the region. Lines of conflict were being drawn, and the cost of change was being exacted.

I read a newspaper story about a nineteen-year-old black man named Angelo Herndon being arrested and sentenced to twenty years in the chain gang in Georgia. The circumstances of the case concerned me very much because Herndon had been arrested and made an example of for leading a group of unemployed people to the mayor's office to ask for food. He seemed to be a very serious, very dedicated young fellow who was willing to stick his neck out on issues that involved the welfare of himself and his people and other people. So I hitchhiked down to Atlanta one day and went looking for somebody that knew more about Herndon. Down on Auburn Avenue in the black section of town in a little hole of an office, I finally found the Herndon Defense Committee, and went in and talked with someone in there and they said they were having a meeting that night in a black theater there on Auburn Avenue and they wondered if I'd be willing to be chairman of the meeting and say something. I finally accepted and after I had spoken that evening and talked with the people further, they made a good case to me of the importance of coming to Georgia to be active in the defense work for Herndon. So Connie and I and our daughter, Ann, who was just a baby then, left Highlander and we went down to Georgia and for a period of nearly two years, I was active in the defense work for Angelo Herndon.

We lived in a little one-room basement in a place over on Georgia Avenue not far from Grant Park. We had an old set of springs with a mattress on it, and had a box for a table and a two-burner kerosene stove; and we managed to live on a total five-dollars-a-week income that we received for living expenses from the defense group. Sometimes we would get a weekly handout from some storekeeper who was sympathetic. There were numbers of small merchants around Atlanta, Jewish people generally, who were sympathetic. They were not well-to-do people, but sometimes they'd contribute a piece of meat or some kind of groceries to help our food problem. And then I went out lots to my mother's farm outside Atlanta where they had gardens and we would get a few things from there. But basically we made it on five dollars a week.

The ILD [International Labor Defense] was the official organization that was handling the Herndon case. It raised funds wherever it could for the defense work, and it had hired a black attorney there in Atlanta named Benjamin Davis, Jr. There were a number of black leaders—black ministers particularly—like Maynard Jackson, Sr. [whose son was later mayor of Atlanta] who participated and were concerned with the case; and as it got well known over the country, many others got involved and would come down to Atlanta to talk and help do some planning. Matter of fact, I drove John L. Spivak from New York to Atlanta once and he did some writing on the case. Other writers got involved too. I don't remember any white preachers that really took a stand, or representatives of labor. It was too risky at that point for the unions at that time to take much of a stand. But there were some white university students and a number of white professors who did. People like Mercer Evans at Emory and C. Vann Woodward at Georgia Tech. They showed real concern—and real courage because at that point, it took courage for a person who wanted to be a professor in a white university to come out on an issue like that. And there were some white cotton mill workers over at Fulton Bag and Cotton Mill like Walter Washburn and his wife who were very much concerned with the Herndon thing and worked in the defense work quite actively. It was not any great mass thing, but quite a number did get involved.

It was very difficult to work in Atlanta at that time because the police were watching anybody and everybody who undertook to do anything for the benefit of black people. Our committee was putting out handbills, for example, that we wrote and mimeographed as part of an educational effort to reach people to help them understand what the issue was: why Herndon was particularly singled out and why he was arrested and what he had done because he was fighting not only for himself and his own freedom, but he'd been fighting for the welfare of both white and black poor people. We emphasized particularly the necessity for a feeling of unity between whites and blacks in the working class. But these handbills had to be put out very carefully late at night because policemen would arrest you for that kind of thing. Usually the best time was after midnight when everything was quiet and still and there were no policemen around much and everybody was asleep. We would go from door to door and stick them behind the screen door and do it very quietly and very carefully. And you looked very carefully up and down the streets as you worked to see that there were no cops around on the block. I've been amused by the so-called underground press that puts out papers with the name of an editor and an address on them. That's sort of amusing to those of us who had to *really* work underground. I remember when Max Singer's place was raided. He was a very dedicated Jewish merchant who let us keep the mimeograph machine upstairs in his store. Connie was upstairs in his kitchen running off handbills and the police arrived and she grabbed the handbills and put them in the trash basket and put on one of his wife's aprons and spread some flour around there as if she was cooking and the cops came in and looked around and didn't even speak to her. They left, still looking for [the source of those handbills].

And then we would have meetings in private homes. A meeting would be announced and you would be told to go to a certain place and then you would be told where the meeting was going to be. Other people would be sent to different places to get the meeting's location. Sometimes the police found out and the meetings would be raided anyway. But the members of the organization were really disciplined. This is a thing I have marveled at in the modern day with so many of the young people. Time doesn't seem to amount to much. Back in that era, if you had to go meet a person at ten minutes after eight at a certain street corner, you got there if you were a member of the organization. Otherwise, you just weren't in it. There was a tremendous amount of self-discipline as well as group discipline, and people who fell down didn't last in it. They had to be responsible. People's freedom depended on it—sometimes, people's lives.

Eventually it got to the point where, although we were underground, it looked like every time I moved the police were right behind me. I remember one time I had gone over to the house of a very courageous black minister for a conference with him, and I had just entered the living room when his wife looked out the window and said, "Oh, there's the police! There's the police!" And she said, "Come here!" And she dragged me into the kitchen and she had a trap door that went down into a basement and had a little rug over it and she raised that up and pushed me down and said, "Get down there now!" And she put the rug over there and the police came in searching for me and they searched the whole house. I heard them walking overhead and then they left. A short time after that they had a bench warrant out for me, and it became impossible for me to be active in Atlanta without the possibility of being arrested. Personally I've never liked the idea of being arrested. I've never been particularly afraid of it if it was necessary, and I have been in jail numbers of times, but I've never courted that kind of thing. A person who is in prison is pretty inactive and there is not much you can do. I like to be outside. I like freedom.

So I discussed all this with some of our committee and they said, "Well, it might be better for you to get out and go to New York for a conference and discuss what's happening." I spent the night with the chief attorney and just before dawn, he took me out to his daddy's car and I lay down in the backseat and he threw some old croaker sacks over me and took me way out beyond Stone Mountain where I could flag down a bus to New York. Connie and Ann stayed out at Kennesaw with my folks.

I didn't come back to Atlanta. Herndon was freed and left the South. Last I heard of him he was running a small bookstore in Chicago. Connie and I and Ann moved to Burlington, North Carolina.

By this time, it was 1934 and there was a general textile strike going on throughout the country. Cotton mill workers had organized the Flying Squadrons that went from town to town and cotton mill to cotton mill trying to bring the workers out on strike even if the mill wasn't organized. They'd picket the mills and encourage the people to come out. Well, in Burlington, North Carolina, several of the local leaders were arrested and given long prison terms—ten years, I believe—so I went to Burlington where the local defense committee asked me to work with building this committee's effectiveness and raise bail money and get local support. I got several professors at the University of North Carolina—like Vann Woodward, who had moved up from Atlanta by then—to contribute and help in the defense. I guess, though, the most able and the most effective help we had was from Paul Green, the playwright. I went to Paul's house one day and I was talking to him about the case and about these men being framed and that we needed bail money. We were sitting around having something to eat at his place and he said, "If I could just be convinced that what you're saying is right and that these men were framed, I'd really throw in and do everything I could."

"Well," I said, "would it be possible for you to come over to Burlington some evening and we'll get the families of these people and some other cotton mill workers together who know about it and just talk about it? Maybe you could bring some of your friends here around the university?"

He says, "All right, I'm interested and I'd like to do that."

So Paul and a number of others came, and he became convinced it was a frame-up—which it was. The company had actually hired a person to throw some sticks of dynamite across the mill fence and the workers, who were innocent, were jailed for it. We needed twenty thousand dollars in cash for bail money, and Paul Green put it up. I've always had a very warm feeling for Paul since. He was committed, and he put his money where his sentiment was. Later we were able to prove in court the men had been framed, and they were set free. But it was a pretty long, drawn-out case.

The militancy that prevailed during that 1934 strike was a remarkable thing. My gosh, there were just thousands and tens of thousands of workers out on strike, and many of them not even members of the United Textile Workers. Some of the members of the Flying Squadrons weren't even members of the union. They would just be people who were enthusiastic and so much stirred up about it that they wanted to spread the word to other places. They'd go for miles and miles and miles, you know, from one village to another, and they would go in great numbers. Sometimes there would be a hundred or more of them going together.

And they would make a great commotion on the mill hill, and shout their slogans out, and they stirred people up tremendously. It was a very, very active and militant type of action. Sentiment got very deep, but unfortunately very little organization came out of it. The cotton mills have been the most difficult in the South to organize. North Carolina, as I understand, is still open shop. It is still pretty unorganized. I think the cotton mill workers' union has just never had the kind of leadership that would take advantage of real organization potential.

After North Carolina, we came back to Connie's home in eastern Kentucky where I was the state organizer for the Workers' Alliance in '35, '36 and '37. The New Deal had come in and there was the WPA, and there was a great deal of militancy among the unemployed and the WPA workers and the men who had jobs, and there was a feeling of a need for unity between all of them. So there was developed one central national organization, recognized by John L. Lewis of the CIO and William Green of the AFL, called the Workers' Alliance for the Unemployed and the WPA Workers. It would take in any poor people—schoolteachers, farmers, anybody who had no organization that represented their interests—because its position was that all these people had a common interest regardless of what they were doing. The Workers' Alliance in Kentucky at one time had between sixteen and twenty thousand members—particularly in East Kentucky where there were so many unemployed coal miners and so many on WPA. I'm amused now looking at the demands we were making. We were demanding such modest things, but they were real then. For example, we were demanding thirty dollars a month for old age pension. There were no old age pensions at that time for these people. There was no welfare, no social security, no workman's compensation, no unemployment insurance—none of these things. At that time, if a man was unemployed, he was just out. Unless he could find some philanthropic organization that would issue him a basket of food or some kinfolks that could share something, he just went hungry, and that was it.

Also at that time in the country they had what was called the Southern Wage Differential. The New Deal government recognized this. When they set the minimum wage that had to be paid in the cotton mills and other industries, that's why industry in the

South could pay a lower wage than it did in the North. The assumption was it was cheaper to live in the South. That was the story. Of course, this has been blown up for a long time. But the government practiced the same thing with WPA. The Mason-Dixon Line was the Ohio River, and across the Ohio River, workers on the WPA received $60 a month for the same number of hours that workers in Kentucky received $22.40 a month for from the same government. And this, to us, was a very sore point. Why should Kentucky workers working the same number of hours on a WPA project receive only $22.40 and just across the Ohio River they got $60? This is what I'm talking about with the Southern Wage Differential. The first time I ever met Aubrey Williams, who was then deputy director of the WPA, I had taken three hundred unemployed East Kentucky miners to Washington to protest the $22.40-a-month WPA wage. Aubrey was very sympathetic. He was a tremendous human being. He said, "Boys, I agree with you a hundred percent, but all I can do is to administer a program that Congress gives me. What you fellows are gonna have to do now is go back home and raise hell with your congressmen." Well, we agreed to that. We knew in advance that Aubrey was not responsible for the discrimination. So we went back home and we did raise some hell and got that changed. . . .

At any rate, with the Workers' Alliance, we had a number of very militant activities going on. For example, we printed placards to go in the windows of businesses that supported us that said, "This business supports the program of the Workers' Alliance and its demands for decent wages." If the businesses didn't support it and didn't have the placard, the membership boycotted the store. Probably one of the most outstanding things we sponsored was the National Hunger March in the 1930s when ten to twelve thousand people from every state in the union came to Washington and camped in Potomac Park for the purpose of petitioning the government to do something for people who didn't have jobs, who were poor, who didn't have food and so forth. There were men, women, and children involved. Roosevelt was President then, of course, and he did approve of the hunger march because he was having difficulties getting some of the New Deal legislation through Congress. He sent the Army out with tents and truckloads of food to feed the thousands of people who were there. Streets were blocked off and people made parades up to the Capitol and delegations from each state went to see their congressmen and senators to put in their pleas and their demands for changing the conditions. So the militancy of the working people had a real effect on the New Deal. When Roosevelt died in Warm Springs, Georgia, and the train came through the little places like Lula, Georgia, there would be great mobs out just to see the train go by. There would be people who'd be weeping. People loved him. He gave them a breath of hope, I think. He gave them a feeling that they amounted to something and that somebody was concerned.

So through my work with the Workers' Alliance, I think I knew most of the pig trails in eastern Kentucky. I remember some wonderful people. One of them was a Holiness preacher named Eli Hugh Trusty—we called him "Li Hugh." He was one of the best speakers I've ever heard. He was a tremendous union speaker and so dedicated. His whole family was just completely dedicated to the union. So after we became acquainted, I used to take Li Hugh around with me on speaking trips talking to the locals. Whenever I was in his area, I used to stay with him. They lived in about a three-room shack. The room I slept in was in the back and if I came in late, I could crawl through a crack in the wall and get in and go to bed so I didn't have to go through the front room where Li Hugh and his family were asleep. I could just go through that hole in the wall and get into bed. And in the mornings, his wife would cook biscuits with lard and flour and water and salt and soda; and we'd have thick bulldog gravy and this was our breakfast. I've eaten breakfast like this with Li Hugh and his family many many times. Always welcome and warm hospitality. But that was the only thing they had. He named one of his daughters after Connie and me.

Then there was Jim Garland, who lived up toward Kettle Island out of Pineville in one of the shabbiest little shacks that I've ever been in. He was an unemployed coal miner and was having a tough time making a living—like thousands of others at that time —and he became very militant and wrote a lot of songs like "I Don't Want Your Millions, Mister." And Aunt Molly Jackson, the wife of a coal miner. I knew her very well. She was a militant, tremendous human being who became very much upset with the way people were treated and turned her abilities and talents into writing. The song "Poor Hardworking Miners" is credited to her, you know.

It was a violent period. Many of the people became very militant, and around there in East Kentucky, they meant business. I remember going over to Paintsville one time to make a speech for the Workers' Alliance and I hadn't any more than got into town before I was arrested and put in jail. After I'd been in just a few minutes, I heard a commotion outside and looked out, and a group of our members to whom I was supposed to speak that night were out there. They came in and I heard somebody asking where the sheriff was, and they got the sheriff out and they said, "Now, Wesley, he's billed to speak here tonight and he's gonna speak." There was a little bit of palaver. And then finally I heard one of them say, "Well, if you don't turn him loose, we're gonna break this door down. He's gonna speak." And that kind of militancy existed with those people, see. So, I was set free and I had the meeting that night. [*Laughter*]

But you were constantly harassed. The coal operators, like U.S. Steel or Consolidated Coal, would import gun thugs from Pittsburgh or Chicago or through detective agencies like Baldwin-Felts, the sheriff would make them deputies, and wherever you went, if they suspected you of talking unions, the gun thugs would be there to arrest you or drive you off. You couldn't go in and visit a man in his home. If you went into a coal miner's home in those villages at that time, you wouldn't be in there long—even on a Sunday—until there would be a knock on the door and the gunmen would be there. "What are you doing here, buddy? You don't live here. You get back over where you belong!" Three people couldn't meet on the street corner and stop and talk without one of these gunmen telling them, "Break it up, men! Break it up! You go this way, you go this way, you go that way. Break it up!" I was once jailed in Pineville for six weeks until somebody raised the five thousand dollars' bond money, and the judge stipulated that I should leave Kentucky, and on the way out of town on those crooked mountain roads all four wheels on the automobile came off. The nuts had been loosened so that we'd get up on one of those mountain roads and run off over the side. It was a common thing for men to be beaten up or thrown in prison or killed. I remember a county attorney in one Kentucky county being involved in plotting to dynamite union organizers' houses.

But the national publicity surrounding these conditions—publicity that had been started back before this period by writers like John Dos Passos and Theodore Dreiser and Waldo Frank and Bruce Crawford, who published *Crawford's Weekly* over at Norton, Virginia—all eventually led to the investigations of violence in the coalfields by the La Follette Committee. The fourteen volumes printed of the investigations in turn had a tremendous effect on Congress and helped bring about the passage of the Wagner Labor Laws and the La Guardia Acts by which workers were guaranteed the right to organize and join unions. And that led to the union eventually being successful in organizing some coal mines.

All through this period, union organizers were red-baited a great deal, but in this particular case it didn't work as the instigators hoped it would because the working people of East Kentucky learned to take the attitude that, "My goodness, anybody that's for us is gonna be called a Communist. So, if somebody's called a Communist, that must mean he's for us, or for poor people." So it always didn't work as they hoped it would. I think sometimes red-baiting became more effective later on, after the McCarthy period, you know, than it was then.

For the continuation of Don West's interview, see Chapter Three (page 194). And for the continuation of May Justus' interview, see Chapter Four (page 266).

The Plant, A Little Café, and Lots of Coffee
Zilla Hawes Daniel

As a young Vassar graduate, Zilla Hawes was lured to Highlander in 1933 by some of the same forces that had influenced Don West and Myles Horton—namely, the European folk school concept and Reinhold Niebuhr's vision of a "Southern mountain school." And she quickly demonstrated talent. That same year, this descendant of suffragettes organized the first Amalgamated Clothing Workers local in the South.

By 1934, Zilla would be listed as one of five incorporators when Highlander obtained its charter from the state of Tennessee. She would also serve on Highlander's first board of directors. But her memories of that era's union-organizing efforts reveal how factories in the South cast long shadows across the green lawns, white-painted frame houses, and porch-talk friendliness in the small towns where she worked. Often, alone.

My mother was Ann Day Hawes. Her mother was Elizabeth Day. She moved over here from England to marry H. Kent Day, whose father, Charles, had also come from England. They settled in Germantown, Pennsylvania. Both my mother and grandmother were suffragettes. They paraded in Philadelphia.

My father, Oscar B. Hawes, was a minister of the Unitarian Church. I was born April 3, 1908. I have two sisters—one younger and one older.

As a small child, mostly I remember what to me was a perfectly lovely big yard around the parsonage where we lived with mock orange and beech trees and good places to hide and play; then in the spring, the grass was dotted with flowers with white petals called stars-of-Bethlehem. I've since found some more up here. They're lovely.

In those days, clergymen had the summers off. After I came very close to dying of typhoid fever when I was two, Dad began bringing us up here to the Maine seacoast at Hancock Point. That's just one peninsula over from where I live now.

From then on, Hancock Point and the coast and the Atlantic Ocean became the most important things in my life. I'd wait for summer. We came sometimes in an old touring car part of the way, and later took steamships the rest of the way. I remember when the old touring car got stuck in the mud and farmers pulled us out with their teams of horses. . . .

We rented [a house] for years and years and that was the house of my life, too. Juniper Cottage. It's still there. I go over and see it every once in a while. Sort of a funky little house with a very pointed gable and crisscross beams in front that make it look like gingerbread, and a porch on three sides. On the front porch was a big old Gloucester hammock, and sometimes when it was very warm I was allowed to sleep out there. When everybody in the house was asleep, I'd get up and go down to the beach, only a couple hundred paces, if that far, and even go in the water at night. They never knew about it, though. They wouldn't have liked it.

Dad had boats. He didn't have a sailboat then, but he had a slender cedar rowing craft with a place for three oarsmen and women and we'd row across Frenchman Bay. He also had two canoes, and he'd take us camping to an inland lake that was quite wild—we'd put up tents and cut balsam boughs and make beds out of them—and we'd learn how to use those canoes there. He taught us to paddle, and how to right the canoes after we'd tipped them over in the water, and all kinds of things that are good to know. We loved it on those lakes, and on the saltwater. We'd play on the beach by the hours and climb mountains, and pick wild raspberries and strawberries.

I went to the Germantown Friends School for kindergarten and first grade. Many of Mother's friends were Quakers. Then in 1916, Father changed parishes and we moved to Newton Center,

Massachusetts, and I went to the grammar school there. Shortly after we moved, we'd gone into the war and Father went over to France to serve in the French version of a YMCA. I remember that the parishioners all had Victory Gardens, which was unusual because hardly any of them had ever had a garden. We planted vegetables and grew them, up on a hill.

I loved the years in Newton Center. I think they were some of my happiest years. It was a very small town at the edge of the country. I remember the chestnut trees behind our house. We picked pink lady slippers in the spring, and in the winter we'd ski; and the men all made a toboggan slide with a big bump in it that we'd go tearing down. Plenty of places to roam. It was really almost country, which was important for me. It turned out that I'd have to have country—trees, hills, fields—around me all the time to be really happy. And the ocean.

After Newton Center, when I was about to go into high school, we moved again, to Summit, New Jersey, which I didn't care for at all. Dad enrolled us in a private school where the motto was "Kent Place School for Girls where manners makyth man." It was pretty snobbish, but it was good academically. We had to take Latin all four years.

Dad was determined that we'd all graduate cum laude from college, but none of us did!

I wanted to get away from home. Mother was an outgoing, warm person with a beautiful personality, but Father was a very hard taskmaster and he had a hot temper. There was no doubt about his love for us, but he was such a perfectionist that I'd give up. In the summertime, for instance, he had a grass tennis court and an archery court, and if I didn't do exactly as he instructed, he'd lash out at me to the point where I just withdrew into myself.

So I entered Vassar in 1925, and I majored in English, minored in philosophy. . . .

I can't remember any particular awareness [of social conditions, such as poverty]. I was just intent on my own life and getting away from home. I can't even remember thinking very specifically about a career. I remember some of the courses though—Russian history, philosophy, geology, paleontology. I loved Italian. One poem I still know all the way through is in Italian. A course in comparative religion struck me very much because I'd found Unitarianism so arid and uninspiring.

And summers, except for a summer when my grandfather sent my older sister and myself to Europe, we stayed in Maine. One summer I went to Sea Scout camp where the Girl Scouts were the crew on a ninety-two-foot schooner. I have a boat now, a rowboat. It's sitting out back. Its name is the *Lully Lulay,* which is really the name of a very old, old Christmas carol that I used to sing to my second son, Jim.

When I graduated from Vassar in 1929, I went straight from college with a friend to the John C. Campbell Folk School in Brasstown, North Carolina, as a volunteer worker, doing everything from whitewashing the creamery to shoveling silage and taking care of the horses. We loved every minute of it. That's when I first saw the Smokies. Olive Campbell's husband had started the school, and modeled it on the Danish folk schools, and she was carrying on. She was very cultured and educated, and she believed in going to the people, wherever they were, and improving their skills and widening their knowledge to make their livelihoods easier. Sigurd Neilson and his wife, Kirstine, were there from Denmark running the cooperative creamery, and George Bidstrup was running the farm, and the local people would come in every day and take courses in animal husbandry and farming and canning and so forth—skills that would help them in their homes and make their lives easier. We learned Danish folk dancing in the evenings.

At the end of the summer I knew that I wanted to go back. The school had asked me to come back and take charge of a crafts program. Many of the local men made chairs and wood carvings, and some local women were weaving and making quilted seat mats. I didn't know any crafts myself, but I wanted to help with that, so I went home to tell my parents, but they refused to give me permission. Dad wanted me to go back to school to become a professor of English, and I was not about to do it. So I left home. I went back to the folk school and spent the winter there mainly going out into the hollows and finding the old mountain men— just the kind of people that are in the *Foxfire* books—that were making chairs or carving or making brooms. That broom over there by the wood stove, in fact, is from the John C. Campbell Folk

School, and it may be the one I brought to my mother in the thirties. So I handled this program, which got me back out into the hills and hollows where these people lived. I took down some of their songs. I remember my mother was very interested in that. I showed her the songs that I'd written down that winter. I learned from the mountain folks. I learned a tremendous amount from their honesty and their straightforwardness—you know, calling a pole a pole—and how hard it was to hew any kind of a life out of those hills.

When I got back home, a college friend, Kay Bennett, invited me to a house party on Heron Island, Maine. Her brother, John, who had recently graduated from Union Theological Seminary, was going up, along with some of his friends. So I went with them —James Dombrowski and Franz Daniel and King Gordon. They had all graduated from Union Theological, and I had never met them before. Reinhold Niebuhr came up for a couple of days, and I was just swept off my feet with the discussions and the questioning and the aura and the talk of Marxism and socialism and religion and the sense that we've got to pay attention to all the people in America and what they need and what they want and where they're going. That is where my social awareness was really opened up for the first time. I hadn't really looked at all the social forces at work in the country before then, but this was a social awareness era, and all these fellows out of Union were going into some form of social service. It was all very new to me and very intellectually exciting and stimulating. I wanted to know more about it.

Franz Daniel had joined the Socialist Party after he got out of Union and was being sent to Philadelphia as a Socialist Party organizer, so I decided I'd get a job in Philadelphia. I got a job that was pretty dull, but at least it gave me a living. It was with a very, very nice, extremely well-intentioned woman who was in charge of a recreation program after school in the poorest, most run-down, most highly industrialized section of Philadelphia. We used to travel by trolleys forever to get there, and then take these kids and put on some sort of recreation program in a school yard that was nothing but concrete. If it rained we were indoors in the schoolrooms. And the kids couldn't have been less interested. We really tried, but it felt ineffectual from the very beginning. I just actually hated every minute of it. . . .

[M]eanwhile, I'd become quite active in the Socialist Party and in the YPSL—the Young People's Socialist League. We were in touch with trade union people, many of whom belonged to the Socialist Party in Philadelphia, so we were pretty close to the labor movement of that day. Franz and I and several others all rented rooms in the same house—all of us socialists—and we'd have dinner there together at night, and evenings of discussions and arguments, and then go our own ways in the daytime. At some point I decided I wanted to learn more about the labor movement, so when the school term ran out and the recreation program ended, I went to work in a necktie factory at six dollars a week. Finally I went to another necktie factory and made nine dollars a week.

. . . [O]ne time I was pulling the stitches or basting out of a necktie and I leaned back in my chair and the floorlady told me, ''Sit up straight!!'' You couldn't even slump in your chair. How many months I did that, I don't know. Several months, anyway. I soon found out how degrading that work is and how totally destructive of anything creative and anything really alive in a person —anything other than survival instincts really. What came naturally after that was, ''Well, I'd like to find out even more about the labor movement.'' So I went to Brookwood Labor College in Katonah, New York, for a year and studied labor journalism, labor history, and labor economics. Many of the students were miners and textile workers and factory workers who would go back to their own local unions better informed and with a deeper background. The point was to make their local unions better.

By the time I finished Brookwood in the spring of 1933, I had decided to go to Highlander. Myles had asked if I wanted to help get it going. I knew about the school because Jim Dombrowski had already gone down to help Myles, and Jim and Franz were always in touch with each other. So that spring I bought a car for forty dollars from an autoworker at Brookwood, named her Mother Jones, and I and Stan Reece—an architect who also worked at Highlander a while—proceeded to drive down. We spent one night sleeping in a pasture and oh, I can remember being waked up by a nice dog licking my face [*laughter*] in this pasture where Stan and I were stretched out sleeping; and that day we got to Highlander.

Of course Myles was there, and Jim Dombrowski, and Mack

Chisholm. Mack later went to Spain and was killed in the Civil War. He wore my boots over there, I'm glad to say. He had small feet, and I had these fine boots. I don't know where I got them, but they went with him. Zilphia hadn't come yet, or Teffie [Ralph Tefferteller], so the Highlander I remember is way back in those first couple of years around '33. It was just a small, close group in those days. I remember Dr. [Lillian] Johnson coming over once in a while to visit the school, and I know we were always concerned that we were doing the kind of thing that she would understand and, we hoped, approve of. She did give us pretty much carte blanche. And I remember Mom and Dad Horton, Myles' parents. It seemed to me like Mom, that lovely sweet woman, spent the whole time cooking, bringing in a big pan of cornbread every dinnertime along with everything else that she cooked. I can see the kitchen now in that old house at Monteagle. And when somebody would bring up the question of vitamins, Dad Horton would say, "I don't want none of them things running around on my plate." [*Laughter*] And he'd go back out and go to work in the garden, and we all, of course, washed and cleaned up. And I remember playing volleyball. We had quite a few games out on the volleyball court in the back.

In those earliest days, though, there were almost no students. Myles and I would take off on trips in Mother Jones into the mountains recruiting students for Highlander. Zilphia came first as a student and later married Myles. I taught labor history at Highlander, and I remember Zilphia and I and the others enacting little scenes from workers' history. And music. Music I associate with Zilphia, very much.

Then there was one summer at Allardt with Joey Marlowe and Dolph Vaughn and the others quarrying rock on Joe Kelly Stockton's farm. Berthe Daniel and I cooked. Jim was there. Joe Kelly I could never forget as long as I live. We ate his pork. We ate his bacon. He supplied us with vegetables. We'd go to eat at his house and he'd laugh and say, "Eat some more. It won't hurt long!" [*Laughter*]

So in the very early days we were a close group. There was an emphasis on establishing the school in the community. Later, the school went through more difficult times. I don't know if I'm making this up or not, I hope not. I honestly wish, honestly wish I could remember more of those early days and exactly who was what and what happened and when. I've tried, but it just hasn't worked. But I know that as more people became associated, and in an atmosphere like Highlander which was then an ideologically directed place, there was a greater chance of minds often going off on tangents. When three or four people had three or four different ideologies, why there was a good bit of not only confusion, but argument. Most everyone there had a different approach, and I've learned since that when you approach things ideologically, you seldom get a meeting of minds. There may be meeting of hearts, but that doesn't overcome it. And we weren't always open and loving and supportive, even though underneath we did love each other.

I think that's one of the reasons why Jim and Ellen, his wife, finally moved on. I think Jim did not care for confrontation, and there was an awful lot of it at Highlander. I felt that it kind of wore him down. That, and the fact that some people simply aren't suited to that sort of community life. It was very difficult for both of them. . . .

[Most of the conflicts centered, in part, around approaches to labor issues] or conflicts over the school's open-door policy. Of course I can see much better now than I did then Highlander's point of view that we work with anyone. It doesn't matter what they believe or think, or whom they're affiliated with. I seem to recall Communist Party organizers coming to Highlander from Chattanooga, and they were made as welcome as anybody else. But there was some feeling among some members of the staff about whether or not Communist organizers ought to come because of the repercussions that might ensue.

I often found myself raising doubts about our course of action. I sometimes represented a divisive point of view—and I was often overruled. I don't know if I was right or not, and I'm not going to be critical of myself now, but I did tend to be domineering then. Dominating if not domineering. There's a difference, I hope. And that's one of the things I've since tried to straighten out in myself. But I was sticking by whatever principles I had then, in the midst of a search for identity on my part as a woman with at least two other men who were there all the time, and I had to sort of stand up and shout sometimes. So there was a clash of personalities. There was no question about it. And the sound of cymbals could be heard afar, if one wanted to hear it. [*Laughter*]

. . . Franz and I were married in November of '34. Earlier, Amalgamated Clothing Workers of America had taken over the organizing of shirt workers. When they decided to organize the shirt workers, the plants were moved South to get away from being organized. The Liebovitz campaign was the first I was actively involved with. It was a successful campaign because the Liebovitz plants were already organized in Pennsylvania, and the workers there refused to sign a contract until the Liebovitz plant in Knoxville came into the union, too. That's why we were successful.

That's not to say it was easy. At that time, the Amalgamated was not in the AFL, and that was all long before the CIO, so we couldn't meet in the labor temple, but somebody got us another hall. And we had a hard time getting the people together because of the company's spies and the foreman riding up and down in front of where he heard, through his spies, that the meeting was going to be; and us coming in through the watermelon patch in the rear, or else holding the meeting somewhere else. But as for the strike, that was very well planned and laid out. The committee was going to go in and ask for an increase in pay and the other things, and if the management said no, the committee chairman had a whistle and would blow it, literally, and then everybody would pour out on the street. It was classic. . . . [T]hey said no and they poured out. . . . I was waiting outside.

We won that strike. And you know a remarkable thing? Even though that mill has been completely closed down for years, some of the union people still have a reunion every year. I've never heard of that happening anywhere else. That strike had a tremendous impact on those people. . . .

So when the first convention met to set up the Textile Workers Organizing Committee—composed of the Amalgamated Clothing Workers and the United Textile Workers—I was there. Franz was made director for the whole campaign in the South. I went on being paid by the Amalgamated as an organizer, but I was assigned to TWOC. There were three or four men working with me.

In the initial stages, though, we'd work alone. You were simply sent cold into a town to find out what could be done. "Go in, see what you can do; you're on your own.'' Then based on what we found in terms of interest among the workers, we'd decide whether or not to continue working on such and such a mill. If there were enough names and enough support, and you had reason to hope something might happen, you'd stay around. If not, you'd move on. But generally you were alone. I didn't even work on Franz's campaigns. There's no reason just because you're a man and wife to work as a team. I would try to meet him sometimes wherever he was at, or sometimes he'd come where I was at, but we had no home base and we didn't organize together.

I think that Greenville, South Carolina, was my first TWOC campaign. I was chairman of the organizing committee. There were several people working with me there once we had decided to go ahead and try to organize two big companies: Woodside and Brandon. Woodside is where we won the labor board election by the skin of our teeth. It took ages and ages. At one point in Greenville we called for an election and they burned crosses—I'll let you figure out who "they" were—in front of the homes of the local leaders in the mill towns. That happened at least twice. . . . They're still doing it. Gee, they learn slow.

[But going into a town cold, to find out whether or not there was enough interest among the workers to warrant staying], you'd go drink a cup of coffee in a little café pretty near the plant and just kind of start talking in a casual sort of way with the fellows there. After the Amalgamated had joined the AFL, you'd go to the labor temple and the existing unions and see if you could get any contacts there. Then if you got one or two, you'd go visit them and introduce yourself and talk about the weather, admire their children, anything to break the ice, but not in an obvious way. And then you'd get around to where they worked and whether they liked it and how was the work going; and then most of the time you'd tell them who you were and what you were there for. Leave some literature, take their name, phone number, and address, and see if they would give you any other names to go visit. If there was only a day shift, you would have to go at night. If there was a night shift, you'd be careful to go in the late afternoon. You didn't want to disturb them while they were sleeping. Just casually and very gingerly you'd get the first contacts and use them to go on to others.

You'd have to use your own judgment as to how far to pursue those contacts and as to whether or not something could be developed in terms of a local union. [But even that much contact would come to the attention of the company within twenty-four hours.] You know—the strange woman in town. The towns were mostly small so you were known very quickly.

Sometimes I was afraid. Not for myself, but for some of the people I worked with, because I could not promise that they would not be fired for union activity. I could say that we would do everything possible to get them back on the job, but that was before their local was even organized, not to mention recognized, not to mention made legal. So I tried to be careful—I don't say I always succeeded—and to be honest about it, I was asking them to take a big chance. I mean "I" in the name of the union—not me personally. But I was very well aware of what was involved in their lives and the more places I went, the more this was apparent. The fear that had been in them since they left the farm and the company had gotten hold of them was obvious—and justified. The company almost owned many of them. Often there was a company store and they always owed them something, so their pay was always goose eggs: zero, zero, zero. Week after week after week.

. . . Greenville was the most threatening [situation]. I drove down to Anderson, South Carolina, once, which is close to Greenville. We knew it was company dominated, and we knew the deputy sheriffs were on the side of the company and that they didn't allow any strangers in Anderson. But being the head of our little organizing committee I thought I ought to drive down there. I can't even remember talking to anyone—if I did, I'm sure I didn't say I was a labor union organizer—but they had their stooges out, and being a stranger, I stuck out like a sore thumb in that little town. I got just beyond the city limits on the way back and heard this blast, and the rear end of the car was loaded with buckshot. My knees shook so much on the way back, I wasn't sure I could keep my foot on the accelerator, but did, of course. And all the time I hadn't been sure that my car was even shot at till I pulled it into a garage and looked at the back. But I think you can't function if you are going to allow yourself to be fearful. I didn't give it any thought because fear is a negative emotion.

Besides, the work with the Amalgamated—with *any* union,

particularly in the early days—was invaluable because working people *had* nothing else. Whether they knew it or not, they had no other hope. I know as an organizer the thing I had to do was try to inculcate within people enough self-confidence to allay their fears and to give them a sense of self-respect. That "I am worth every-thing possible to get a decent life for me." That is what was hap-pening during that period.

[By that time I was no longer a member of the Socialist Party.] When the New Deal came along, both Franz and I became Rooseveltian Democrats after a lot of heart- and mind-searching. [Then we finally settled down to a personal life.] Franz was told in 1939 that he was going to be located for a period of time in New York City with the laundry workers union, so I quit everything and we got an apartment in Greenwich Village. Of course, in three months he was sent to New Orleans [*laughter*], and I was pregnant. I was working with the CIO War Relief Committee. After Franz left, I had a miscarriage. Then I joined him in New Orleans. After nine months there, he was assigned to Philadelphia as a city orga-nizer, and in '43, Georgie was born. Then we were transferred to South Carolina where Franz was state CIO director. We lived ten miles out of Spartanburg, out in the country. Georgie was three years and less than two months old, and four days after he had been examined by a pediatrician and declared perfectly healthy, he died in my arms on the way to a doctor—the company doctor, it turned out. A neighbor drove me because we had no phone—couldn't get one during the war—and Franz had the car. The pediatrician signed the death certificate because the company doctor refused to.

Jim had been born by then. He was nearly two. But Georgie's death paralyzed us. Friends came to be with us and said, "Well, Franz and Zilla don't seem to be grieving." We were numbed. The whole situation there in South Carolina was comparable to what Highlander was going through when it was under attack at Monteagle. We were "Communists" and we didn't really have any friends in the community of Wellford where we lived. Our whole social life was with Franz's staff of organizers who would come to the tenant farmhouse where we lived for picnics and roasts and watermelon and homemade ice cream. There wasn't any other social contact. It wasn't allowable. Except we did develop awfully good relations with the local Negroes. There was one who lived right close and who came over and did our wash in a big pot in the yard. Nanny always wore a hat, even when she was scrubbing the clothes. Jim used to run through the bushes over to her house about every day. She was scared he'd get snake bit. The day when Nanny and her brother and his wife and all the other blacks registered to vote was a great day.

★

Known as "Those Reds" Down at Joe Kelly's

Ralph Tefferteller

Young and enthusiastic, he joined the Highlander staff in 1935—the same year that Myles Horton married Zilphia Johnson. It was an invigorating period at the school, and "Teffie," as Ralph Tefferteller was nicknamed, brought to Monteagle a particular combination of qualities: Because he had been reared in the Tennessee mountains, he "spoke the language" of Grundy Countians; and because of his Union Theological Seminary experiences (described below), he could communicate solidly with the others whom Reinhold Niebuhr had influenced toward social consciousness.

At points comic, at others insightful, Tefferteller's memories of the conflict-ridden thirties depict the ever-growing contributions that Highlander offered workers and unions in the region.

. . . I was a maverick. None of our people had ever gone north of the Mason-Dixon Line. I caught the Greyhound bus in Maryville with my duffle bag and I got off on Thirty-fourth Street and Eighth Avenue in New York City. Fortunately, of the three people whom I knew there, two of them met me, and they took me to the Lower East Side. First thing they did was to put me on a subway. Here this thing came roaring along—first time I'd ever seen such a thing as a train underground in my life—and they hopped on when the doors opened and there were some other people hopping on and I kept stepping back because there were people who seemed to want to get on more than me, and I'll be darned if the doors didn't almost close right there in front of me. They finally jerked me inside. I was being too polite, they said. I'd have to learn. [*Laughter*] Yes, I had to learn all right. Then they took me down to the lower end of Henry Street, near Chinatown, at the bottom of the Bowery. "Bowery," of course, is the word for "farm," and there was a little Presbyterian church there where one of my friends was doing his fieldwork for Union that was known in the early days of the city as the Kirk on Rutgers Farm. The old church was still there. They'd had an organ put in by this time up in the rear balcony and you had a little "bellows monkey." A little boy would strip himself down into shorts and he'd pump the bellows while Teresa, the organist, played on Sunday.

So through my friend who was doing his fieldwork there, I was introduced to life on the Lower East Side. And up at Union in the rarified atmosphere of Morningside Drive and 122d Street, I began exploring a different world. Reinhold Niebuhr had arrived some four years earlier. And Dr. Harry F. Ward was there, and Dr. Henry Sloane Coffin, great scholars of the Old and New testaments. Great philosophers. And that's where I holed up for three years.

One of the magical things about the place was the accessibility of these great men. One of my great courses was in Christian ethics under Niebuhr, but we all called him "Reiny" because he was also a friend. Here was this great intellectual who never read from a note in his life no matter what lecture he gave, always scratching his head and speaking extemporaneously. He just baffled us with his ability to do that. And he loved to play handball, and we would go into Union's handball court and bang away trying to beat the hell out of each other, and come out of there just wringing wet. That was one of his escapes—one of his relaxations. This great mind.

And at the same time there was Dr. Ward, who had as much or more influence on me than anybody else at Union. He and his family lived over on the Palisades along the Hudson River, and they knew that certain young people like myself, far away from home, were homesick at Thanksgiving time; and sure enough, that very first Thanksgiving an invitation came from the Wards for me to come over and have dinner there with them. Believe you me, I went! In fact, I went all three Thanksgivings I was at Union and treasured each experience. We had a certain kind of program when we went there. Before dinner, Dr. Ward would put on his old slouch hat and his hiking boots and get his walking stick and we'd head out walking along the Palisades. He had a trail that he liked to hike on, and usually the trail was so darn narrow you couldn't walk abreast so we'd just trail along behind this little guy; and then we'd catch up in some places and we'd talk about this and that. Then finally back into the house and by this time, the ladies would have the dinner ready and on the table and so we had a feast. And then they loved to clear the table away and roll up the rug, and their son Gordon, the teacher, would get out his accordion and they'd expect me to direct them in a little square dancing—the Virginia reel and so forth.

We followed this same ritual each of the three Thanksgivings I went there. I did my master's thesis under Dr. Ward on the social programs that were being developed by the Methodist Church with Dr. Ward's leadership. My good friend, Carl Voss, helped me edit it. He lived next door to me in Hastings Hall, and later became a fine scholar—Dr. Carl Herman Voss. He was some guy. He'd come from a German-American background. His father was a preacher in Pittsburgh. And Carl had retained the language. When Paul Tillich arrived at Union knowing very little English, Carl became his tutor and came to know him better than anybody else in America—the great Paul Tillich who got his fresh start at Union.

I really only got into trouble once at Union. During my senior year I headed up a weekly forum, and we brought in some masterful participants to speak. We were known for asking very sharp questions of the visitors who came there. One of them was Sherwood Eddy, and we were trying to embarrass him because he had been flying over battle areas in U.S. planes with Chiang Kai-shek, and we asked him such pointed questions he put in a protest to the dean that went all the way up to Uncle Henry—Dr. Coffin— the president. He sent me a summons: "Dear Tefferteller, You will report to my office with your colleagues tomorrow morning, nine o'clock, and I advise prayer beforehand." [*Laughter*] This was to put us on the rack for being so inhospitable to Sherwood Eddy at a time when we felt that he was being a dog.

We also established the Agenda Club at Union, which was

really the social action crowd amongst the student body. Whenever there were strikes, like the one when the workers at the Waldorf-Astoria Hotel walked out, or in New Jersey mill towns, we'd send members out to go and investigate and bring reports back. Sometimes we'd arrange for speakers to come in.

While I was a student there, of course, I was also expected to do my fieldwork. I was shown a number of available placements—a lovely suburban Congregational church in New Jersey, for instance —but I finally decided I'd take that first church I saw in New York. Then, rather than being called the Kirk on Rutgers Farm, it was known as the Church of Sea and Land, where the people of the sea met the people on the land and worshiped together. There was an English pastor there in the morning, and an Italian pastor in the afternoon. The Italian pastor was a minister to both the spirit and the physical body. He had completed his work as an M.D. and also had his doctorate in theology. Imagine! We called him the St. Francis of Henry Street, and he was! If his subjects came in to see him at the church and something was physically wrong, he had his cabinet there filled with all he needed. He was ministering to the spirit and the mind and the body in a great way. We loved him. The Italian population had grown right there in that neighborhood, and in one of the first slum clearance projects, the French corporation had put up the Knickerbocker Apartments. One of my boys eventually was killed while skating on the sidewalk of that apartment complex. It was a gruesome story. He was shooed away from the place and was run down by a truck.

But it was my first experience meeting ethnics, other than blacks, but my mind had been so opened up I was ready for the big experience and it didn't take me long to get right into it. There were people everywhere who had come from different parts of Europe and were poorly housed and poorly fed, struggling to survive at a time in the country when the adult population in the tenements was practically 50 percent unemployed. I'll never forget the fall of '32 as the interest and the fever built up over the election, and on election day, scraps of wood that had been hidden under the stoops of Henry Street were pulled out and piled in the middle of the street on every block. At night, when the returns started coming in, they set these afire, and there were huge bonfires and dancing in the streets when Roosevelt was elected. It was a grand, grand, stimulating occasion in the lives of people.

For the three years I was at Union, I continued my fieldwork in that same church, going from Riverside Drive all the way down on the West Side on the subway, and then walking across Chambers Street and through the arch of the city office buildings, and then walking down Park Street to the end of the Bowery and then turning up Henry Street; and walking carefully because it was fall and it was wine-making time in the Italian community and if you didn't watch, Mama might throw out a load of grape pulp meaning to hit the gutter but sometimes missing!

And there at Henry and Market, the Church of Sea and Land, the boys and the girls were ready to test the newcomer. They tested me in the beginning! Here I'd come fresh from college and the summer at Blue Ridge, and I was strong and physically fit and I was a wrestler and I wasn't going to let *any* smart alecks get the better of me. I was sure going to see that they got workouts. We had a little matchbox gym where basketball was played, and we had some old dirty mats—oh, my gosh, they were dirty—and there wasn't any place to shower or clean up afterward. You had to just pull your clothes back on. So I'd strip down and I'd take three or four of these boys and challenge them and we'd go to the mats and they'd try to put me down, but I knew a thing or two about wrestling. And that's how I established my turf with those kids, by showing them that I wasn't a pushover and we could have good fun together. And so we started off on this three-year journey of ours.

That first year I also met Chuck Black and his brother—two extremely tall Californians who had graduated at Union, and one was a minister and the other was working in the Lower East Side in one of the settlement houses—Madison House. Through him, I began to meet the young people involved in the settlement movement with their boys' clubs and girls' clubs. They also had a summer camp, and they soon had me talked into being a counselor at their camp near Peekskill, New York, that first summer of 1933. It was about 99 percent Jewish, and *this*, I mean, was a chance to live and learn. They taught me all summer long.

But I'd tell them stories about the Smoky Mountains, and read traditional stories to them in dialect, and they loved it. Some of them went back to their schools in the fall talking with Southern accents. What a rich summer!

And do you know it was that same summer that I met my future wife, Ruth. She was just a strip of a thing—fifteen years old —and taking care of the lady camp director's son. He took up all of her time practically; except that she was always drifting around and sitting on the edges of our counselors' staff meetings as we'd gather out under a tree or somewhere—always nosing around trying to hear what was going on. I was teaching tennis that summer, and I taught her to play tennis, and I told her about my younger sister back on the farm that she reminded me so much of. At the end of the summer I sent her a letter and I addressed it to "my little sister" in quotes.

Do you know that seven years later, *seven years later* in another camp, I met up with her again, and not long after, we were married.

It was shortly after I got to Union in the fall of 1932 that I found the trail of Myles and Jim Dombrowski. I didn't meet either one at the time. Jim was finishing his dissertation in philosophy at Columbia, and Myles had gone on, but I had learned what was being planned at Monteagle from Reinhold Niebuhr, who was an avowed supporter right from the beginning of the work at Highlander. I decided I had to find out [what was happening], and so in the winter of '33 I made my first visit.

It was in 1933 that things got pretty rough at Highlander. It didn't take long to stir up trouble there, and opposition forces like the Tennessee Coal and Iron Company had decided that little nest of troublemakers should be eliminated. Jim Dombrowski—I always called him "Skipper"—had decided it would be best to develop a fallback position because the intimidation of Highlander at Aunt Lillian [Johnson's] place was so imminent and so active that it didn't look as if Highlander would be able to continue there.

A dear friend of Myles', Mr. Nightingale, knew Joe Kelly Stockton, this old agrarian socialist who was a rock on the mountain, so to speak, near Allardt, Tennessee. He had the land. He had a farmhouse that wasn't being used at the time. There was good spring water and a barn, and a place where we could set up our little "commune," right in Sergeant York country. Joe Kelly arranged for us to open up a little quarry and quarry flagstone with a work crew so we could get enough that we could, if necessary, start building a new structure for Highlander right there on his farm.

So in the summer of '34, I went back to Allardt with Charlie Webber and his wife to join Highlander's people. Skipper was there, and Zilla [Hawes Daniel] and Mack Chisholm, and Griscom Morgan [son of Dr. A. E. Morgan, director of the Tennessee Valley Authority]. I'll never forget Griscom trying to convert all of us coffee drinkers to the virtues of having warm water in the mornings instead! And Skipper, this clever person, had arranged with several Eastern colleges to send some young men down to mix with mountain people, so they came down as part of the work force. And there were some local people there like Bill Marlowe and Eldridge Kilgore.

That was a great summer. There were campfires at night where we would sing, and we'd work on the weekdays. We had an old keg with a bunghole, and we'd carry water out to the work site on the mountain each day. On Friday evening, Bill Marlowe and some of the locals would seek out the nearest still and get it filled with moonshine. Sometimes on Monday morning not all of it was gone, but they wouldn't pour it out. They'd go down to the springhouse and fill it the rest of the way with water! But that's the way it was on weekends. They'd hide it out in the crabgrass because liquor was not allowed in the "commune," and it kept sort of chilled out in the crabgrass. Some of these Eastern fellows got their first introduction to white lightning that way.

We actually quarried a lot of flagstone. It comes in different thicknesses, you know; but getting that stuff up from its layered beds with crowbars is a very ticklish and hard job. We didn't have any modern equipment. All we had was just hand tools in getting it up. Heavy?! Oh, it is so heavy! And then loading it on this old flatbed truck which we'd acquired. Then we'd go in through Jamestown (known locally as Jim Town) at the end of the day with our flagstone. And we always liked to stop. There was a place there where you could get beer in fishbowls, and we'd go in and have some beer in these wonderful fishbowls. Boy, we were thirsty! Out on the job, we found a farmer nearby and he had buttermilk in his springhouse, and so we got buttermilk from him for lunchtime to have with our lunches. But that beer was a great thing. We'd go in, singing along the way, you know, on the flat-bottom truck. Naturally we became conspicuous in the town, and we almost got ourselves killed off by becoming identified as "those reds" down at Joe Kelly's.

There we were in Fentress County. The town of Wilder, where Barney Graham, the mine union leader, was shot was located in that county, and violence was not far off at any time. The incidents of violence could start over the most insignificant things, but this has been true in the lives of hill people for generation after generation. So Charlie Webber and I tried to make as much contact with the community as possible. We did some square dancing in the summer, and we also reached out through baseball. Charlie loved to play baseball and I did, too. We organized a team from our side, and they organized one, and we played in a little rough field right there at the little crossroads community of Allardt. We made a lot of friends that way, showing them that we were no different than they were and that we liked the same activities and recreations that they did. Not far from there was Rugby, you know, the English attempt to establish an English colony in the Cumberlands.

At the end of that summer of '34, several of us went over to Knoxville to join the picket line outside the Cherokee Spinning mill. It was the first general strike in textiles. That's where we met Lucille Thornburgh. We were singing songs and marching and carrying signs and so forth in support of those people. At one point, I was on the verge of being arrested by a policeman, but something diverted his attention and I got free. I didn't have any money, and I had to get back to Union [for the fall term]. Luckily, Zilla Hawes' sister had come down in her little two-seater rattletrap, and she was driving back to New York, so I hitched a ride with her. We came straight through to 122d Street and Broadway nearly without stopping, to my last and very full year at Union. Back to my cabbage patch. That was my place. By that time I had so identified with it and with the youngsters down there in the ghetto that I would hardly go anyplace else to get any other experience. I began to introduce them to drama and Eva Le Gallienne's repertory theater. I would get tickets and passes to the repertory theater and we would buy these hero sandwiches for a nickel apiece and we'd start out walking toward Sixth Avenue and Fourteenth Street from down there on the Bowery, eating away at these long sandwiches.

We'd eat our way up [*chuckling*] to the theater and have a great
time; or go to the circus at Madison Square Garden, or have a
picnic along the Hudson River. Those were great, great occasions
with those youngsters!

The next summer, I was a counselor at a camp established in
Sturbridge, Massachusetts, by a very creative camp director, Josh
Lieberman. Then, before I knew it almost, I had graduated from
Union. That winter of '35–'36 was a memorable time. Here I was a
graduate of Union Theological Seminary and during part of that
time I was on public relief, because the jobs in New York City were
so scarce. Settlement house work was such that they couldn't take
on new workers, and I remember at one point, during the winter
when I was so short of funds, I sold blood. But I was so deeply
involved in all that was going on in New York, I wanted to hang on
for a while longer. Margot Mayo and I, for example, organized the
American Folk Dance Group, and we met regularly and taught the
dances of southern Appalachia to other ethnic groups through
the Folk Festival Council, which was a new instrument for such
purposes at the New School for Social Research. Every Sunday
night during that fall and winter, we had exhibitions of ethnic folk
songs and dances that were taught to the people who came.

From the moment I arrived in New York, I had found myself
among interesting, interesting people who were almost like folk-
lorists in that they were fascinated by ethnic customs. Here I was
an example of an Appalachian having made it out of the hills, and
I was expected to know how my people lived and how they recre-
ated, what songs they sang, what kind of dances they danced, how
they made their living, and so on and so forth. And this really
opened my eyes to the value of transmission of cultural modes and
forms across regional lines. Almost as soon as I got into New York
City and met some of those people, I knew my fate was sealed. I
had to be a square dance caller and teach the Southern style. And
every time I went back to Tennessee, it was like going back to sup
at the table. I wanted to get as much as possible so that not only I
could be enriched, but so that I would also have some content to
pass on to others. And so the play party games I grew up with, and
the customs at the church socials when there might be pie supper
socials or ice cream supper socials—with homemade ice cream
that would freeze the top of your head off—and the dances like

the Virginia reel and other line dances and the circle dances, all became very important to me. I suddenly realized that this was a part of my past and my growing up, and when I came in contact with others who were trying to save this, or collect it, like Neva Boyd had already done, I wanted to put in my little mite too. And so I became very, very active.

In fact, Margot and I, the spring before that brutal winter, had made a trip down into eastern Kentucky, where her ancestors originated, and then on into my home base, seeking out the folk forms of that time. Wherever sacred harp singing was taking place, or square dances were being held, we were there. I remember taking her to the Walker home near Townsend, Tennessee, where they lived in a little log cabin up the creek at the foot of what was called Rocky Mountain. The grandmother, Aunt Liddy Walker, was one of the best natural folksingers in the mountains. Her songs had been handed down to her through the ages by word of mouth. And the grandfather, Smoky Joe Walker, played the fiddle, and the father played the banjo. When we got there, the grandfather was on a religious tear at the time and wouldn't play the fiddle because it was violating certain religious principles. He belonged to the Primitive Baptist Church, and he'd hung his fiddle up on the wall of the cabin and wouldn't take it down. We had one heck of a time. Finally, we got him to take it down. And here was the grandfather and his son and his granddaughter, Marie, all making music. And it was wonderful to behold. Even though all the others are gone now, I still stay in touch with Marie.

But that's the way it was when you went into the mountains. And Margot had this wonderful facility of being able to take a blank sheet of paper and a pencil and draw the lines off and the staff and she'd note any melody right there in the palm of her hand. She had that skill. She could pick up a tune that way and then get back to a piano and do the whole thing.

At any rate, the winter passed. All this time I had stayed in touch with Highlander, and I had been moving since my summer there toward making a commitment to join the staff full-time. Now, one must remember the setting and the times. Here I'd been trained as a minister with a great deal that Union had to offer ministers in those years, and I'd come from a very conservative part of the country and I knew the governance group of my Presbyterian church would never approve me as a minister there. I was following pretty much in the footsteps of others who had been to Union and who, during those days, felt that the church was not the proper organization or vehicle for addressing the needs of the people in the depths of the Depression—that the churches were failing and that you needed a different approach. I felt more and more that people like Jim and Myles and John Thompson and Franz Daniel and the others who were pitching in together into the outer parts of the labor movement [were coming closer to really helping those in need than the churches].

In the spring of 1936, the National Federation of Settlements and Neighborhood Centers decided to hold their national conference at Norris Dam. The dam had just been completed by TVA, and the barracks where the workers lived were being vacated. The recreation hall was free and they booked it and they asked me if I would come down and lead them in square dancing, and I agreed. I went down along with some other settlement people, and after the conference, I made my way from there to Highlander for the beginning of a rich and rewarding time. I don't suppose any other experience in my seventy-one years has had as much or more influence on me than the experience of being associated with Highlander during these years. And even though I was on the staff for only a short time, it was a formative period and a formidable period for Highlander because they were at great risk. Events which later culminated in the closing down of the school hadn't gathered up enough steam by that time, but if their opponents had had their way, they would have been wiped off the face of the earth.

When I got there, I just fell into whatever needed to be done. Myles was often away on extended trips into North Carolina organizing for the Textile Workers Organizing Committee, and Zilla and Jim and Zilphia were constantly responding to demands being made on their time, so there was always work to do. The Unemployed League of Grundy County, for example, was being formed when I got there, and the local unemployed miners were coming together: Dolph Vaughn, who was like a piece of indestructible material at that time—philosophical, very experienced, a natural leader—and Lige Birdwell—fractious and impulsive and emotional and outspoken. If Lige hated you, you were at risk. And so I picked up and began working with Dolph and Lige. Highlander people would work as a team with them and go with them to their meetings out on the mountain, or get them transportation if they needed to get to Chattanooga or Nashville—or just stand by them to give them support.

And it was really with those unemployed coal miners that Highlander made such a contribution at that time. Here were people who were really down and out, and they were trying to deal with a bureaucracy that had been established by the federal government but was controlled locally by the states and the districts in those states. That's why, whenever I hear talk of dismantling the federal presence and returning control of certain monies or programs to the states, I get nervous, because those of us who are a little older remember what happened during the Great Depression when the states ofttimes were the most obstructionist of all the governmental forces. And if you acted a bit out of line in the judgment of the local bureaucrats, you were to be penalized and stricken off the list for federal aid. This was really the case there in Grundy County during the days of the WPA when the unemployed coal miners were trying to deal with the bureaucracy. Here were the state forces and district forces that were really their enemies, really against them, and not willing to give them justifiable aid. The excuse they used was the relationship of the miners to Highlander—this red, subversive group—but if it hadn't been Highlander, it would have been the fact that they had once belonged to the United Mine Workers of America, or something else. The scourgers always find a reason to scourge.

Dolph and Lige knew this, and they saw it very clearly, and that's why they became fast friends and allies of Highlander. They knew that Highlander had their best interests at heart and was willing to go the second mile and beyond to help them out, and that's what did happen. It was really through Highlander that these local people were able to leapfrog over the local bureaucrats in the state and go all the way to Washington and find the friendly, receptive, understanding, giving hand which eventually reached out all the way to the unemployed miner there in Grundy County. Without Highlander's help, these men were at a great disadvantage.

It was also during this time that there were disturbances oc-

curring in mills and factories in the lowland—especially around
Chattanooga. One of the most influential labor leaders in Chattanooga was Joe Dobbs, who headed the labor council there, and
when it came to the crunch and a crisis occurred, Joe would call
up to the school and say, "Hey, we've got a strike on and I need
help. Come on down!" Many a morning I can remember getting
in the old rickety station wagon—some half dozen of us—and
making the run from Monteagle down to the picket line to reinvig-
orate tired folk and let them know they had friends who would put
themselves out and stand to help a flagging spirit. This was one of
the functions of a place like Highlander. It meant that there were
informed, finely honed human-service skills in the Highlander
community that could be summoned in time of crisis. Whenever
there was trouble, there was usually a way in which Highlander
could make a contribution. And this principle, you see, has come
down to today. It's still, today, one of the vital contributions Highlander makes.

And one vital aspect of that contribution and that spirit that is
still carried on today at Highlander is that of music. When people
like Zilphia would get songs going on the picket lines, you could
feel people's spirits rising. Or in workshops. If ever there was a
person who could invigorate and move a group of adults with
musical participation, she was the prime example of an artist at
work. The walls of the old building at Highlander—Aunt Lillian
[Johnson's] house—rang with the songs of people during those
years, and with the music which she generated and was always
encouraging individuals to create in their own way and to bring as
contributions to the sessions that were held.

She knew, and would use, anything that seemed to suit the
occasion—popular music of the late twenties and early thirties,
Broadway tunes, old tunes. I'll never forget how effectively she
used the song "Brother, Can You Spare a Dime?" in little playlets
to arouse the emotions of either working people or people to
whom she was trying to give some appreciation of what the life of
the unemployed worker was like. It was just a joy to be a part of it
with her and to sit in any group and to see how they would respond. She had an infectious type of presentation that enveloped
you and drew you in. You weren't on the outside as a spectator—
you became wholeheartedly involved with the moment. And that

was singing either one of the traditional labor songs, which spoke of the struggle of years past and had application to today, or a new song that had been brought in by a participant in one of the workshops, which was then ingested and became a part of the collective material and would eventually appear in print as a part of a little songbook.

"No More Moanin'," for example, was literally put together right there in the kitchen at Highlander. People coming from wherever—factories, sharecropper country—brought a little of their lifestyles with them to workshops, and ways they had learned to communicate with each other, and singing was one of those ways. The old songs became vehicles for carrying new messages, and singing became a unifying force. And because of those deep-rooted traditions of singing in churches and homes, it was very natural that singing should develop in the Southeastern part of the country as a natural adjunct to the struggle to overcome inhuman situations and to deal with them in song. Preachers and workers all had this sort of experience, whether they were blacks or whites.

Because music was one of my real loves, Skipper, who had arranged one of the periodic Highlander fund-raising tours, asked me if I could set up a program that could be taken to Washington, Philadelphia, and New York. So that was another of my projects as a staff member. In each place, we'd have a party and have people come. So I agreed, and then I had to get my musicians.

The first place I went was up toward Gatlinburg, Tennessee, to Wiley Oakley's place, because he was the best tall-tale teller in the Smokies. He could really entertain you. Great around a campfire at night. Some of his stories are just classics. One of his tales was about being in the mountains one day, and he heard a big noise up the mountain from him, and all of a sudden a *great* snake came slithering past him and he just didn't know what to do. He hadn't seen a snake that large. "And you know that snake was traveling so fast," he said, "that it was setting the leaves on fire." He said he had to get a little "whup" there to "whup" it out because he didn't want to have the forest on fire. But while he was doing this, he heard another noise up the mountain, and along come another big snake. And he said, "You know what, this second snake that was coming down was a weepin' and a cryin' so that the big tears that were coming out were puttin' out the fire. She was going after her mate," he said. [*Laughter*]

He had a habit before he'd have a storytelling session of saying, "Now, I'd like you folks to know that after I tell a story, if I yodel a little, you don't have to believe that story; but if I don't yodel, hit's the truth." [*Laughter*]

Wiley became a legend in the Smokies because of his knowledge of the flora and fauna of the mountains. So there was Wiley in his boots and his large hat and his plaid shirt and his corduroys, and Wiley sort of got interested [in going on the tour]. And then I looked up Long Jim Trentham, who played the fiddle, and I tried to get him interested and I had a hard time. He made fiddles and then played the fiddle and I wanted him so much. Mind you, I was trying to get together this party of musicians and take them all this way to New York and back. Well, I finally got him, and then I went across a mountain stream on a swinging bridge to get to Ashley Moore's house, and I got him interested. He had only one leg, and he played the banjo. He had lost one leg logging there in the mountains. Then Harvey Oakley, Wiley's son, was interested in going and playing the guitar. Then Fred Maples, his friend, was interested in going and playing the ukulele. There, we had it! All those instruments and a good storyteller in Wiley Oakley; and I would do the calling. So we could go and have one-night stands and raise a little money for Highlander, and by golly, we did that!

We had some marvelous experiences along the way. The National Folk Festival was being held in Washington, so we played there, and the World's Fair was on in Flushing Meadow, so we put on a Tennessee Running Set exhibition for the audience on the stage there, and the Amalgamated Clothing Workers were holding their national convention in Atlantic City, so we led them in some square dancing there. But the next morning after the Atlantic City stint, the men with me confronted me, and they said, "We've been traveling with you for three weeks now, and we're tired and we want to go home. Trout season opens the fifteenth of this month and we want to be there when it opens. You talk a lot about Highlander and strikes—well, we're about to go on a walkout. [*Laughter*] We want to go home."

That was the fourteenth of the month, and I knew I couldn't get them to stop in Washington again on the way back, so we turned that car toward southern Appalachia and headed down the Shenandoah Valley and made it back to Gatlinburg on the day that trout season opened! [*Laughter*]

It was also during the time I was at Highlander that we made the movie *The People of the Cumberlands,* featuring the Barney Graham incident and these coal workers and lime workers and so on. I would serve as the prototype of the organizer working with them, and Dolph and Lige were involved, along with the young folks dancing to the tunes of J. D. Marlowe and others. J. D. Marlowe loved to go squirrel hunting, and sometimes he would take Zilphia with him and teach her to shoot. She became quite a marksman herself. The Marlowes were great friends of Highlander.

Anyway, that film was used often in Highlander workshops. It was filmed by Elia Kazan and Ralph Steiner.

In August of 1938, the time came when I felt I should move on. Griselda Kuhlman, the Amalgamated Clothing Workers organizer in Nashville, had urged me to join her staff full-time in organizing, and I wanted very much to do that. And within a few months of my being in Nashville, I was asked to go to New York and work with the Amalgamated office that was in charge of cultural and educational activities for the union members. Several unions had this kind of operation. The International Ladies' Garment Workers' Union had an education department, for example, headed by Mark Starr. J. B. S. Hardman headed up ours. The kind of thing we were to do was help union members form drama groups to develop plays that had some social content with which they could entertain their coworkers; or hold seminars on the meaning of industrial democracy in America, or the history of the labor movement, or of various types of industries to help newcomers to the industry understand what the old-timers who fought to bring about organization went through, and understand what they had inherited without having to fight for it—that kind of thing. So I began to work out of New York, going to locals in the eastern part of Pennsylvania, or Rochester or Boston or Cincinnati or Buffalo—wherever they sent me.

At one point I was traveling in Massachusetts in 1940, and I stopped off to visit my friends the Liebermans at the Sturbridge camp where I had once been a counselor, and there was Ruth. This fifteen-year-old strip of a girl had become a woman seven years later and was a counselor in the Sturbridge camp herself. What about that? She no longer reminded me of my little sister at all.

The next year I was near Joplin, Missouri, working to organize in the little factory town of Webb City, and there, on Route 66, I decided it was time to take myself a bride. [*Laughter*] So I wrote Ruth a letter and I said, "Now or never," and she wrote back and said, "I'll be on the next train." And this year we're celebrating our fortieth wedding anniversary. She took the train to Kansas City, and I met her at the railroad depot. I put her in the car and headed south toward Joplin, Missouri, and on the way we came to a little community called Nevada, Missouri. We said, "This may be as good a place as any to get hitched." It was just about sundown and we turned in and started looking for a justice of the peace. Well, all office hours and everything were over, but we found the justice of the police court at home in his undershirt, mowing the lawn. So we drove up and we said, "Would you please?" And he was amenable. He said he would call his wife, and his wife came out wiping her hands on her apron and she stood up as witness and there is where we were married. And then after all of the customary adieus and so on, we got back into the car and continued driving south to Joplin, Missouri, and to the Keystone Hotel. [*Laughter*] They prided themselves at the Keystone Hotel on having the best hamburgers east of the Pecos, so we had a couple of hamburgers for our wedding dinner sitting there at the counter! [*Laughter*]

Ruth began helping me organize. Not long after, we had to go back up to Kansas City to confer with the nearest Amalgamated official; and there, Sunday morning, we heard, "This day will be remembered as a day of infamy," and we knew then I would have to go into the service. I was thirty-two years old.

★

Ten-Hour Night Shifts on the Universal Winder
Lucille Thornburgh

If cafés or hotel rooms were the earliest meeting places for mill workers and union organizers in eastern Tennessee, the implications were clear: In the event of serious trouble, the organizers might escape but not the workers. For the latter, these factory towns were home and family and heritage. In 1934, this became particularly true for one Cherokee Spinning Company worker in Knoxville: Lucille Thornburgh's first participation in a strike caused her to be blacklisted in the region for years.

Despite this discrimination, she did not forsake union causes. After studying at a British labor school, she would return to Knoxville and, starting in 1948, would serve as associate editor of the East Tennessee Labor News. *By 1966, she would become its editor.*

Thus, her memories of the Depression era reveal the human costs when strikes fail, contracts go unsigned, and union organizers move on to the next town, the next cause.

Our family was from the country—from Jefferson County, Tennessee. My grandparents were farmers. Grandfather Thornburgh made his money on hogs and bees. His specialty was hickory-smoked hams, and he raised all the family's food. . . .

My father ran a little general store at Rolling Hills, sixteen miles from Dandridge, the county seat. It was the only store around. He was also the justice of the peace for thirty-five years up there. He was always performing marriage ceremonies, and he would perform them anywhere. People would come to the store or our house. One time he married one couple that was eloping, running down the railroad tracks with the girl's father not far behind with a shotgun. He never cared. He never asked any questions. And he never charged a penny.

All the people in the surrounding area got their mail at the store. The mailman delivered it to the store in a horse and buggy, so the store was really the center of the community. During the winter, people would come in and sit around that potbellied stove and spit tobacco juice everywhere, you know. And they would tell big tales, and I would sit there and listen until I would go to sleep at the tales they would tell. I particularly liked scary tales. After they told those big tales of things that happened all around there, I would have to stay until the store closed so I could go home with my daddy because I was afraid to go by myself.

I was born September 19, 1909, there in Jefferson County. I had four sisters and one brother. The other sisters helped my mother with the housework, but I didn't like that housework too much so I learned to milk and feed the cows. I was milking our cows twice a day when I was eight years old—I preferred that to washing dishes and making beds. We had a big garden, so we all helped with the gardening and canning, and any of us kids could keep the store if our father was gone.

For games, paper dolls was our big deal. You know where we got our paper dolls? We cut them out of the Sears, Roebuck catalog. The clothes too. Everything. We would just have rows and rows of those dolls. And I can remember when the Sears, Roebuck catalog did not have any colored pages in it. When the first colored pages came out, we fought over who was going to get them. We educated every doll in the Sears, Roebuck catalog, [because] we played school with them all the time.

I started to school when I was four years old. Piney Grove was a one-room school, and my older sisters took me one day and that was it. I went from then on. The teacher didn't seem to mind and he let me stay. The school wasn't filled anyway. Actually, from that and from hearing my mother working with my brother and sisters on their lessons at night, I was bored in school up until about the sixth grade because I had heard it all twice.

We were the only white family in that little immediate community. The rest were black. The black men worked at the Mascot Zinc Mines and on the Southern and L and N railroads. They'd gather there at the store when the Knoxville papers came, and by the time I was six, I was reading the papers to them.

We had never heard of segregation or integration. Our play-mates were those little black kids up there. We never even thought about it. But they had to go to a different school, and a different church; when we were walking the two miles to our white school, we would pass the black kids walking to theirs. We played together and ate together in each other's homes, but we couldn't go to school together. We always thought that was so foolish.

As I got older, I began to think about what I was going to do. When my father had to go to Knoxville to buy things for the store, he'd take one or two of us with him. When it was my turn, I remember seeing a woman sitting at a typewriter, and I thought that must be such a glamorous job that I decided to learn how to type. And then I had a dream of someday going overseas, and I had a dream of working in New York City. The reason I got inter-ested in New York was that somebody had sent us a postcard from New York of the Woolworth Building (at that time, you know, it was the tallest building in the world). And I said, "Oh, I want to work in New York City." I didn't know what I was going to be doing, but I wanted to work there. It was a strange thing, but when I *did* work in New York City for the labor movement from 1942 until 1946, from my desk window I could see the Woolworth Build-ing. I would always think of that. In fact, both that dream and the one to go abroad eventually came true.

When I was fifteen, my father moved our family to Dayton, Tennessee. They thought it was going to be a great improvement, but it was the biggest mistake that the family ever made. My mother and father both thought that there were no educational opportunities for children in Rolling Hills. So my father sold the farm up there and bought a meat market in Dayton. It was a mistake. He was a country boy and he wasn't a butcher. He didn't know anything about it. It was a mistake—especially with the De-pression coming on. We stayed there long enough, though, for me to graduate from Rhea County High School just one year before the John T. Scopes trial.

When we moved to Knoxville, my father opened a grocery

store and operated it until the Depression hit in 1929. Meanwhile, the rest of us had to work to help out. We didn't have training enough [to get good jobs] so two of my sisters started working in a glove factory, and my brother and I got jobs at the Cherokee Spinning Company. They took raw cotton all the way through from the card room to the spinning room to the winders on to the weave shop, so they took it all the way through to finished cloth.

The first job I got there was in 1925. I was on the night shift. I went into work at five in the afternoon and put in a ten-hour shift. My job was to stand there all night at a universal winder, which was a machine that wound thread from cones onto little spools to be taken into the weave shop.

I never will forget that first night as long as I live. I had never been in a cotton mill before and this woman was showing me how to run this winding machine, and I thought, "Oh gee, it's going to be time to go home soon. It's time to go home. I know it is." I was standing there and I started to get sleepy, you know, with her showing me and the hum of that machine and all. [But when] I went back to the water fountain and looked at the clock, it was only eight-thirty. I thought, "Oh, can I make it? I don't think I can make it." I hadn't been there but three and a half hours!

I finally got used to it, but I used to get so mad. The National Recovery Act hadn't come in yet with the eight-hour day, so you'd work ten hours for eight dollars a week—that's if you got to work a full week. Sometimes you'd only take home four or five dollars to put into the family kitty. But I used to get so tired and mad and sick of standing. Even though I was young, I wasn't strong and robust. Also you had no sick leave, no hospitalization, no vacation. You worked strictly on piecework. They always gave us the Fourth of July off, and they thought they were doing us a big favor, but we weren't paid for it. No paid holidays at all.

That's why, when the AF of L sent a general organizer into Cherokee in 1933 to organize textile workers, I was ready to talk to him. I was the first person he called—probably because he had found out I was always mad about something—and I got a group of about ten coworkers together to meet with him in a hotel room in Knoxville. We knew the boss would fire us if he knew about our meeting, but we were so full of enthusiasm and ignorance that we took the chance. . . .

Another thing he did that impressed us was that more than talking about hours and wages and working conditions, he pointed out where united we could do something, as individuals we couldn't. He made [it] very clear that if we wanted to get the things that we were after there, we were going to have to be united. . . . He was a good organizer . . . , a railroad boiler-maker, an old-time trade unionist. I did not understand all the things he told us but I was certainly interested when he said the union could get us higher wages and better working conditions. By this time the National Recovery Act had brought in the eight-hour day and the Wagner Act had been passed, giving "workers the right to organize without coercion or intimidation." We listened carefully as he gave a short history of the labor movement. He told us about the Haymarket Riot, the railroad strike in 1921, and how Ella Wiggins was killed in the Gastonia, North Carolina, textile strike in 1928. We were truly inspired by these stories.

We began holding meetings in homes, secretly, of course. Each meeting would bring in a few more members. We only needed seven members and seven dollars to get a charter. We passed the hat, got the money, and ordered our charter. Now we were a bona fide labor union. We appointed delegates to the Central Labor Council, and I was the only woman delegate and the first woman to hold office in that body since it was organized in 1888. We had men delegates from our local union but they were not yet certain that the labor temple was any place for a woman!

Then we started holding meetings downtown in the Moose Hall, the only place we could get a room. Meetings were held on Saturday morning. That was when the workers were off from work and since everybody went to town on Saturday we had good attendance. East Tennessee has always had a lot of itinerant, street-corner preachers and we had several of them in our union. They were accustomed to speaking before groups and our meetings were lively. Sometimes they would argue among themselves and tell me, on the side, that so-and-so is a false prophet. But no matter how heated the meeting might be the preachers made us close by holding hands and singing a church hymn. Good fellowship. In fact, the president of our union was a Holiness preacher–loom fixer and he was a good leader. Like myself he was blacklisted later. . . .

Then we drew up our contract and presented it to the company. There was no argument about us having a majority of the workers. We had signed up all of them! Our contract was a crude, simple document. All we asked for was a small increase in wages, decent restrooms, a seniority clause, and elimination of the "stretch-out system"—where we were required to operate more machines than we could handle, for the same amount of pay. We never thought of asking for anything like insurance, paid holidays, sick and vacation leave, or any of the benefits that today are standard clauses in all union contracts.

However, the company was negotiating with us and we possibly could have gotten a watered-down contract and saved our union. But, amid all the unrest in the country, the United Textile Workers of America (AFL) called a nationwide strike of textile workers. "Textile workers" was a new title for us; we had always been called "cotton mill hands"—we liked our new title.

Our local union voted not to strike and continue with negotiations but the UTW ordered us to strike or give up our charter. We called the strike and I was elected strike leader. We all thought if we didn't win we would just go back to work. We knew nothing of blacklists. We closed the mill and for three weeks carried on a good strike. The members remained loyal and members from other unions helped us picket.

The mill owners were staging a tremendous fight against unionism all over the country. Martial law was declared in several places; the National Guard swarmed in to break the strike. They never came to Knoxville but goon squads were sent other places to terrorize strikers; Pinkerton spies were used and scabs began appearing at the gates to replace the strikers. Our local union was served with an injunction. In all, sixteen strikers were killed in the South and many more wounded.

Locally, with the news of all the "terrible things" the strikers were doing being blared over the radio and printed in the newspapers in detail, we had no allies. Neighbors hearing these stories were against us; families were divided pro and con. The churches took an active part against us. To add to our troubles the president of the company died of a heart attack in the fourth week of the strike. Many of our members were fundamentalists and had guilt feelings that the strike had caused his seizure. Of course, the strike had nothing to do with it, but it dampened the spirit of the strikers and was one more obstacle we had to overcome.

In looking at our situation in retrospect I can see why the people were confused and afraid. We were not out of the Great Depression, jobs were still scarce, and FDR's New Deal was just getting under way. So our members, especially men with wives and babies to feed, began drifting back to work when the mill opened. I couldn't really blame them, with the entire community against us, preachers telling them how "sinful" it was to strike, and wives nagging them. International union representatives who came in told of how men and women had fought, bled, and died to establish a better way of life for all workers. But our members, with the ink barely dry on their union cards, could not grasp this and were not willing to sacrifice their livelihood for a cause they did not understand.

The UTWA had no strike benefits and with no real leadership our local strike broke down, as it did all over the nation. I learned later from a veteran unionist that during grievances, negotiations, and even strikes, the overriding thought in the leader's mind should be "save the union." Then go back, increase your membership, garner allies, and come back to fight another day. How true. When the local union is lost (dissolved) you are back to square one. That's just where we were in Knoxville.

It was bad timing for a strike. I agree with the J. P. Stevens worker quoted in Mimi Conway's book, *Rise Gonna Rise:* "They [UTWA] had no business striking down South because they were weak here. We didn't have no backing. I think what happened in 1934 has a whole lot to do with people not being so union now."

With the strike over I was blacklisted, along with fifteen thousand other Southern strikers. Even with my experience as a winding machine operator I could not have found a job anywhere in the industry, nor could I today. Blacklists are permanent.

Let me say right here, some people who don't know, or don't want to know, think that all organized labor does is strike. This is far from the truth. While the strike is the only real weapon the working people have, it is only used as a last resort. Writers and poets have dramatized and romanticized the strike as "dedicated men and women standing shoulder to shoulder on the picket line, singing their solidarity songs, to better the fate of all mankind."

It might be dramatic for the first two weeks until the money from the last payday is gone; then it gets rough. House payments are due, the baby needs shoes, the wives are nagging, and the strikers find too much time on their hands after they've done their stint on the picket line and they become bored. Nobody really wants to strike, but it's like I said, withholding our labor is the only weapon we have and we use it as the last resort. I wouldn't sign a union contract with a no-strike clause in it. I would be signing away the only weapon I have.

Our Cherokee strike had long-lasting results. Mill owners told workers, "See what happened at Cherokee. They couldn't win and you can't either." Cherokee moved to Sevier County many years later. The strike had nothing to do with it. It is the general belief they moved because of tax incentives. . . .

In 1934, I went to work for TVA as a secretary in the filing department. They didn't mind that I was blacklisted. TVA was very liberal and pro-union at that time, and they had an office workers' union—the American Federation of Office Employees, which I joined—so they were used to dealing with unions.

All the time I worked for TVA, I stayed active in the labor movement as a delegate to the Central Labor Council and a volunteer organizer through their general organizing committee. There was a group of railroad men and motion picture operators and myself that would go out at night and visit in various homes— especially the homes of bakery workers and laundry workers. Those were two groups that were so low-paid we were interested in them. We weren't paid a penny. We were doing it because we wanted to. And we did manage to organize a laundry workers' union here [in Knoxville]. . . .

While the organizing among textile workers had come to a dead stop, other workers were flocking into the union. The Committee for Industrial Organization (CIO) had been formed in 1935 to organize the unorganized in the mass production industries. The AFL had concentrated on skilled craftsmen. In February 1936 the CIO struck Goodyear Tire and Rubber Company, Akron, Ohio, with its fourteen thousand rubber workers. They won [that] strike and the CIO was off and running.

The AFL was not asleep. They staged organizing drives among

the skilled workers, especially the building tradesmen, until in 1936 we had a pretty strong movement in Knoxville.

On Labor Day of 1936 we put on the biggest and longest parade this part of the country had ever seen. We marched down Gay Street (our main street) to the tune of five high school bands. Every local union, under the banner of the AFL, had a big float. The painters were dressed in their white overalls. After walking the mile down Gay Street we loaded into cars and went to Maryville/ Alcoa to join the Aluminum Workers in another march. We had a beauty queen, a wrestling match, and free barbecue—all the hoopla that goes with a celebration. The day ended with a grand march led by AFL president William Green and our beauty queen. This day was the talk of the town for several years. . . .

While I had no social philosophy at that time, I knew something was wrong when men and women spent their lives in drudgery jobs, never getting ahead, barely eking out a living and going to an early grave. Surely, I thought, this is not the American way of life! So I began searching for a way that I might help change things. Through reading all the labor books I could find and listening to unionists talk at the Central Labor Council, I decided changes could be brought about through unity of action by the workers.

This was a time of learning for me. My thinking was influenced by listening to such speakers as a representative of the League for Industrial Democracy (LID), who had come to Knoxville to talk with the WPA workers; Clair C. Killen, director of labor relations at TVA, was a member of the Industrial Workers of the World (IWW) and I worked closely with him. Then too, I remembered things that Myles Horton, Highlander director, had told us when he was there helping with our strike.

This is an amusing sidelight on the LID speaker: He spoke to the WPA workers at the old ramshackle Market Hall. He was a small man, with rimless glasses, articulate, and very much an intellectual. The following day the Knoxville *Journal* came out with a screaming headline on page one: WILD RED URGES BLOODSHED. Then went on to say how he had advocated a bloody uprising among "our" people. I'm certain the reporter for this story had not understood a word he said.

We were always having mass meetings with liberal speakers

from all over the country. These meetings were very educational for me. . . .

[In 1941] I left Knoxville and TVA to work with the U.S. Army Corps of Engineers at Fort Belvoir, Virginia. I was not a good government employee; my heart was in the labor movement, so after fifteen months I left that job to join the AFL's Southern Organizing Staff. I stayed with them a year and left to go to New York with the Labor League for Human Rights, the relief arm of the AFL. On this job I was sent to cities across the nation, encouraging union members to serve on the boards of the American Red Cross and community chests and to contribute more money to them. This was a good program, and the forerunner of the community service committees that are now a part of all central labor councils.

For the continuation of Lucille Thornburgh's interview, see Chapter Three (page 191).

★

"When People Betray Their Own Kind . . ."
Ralph Helstein

Events in the late thirties led to more substantial contact for Highlander with union officials outside the South—in particular, with leaders from the Congress of Industrial Organizations. One of these men was Ralph Helstein, who served at the time as CIO attorney.

Throughout the forties and early fifties, he and other union leaders would become increasingly supportive of Highlander. By 1943, for example, the CIO would hire a Highlander staff member to conduct a six-month program for its membership in Knoxville, Tennessee. Following that program's success, Highlander would operate seven other monthlong CIO schools between 1944 and 1953.

More specifically, after Helstein became president of the United Packinghouse Workers of America in 1946, that CIO-affiliated union contributed substantial sums to Highlander. Then, for two years in the early fifties, Myles Horton served as UPWA's educational director.

However, as a prelude to these years, Helstein discusses the Wisconsin background that contributed to his subsequent career in the labor movement.

My parents were both immigrants. My father came to this country with his family from eastern Germany when he was about nine or ten. At the age of eleven, I've been told, he was practically supporting and running the family. They lived in Superior, Wisconsin.

My mother had come to this country at the age of fifteen or sixteen to join a sister of hers who was also living in Superior, and that's where she and my father met. I never did hear the story of how they met, but the one touch of romance that she would tell me about with great pleasure was how he came to call on her the first time. He was driving a wagon or buggy of some sort that had four white horses, and he was handling them with one hand. That, I gather, was an accomplishment, although I wouldn't for the life of me know from my own experience.

At any rate, when my father was nineteen and she was twenty-one, they married. My father in those days ran a furniture store of some kind in Superior, and stories would be told of his quite amazing strength. Those were the days when all the cooking was done with wood and coal stoves and the big cast-iron implements were used, and stories were told of how he would pick up one side of a stove alone when it would take two men to lift the other side. Though he was only about five feet six inches, he had very big shoulders and was heavily boned. He was also a very strong person emotionally with many puritanical traits. For example, he never smoked and he never drank.

At some point they moved to Duluth, Minnesota, where I was born; then to St. Paul when I was very young; and then to Minneapolis where I was raised from the age of four. I was the only boy, though I had two older sisters, and being the only boy in a semi-orthodox Jewish home was terribly constraining. We ate only kosher meats, for example, and I couldn't go on overnight hikes as a Boy Scout or go swimming on Saturdays. Much of that, rather than being part of the Jewish tradition (although it may have been consistent with very orthodox teaching), was probably my mother's desire to keep me tied down. At any rate, it was an extremely protective environment. Everything had to be neat and clean and orderly—which I confess is one thing I inherited from her that I still have a desire for myself and observe to this day.

Both my sisters were a strong influence on me. One had a serious disease at the age of five that required her to spend the rest of her life institutionalized, and at my mother's insistence, we would take the train from Minneapolis almost every week to the town where the institution was located to visit with her. That was an experience that exposed me at an early age to this kind of tragedy.

My other sister was thirteen years older, and when she graduated around 1915 from high school, she went to the university over my father's objections. He felt that it wasn't right for women to go to college, but my mother absolutely insisted. We couldn't afford very much in those days, but Mother put an ad in the paper, had people come to the house, and she sold her carpets in order to raise money for tuition, and my sister went off to the university. She was the first person in our family who went to college. She got her B.A. in 1920, and then she decided to get her master's degree—and by this time my father wasn't even arguing the point—and so she went off to Columbia where she got her master's degree in history. This was practically unheard-of for a woman in those days, at least in our circles. She was a tremendously strong influence on me in terms of my education. She insisted, for example, that I take Latin all the way through high school. I thought it was a terrible waste of time, but when she said I had to take it, I had to take it. It was that simple.

When I was just starting high school, she married a man who had one of the finest libraries in the state of Minnesota—a library not just of substantial size for those days, but one that was also very catholic in its tastes. Before I was through high school, I had read Gogol and most of the other Russians—all except Tolstoy, which came later. Good thing, because I enjoyed him more. And I had read Marx, Confucius, The Book of Mormon, Chaucer, Voltaire— you name it. I had exposure to literature of all kinds at an early age. And I had a compulsion not only to read it, but also to talk to her husband about the books and ideas.

I went through the public school system and then enrolled at the University of Minnesota, where I majored in English literature with the intention of teaching. But in the midst of that, I had an experience that was extremely difficult. In one of my English classes we had a teacher who was a writer of some note and who was there as a visiting professor. After I had given a paper on Cardinal Newman's *Apologia,* she called me into her office and said, "Young man, that was a fine job." She went on and said, "I sense that you have ideas about going on and teaching English in college."

I said, "Well, I dream about that. It's one of my fantasies. I'm going to try."

And she said, "Well, this is very difficult for me to tell you, but I think you ought to know before you get yourself completely involved in that career that at this point in history, it is practically impossible for a Jew to get on an English faculty in any college of any consequence in the United States. As a matter of fact, I don't know of a single one."

Well, of course, that has changed very substantially since, but at that time that was the case. Well, I'd had a tremendous interest in Chaucer at the time, and Middle English, and I saw that dream slowly fading away from me. But the problem then was, "What do I do?" I finally decided, "Well, maybe I'll become a doctor." After all, as a doctor I would be making some contribution. I already had this strong moral urge that unquestionably reflected my family's strong drives toward responsibility to the community. That sort of thing came out of the Jewish immigrant background, you know, and there was a conviction that one had a moral responsibility to do good—not in the cynical manner that our friends in Reagan's administration would speak of it, but really in the sense that you had an *obligation* to help people.

I had absolutely none of the prerequisites for medical school, and it meant going through chemistry, physics, all that kind of thing, which I looked at with real foreboding. But since I knew French, I started out with a course in scientific French. Near the end of the first quarter they announced that they were going to offer an exam and if you passed the exam with a B or better, you'd get credit for the whole year. Well, it was a stupid course, and that was an invitation I couldn't turn down. So I took the exam and when I went to see if my name was posted, it was not, which of course meant that I had not gotten a B or better. It seemed a little strange to me, but that's the way it was and so I accepted it and went off. The interesting follow-up to that story was that when I got my transcript at the end of the year, I had credit for a whole year of French. They had obviously made a mistake in posting. But that mistake had by then caused me to drop my plans for a career in medicine. As a result, though I got my B.A. in English, I came out of Minnesota with a sense of uselessness. I couldn't figure out what I was going to do with my life that would be meaningful.

Finally I decided just to go to New York City, partly to break the apron strings my mother and sister had on me as the only son, and partly to figure things out. I got there a month or two after the stock market crash of 1929, and moved in with a friend of mine from Minneapolis who had preceded me there. Both of us were having a hell of a time finding work of any kind, but luckily I had some savings I could live on and I finally got a job working for an insurance company. . . .

The thing that brought me home was that the clothing manufacturing business my father had started when we moved to Minneapolis was having serious problems because of the Depression and he wanted my help. It was in that same business that I had had my first taste of labor problems the summer when I was sixteen. . . . And one of my jobs that summer . . . , since there was a strike at our plant, was to drive over to St. Paul to pick up this guy who was a scab. In those days it was a trip of over an hour, but I'd go pick him up every day and bring him to work, and he'd go walking through that picket line.

I've thought about this many times since. I don't think my father was insensitive to his workers. I just don't think he ever did any independent thinking about such a situation. He was a member, along with almost every firm in Minneapolis, of an employers' organization known as the Citizens Alliance, which would show up as soon as a strike appeared and tell the owners, "You've got to fight this. You can't recognize them. What they're asking for is completely unreasonable."

And I don't think my father thought he was unreasonable or unfair as an employer. I'm not sure he thought it through. He probably followed the advice he got from the Citizens Alliance believing they knew more than he did. Eventually the workers lost the strike, and he took them back.

At any rate I had to go pick up this scab every day, and finally one day I said to my father, "You know, I don't understand this. Here's this guy working here, and those people down there are out on that picket line. Whether they're right or they're wrong, they're out there. Shouldn't he have some sense of loyalty? What sort of person can he be?"

So he says to me, "He's no damn good!"

And I said, "What do you mean, 'He's no damn good'?"

He said, "Well, for the very reasons you stated. He doesn't have any loyalty. I wouldn't trust him. If I didn't *need* to use him, I wouldn't. I certainly wouldn't ever have any confidence in him. When people betray their own kind—the people they're expected to be with and support and be supported by—they are not the kind of people you can trust and rely on."

Well, that had a tremendous impact on me. That was when I was sixteen, and I'm seventy-two now, so that was quite a long time ago. But it still seems very fresh, that incident.

When I came home from New York to work with him again, he had me buying yard goods. I remember one day I bought ten thousand yards of what was called eighty square percale, which was a certain kind of cotton, and I paid eleven and a half cents a yard for it as I remember. When it was delivered, it was worth only nine cents. And I said to my father, "How can this be? Was it worth eleven and a half cents?"

And he said, "Well, at the time you bought it, that's what the market was. Obviously it was worth eleven and a half cents."

I said, "That isn't obvious to me at all. It was either worth it or it wasn't. If it was worth it then, it should be worth it now. I don't like this kind of a market operation. It doesn't make sense to me."

He said, "Well, it may not make sense, but that's the way it works."

And I said, "Well, not for me. From now on I'm going to see to it that whatever inventories I have are under my hat. They're not going to be on shelves."

And he said, "What do you mean?"

I said, "Well, I'm going back to school." That's when I decided to go back to Minnesota to law school.

While I was in law school during the Depression, there were beginning to be rumblings of labor unrest and labor problems; and a number of us at law school were very sympathetic to some of these causes, and we would go down and get on the picket lines and march around. One day we got into a jam—I don't even remember what it was, but it wasn't very serious—and the cops pushed us around and we ended up in jail. I called my father and he came down and got me out. He said to me, "You know, I understand why you do this. You know I probably don't agree with you, but I don't want to argue with you. If you feel strongly enough to want to do it, do it. But can you please do it in such a way that you don't get thrown in jail? I find this very difficult." [*Chuckle*] Well, that didn't seem so unreasonable. I expected a much more difficult session with him than that! [*Laughter*] After that I got deeply involved in Roosevelt's campaign, and I became a somewhat important cog in that machine. This was my real introduction to issues on something other than an intellectual level. You know I told you earlier I had read extensively—Guy de Maupassant, Balzac, Flaubert, Aristotle, Lenin, Dickens—all of these books that gave you the kinds of insights into human behavior that one doesn't ordinarily get unless you're out there digging ditches or working in the farms. I hadn't been. On the other hand, because of what I was exposing myself to intellectually, I understood some of the problems such people had. The real question was, how did I translate that into emotional terms?

My father died in 1932 just a week or two before Roosevelt was elected, and I had the responsibility for liquidating the business and making sure the family was supported while I continued school. I got my L.L.B. in 1934.

After I got my L.L.B. [through my connections with the Roosevelt administration] I was offered a job to work for the National Recovery Administration, which I accepted, and after a few months, I became the labor compliance officer for the whole state of Minnesota. The NRA was divided into two parts, as you may know. There were codes of fair competition for various industries and each code contained fair trade practices and labor provisions. My job was to enforce that part of the code that had to do with the labor provisions. And it was fascinating. It was just what I needed to give me some notion as to where I wanted to go.

I ran into a lot of trouble on some things. Hugo Black, who was a senator then, gave me a very bad time on an occasion when I had gone to Washington to appear before a committee. This was before he went to the Supreme Court. But he was convinced that the NRA was an instrument of fascism—particularly the fair trade practices provision because what it was doing was undermining the whole antitrust concept and making it possible for big business to get bigger and to consolidate its power over the economy. And, in retrospect, I think he was absolutely right and I think, by the way, that the labor provisions contributed to that end in an indirect but still a meaningful way. In any event, the NRA experience gave me a degree of sophistication that I'd never had before, and I also got a sense of power because I was beginning to represent the government and for the first time, even though I had been able to intellectually understand what Lenin meant when he talked about the state as being potentially an instrument of force and violence in the hands of people who control it, I had a chance now to see it firsthand. It was surprising the things I could do. Even though the maximum penalty we could enforce was to take away the employer's blue eagle, people felt that that meant something, and as long as they felt that, it *was* something.

Well, during this period, I got to know a number of labor people. Truck drivers would come in, retail clerks would come in, machinists would come in—or their union representatives might come in if they happened to be organized, but this was in '34 and there wasn't much organization. But they would come in with complaints about violations of the minimum wage laws, or failure of their employers to pay overtime after they had worked forty hours, and these would be the people that I would then help by taking up their cases.

In 1935, the NRA was declared unconstitutional, and I was asked to come to Washington and do some work with a committee they were setting up to evaluate the NRA, and I did. Of course, the Washington experience was another one of those experiences in giving me insights into the way power operates and the relationship between different forces in society.

I stayed there until 1936 when I came back to Minneapolis, took my bar, and started practicing law. And I practiced any kind of law I could get: criminal law, corporate law, divorces—everything. In the summer of '36, the Teamsters Union of St. Paul asked me to handle their negotiations for them that year. I'd never done anything like this before, and I was very green, but I agreed willingly, and it just opened up a whole new area for me—an area of talent which I expanded and refined and developed and sharpened over the years.

Luckily, that year, we were able to work out an agreement without a strike. They didn't think we were going to be able to avoid one because in the early thirties they'd had those terribly nasty organizational strikes in Minneapolis. Those Teamsters' strikes had been some of the most violent ever. At that time, Roosevelt was not backing the Wagner Act. You will remember that prior to the Wagner Act, in spite of a number of legislative efforts to protect the right of workers to join unions, in 1934 it was regarded as a criminal conspiracy for workers to combine together to raise wages, and so unions, per se, were a conspiracy and illegal. The Wagner Act, for the first and only time in American history, gave workers the right to join unions free from interference by an employer. Well, after the NRA and the Agricultural Adjustment Act were declared unconstitutional by the courts, Roosevelt got mad and finally supported the Wagner Act, and that helped us in 1936 with the Teamster negotiations.

So I then started representing unions—not too many at first, but a number—and I began to see the difference in treatment that was accorded me as a lawyer representing unions and the lawyers representing companies. The judges would just shove me around unmercifully. The Norris-La Guardia Act had passed during the time of Hoover, but most of these judges had never heard of it. All an employer had to do to get an injunction was to walk into court with a piece of paper and the judge would sign it. If I'd come in and say, "But it's illegal, you can't do it," they'd throw me out, for all practical purposes, and by the time you finished your appeal, the strike was lost. These judges treated you with complete, absolute contempt. All except two Scandinavian judges. One was Luther Youngdall, who subsequently became governor, and then a federal district judge—and an excellent one—in the District of Columbia. The other was Lars O. Rue. They understood the law, and they would enforce it, and if I ever got a case in front of either of them, I'd get the injunction thrown out. These employer attorneys used to scream their heads off if they ever got cases involving labor in front of these guys, and they'd just move heaven and earth to try and get them changed to another court. But with the exception of those two judges, it was a misery practicing law until the [National War] Labor Board came around. After that, just the reverse happened, and I was riding high. It was lovely then. I liked it. [*Laughing*]

So I went through this whole period of the development of administrative law in the labor field, practicing law. Then in the fall of '37, the CIO began organizing Minnesota, and a group of them asked me if I'd be willing to handle all the CIO cases in the area. Well, you can imagine I accepted that with glee and joy. My only problem was I never could figure out how much to charge. I remember [my wife] Rachael and I [*laughing*] worrying over whether or not I should send a bill for twenty-five dollars for a case that I probably worked on for weeks!

During that whole period I got lessons intellectually as well as emotionally and tactically that I would never have gotten anyplace else. And Minneapolis was the perfect place to get them. Labor history is the story of class violence, and much of it happened in that part of the country. . . .

One of the events that broke that period of yellow-dog contracts [after World War I] was the famous Teamsters strike led by the Dunne brothers [Ray, Miles, and Grant] and Farrell Dobbs out of the Teamsters Union in Minneapolis. Dobbs later became the general secretary of the Socialist Workers Party. Dobbs was an organizational genius—one of the really great organizers in the country. He was the man who conceived of the conference idea that the Teamsters used to cover the country, and of course it is now *the* basic accepted method for organization on the part of the Teamsters Union.

But Minneapolis was a strange city in many respects. It had Scandinavian and German radicals. It had a very large German Lutheran population. It had this whole conglomerate of radical populist leaders. The Farmer-Labor Party tradition was centered there for a while. There was tremendous anti-Semitism there. It had the strongest Trotskyite group anywhere. It had one of the strongest Stalinist groups in the United States. It had the biggest Silver Shirt group—fascists. As a matter of fact, Eric Severeid broke into prominence because he infiltrated the Silver Shirts and wrote an exposé for the Minneapolis *Star-Journal*. He was at the University of Minnesota a year or two after me. Harrison Salisbury of the New York *Times* sat next to me in a course in drama. Harold Stassin, who became governor in '38, was a senior in law school when I was entering. [*Laughing*]

It was a part of the country that generated tremendous extremes. One of the more stupid things I did in my career happened when I was representing the CIO. A good many of them had strong Stalinist influence, and they were in a constant fight with the Teamsters Union, which was the other power base in Minneapolis and influenced by the Trotskyites. I said, "This business of constant fighting and haggling is perfectly ridiculous and makes it more difficult to make progress. Together we ought to be able to take over this town." Remember, I'm the lawyer for this one group and I'm all of twenty-six or twenty-seven at the time. So I decide the thing for me to do is I'm going to get these guys together and bring peace and harmony and they have to understand that they both have the same interests, and we're going to get unity here. And so I get them in the same room. Well, I think it took two minutes exactly for them to take out after each other, and I couldn't get a word in sideways. I finally just walked the hell out of there. No sense in staying in there. They weren't ever going to make their peace. They were more interested in their ideological conflict between Trotsky and Stalin than they were in what happened in Minneapolis. I said to them separately afterwards, "This is insane! And someday you may learn to realize it." I don't think they ever did, frankly.

These were very bright people, though, in an organizational sense. Very knowledgeable. There was one guy who I was especially taken with and who taught me a lot of what I knew. He was thin, redheaded, sunken cheeks; he looked tubercular, sort of humpbacked. I will never forget this guy. There would be a mass of people—several thousand—and there'd be a microphone, and he was one of those characters who would walk up and throw the microphone off to the side and start speaking without using it and getting everyone to say they could hear him. Whether they could or not was another matter, but they said they could. One time we had a strike at the Honeywell plant when we were in the process of organizing. He shows up at the picket line, walks up to a cop, and with no reason—the cop wasn't bothering anyone, actually—he picks a fight with him and takes that little thin chest of his that could hardly be called a chest, shoves it into the cop's big stomach and starts pushing him. [*Chuckle*] And you know, the cop was so surprised he couldn't figure out what the hell was happening. This little guy pushed him until he almost fell off the curb. Finally the cop began to push back, at which time Bill disappeared. And later when I saw him, I said to him, "What the hell did you do that for?"

He said, "Well, don't you understand, Ralph? People have to feel that you can challenge authority, and I did that because I wanted our people to feel that if they had to, they could."

And let me tell you, it just buoyed their spirits way up. "Bill is shoving that great big guy!" They were telling stories about that for years. Well, you know, it was true. The tensions of that period and the strategies for dealing with them were such that Minneapolis was an extremely valuable place for me to have grown up. That city had the biggest WPA strikes in the country, and I went through those and defended many of the people who were arrested. Another incident I'll never forget was standing on a street corner and watching cops shooting tear gas into a group of people down at the courthouse asking for food, and seeing them catch the canisters with their bare hands and throw them back into the courthouse.

I was the only CIO lawyer at that time. There were a couple of AFL lawyers, but not even too many of them this early. Now remember, I'm talking about 1937.

So I represented the union institutionally. I handled much of its collective bargaining. I handled its legal problems. I drafted contracts. I would handle grievances. I would do all that sort of thing. But in addition to that, the union members began coming to me with their own problems of divorce or financial problems and this gave me new insights into people's lives that I had never had. I even found myself handling a number of cases involving the Children's Protective Society, which would take children from the parents because they felt they were being abused or not properly taken care of. Most of these people were unemployed and couldn't pay me anything—or if they did pay me something it was five dollars, you know, a real pittance—but it all gave me an insight into the lives of these workers that began to humanize many of the intellectualized ideas that I had. I began to translate into human and emotional terms many of these intellectual concepts about the relationships of power and politics and our notions of the relationships of man to man and to power.

Finally, one of the clients I took on was the Packinghouse Workers. There was a big Hormel plant in Austin, which is a hundred miles south of Minneapolis, and the workers were having some troubles, so I went to Austin and negotiated on their behalf with Jay Hormel, whom I found to be one of the most remarkable men I'd ever run into—especially as an industrialist. He was knowledgeable and extremely bright. Not only was he way ahead of other industrialists in labor concerns, but also in the way that he could take those labor problems and turn them to his advantage so that he dealt with the concerns but he didn't get hurt in the process. He would benefit by the settlement too. He was a very skillful guy, and I developed a great deal of respect and admiration for him, actually. It turned out to be mutual over the years. We had a very interesting relationship.

Anyway, I went to Austin, and the first thing I knew I was in negotiations with Hormel for a guaranteed annual wage for his workers. In about January of 1939, we signed the first guaranteed annual wage contract negotiated in packing, I believe, in the country.

To show you what I mean about his ability to turn that to his own advantage, he said to me afterwards, in speaking about the rest of the industry's leadership, "You know these jerks don't realize it, but I got publicity out of this settlement that I could never have bought." He went on, "This was on the front page of every newspaper in the United States. Seven million dollars' worth of space, and they wouldn't have sold it to me because I could never have gotten ads on the front pages for Spam or some other Hormel product."

. . . Oh, [his peers] used to call him a crackpot; but not in front of me after a while, because I would say to them, "Your problem is that you're not that kind of a crackpot; if you were that kind of a crackpot we wouldn't have the kinds of troubles we have!"

For the continuation of Ralph Helstein's interview, see Chapter Three (page 145).

3
1940–50
The War That Turned Industry's "Labor Problems" into Short-Term Solutions

True, the New Deal had created jobs and restored self-esteem for millions of Americans. Still, there were ten, eleven million walking the streets, riding the rods, up against it, despairing. All this changed under the lowering sky of World War Two. . . .

Our huge industrial machine shifted gears. In a case of Scripture turned upside down, plowshares were beaten into swords (or their twentieth-century equivalents: tanks, mortars, planes, bombs). In the words of President Franklin D. Roosevelt, Dr. New Deal was replaced by Dr. Win The War. . . . And prosperity came. Boom had a double meaning. . . .

It is exquisite irony that military work liberated women from the private world of *Küche, Kinde, Kirche.* . . . [And] like women, blacks were called upon. Their muscles and skills, usually by-passed, were needed in defense plants. The perverse imperatives of war brought about relatively well-paying jobs for black men and women who would otherwise have been regarded with less than benign neglect. Even this might not have come about had it not been for the constant pressure from the black community.

"I got a call from my boss. 'Get your ass over here, we got a problem.'" Joseph Rauh, working in Washington, remembers June of 1941. "'Some guy named Randolph is going to march on Washington unless we put out a fair employment practices order. The President says you gotta stop Randolph from marching. We got defense plants goin' all over this goddamn country, but no blacks are bein' hired. Go down to the Budget Bureau and work something out.' ''

[So] it was not noblesse oblige that brought forth Executive Order 8802, establishing the Fair Employment Practice Committee. . . .

At war's end, [however, the] newborn working women were urged, as their patriotic duty Over Here, to go back home where they "naturally belonged" and give their jobs back to the boys who did their patriotic duty Over There. [But] the taste for independence was never really lost. . . . No matter what the official edict, for millions of American women home would never again be a Doll's House. . . .[1]

—*STUDS TERKEL*

[1] Studs Terkel, *The Good War* (New York: Pantheon, 1984), 9–13.

★

Can't Strike the Government? Tear Down the Wall
Ralph Helstein

Even though World War II produced higher wages for workers in some industries, and at least better jobs for women and blacks, the wartime labor policies also frustrated many union negotiations. Strikes had always been a union's ultimate weapon, yet striking during a nationwide war effort seemed unthinkable. Or was it?

In 1942, I was asked to come to Chicago and be the attorney for the [United] Packinghouse Workers [of America]. At that time there was tremendous unrest within that union. Part of it was due to the fact that they wanted to be an international union, and they felt [John L.] Lewis and the CIO had promised it to them, but they were still being kept as an organizing committee—in fact, their real title was the Packinghouse Workers Organizing Committee—and they had no autonomous right to elect their own officers, write a constitution, or be self-governing. [They were completely dominated by the CIO.]

On top of that, when I first got there, their case for a wage increase, which had been presented to the National War Labor Board by an attorney the CIO had sent down to handle it for them, was still pending and our people didn't know where they stood. At that time, the Labor Board was making its decisions as to whether or not to grant wage increases on the basis of a case involving a little steel company in which they had allowed an increase of five and a half cents an hour. Out of that case, they had developed what they called the Little Steel formula, through which, they said, they could prevent inflation. At the same time, they claimed they were controlling prices. But any case that came before them for a wage increase had to fall within the purview of that formula or it would be denied.

I got to Chicago in late 1942, and on February 9, 1943, the decision came down from the Labor Board reversing the panel of the board and denying the Packinghouse Workers a wage increase. That union was ready to blow. They hadn't had an increase for I don't know how long, and the cost of living had been going up because of the war, and those workers were really resentful. On top of that, there was a no-strike pledge that the labor movement had given the government because of the war—only Lewis and the coal miners had refused to give a no-strike pledge—and so our job was to see to it that our guys didn't walk out. Well, it was a very difficult problem.

The last thing the chairman of the PWOC wanted was a strike, because the CIO would have jumped down his neck. He knew that. The real question was, how do you avoid it? And so I said to him, "You know, there's only one way to avoid it. That's to call a national conference. Get all our people in and explain the situation. They have to understand." This is one of the things I'd learned in Minnesota, that one of the crucial things was to make sure that people understood what it was you wanted them to do and why. Your job was to try and convince them that it was right. You might, or you might not, but you had that responsibility. I convinced him and we had this meeting. At the same time, we put so much heat on the CIO that we got an agreement that we could have a convention by October at which time the CIO would issue the Packinghouse Workers a charter. Well, to a lot of guys in the union, that meant more than the five and a half cents an hour because it would give them a certain independence.

While all this was going on, we called meetings of our people all over the country to get them involved in creative solutions rather than strategies for tearing things apart. So we avoided the strike, had the convention in October, and elected a president, and by that time I had worked out a strategy for approaching the Labor Board again and reopening negotiations under a special provision they had for "rare and unusual cases." Our guys had to come to work and change clothes—change into white coats and all. Then after work, they'd have to shower and change again because they were all full of blood. Well, this wasn't true in all departments such as sliced bacon and sausage-making, but many of our people had that problem. I felt this was comparable to what miners had to do—the same kind of argument they had used to win their portal-to-portal pay decision. So I spent many days in Washington convincing the members of this board that they owed it to us to give us this clothes-changing time, and we finally won that decision. We got twelve minutes a day. That meant if you were working eight hours, you got paid for nine, so that was a wage increase by indirection, and we were able to get it retroactively. So that was a big victory, let me tell you. It nearly drove every company in the country crazy because they didn't know where this was going to end! [*Laughing*]

By 1946, a couple of years after our clothes-changing-time success, [Walter] Reuther had pulled a strike at General Motors that went on for months and had gotten an increase of seventeen cents an hour or something like that. Steel had gotten an increase of seventeen cents too, and we were saying we wanted the same. Truman was President, and he announced his plan to seize the packing plants because we were threatening to strike. The Secretary of Agriculture, [C. P.] Anderson, was appointed as Truman's deputy to run those plants under the United States Government.

I recall a meeting of our people and saying to them, "We're gonna tell them to go to hell. . . ." I said to them, "Let me make a point to you. Whether or not we can actually pull off a strike against the government if they once take over these plants is a matter that we can't really resolve here. We don't know. But there's nothing that says we can't threaten to do it and just see what happens. We can say that we're not going back to work. And don't ask for too much. What we want from them is simply a commitment that whatever figure the panel that they have set up gives us, they will put into effect right away." In the case of the autoworkers and the steelworkers, they didn't demand that and so they had to keep their strikes going for months before they finally got what the panel had said they were entitled to.

So I said, "All we want out of Anderson is a commitment that whatever that panel recommends, they will implement. And the way to do that it seems to me is to tell them to go to hell." So we argued. I can still see the office. We sat in that office and argued, and the conservative guys were opposed to it. "You can't tell the government to go to hell," and I'm saying, "No reason why you can't. You can tell them anything. The question is what you do, it's not what you say. Now, this is what we're gonna say." And I wrote a statement. I wish I could find it. I have looked for it and I can't find it. But we were spending money hauling Chiang Kai-shek's troops to places where they could attack Mao Tse-tung and the Chinese Communists when we couldn't even take care of our own labor problems, you know. And so I put the two together.

Anderson had been a senator for many years, and I knew he understood the politics of this. I knew he knew he couldn't move in on us. What was he going to do? Drive us in to work? We could say, "We don't care if the government is operating the plants. We don't have to work for the government," and he knew that was true. He also knew he couldn't take the risk, and we knew that he was a politician and he would understand what the risk was. . . . We also knew that we had limits on our power, because our people were not completely prepared to tell the government to go to hell. It was a question as to who would fall first. . . .

If we had said to Anderson, "We won't go back to work unless you give us seventeen cents an hour," I think he would have said, "Well, we'll have to see that out." But we didn't. We made it easy for him because we said, "All we're asking you to do is what your independent panel says you should do, and that's what we want you to implement."

Well, I got the agreement from my people with only a couple of dissenting votes, and we sent out the statement I had drafted. I never will forget the following morning. We called in all our people from around the country to a meeting to get them ready to call a strike or not call a strike, depending on what happened. The order had gone out to seize the plant. The press was headlining our announced refusal to go back to work. Our meeting was at the Amalgamated Clothing Workers Hall over on Ashland, and the president of our union was standing at the mike, and the telephone rings and it's Anderson.

I go over to our president, and I say, "Now we just laid the law down to him. We can't give an inch. We get that commitment or he can screw himself."

Anderson is pleading with him, "You can't do this. You've got to go back to work. You can't challenge the government."

And I told our guy, "Tell him we don't want to. Tell him he's creating a situation where we have no choice. Either we get a commitment that whatever that panel recommends goes into effect or he can seize the plants, but there won't be a goddamn person there to run them."

Well, Anderson just caved completely, and he says, "Okay, you got your demand. I'll send you a telegram making it clear that I will personally see to it that whatever that panel recommends will be put into effect."

I knew he would give in. It was obvious. You didn't need the Talmudic training that I had had to know that. By the way—it never hurt me to have that training. Served me in good stead, I will say.

At any rate, I left before that meeting was over because we had the first meeting of the panel that was going to hear our case in a hotel in the Loop. I walk in there and I am met with this two-inch-high headline in the Chicago *Daily News* that says something like PACKINGHOUSE WORKERS DEFY GOVERNMENT. So it was already in the paper—well, that wasn't an accident entirely. So these guys on the panel are asking me about it and I'm saying, "I don't know anything about that. We're not defying the government. What do you mean we're defying the government?"

"Well, you're refusing to go back to work."

I said, "Oh, is that what they're doing over there at that meeting? I'm not so sure. I think a lot depends on what you guys on this panel do and you'd better get going."

Well, they got going, and we got sixteen cents an hour in the end. They almost made it fifteen cents because the stupid head of the meat cutters' union made a public statement that the meat cutters would be happy with fifteen cents, but I went to see Ed Witte, the chairman of the panel, in Washington at the last minute —I don't know if that name means anything to you, but he was one of the great men in America, the father of Social Security— and I sat up with him until two in the morning arguing for sixteen and a half cents, and he finally caved in and made it sixteen and I left.

At four in the morning the phone in my hotel rings and this guy I'd been friends with for years who was then an adviser to the head of OPA [the Office of Price Administration] is on my line saying, "When the history of this period is written, the Packinghouse Workers will be known as being responsible for inflation."

I'm half asleep and I said, "Do you have to carry your Calvinism to this point? What do you mean the Packinghouse Workers are going to be responsible for inflation? Nonsense! You don't mean it! And you can't, you're too intelligent."

So he says, "Yep, you're gonna be responsible for inflation."

So I said, "So we'll be responsible for inflation. What are you going to do, call us names?"

"Well, but you've got to understand what you're doing."

I said, "Why? Because I talked Ed Witte out of another penny, that's gonna make us responsible for inflation?"

He said, "But it's the principle behind it. If it's a penny here, it'll be a penny there. Someone else will get . . ."

That was before the domino theory. If I'd known about the domino theory I would have used that. Well, we argued I don't know how long. I'm so tired I can hardly move and here's this guy telling me at four in the morning we're gonna be responsible for inflation. So I hung up the phone on him.

Finally the next day the decision came out and the sixteen cents was put into effect and did we have fun then. We got that raise for everybody in the union. The more stupid people who read about it thought we did this because we were communist. Well, if we were communist, we wouldn't have done it, you know. [*Laughter*] It was just because we weren't communist that we did it. [*Laughter*] The smarter ones understood that. We were just essentially agrarian populists. But the union had never had this kind of leadership before where you don't burn your bridges, but you play your cards out and push them as far as they can go. Until then, the members of that union had really gotten pushed around. They hadn't even been able to get that five and a half cents before. Now some wrongs had finally been redressed.

Well, the net result of all that, and the reason I've spent this time telling this story, is that at the convention that year in Montreal, I was elected president of the union. I've been told that this is the first time in the history of the American labor movement that a lawyer was ever elected president of a labor union. And, with the exception of the needle trades, there were also no Jews that were the heads of any labor unions that I knew about.

In 1946, immediately after I became president of the Packing-house Workers, we became involved in civil rights. The majority of our union was white—during the war when the black enrollment in meat packing and steel and in all unions increased, I think the War Manpower Commission estimated that the black membership of our union was something around 30 percent. But when I became president, we started the policy of refusing to sign a contract that did not have a provision that stated that there would be no discrimination against an employee or job *applicant* because of race, creed, or color. We had a hell of a lot of trouble with the job applicant part of that provision—especially from companies like General Foods that said we were trying to run their hiring policies and they weren't going to let us. I knew that the head of General Foods was at that time chairman of the board of the Conference of Christians and Jews, and when it came time to negotiate our contract with them, I arranged to make that known—and they signed the contract.

But we had real problems breaking through on some of these civil rights questions all over the country because I wasn't prepared to simply accept what I thought was the CIO token kind of approach that just said, "All people have a right to join the union." I thought it should go far beyond that. We wrote into our constitution that discrimination because of race, creed, and color had been a divisive element that had been used for years to keep people from uniting. Therefore, it was outlawed. And I took the position that interpreting that was one of the responsibilities that I had under the constitution. I said, "This means that any kind of discrimination is outlawed. It's illegal under the terms of our constitution." That meant separate dining facilities were illegal. Separate rest rooms. Separate dressing rooms. Many things that unions had not insisted on yet. We started this a long time before most of the others.

Sometimes it caused problems. We got a call one day from

our organizer at the Armour plant in Fort Worth, Texas. He had laryngitis and could hardly talk. And so I say to him, "What the hell is the matter with you? I can hardly understand you."

He says, "Well, Christ, there are almost a thousand people marching in the hall. I'm scared stiff they're gonna kill me."

I said, "What do you mean, they're gonna kill you? What's the problem?"

And he said, "Well, you just told the company they had to take down the wall between segregated eating facilities and they're about to remove the wall."

And I said, "Yeah, but what do you mean they're going to kill you? No one is going to kill you."

He said, "Well, boy, they sure look like it."

He *was* scared, so I said, "Okay, forget about it. Don't do anything. Get the hell out of the office and go away somewhere."

We had a vice president who was black and a secretary-treasurer who was out of Atlanta, and I figured these would be two good guys to send down there. They could talk to whites; they could talk to blacks. So they go down there, and they come back and they say, "This place is terrible. It's impossible. You can't talk to them. They've got guns and knives, everything, and there's a thousand people participating and we couldn't talk sense to them."

So I said, "Well, we're gonna get that goddamn wall down. There's going to be no segregated facilities in that plant. That's our commitment." And I called the Armour Company's vice president in charge of labor relations, and I said, "You and I are going to Fort Worth."

He started laughing, and he said, "Yeah, you've got some problems there, haven't you?"

And I said, "Yes, but so have you."

He said, "What do you mean? I haven't got any problems there."

I said, "Oh, but you have." I said, "You're either going to come to Fort Worth with me or I'm going to get on this telephone and I'm going to call every Armour plant in the country and tell them the way you're living up to your obligations under our contracts." I said, "I think you are violating them, and I don't know why your employees should show up at work tomorrow."

He said, "You can't do that!"

And I said, "You want me to try?"

He said, "I'll call you back."

I knew goddamn well he didn't have guts enough to take that kind of pressure. I would have done it. I would have shut every Armour plant down over this issue. I would have been prepared to make this a national issue. First of all, I couldn't have lost it.

So he called me back in a few minutes and he says, "Look, I can't go. I've got this problem, but I'm going to send Dean Hawkins, who is my assistant." I would rather have had Hawkins anyway, because Hawkins was a more intelligent guy and he was more sympathetic to this whole issue of discrimination.

I said, "Okay, tell him I'll meet him there at such and such a time."

So we go down there and I have our local people get the union committee together and I get the company to get their supervisory staff in the same room, because I was convinced the company's supervisory staff was behind a lot of this, you know. And we get in there in a meeting, and I start. I raise the question and some of these whites begin on me: "You can't ask us to do that."

I said, "What can't I ask you to do?"

"Well, we don't want them to eat near us."

And I said, "Why? You work with them, don't you?"

"Well, but that's another matter."

And I said, "Well, I'm not so sure it's another matter. I don't know how you can possibly have any real feeling of unity and a sense of purpose unless you do all these things together."

And then one guy comes up to me and whispers in my ear, "You don't expect me to use the same toilet with one of those guys, do you?"

I said, "Why? I don't know why. I would. What's your problem?"

Says, "Well, they all got syphilis."

I said, "Oh, really! Are you sure?"

Says, "Yeah."

And I said, "I'll tell you what we'll do. Let's go down in the public library and go into the medical section and get a book on syphilis and find out whether that's a racial characteristic."

He says, "You're not serious!"

I said, "I'm just as serious as I can be. There is no better way of dealing with a problem of this kind than finding out."

He said, "Oh, well, I-I won't. No, no, no."

And I look at him for a minute, and suddenly it occurred to me. I realized what his problem was, and I said, "You can't read, can you?"

He looked at me. He froze. He said, "How did you know?"

I said, "I didn't know. You told me. You don't *want* to understand and one of the reasons you don't want to is you don't know *how*. It's not that you're a bad guy. It's just that life didn't give you any breaks. You can't read and you can't find out, so you come up with stories like this. You better forget them, because they're not true. They're lies, and you shouldn't spread them."

But he walked away dragging his tail.

Almost immediately a very reasonably well-dressed woman working in the plant comes up to me. She pulls open her purse and says, "You see that?"

I look at it and it's a gun. I said, "Yeah, I see that. I don't particularly like it, but I see it. Why?"

She said, "When one of those bastards walks close enough to me so that the wind of his passing rustles my dress, I'll kill him."

So I said to her, "What?"

She said, "Absolutely!"

I said, "Jesus, isn't that an awfully heavy penalty for such a small offense?"

"You just don't understand!"

I said, "Well, I don't know what it is I don't understand, but let me tell you something. I come from Chicago. Chicago has a reputation, as you probably know, of being the most lawless city in the country. We have rapes every day. Black men raping black women; white men raping white women; black men raping white women; white men raping black women. Goes on all the time. Now what is it I don't understand? I never knew that biology had anything at all to do with color. Do you really think it does?"

She slammed her purse closed. "You don't understand!"

And I said, "I'm afraid you're the one I don't understand." I said, "Let me tell you and all the rest of you, we just negotiated a contract that gave you people benefits that you've never had before in your life!" This was true. "We've put you on the same wage rates that Chicago had," and that had never been true before. "You got sick leave benefits, vacation benefits, insurance benefits, benefits that you never would have believed that you would have gotten working in a packinghouse."

"Oh," they kept saying to me, "Well, the steelworkers don't require this. Other unions don't require this."

And I said, "Well, that's their business; this is our business. Our constitution requires this kind of behavior. You are either going to live by it or you can get the hell out of the union. Now these are the contract benefits we negotiated. If you want them, stay in the union; if you don't want them, get the hell out. We don't want you! But this is the way it's going to be in this union."

I turned to the company representative, and I said, "Look, Hawkins, you tell your superintendent what I told these people in his presence and in yours, because I am absolutely convinced that he has had his foreman going around whipping these people's sentiments up."

So he said, "Oh, I don't believe that. He denies it."

I said, "What the hell do you expect? You expect him to admit it? You tell him the way I told them. Tell him! Tell him that we're going to get those walls down, and if there are any problems, you're going to hold him responsible. Tell him that in my presence and in the presence of all these other people from the plant."

And he did. And so as we left there, I said, "Now look, you don't do nothing until I tell you."

So he said, "Okay."

We had a provision in our contract that said if you don't work a day before or after a holiday, you lose the holiday pay. There was a holiday coming up about a week later, and two days before the holiday, I called Hawkins up and I said, "Hawkins, take the wall down."

So he said, "Okay." He did it. The employees came in and they knew damn well that it was just before the holiday, and they didn't want to lose the holiday pay, you know. There's nothing like a buck. They worked. There were no walkouts. That was the thing that bothered me the most, because if there had been a walkout, the company would have had a basis for screaming at us. But they worked the last days before the holiday—no problems—and they came back the day after the holiday, and by that time the thing had passed over.

We had an election in that plant a couple of weeks later in which there were two slates: one a completely white slate and one a black and white slate. The black and white slate won two to one.

And we weren't hitting at discrimination just in the plants. If you ever had occasion to take a look at our constitutional conventions, you'd see that we had resolutions in almost every one of them in which we made it clear that it wasn't sufficient to deal with discrimination just in the plant; you had to deal with it in the community too, because whatever you were able to do in the plant didn't do the guy any good if he couldn't rent a house in the community where he wanted to live at a price he could afford to pay. You might eliminate the discrimination on rates or seniority in the plant, but if you didn't take care of these other questions you weren't getting anywhere. And so we started trying to do that too. We began in Kansas City trying to break down discrimination in eating places and in bars across the street from the packinghouse in about '49 or '50—long before the *Brown* decision. And *that's* when we began to develop these relationships with Myles [Horton], you see, because he understood where we were at and [*chuckle*] he knew that that meant we were with him and we knew he was with us. There was no question as to whether or not you meant what you said. That's why we get along so well [*laughing*], because we both meant it. [We weren't kidding about our commitment.]

. . . Myles and I have been so close for so many years we can't remember when it started. [*Laughter*] My hunch is that we met initially because I had heard of Highlander as a place where one could go without any problems of discrimination, so I think our union first used Highlander in relation to civil rights rather than labor. In any case, one thing was clear. We started very early supporting Highlander, contributing money in substantial sums. Our union used to be one of the major contributors, and then we used the school for sessions and workshops down there. I knew that when I got to Monteagle, I didn't have to worry about the fact that I was traveling with blacks—no problem. On the road down there we had problems. We would have to stop and buy a loaf of bread and cheese and cold meat—whatever the hell it was we bought—in order to eat in the car because we couldn't find a place where they'd let us eat. Even in Indiana, of all places. We even went to a Quaker restaurant and they wouldn't serve us.

For the conclusion of Ralph Helstein's interview, see Chapter Four (page 255).

"She Just Enjoyed Enlightening People"

Rosa Parks

Though the name "Rosa Parks" would become synonymous with the 1955 bus boycott in Montgomery, Alabama—the event that propelled Dr. Martin Luther King, Jr., to the helm of the civil rights movement—this black seamstress's act of courage in the fifties would not be her first. Indeed, it certainly would not be her first encounter with racial discrimination.

During the thirties, she had refrained from joining the NAACP because of the furor over nine black youths being convicted of raping two white women in Scottsboro, Alabama. In the early forties, however, Rosa Parks became active in Montgomery's NAACP chapter, then led by E. D. Nixon. That beleaguered chapter struggled to help blacks register to vote. But they were repeatedly oppressed by poll taxes, a "test" of twenty-one questions, racist registration committees, and the Ku Klux Klan at the polls.

Thus, her memories detail the period that would, in many ways, fuel blacks' outcries in the South during the decades that followed.

I had one brother—no sisters—and he and I were raised in Montgomery County, Alabama, by our mother and grandmother and grandfather. I can't tell you very much about our father because he and my mother were not living together after I was old enough to remember.

My great-grandfather was there with us too. He died when I was about six or seven years old at the age of ninety-six. He was of

Scotch-Irish descent, and he was brought over here to South Carolina from England or Scotland or somewhere overseas as a young
boy. Then he was sold into Alabama. His wife—my great-grand-
mother—was from a little place in Montgomery County called
Pine Level. I don't know where her family came from originally.

They had three children, one of whom was the grandmother I
mentioned earlier, and they were all three born into slavery. My
grandmother was the first child, and then there was her sister and
her brother. Six children were born to them after Emancipation.

My grandmother always remembered her age by saying she
was five years old when the Yankees came through. The Yankees
coming through the South did not necessarily mean the Emancipation Proclamation date, which is January 1, 1863. It would probably be several months' difference from whatever time the Yankees
passed through and let the slaves know that they were free [and
the proclamation date].

When my great-grandfather found he was free, he purchased
a few acres of land. There were twelve acres right on the same
plantation where he lived, and he had a small log cabin. That was
where he made his home and reared his family.

Later on, when my grandmother got to be about age seven,
she moved into the white people's home there joining the same
place my great-grandfather had bought, and she lived with them
so she could look after their daughter, who was a baby.

She married my grandfather when she was twenty-one years
old. His family came from Georgia someplace, but I don't know
where. We didn't have any written record of his family history. He
was crippled. He had suffered a whole lot being mistreated as a
slave boy. Out of the treatment he received was his very strong
dislike of white people even though he was partly white because he
was the slave owner's son, and his mother was a young girl who was
the daughter of a white person too. He had no discernible features of black people. He was [fair-skinned], and he had straight
hair and Caucasian facial features.

During the later years when my grandparents were up in age,
the white people had moved away and they gave their home to my
grandmother for her lifetime. But there was no deed. In other
words, as soon as she passed on, then it would go back to the white
people. So my great-grandfather, my grandparents, my mother,

and my brother and I lived in that house together, and that was the situation there at the beginning of my life as I remember it.

Great-grandfather, as I said, died when I was six or seven. Grandfather was ill a long time and I was ten when he died. And then I was sixteen when my grandmother passed, and after she passed [the house went back to the estate.] All the family had died. Their remaining descendants had moved away, so my mother moved to another place in the same community and we lived there for a few years. When I got married, I went to live in the city of Montgomery. Then, later on, she did too. She came to Montgomery.

ELIOT WIGGINTON:　You said you didn't have any written records of your grandfather's family. Do you think it's important that families, to the extent it's possible, write all that family background down?

ROSA PARKS:　Yes, I do think it's very important that they have documented all the history that they can. One of the mistakes that we made was that we didn't take the time to write or record all our historical background or beginnings. [When it is written down, the young people can] know their ancestry and some of the things that were accomplished. Or if they didn't accomplish anything spectacular, at least they would have some family history and could appreciate the continuation of the family from one generation to another.

E.W.:　Did your grandparents or your mother have a chance to go to school?

R.P.:　Well, my mother went to school. I don't know about my grandparents. I imagine they could read maybe a little, but if they attended school, it was not enough to mention. But after my mother went through grammar school, she was interested in teaching, and so my grandfather had her to go to school in Selma, Alabama, at Payne University, and then she also attended what was then called the State Normal School, and later called the Alabama State Teachers College for Negroes. Now it's called Alabama State University. It wasn't really like going to college today, though. Out in the country, they didn't have any high schools at all, and even grammar schools didn't have any full nine-month terms. When you finished grammar school, if you wanted to you could go to one of these state teacher's schools and get enough education

there to take a state examination and get a teacher's license. And
then she'd go to summer school in the summer.

Relative to her time, though, she was well educated. Yes. And
she was really interested in teaching. You had to be dedicated,
because you made very little money. The highest my mother ever
earned was in another county—not Montgomery County—and if
it was fifty dollars a month, that was pretty good money. And then
she'd have to pay room and board to live in someone's home. Paid
all expenses and made most of her clothes.

But she cherished education. She believed in teaching anybody who desired to learn to read and write, and she *could* teach
them. She just enjoyed enlightening people. I can recall once
when she was teaching this young man who hadn't gotten beyond
the first grade, but he wouldn't drop out of school, and the little
students in the lower grade levels would be in the same class, but
he would still go to school every day. So she called him aside and
asked him why was he still in the first grade, and he told her he
just didn't quite understand how to read, but he still wanted to
learn. So what she would do was tutor him during the time the
other children were at recess, and after school, and give him a
little special attention just by himself. He was probably what they
call a slow learner today. But he learned to read, and he learned
to write, and I recall him and his wife, after they were married,
coming by to visit, and he was happy and very proud of the fact
that he had learned to write a letter, and send it through the mail,
and things like that. That was quite an accomplishment. But he
was nearly a full-grown young man and until she started working
with him, he just hadn't been able to be promoted out of the first
grade. Any instance where she could see that a youngster needed
extra help, she would go out of her way to teach them and take a
little extra time.

And of course my mother taught me quite a bit about reading. She taught me the alphabet and figures and counting and
such before I even actually started going to school. In fact, I don't
even remember [a time] when I *didn't* read. I always wanted to
read something. One of the stories I liked was "Little Red Riding
Hood," and I read Mother Goose rhymes, and the comic strips in
the paper. We got the Atlanta *Constitution* by mail at home when
we were living in Pine Level.

The first book I ever read was when I was seven. I was sick that year and couldn't get to school very much because I suffered very much from tonsillitis, and during the time when we could get to school, the weather would be damp and cold and rainy. I spent a lot of time out of school that year. So I started reading a book called *Is the Negro a Beast?* Awful. It was written by a man named Shell in answer to a book called *The Negro, A Beast.* That's when I began to actually try to figure out why people of a different color and texture hair had been in slavery, and were not considered complete human beings. I would ask questions about it. From then on I read whatever I could find about racial subjects. I had thought about it before. There was this thing about the Klan right after World War I and how they were moving around through the community and some churches were burned and people were often flogged or found dead. There would be not much said about it, but you could just feel that something [was wrong]. My grandfather didn't ever know when our house would be invaded. He kept his gun close by and we stayed up at night and didn't go to bed sometimes. Didn't even undress [in case] they should come and we'd be taken by surprise. I guess that is really the first real harsh realization that I had of our [situation as blacks]. I was five or six then. You just never knew what to expect. It wasn't that the Klan did so much in our community, but we'd hear about it in other places. We didn't have any other media other than the newspaper, and I could hear my mother reading the paper, but they didn't put too much in it. Usually you'd hear just from one person to another. They didn't put much in the paper about all that, and if there were any black publications, we didn't know about them.

But I'd hear people talk, and hear the older people discuss the hardships of slavery, and then I could see for myself the difference in the new building where the white school was—I remember when it was built, in fact—and where we went to school. It was just a little one-room shack, I guess you'd call it. Just a little building. No paint, no windowpanes. Just little wooden shutters. And it was cold enough for the shutters to be kept closed. We didn't have very much light to see how to read in the schoolroom. But we enjoyed studying.

    E.W.:   What about your more formal education?

    R.P.:   Well, my first teacher was Miss Sally Hill, and then Mrs.

Beulah MacMillan. My mother was my third teacher. She was teaching in our community. She took the place of Mrs. MacMillan, and taught grades one through six, and so I had her for three years. It was always a one-teacher school—a one-room schoolhouse —so she taught all the grades.

Then when I was eleven years old, going into the sixth grade, my mother had me enrolled in an all-black girls' school in Montgomery, the Montgomery Industrial School. The principal and founder of this school was an elderly white spinster from Massachusetts named Miss Alice White. She was an old maid, and the teachers were all white women from the North. It was a private school. You had to pay tuition, but you didn't live there. You still lived at home. And then if you didn't have enough money, you could do some work around the school to pay off the tuition. I was one of the scholarship girls after my first term. My mother was able to get me what was called a scholarship and then I became one of the girls who earned their tuition by dusting and cleaning classrooms after school.

E.W.:   I'm amazed that the white community let her keep the school open.

R.P.:   Well, I think she must've suffered a lot. She and the other teachers were so isolated from the white community, I imagine they just chose to ignore her, and I guess she had a good reputation. She was a very strict disciplinarian with the students. The school only went through the ninth grade, but most of the young women who graduated went on and had good grades in high school and college and so on. Maybe the white community considered that she was doing a worthwhile service as long as she did not violate the segregation laws.

But these teachers and Miss White, the principal, were completely isolated and not recognized in any way by the white community in Montgomery. They attended church, but they had to go to a black church. And more than once before I started there her school building had been destroyed by fire, but it was always rebuilt.

Miss White closed the school the year before I was to graduate. She became too old and feeble to continue to keep it open, and she did not have anyone to succeed her, so it was closed after forty or more years. I have often thought that if she had been able to integrate her faculty—even with some of the graduates from her school—it would have had a better opportunity to stay open, but at that time, I guess, it was just about unheard-of to have an integrated faculty because none of her students became teachers *there.*

MILES HORTON: Was it sponsored by some kind of religious organization?

R.P.:   I believe it was. I guess a Congregational church set it up, or she must have been endowed by some contributions from the North.

M.H.:   After the Civil War, the American Missionary Society started schools all around the mountains for white people and in the Deep South for blacks. It's the same period, so I would guess it might have been one.

E.W.:   In the private school, did any of the teachers get in any discussions of things other than straight academic subjects? Did they talk about the possibility of change sometime in the future, or the politics behind segregation, or about things that you might try to do as an adult that might make a difference?

R.P.:   I never remember hearing anything like that. I don't know how they felt about it because I never heard any discussion of that nature in the school. The nearest that I remember was when Miss White herself was teaching a history class. The first year that I was there, the subject of slavery came up, and she said that some good could have come out of slavery in that if there had not been slavery, and our ancestors had not been brought from Africa, we would probably still be savages climbing trees, and eating bananas. So I guess they thought about it, and in fact I even thought about it then, but we wouldn't dare get up and say anything because at that time, you just listened to what they had to say. And what she said was just the way she herself had been taught. It was not that she was a bad or bigoted person, but that was just in her background. She just didn't have the knowledge that there had been civilization and culture and so on among black people even hundreds of years back. In my case, beginning with this first book that I read called *Is the Negro a Beast?* and then hearing remarks and seeing how things were, I just began to be very concerned about learning, and reading everything I could about not just black history, but all history, because history did appeal to me, and it was my favorite subject during my school years.

Anyhow, the year before I would have graduated, she gave up the school and went back to Massachusetts. My mother was a little bit bothered. She said, "Oh, I had wanted so much for Rose to graduate from Miss White's." If I had been a grade ahead, I would have, but I received my last year of junior high school from Booker T. Washington Junior High.

Then I went to high school, but during the second year my grandmother became ill and helpless and my mother had me to come home to look after her up until her death. Then not too long after my grandmother passed, my mother became ill and had to give up teaching and so I wasn't able to continue in school. I took care of my mother through a long illness until she recovered. Finally I *did* go back and finish high school after I was married. My mother was anxious for me to get my diploma, and my husband was willing to have me do that and then it was not really that hard to do because I was living near the school on the same street. It took a couple of years, but I finally graduated. I didn't get to go to college at all. I have received several honorary degrees.

If I had gone to college, I don't know what I would have chosen as a career. I didn't want to pursue teaching from the time I was a youngster, because of the way my mother suffered to try to teach and be a real teacher facing some almost insurmountable odds. The teaching profession is a very worthy one, but I never wanted to teach under the conditions she had to work. The segregation and the humiliation and intimidation they'd have to take from the board of education and the officials just didn't appeal to me then.

The only thing I can recall I might have enjoyed if I had had the opportunity to have a professional career—I guess because there were so many ill people at home during my childhood—was nursing or some type of social work that would help people to be relieved of suffering. It seemed like I had an affinity for that. And I enjoyed the domestic science of home economics—cooking and sewing and things like that. I guess I just never was that career-minded after I was married. If my husband had been able to earn enough income for me to have kept house, I probably wouldn't have worried too much about going away from home to work at all. He was a barber, and so I helped in any way I could to bring home some extra income.

E.W.:　Can you talk a little about the kind of work you wound up doing?

R.P.:　As a child, I had done work in the field on the farm, working in the cotton and corn and whatever else was growing around, and looking after the house and things like that. But during the time when I was going to school in Montgomery, I was living with my mother's sister, who was a widow who had five children. We were living with a lady who prepared food and took it on jobs where people who were working would take their lunch hour. I did that some and whatever else we could do. We'd pick berries —just do things to have a little money. My aunt, being in very frail health, was not able to hold a job unless she took some of us youngsters on the job to help her with her work, so that's when I first got into whatever work she was doing. Sometimes domestic work for a private family, and once she worked at the Jewish country club cleaning the building.

Those of us who didn't go along and work with her would have to be doing something else like looking after a little garden that we'd have, or doing the laundry and housework, and maybe finding a little extra job somewhere for some of the neighbors for whatever they'd give us. Sometimes they might not give us any money at all. Maybe they'd pay us with an article of some kind. Then, when school was closed, we would come back down to Pine Level and look after the place around there until the time for school to open again. Even after I received my high school diploma, the only work that was available was some sewing for our neighbors and looking after my husband's clothes and just various jobs such as domestic work. Then in 1942 I started working at Maxwell Field Air Force Base in their guest house cleaning rooms. I worked there until 1946 when I started working for the Atlanta Life Insurance Company as an agent. I didn't do very well as an agent so they gave me work in the office as a clerk.

And from that I started working in a private tailor shop and later I worked in a menswear store doing the alterations. In 1954, around Labor Day, I started working in the tailor shop of the Montgomery Fair department store doing men's alterations. That was where I was working at the time I was arrested on the Montgomery city bus.

E.W.:   During the time you were working as a seamstress, weren't you also doing volunteer work with the NAACP?

R.P.:   Yes. The first time I knew of the NAACP in Montgomery, my husband was a member and had a membership card. But I didn't go to any meetings. Sometimes I would ask him if I could go —especially [during the early thirties] when he was trying to work for the defense of the Scottsboro boys—and I would want to go along with him to meetings and hear discussions but he'd always say it was too dangerous. I didn't want to displease him, so I didn't get right in it then.

After that was over and the Scottsboro case faded off the public's view, I finally attended a meeting. Johnnie Carr was the influence that led me to enter an NAACP meeting. She was the secretary, and since I remembered her as my former classmate at Miss White's school, I thought maybe I should go and see what they were doing. I finally went to this meeting, and it happened to be their election day, and they asked me if I would serve as secretary. Just being at the meeting for the first time, I didn't have the courage to say no, and I didn't know what to say, so they took it for granted, I guess, that I was willing to accept the office. That was one of the days Johnnie wasn't there. There were just a few men there.

E.W.:   So with the first meeting you were in over your head?

R.P.:   I was! [*Laughing*] I think the first assignment that Mr. E. D. Nixon gave me was the case of a serviceman in the Army who had been accused of raping a white nurse on the base where he was stationed at Fort Benning in Columbus, Georgia. His father brought that problem to the NAACP and I worked on that, trying to get the affidavits together. I can't recall too many details about it now, but from time to time there would be incidents happening that involved people who were intimidated in some way racially. Our biggest problem during that time when someone would make a complaint or say that they had been mistreated or violated in some way by white persons, was getting them to be willing to sign an affidavit. Some of them wouldn't mind talking about what happened, but when it came to putting a signature on a statement and filing it with the Justice Department that was another story.

So that part of it was hard. Sometimes it didn't seem like we made any progress. Another problem was that we didn't have any [sympathetic] lawyers in Montgomery at that time. The only white lawyer who would take a case in those early days was a nephew of Mrs. Virginia Durr, and the strain of ostracism and the pressure put upon him by the white community made it so difficult he couldn't continue working with us long. And there weren't any black lawyers in Montgomery at that time.

But we did whatever we could to help individuals in their distress. We were concerned with trying to alleviate the suffering of people that were being oppressed as much as possible. If we couldn't, at least we could try. We did lose some cases. We lost at least two young men to the electric chair. They were executed for what they were accused of.

And then people were also trying to figure out how to get blacks registered to vote. See, at that time—this is in the early forties now—first you had to pay twenty dollars, and then a dollar and a half poll tax for every year of your age between the ages of twenty-one and forty-five to vote. Most of us didn't have that money. Then even if they did, a black person couldn't even approach the board of registration unless they were vouched for or accompanied by the recommendation of a responsible white citizen, and then there were not many white citizens who were willing to see the Negroes become registered voters so there was another holdback. And if you could get that recommendation, there still were very few black people that we could get to say they would be willing to register because the voter registration board was so hostile. If they didn't come right out and be abusive, they would act as if you just weren't supposed to be there even *talking* about registering to vote.

People were real discouraged. My husband was very interested and concerned about black people getting registered to vote, and he was a member of what they called the Men's Social Club. He tried to get them—instead of having coming-out balls or parties where they would spend whatever money they had in the treasury each year—to try to get registered. Then if anybody did get registered, they could take a portion of the money from the treasury and help pay that poll tax. But that didn't set well with his fellow club members and he lost interest and dropped out of that.

Then he tried on his own to interest people in getting registered, but it was just considered too dangerous or too risky, and they felt like they would invite the disapproval of the white leaders.

Mr. Nixon was trying to get people registered too. In fact, the first time I met him was when he came to my house with a book on the requirements of voter registration, and I think he asked me if I had ever gone to register. I told him I hadn't so he gave me that book to read, and asked if I was interested. I told him I was. During that same time, Attorney Arthur Madison, who had gone to New York to practice law but whose family still owned a large area of land outside Montgomery, was invited by Mr. Nixon to come down to conduct meetings and classes to get people acquainted with registration. He came down, and I went to the classes. I know we had twenty-one printed-out questions we had to answer correctly. But I failed a couple of times to get registered to vote in 1943 and 1944. I finally did after two years, in 1945, two years after I started working actively with the NAACP. Mr. Madison wanted to get us registered without our having to go to a white person and be vouched for and be recommended or approved of, so that was a pretty rough time during then.

M.H.: In addition to twenty dollars on the barrel for permission to vote, they had to pass muster of a white racist committee even after they paid that poll tax before they could be certified to vote, and then they were quite often stopped at the polls by Klan violence when they tried to vote, and if they succeeded in voting, quite often the votes were thrown out. Despite that, some *did* get registered, didn't they?

R.P.: Well, they were very few. I guess they would let a few of what they called the leaders—maybe insurance officials or a teacher, doctor, or somebody like that. I kept an article for a long time where they had the names of the registered voters published in the paper, and I think there were thirty-one in Montgomery County who were voting, and there were several thousand who were voting age. That was not even token representation.

So we were working on that. And then every year we would write letters to Washington out of our NAACP office and request that the antilynching bill be passed, and then that would always be struck down.

E.W.:   It sounds like the situation was almost hopelessly frustrating. It doesn't sound like you were able to find any ways to take direct action that could get real results. If you had a real commitment to making things better, it doesn't sound like you had many ways to express that and see any progress.

R.P.:   No. There were almost no ways to express that.

E.W.:   I have a vision in my head of lots of people gathered together in rooms just saying, "What do we do? What do we do?"

M.H.:   You have a vision of the Highlander workshops during that pre–civil rights period. That's exactly what we were doing. Trying to figure out what you could do that was within the law, but we couldn't see any way within the legal framework to do anything, because every time you got outside of that, you got talked down. We were all working within the legal custom . . .

R.P.:   . . . of segregation . . .

M.H.:   . . . and the social-custom framework of segregation.

R.P.:   Yes, that's right. . . .

For the continuation of Rosa Parks' interview with Myles Horton and Eliot Wigginton, see Chapter Four (page 229).

★

"Don't Worry, I'll Be on the Train Tomorrow"

Bernice Robinson

During the forties in New York City, this black woman learned to enjoy "beat" music at the Apollo Theater, or jazz concerts and classical music at Carnegie Hall. To her initial surprise—having come North from Charleston—seating in Manhattan was not by race.

Meanwhile, nothing seemed to change back home in South Carolina. Cinemas remained the only entertainment, and black moviegoers were allowed only in the balcony, or "buzzards' roost," as it was called. And by 1948, circumstances in Charleston worsened when white delegates from South Carolina and Mississippi protested a civil rights plank in the Democratic platform. Instead of supporting Harry S Truman, these segregationalists walked out of the convention, formed the Dixiecrat party, and rallied behind South Carolina's Strom Thurmond as a presidential candidate. Once again, politics was the forum for arguing civil rights.

Although Bernice Robinson had first gone to New York City with the intention of becoming a musician, she returned to Charleston with a politically valuable skill. As a beautician, she could maintain economic independence from what, at the time, was a virtually all-white business community. This meant that she could work for the NAACP without fear of financial reprisals. And she did.

By 1956, she would attend a Highlander workshop and return home to become the first teacher in Septima Clark's "Citizenship School." Her students would learn their lessons well: If politics was the forum, then blacks had to register to vote if they were ever to be heard in the debates.

I was born in a little town called Charleston, South Carolina, on February 7, 1914. The day I was born was the first time that they had had snow in maybe one hundred years. I brought the snow to Charleston when I was born, and this meant that I was going to spend my life disturbing the elements—or so my mother thought. She called it quits after I came along. No more children after that. I was the ninth child, and that was the end of that.

But my childhood was a happy childhood. We weren't rich. My daddy would refuse to let us say that we were poor, but he didn't make very much money. He was a bricklayer and tile setter and a plasterer—that sort of thing. My mother just took care of the home and children and did sewing, and she was the stabilizing factor, I guess, in the home. She was always quiet and soft-spoken. I didn't take after her at all. [*Laughs*]

My father was a very strong man, and most people were afraid of him because he always looked so stern. He was of Indian descent—Cherokee—and he very rarely smiled. He just went around looking mad all the time. His lips were thin and tight and he had this big long nose and high cheekbones and was ginger-cake brown. I wish I had thought to get all the background of my people while some of the older ones were living so I could really trace it back. All I know about my mother's people is that they came from Florida. Her grandmother was a Seminole Indian and she married an Italian sailmaker. Whew, what a combination! And they moved from Jacksonville, Florida, to Charleston because there was more work for him there.

Even though my father looked stern, he had a big heart and he was concerned about people at all times. He always said you never had so little that you didn't have enough to share. And that has stayed with me over the years.

One of the first examples of that kind of thing that I remember was when I was in the third grade. We had a contest that day writing all the capitals in the United States, and we had to write them with ink and the straight pen you used then, and my paper was correct. I had no mistakes at all. There was another girl in the class whose parents had told her that she would have to win that contest. I was never pressured like that by my parents. The prize was just a pencil box. It was no elaborate award, but it was just the idea of giving us some incentive. And this girl had a small *o* for

Ohio, and, of course, that was one point against her. I had a perfect score.

Well, she got together her little group to take this pencil box from me. It was just a little thing that held about two or three pencils, but she was going to take it from me and take it home, because she did not want her parents to know that she lost the contest.

I was scared because I had never been in anything like that before. But there was this girl—big for her age—who followed me all the way home. She said to them, "You are not going to touch a strand of hair on her head." Her name was Jenny, and we used to call her the bully, and I couldn't understand why she was protecting me. But she walked me all the way home, which was several blocks past her house. When we got just about half a block from our house, she said, "You don't know why I stood up for you, do you?" And then she said, "The only time I enjoyed a Christmas was when your father brought fruits and toys over for us kids to our house. My mother is in your father's class at church, and we never knew what Christmas was like because we had never had any money to have anything, but your father brought us some toys and fruits for Christmas, and that was the best Christmas I ever had in my life. Nobody was going to touch you." And I have never forgotten that. Those are little things that happen in your life that go with you throughout your life because you get help from sources and you don't know why it's coming, but it's because of some good thing that somebody else close to you has done. My father was a man like that.

We had very little, but there was never a meal in that house that there weren't other kids in there enjoying it with us. My first two brothers died before I was born, but I grew up with five brothers, and they had their friends coming over all the time. Most of their friends' mothers were doing domestic work and they left home early in the morning, so the kids would come by to pick up my brothers on their way to school, and get hot grits and whatever we had to share. The only time we had eggs was when the chicken laid them, and if there was only one or two eggs, then my mother would make what you call a sweetbread. She would put that egg in her sweetbread and then we could all have a piece and get the nourishment from the egg. Whatever we had, my mother would share with them because she knew that their parents had had to leave early in the morning to go and prepare breakfast for the white people that they were working for and the kids were just left on their own. So I had knowledge of the act of sharing and caring from an early childhood, and I began to do a good bit of that kind of thing myself as soon as I was able.

We had courts and alleys around in the city, for example. Nowadays if a person lives in a court it's called a plush section. You would think that only middle-class people were in a court. But at that time if a person lived in a court or alley it meant that they were very, very poor. In our town that was usually where the blacks lived when they had practically nothing. These kids would be out there in the sand and dirt all day long because they usually came from a single-parent family, and the mothers had to go to work and leave early in the morning and the kids would be out there just playing in the dirt with nothing to eat. On the way home from school, if we had any lunch left over in our little lunch boxes, they would beg it from us, so I got in the habit of bringing some of my lunch back for them. I'd eat a piece of my sandwich and leave a little piece. If I had an apple, I'd leave a little plug of apple in my lunch box to give to them. Then sometimes I'd bring them home. They were dirty and you know how kids are with stuff running out their noses and everything—and I would bring them home and get the big washtub out there in the yard and I'd wash them off and give them some of my food.

It used to really worry my mother. I had been very ill as a young girl just before I started kindergarten. I had typhoid fever and they couldn't get that fever down and I was in bed for months. It started at the beginning of the school year and it was spring by the time I got out of bed. They really didn't think they were going to raise me at that point. I don't remember anything much about it except in the spring when I looked out the window and I saw the blossoms on the peach tree in the backyard, and I got out of bed to go downstairs to play because I liked to feel the blossoms off the peach tree falling all over me. It was the first time that I had been out of the bed, and they were shocked when they saw me coming down the steps. The doctor had given me up because he couldn't break the fever, but my father's sister came over with a whole sack of raw red onions and they sliced onions all night and wrapped me in a sheet of onions. The fever was so high that the onions would just shrivel when they put them on me, but they did that all night long and that finally broke the fever.

For that reason, my mother was afraid that she wouldn't raise me. I was very frail after that, and when I started bringing these dirty kids home, my mother used to worry so. She'd say, "Jimmy," which was Poppa's name, "Jimmy, Bernice is going to get sick fooling with these kids that's so dirty that she's bringing in here. I'm just so worried about her." My father would stand on the porch and say, "Nothing's going to happen to her. That's my little missionary." [*Laughing*]

Then I started working with these kids, teaching them how to spell, do numbers, tell time, and different little things like that. I worked with them that way until I got to the point where every summer I'd have some kids there that I had to run a little school with. [*Laughs*] There is a funeral home about two doors from where I'm working now, and the guy who's running the funeral home now was a kid that I taught his ABC's and how to spell. His family came here to Charleston from the country, and the children hadn't been in any school at all. They moved right next door to us and their mother wanted me to work with them over the summer so as to prepare them to go into school. So I taught him and his older sister.

And when my daughter was in high school, her teacher looked at her and said, "You know, you remind me of a woman I knew very well. What's your name again?"

"My name is Jacquelyn Robinson."

"That's the woman I remember, but this woman's name was Bernice Robinson. You look so much like her."

And my daughter said, "That's my mother."

So she said, "Well, your mother taught me. She was the first teacher I had."

My daughter came home and said, "Mama, I thought you said you never taught school."

I said, "I didn't."

So she said, "Well, my teacher said that you were her first teacher."

So I said, "What's your teacher's name?"

She told me and I said, "Yeah, I did teach her, but not in a classroom.'' She was being raised by her grandmother in the country and her aunt went up there on a visit and stole her—just put her in the car and brought her back with her to Charleston. When they were driving off down the road, the grandmother was running down the road behind her yelling to bring her child back. But her aunt realized that the child wasn't getting any schooling and she would grow up ignorant out there, so she just stole her and brought her on. The grandmother couldn't follow her to Charleston so she kept her and she wound up being a very smart woman. She was about eight years old then and had never been in school, so her aunt had me to work with her over the summer to get her ready, and I did teach her. She was a very eager person, and it was really easier to work with her because she was anxious to learn; and not having had any school, it was all fascinating to her.

The Delta sorority just recently had a big workshop to register a great number of people in the community to vote. This same woman is a member of the sorority. I was over there to speak on a panel that morning, and she came up to me and said to the whole group there, *"This* young lady has *been* in the movement for years and years.'' Says, "When she was knee-high to a duck, she was out there working hard."

But, you know, at that time I didn't even think about what I was doing. I just did it because I was interested in the kids and I guess the feeling of caring was handed down from my father and my mother. To me, I was just doing what I ought to be doing. I mean, I never thought about any movement or activity or that.

My father had been involved in organizing, but I never knew about it. I really don't know how he ever did it, but he and two other men got together and reorganized a bricklayers' union in Charleston in 1900. When he died and I was going through some of his papers, I found his NAACP card. He'd never mentioned it, but he had been a member of the NAACP, I guess, from its inception. He just never talked about it. I didn't have to wonder why I was doing some of the things I was doing later when I found out all he had been involved in.

And, as far back as I can remember, my father never called a white man "Mister." He would say, "Wigginton" or "Shumacher" if he was talking to you directly. I've heard him standing out in the yard talking to a white man and saying, "Why, Shumacher, that's going to take a while to finish that job."

Another thing like that my father did was that he never would let the boys work as errand boys for these stores. A lot of times that was the only kind of a job black kids could get, but he had an eye for the future at all times. He taught every one of those boys how to do brickwork and carpentry and they all wound up being independent. At an early age, he also rented a tailor shop and the boys used to press clothes for people. I used to go over there and do it too sometimes when they were busy. It was thirty-five cents to press a suit, and I learned how to pull the knee out of the suit and everything before you press it and steam it down. You used charcoal irons too. Big sixteen-pound irons you pulled down to press the cloth. So he opened this up so the boys would have something to do in the afternoon to make a little money, rather than to have to ride these bicycles and deliver groceries and work for drugstores, because they used to pay practically nothing and treat those kids like dogs. Yell at them like they were just garbage, you know. My daddy said he wasn't going to have his kids going through that.

My mother was a beautiful hand sewer, and she could make you a whole dress by hand. So my sister took that up and she would do alterations at the tailor shop.

And one of my brothers partitioned off a little part and made a kitchen and he used to make candy. He took a correspondence course in that, and he used to furnish all the little sweetshops with these peanut bars and different kinds of candy and taffy. These are the types of things that my father promoted. Daddy made preparations for us to be independent. If you come in contact with any of my brothers, you can see that independence in them. I got it too. . . . Like if a light plug goes bad, I just fix it. I maneuver for myself and don't have to be wholly dependent on someone to do everything for me. . . .

I completed high school—well, the schools only went through the ninth grade. But we did get to go nine months in Charleston, whereas the kids on the islands off the coast were lucky to go three or four months. We had a much better education than that. Those kids on the island had it pretty rough, because anytime the whites wanted, they would come and knock on the building and take the kids out to go into the fields; so their education was interrupted at any time that the whites felt they needed them out there.

And our teachers were pretty rough. If the teacher said something, you might mumble back, but you did *not* challenge. You just accepted. I went to school one day in a pretty little pink dress my sister made for me. The sleeves were slit here [*points*] and she had little lace running around the slit and all around the sleeve. I slipped out and went to school and dodged my mother because I *knew* she wouldn't let me wear one of my *best* dresses to school. You know what happened when I got to school? My teacher sent me back home and I had to change my dress. You didn't come to school dressed up like that. [*Laughing*] She sent me right on back home. She knew that Mrs. Robinson wouldn't have sent me to school with that dress on. That's the control that the teachers had in those days.

They were really dedicated. The teachers didn't even get married when I went to school. If they married they would lose their job. There was this big thing about the teachers marrying, because they might become pregnant and you didn't teach kids while you were pregnant. You would have to get somebody else to take your place and all, so these were all old maids except for the men in the shops and the principal.

So I think they were a heck of a lot more dedicated than some teachers are today. They taught because they wanted to teach, and when you really have to give up your personal life in order to teach, you are dedicated to the cause. They were more strict about your getting your lessons properly. You would do a grade over if you failed, where now they have the social promotion thing going where they put you on up whether you make it or you don't. So in essence we really did get a much more solid education. When you came out of high school, you had a pretty good education. You couldn't get many *jobs* being black, you know, but the best proof of it is how many blacks did go on and become lawyers, doctors, scientists, and that sort of thing.

I'll never forget Minnie Burroughs. She was my English teacher in the ninth grade. There's a woman. I heard Myles [Horton] say to some guy one time that if you put Bernice in a room and you've never met her and you listen to her talk, you wouldn't know what color she was. She was really strict on grammar, and she was very particular about your *diction*. You have to speak clearly. [*Mrs. Robinson very exactly pronounces the words in this statement.*] Because of her, I used to make it a habit when I'd hear different people speak that if they used words I didn't know the meanings of, I would write them out on a little piece of paper and I'd go back home and I'd check out the dictionary to see what they were talking about.

We also had to learn how to wash and we had to learn how to iron. You started that in the seventh grade and went through the ninth grade in that. Cooking, sewing, and laundry. You didn't ask whether you had to take it. You took it. I remember a teacher that had me to iron a white shirt over and over and over again. And I had to wash that shirt every time I ironed it. I had to wash it out first and then I had to starch it and iron it again. The reason why is because on the collar I would get what they called "cat faces"—creases—and I couldn't get it right. We didn't have any electric irons. We had the flatirons heated on charcoal, and I'd smear it and crease it. Oooohh, I never wanted to see a white shirt again in my life. But I betcha I can iron a shirt today. I can iron a shirt.

Then the boys were trained in the carpenter shop and they had repair shop and this was the kind of trades *they* were taught.

Of course, *all* of what was taught was dictated by the white Charleston school board. They set the curriculum. They sent you the books. And all our books were used books because when they got too old for the white schools, they were shipped over to our schools. It was all definitely dictated by the school board. No ifs, ands, and buts about that! They ruled it. All the superintendents were white. We had no choice.

And in history, there was *nothing* about any black leaders. I learned more about black leaders in the civil rights movement than I ever knew before. No discussions at all about integration. Segregation was just an accepted fact. In a sense, you were almost isolated. You just didn't give it any thought, really. It was just an accepted fact that you live in one section of town where everybody you see is the same color as you, while three or four blocks from there it was a completely white neighborhood, and you just didn't even *walk* through those neighborhoods.

ELIOT WIGGINTON: I was raised in Athens, Georgia, and I can remember very distinctly as a kid going into the five-and-ten-cent store in Athens and seeing a white water fountain and a colored water fountain, and there was a men's and women's rest room and then a colored rest room; and I remember at the Seaboard station, there was a colored waiting room and a white waiting room. And I remember in the movie theaters there were separate entrances, one entrance we went in and there was a side entrance . . .

BERNICE ROBINSON: . . . side entrances and everything. Same all over. That was a way of life. You didn't know anything different, so you questioned nothing. When we had the fair in town, there was a week that it was a white fair, and then there was a week for colored.

E.W.:   I remember all this *real* distinctly, but I also remember never thinking that that was strange.

B.R.:   That's right. Nobody ever thought it was strange. We just went our separate ways and thought that that was the way we were supposed to go. Nobody ever discussed it.

E.W.:   Right. It was never discussed once in my family.

B.R.:   The only thing that was ever discussed in my family in reference to the whites was that my mother said, ''Well, I don't ever want any girl of mine to do any domestic work or work in these white folks' kitchens,'' and my daddy said, ''I don't want any of my boys to be errand boys for these white folks' grocery stores.'' I know that my mother's mind was dealing with the slavery issue. It was still prevalent with domestic workers working in these white homes that the white men would take advantage of them, and they were not able to say anything about it. Of course, now the people speak out about it a whole lot more. But I *know* that. As I grew older I understood that what was in her mind was that if you do domestic work and the white man comes home and he wants to have sex with you, you can't do anything about it. You have to give in. That was what her thing was. She wasn't going to have that with her girls.

But we accepted that way of life, and it was never discussed in school, and those teachers didn't *dare*. When Septima [Clark] taught, she would try to teach her kids some black history. She was injecting it into her class. And she was warned by her principal that you just don't do things like that. We had no teacher that would dare. . . .

After I finished high school, I had great hopes of studying music. We were a very musical family. My father had an old organ in the house and every Sunday morning he serenaded us with that organ. He was the choir leader in his church for fifty years, and he could be conducting a group of about twenty people and if someone hit a sour note, he'd say, "Eliot, you had a sour note over there. Get it straight." His ears were tuned in to music. He had a bass fiddle and a mandolin and a violin in the house and he could play them all. He tried to teach me violin and all I could think of was getting outside to play with the kids. Oh, I would struggle through that thing real fast so I could go on outside to play! [*Laughs*] But on winter evenings the family was together and my mother would be sitting there sewing up the holes in the socks and mending the holes in the back of the pants, patching them with any color material she could find. The boys used to call those colored patches "eyes" and they'd laugh and say, "Let me see how many 'eyes' you got." One would say, "I got two eyes, how many you got?" "You got two eyes on there!" [*Laughs*] So my mother would be sitting there doing the patching of the clothes, and we had a big wood stove and we'd be sitting around that together, and Poppa would be playing the bass fiddle and my brother would be playing the mandolin and we'd have a good time and just sing through the night. Music was in the family, and I grew up with it and I wanted to play. All of us played something. Poppa didn't have enough money to pay for lessons for all of us, though, because music lessons were something like twenty-five cents apiece and those twenty-five cents were hard to come by. So he sent my brother Hilliard to get piano lessons, and then Hilliard would have to teach the next brother, Fletcher, what he had learned, and so on. [That way we could stretch those quarters a long way.]

So I was interested in studying piano. My sister had gone to New York City to work in the garment industry, and her godmother lived in Boston. My sister's dream was to send me to the Boston Conservatory of Music and have me live with her godmother while I was going to school. I went to New York to work through the summer to earn some money to help my sister with the tuition, and that summer she got very ill and had to have an operation and quit work, and since my parents couldn't afford to send me there, that threw those dreams out the window, so I came on back home and got married, and had my daughter. But the marriage didn't work out. My husband was working as a waiter at the country club, and it closed down and all the guys lost their jobs, so he moved away to find more work and the money stopped coming in. Meanwhile my daughter was about two years old and growing and stretching out her little undershirts and everything, and we had to have money, so I took a job as a maid at a hunting resort on Bull Island. My mother cried when I did it because she had never wanted any of her kids to work in a white person's place like that, but I was always a realist, and I knew that when you've got to do it, you do it and get it over with. So my mother kept my daughter, and I moved out there. During hunting season, you'd live out there for a month, and then you'd get your pay and a couple of days off, and then they'd pick you up and carry you back out to the island for the next month. . . .

Finally I realized that I wasn't going to be able, with my education, to find anything to do in Charleston except to work seven days a week as a domestic making a dollar a day. So about 1936, I left my daughter with Momma and moved back to New York to a job in the factories in the garment industry. . . . You know how they used to advertise for jobs in the garment industry? You'd just walk down in the garment area and they had these pasteboard signs hanging outside: "Need seamstress on such and such a floor." You were supposed to have experience, and they would ask you where you worked before, but you would tell a little white lie the first time you'd go there. My sister taught me that. She said, "Now, when you go in there, you just give them the name of the people I work for, and you say that you know everybody does things differently and if you'll show me *your* way I'll do it that way. Then you just watch them when they sit down at the machine to show you their way, and then you sit down and you do it." [*Laughs*] It was awful coming from a domestic machine to a power machine, but she had explained all that to me. She said, "Now, don't go pressing down too hard, or that machine will 'zip' like that, and the garment will go everywhere. Then they will know that you don't have experience. So you just start it out nice and slow until you get the feel of it, and then you'll know how fast to go with it."

So I was there on the assembly line making women's clothes —dresses, coats, blouses, things like that. And you had to maintain a quota. You might be working on just sleeves, you know, so you'd get a whole box of sleeves to sew up, and then somebody else would do another part, and somebody else would put the whole garment together. At one time, I was just working on a snap machine. You'd have a dozen machines right in a row here, and then you'd have another dozen machines facing on that row. They were all controlled by one switch. When the guy would pull that switch down on that switch box, all those machines would be ready to move. And they wouldn't say anything until it was closing time. Then they would just go and flip that switch and the machines would all cut off. If a garment was left in there, you'd just leave it there until the next morning.

I made good money there—about thirty-five to forty-five dollars a week—and I probably would have stayed in that work, but the problem with that was that in a garment factory that salary was not *steady*. It was only steady for a period of time. Maybe for two months straight, you are working real hard and steady to get the winter clothes out, and then it slows off because you've gotten everything ready for the winter season. Then it slows until they start making the spring goods. I had to *know* that I was going to have money coming in every week, because I was sending money home to take care of my daughter, and I had to take care of myself.

That's when I said, "I need to get into something that's steady," and I began to take courses in beauty work. And it really *was* steady. When I finished beauty school, a friend of mine, who worked in the same beauty shop where I worked on weekends getting experience, went in with me and we started our own shop on 145th Street between Convent Avenue and Amsterdam, right near my apartment. Her boyfriend knew of a shop that was going out of business and he got the equipment for us very reasonable and we just made payments to him for the equipment a little at a time. What I did was I said, "Now, Lillian, I'll tell you what I'm going to do. I'm going to take a job in town in a drapery factory, and you run the shop and just make appointments for me for weekends until we can get on our feet. That way I can take care of my end of the expenses.'' And we started out like that, but I wasn't able to stay on the drapery job more than three weeks because we got swamped with work. We had opened up in an area where there wasn't any shop, and business just grew until Lillian said, ''I hate to tell you this, Bernice, but I just have too much business to handle for myself. I've been turning away people.''

So I left the drapery factory and went in with her, and we really did well. Sometimes my tips alone would run thirty dollars a week. I really made good money. But then I started getting it from all sides from my family. They were all worried about my health because I was working eighteen hours a day in that shop.

About this time, the war broke out. My sister who had lived in New York had moved to Philadelphia, so I followed her there and took the civil service exam and got a job with the Philadelphia Signal Corps. But I didn't like Philadelphia. And all this time I had been worried about getting my daughter back and sending her to a good school, so finally, even though my parents didn't want me to, I moved back to New York, took the civil service exam again, was sent to work in the Internal Revenue Service, and I got my daughter back. We moved into an apartment all the way up on 165th Street and Amsterdam. I took that apartment there because I wanted my daughter to go to that school right there on the corner. She didn't even have to cross any streets or anything. It was just about two doors down. That apartment was kind of expensive, but that's when you had the rent freeze and I was able to get it in an area where at one time only whites had had these apartments. So we stayed there.

In 1947, I sent my daughter to Charleston to spend the summer with my parents. By that time, I had moved from the Internal Revenue job to the Veterans Administration, and on August 24, I was supposed to begin work with the Treasury Department making seventy-five dollars a week. My daughter was about to come back to start school again when my daddy called and said she wouldn't be on that train the next day because my momma had been sick all week and couldn't pack her clothes and my daddy never could do anything around the house other than construction stuff, so my daughter was cooking dinners and all for them, and he really needed her. He wasn't well himself anyway. So I said, ''Don't worry, I'll be on the train tomorrow." I figured that I would be there for a couple of weeks, so I sent the Treasury Department people a telegram and said that I had an emergency come up at home and that I couldn't report to work that Monday morning and I would let them know later when I would be back. I came down with a little overnight bag and I've been in Charleston ever since. [*Laughs*]

It's almost like I haven't had control over the destiny of my life in certain aspects. I went to New York with all intentions of getting my music, and that didn't work. I came on back and got married. *That* didn't work. I went back to New York and just as I thought I was getting my life all straightened out again, there was this emergency at home. I saw what the conditions were there and I just wasn't going to leave my mother and father in that situation. They were still cooking on the wood stove and they still didn't have hot water in the house. They had a bathroom, but they would heat the water in big pots and pour the water in the bathtub. I just couldn't walk off again and leave them like that.

Finally I found a job. You know the best job I could find in that city was working six days a week for an upholstery man making cushions for fifteen dollars a week?

E.W.:　That must have been a real shock coming back to South Carolina and segregation and low wages in menial jobs after being used to New York.

B.R.:　I'll say. I went to New York in the first place to get away from all that. There you could go to the theater and sit anywhere you wanted to sit. You could get on the bus and sit anywhere you wanted. You had a certain amount of freedom there that you didn't have elsewhere. You could speak up if you didn't like something. There was subtle segregation in New York at certain exclusive restaurants. They'd just let you sit there all day and they simply wouldn't serve you. But we didn't go to them anyway since they were so expensive, except for one time when my girlfriend and I, just for fun, got these wraparound turbans and put them on our heads. [*Laughs*] We went into this segregated restaurant looking elegant. Had on great big earrings and a *lot* of jewelry and stuff, and boy, we got the royal treatment! We made believe we couldn't understand exactly what was being said, and they treated us like some African dignitaries or something. [*Laughs*] And they served us. We kidded about it because they didn't serve colored in there, but you could get away with anything like that because there was such a mixture of people in New York. As long as you didn't open your mouth except to speak some gibberish and make them think you were a foreigner, you could be served. [*Laughing*]

Also in New York you could register to vote. I couldn't register in South Carolina. And blacks could run for office. In fact, my first taste of politics was through a friend of mine who was a lawyer and who had been an assemblyman for twelve years. He hired me to go over to his office after work and help mail out cards and letters to his constituents. He was originally from Sumter, South Carolina, and we got to know each other because my brother lived in Sumter and we all knew some of the same people. And that was in 1944 —a long time before that kind of thing happened in the South.

And on top of that, I could take my daughter to concerts and plays downtown at Carnegie Hall and Town Hall. I used to take her to hear Dean Dixon conduct. He was a black conductor who I had met personally because I did his mother's hair. We'd hear Duke Ellington—all of them. I used to try to expose her to music like that. Of course, she just liked the boogie beats then. I broke an umbrella over her head one time for slipping off and going to the Apollo Theater! [*Laughing*]

New York really prepared me to live in an integrated society. Even the work in the garment industry contributed because there you had Armenians, you had Germans, you had Jews; we *all* worked side by side on those machines. Some of my best friends were German and Armenian. We would go to lunch together, and we would get together some evenings for movies. When I first came to Highlander, someone said to me, "How is it that you don't find it strange mixing with these white people up here?"

I said, "Well, because this is not the first encounter I've had with the opposite race." At work I didn't even give it a thought. I'm out there trying to make some money, you know [*laughs*], and you're sitting next to me, and we get to talking and swapping chewing gum and suddenly we're friends!

Then all of a sudden I was back in South Carolina. I wouldn't even go to the movies in Charleston. I wasn't going to go there where you had to sit upstairs in that little buzzards' roost. I told my sister, "I'm not going to go sit up there in the buzzard roost where if there's a fire or something I can't even get out. And I stopped eating out. Course, you couldn't eat in the restaurants anyway, except for a couple of greasy spoons where the guys who drank would hang out. Black people as a rule in the South just ate at home.

I had to ride the buses because I didn't have a car, but it used to gall me every time because I had to sit in the back. I got into an argument on the bus one day not long after I came back. I was sitting in a seat just above the back door because the back was crowded with black people. Here comes this white guy on the bus, and there were two of us women back there sitting on our seat. He said, *"All right, you niggers, move on back, move on back."* So this woman who was sitting there beside me started to get up. I said, "Where the hell you goin'! I ain't about to move." She was shakin' —nervous, you know, being a "nigger" and in Charleston. I don't imagine she knew what was happening with me, you know, but I just boiled at that point. So he stood up over me and yelled, *"You know where your place is!"* I just looked up at him and didn't move. When I got to my stop, I said, "I'm gettin' off now. Do you want to finish this on the outside? Come on outside. You want to finish this outside?" *Never* had a fight in my life. Hadn't fought with anybody in my life. I thought about it afterward and I wondered what I would have done if the man *had* got off. But he just looked at me. I was so mad.

I got back to the house, and my daddy could see from my expression how mad I was. He said that I always turn gray when I get angry, so he can tell. He asked me what had happened, and I said, "Well, this old cracker on the bus tried to tell me, 'All right, niggers, get in the back.' I was ready to fight him." I said, "I could be lying in jail just because I forgot I was in Charleston." I said, "See, this wouldn't have happened to me in New York." [*Laughs*]

"Well," he said, "don't worry about it. He wouldn't have got off that bus because he was as afraid of you as you were of him." [*Laughs*] I guess he had never had no nigger to face up to him like that.

But I was in Charleston to stay. All my brothers and sisters rallied around and helped our parents with clothes and shoes and all, and they even wanted to pay a housekeeper to stay with Mom and Dad, but I couldn't see myself being content to leave and having them on my conscience. I could leave and make more money and know that they wouldn't be taken care of as well as I could care for them, or I could stay and not make the money and have a clear conscience. So I stayed. A friend of mine helped sublet my apartment in New York, and in January of 1948, I went up there and called in the movers and we packed up the furniture. I was up there for about three days packing and everything, and when I finished, my friends said, "You have been working for three days packing. Why don't you stay over for a day or two and have a little fun."

I said, "That sounds good." But something said, "No, go on back home." So I said, "I think I'm going home." The train got into Charleston around four o'clock in the morning, and I went in home and I went to bed. Later that morning I got up and helped my mother with breakfast. She was moving around a little bit then. That day at dinnertime as Poppa got up from the table, his hand started shaking and he said, "This is—" and before he could get the "it" out, he had a stroke and he was about to fall and I caught him. If I hadn't been there, my daddy probably would have been paralyzed for the rest of his life, or he might have died. My mother didn't know what to do. She just screamed. She went and got the rubbing alcohol bottle and was just pouring it all over the floor. I yelled at her to sit down. While I was in New York, I had been friendly with a nurse and she told me what she did when her husband had his first stroke, and those things came to me like that, and I ran and I put the hot water on. We always had dry mustard in the house, so I used it. I started putting this hot water mixed with dry mustard in a basin to the bottom of his feet. I ripped all of his clothes off and I bathed the opposite side of where the stroke was with the warm water, and after I don't know how many basins of hot water, he said, "It's hot, it's hot!" So then I knew the feeling was coming back to that side. Sure enough, my father's face straightened up, and I finally got around to calling the doctor because my mother was in such a state that I couldn't get her to dial the phone. But I have just thought about what would have happened if I hadn't gone home. But he got out of that, and you wouldn't have known he had had a stroke at all. The doctor put him on a diet and took him off cigars, which hurt him more than anything else! He made it, though.

Later the furniture came in, and I was able to put a hot water heater and a secondhand gas stove in the house and fix the place up a little.

My daddy finally died in 1950 at the age of eighty-four. He had wanted my brother to take the old garage out back and make it into a shop for me to work at home, but we had never gotten it done. I went from job to job trying to get my salary back up to where it had been in New York. For a while I worked in a factory making coats for ladies and children. Then I got a job at a dry cleaning place doing repairs on customer garments. I was really struggling. I had taken the civil service exam for the Navy Yard in Charleston, and I passed the exam, but I was always put on waiting lists, and I was never hired. One time in 1951, they called me for an interview. I guess they didn't know I was black. I went up there to the supply station and went through *all* this interview. They had me to do the work and everything, and the man was pleased with it, but the next thing I knew, I got a letter saying that the job had been changed from a supply clerk to something else that, of course, I didn't qualify for. I knew why it was done, but at that time there was just nothing I could do about it. Even with all my experience, I could never get back into civil service. After Poppa died, though, my brothers built me a beauty shop at home, and I started making it all right. I also took in sewing and while I was doing the hair work, Momma could do all the handwork on the sewing. Even when she was sick in bed, I could get everything ready and lay it on the foot of the bed and she could take care of the handwork. That was in 1954, nearly seven years after I got back to Charleston, and in the meantime, my daughter had graduated from high school and had gotten married and had a child, so I was a grandmother!

E.W.: By this time, you had gotten pretty heavily involved in politics, hadn't you? How did all that come about?

B.R.: Well, the same year I moved back to Charleston, one of my friends who was in the NAACP asked me to join. I said, "Looks like I'm going to be here anyhow, so I'll get in." At that time, I don't think we had two hundred members. There would only be about fifteen or twenty people at the meetings. That was 1947, and our main concern was the voting situation because Judge J. Waties Waring had just handed down his decision that the Democratic Party was not a private club, and that the primary was open to everybody—blacks as well as whites. That was vital, because in South Carolina, since it was a one-party state, the primary *was* the election. Some blacks could vote in the general election if they paid the poll tax and got passes, but it didn't do any good because the primary was the important one and blacks couldn't vote in it at all. . . .

In order to register, though, we still had to read a section of the Constitution. That was bad, but it wasn't as bad as some states where you had to guess how many beans were in a jar to vote. In some places in Alabama, they asked you how many bubbles did you think were in a bar of soap, and all those crazy things. [*Laughing*] To get around our requirement, Esau Jenkins had started teaching that piece of the Constitution to the people he brought over from Johns Island to Charleston on his bus every day to work. He was really helping them memorize the section they would have to read when they would go down to register. Later the whites realized what was happening and started switching the sections you had to read, but they didn't catch on until the late fifties, and by that time we were really teaching people how to read—not just memorize.

For the continuation of Bernice Robinson's interview, see Chapter Four (page 245).

"I Was a Woman, and That Was That!"
Lucille Thornburgh

Following World War II, this young union organizer discovered that American government and industry were not the only practitioners of discriminatory measures against women. U.S. labor unions also reverted to the old peacetime methods that included expecting women to work under conditions that were not equal to those of male union members.

. . . When the war ended my job with the Labor League was over. I came back to Atlanta and rejoined the Southern Organizing Staff. My assignments were always to organize women. Where, oh, where, I wondered, was it chiseled in stone that women couldn't organize men? I was sent to Rome, Georgia, to organize a glove factory, then later to Knoxville to a similar plant. Old methods had been done away with. We couldn't just get seven members and seven dollars, order a charter, and become an official union. We had to have an election conducted by the National Labor Relations Board to prove we had the majority signed up. We lost both elections—later, the Knoxville plant did become unionized. I doubt that the Rome plant ever did, but I believe it could have under the old system, for we would have had our seven inside organizers.

In 1947 after a year of organizing, I saw a notice in a labor paper that the AFL was awarding five scholarships to labor leaders for a year's study at Ruskin College, Oxford, England. The notice specified that the applicants must be free to spend a year away from home. I was free. I applied. I was accepted one week later. Finally, I was going overseas.

On September 7 I sailed for England on the *Marine Tiger,* a reconverted troop ship. Ruskin is a labor college and students from Egypt, Nassau, India, Scotland, France, etc. were on scholarship from their union. I studied political science, economics, English history, and the British trade union movement.

It was a year of serious study. An occasional evening at the Lamb and Flag pub, drinking beer and shooting darts, was about the extent of our social life. Our time was taken up studying and listening to speeches by the liberal member of Parliament who came to the college. In December of that year five students were selected for scholarships for a month's study at Blaricum, Holland. I was one of them. This was a pleasant adventure, in spite of the uncomfortable living conditions in a youth hostel and every lecture being given through an interpreter.

It was a good year. My favorite subject at Ruskin was the British trade union movement. It was so much more progressive than ours. It went back through generations, from the days of the guilds. Children were brought up in a union atmosphere. While here in East Tennessee, in my early union days, there were very few parents to tell their children of their struggles in the movement. We had to wait for the Wagner Act to be enacted, giving us "the right to organize without coercion or intimidation." In England when a strike was called every worker in the plant went out. There were no "blacklegs"—scabs to us. I came home more militant than ever. If English workers could build strong unions, so could American workers! I read everything I could find concerning Samuel Gompers, considered the founder of the American labor movement. He was a Jewish cigar-maker from England and far more militant than most of our American leaders today.

I came back home in October 1948. My father had died in May. After being away for a year on scholarship I was broke and unemployed. I took the first job offered to me—associate editor of the *East Tennessee Labor News,* a weekly paper founded in 1932 and owned by the Central Labor Council. It was supported by advertising, and this I did not like. Regardless of what some labor-paper editors might say, you cannot lambaste a company for its poor

working conditions or its antilabor stance when you are accepting
money from it for advertising. I thought then, and still do, that all
labor publications should be financed by the members, or through
their treasuries. Our paper closed in 1971 when the only union
printing shop that could publish it went out of business. Many
other union publications have closed since then. I think it is just as
well, for they were not serving any real purpose and never will
until the membership sees the need and is willing to support such
a publication.

The editor of the paper was a man, who sold the advertising. I
was completely in charge of the contents of the paper but I
couldn't be the editor. Why? Because that had always been a man's
job and paid more than associate editor. Qualifications, interest,
and willingness were not considered. I was a woman, and that was
that! I was paid a secretary's salary until 1966 when a more liberal
board of trustees named me editor, the job I held until the paper
folded. . . .

*For the conclusion of Lucille Thornburgh's interview, see Chapter
Four (page 259).*

"Some Snoopers Did Come Around"

Don West

In the late thirties, Highlander's cofounder took a sabbatical from union organizing. For a couple of years, he worked on his grandfather's farm in Georgia, and around 1940, he signed on as a deckhand for the riverboat Duncan Bruce.

But Don West could not stay away from involvement in social causes. Not for long. By 1948—a watershed year, politically, in America—he supported Henry Agard Wallace's bid for the presidency. West, like many other liberals of the period, viewed the Iowa agriculturist as a viable national spokesman for liberal concerns.

Wallace had paid his political dues—having served in President Franklin D. Roosevelt's cabinet from 1933 until Wallace's election, in 1940, as Roosevelt's vice president. Then, following the 1944 victory of the Roosevelt-Truman ticket, Wallace had also served a year as Secretary of Commerce. In 1946, however, he won solid liberal support by criticizing the Administration's foreign policy, then resigning the commerce post in protest.

So in 1947, when the Progressive Party nominated Henry A. Wallace to oppose the presidential campaigns of Democratic incumbent Harry S Truman, Dixiecrat Strom Thurmond, and Republican Thomas E. Dewey, activists such as West took hope. Things were happening. Even in the South. That same year, the Congress of Racial Equality sent Freedom Riders into the region to test a recent Supreme Court ban against segregation on interstate bus transportation.

Was it possible that real *social change—so bitterly sought, and for so long—could finally be at hand? Or were liberals only enjoying a moment in the sun before new storms were to descend?*

[In the early forties] I applied for a job as an organizer with the Food, Tobacco, and Agriculture Workers Union, but the president, Donald Henderson, told me, "You're too red for our union," so I went back to Georgia and got a job as a public school superintendent under Governor Eugene Talmadge. [*Laughing*] It was at Tallulah in Hall County, and I didn't have any trouble getting the job at all. Some snoopers did come around checking up on my patriotism, but they talked to people like the town postmaster—who was probably more radical than I was—and the lady I boarded with, who said, "Professor West is the most patriotic man I have ever known," so they didn't get much satisfaction. And we had a very interesting school there. It was a poor mountain community, and we tried to develop there a system in which the school became a community center and the students in the school and the people in the community actually ran the school. We tried to develop a democratic situation with the students really having a voice in the administration and making decisions. At first there was a great deal of questioning about it, but eventually it took on and our kids did remarkably well. Not only were they responsible for discipline and this kind of thing, but each year the seniors would write their own plays. They would never buy a book and put on a play, but they would write their own drama, and it always involved something about the community.

We had a good many things going there. We organized several locals of the Farmers Union. Aubrey Williams came down from Washington, D.C., and spent several weeks with us in the community helping organize. And we had a cannery where anybody in the community could bring anything they grew on their farm or in their gardens and can it in tin cans. We had retorts and a big steam boiler, and we set it up as a co-op type of thing where people could do it just at actual cost. And then we had a welding shop that the school operated and the community had the advantage of the service of; and developed a community library that the students operated. Generally speaking, the school became a community center, which I think education ought to be. A public school ought to be a center for learning, not only for the students who are of school age, but anybody in the community who is concerned or interested, and it ought to serve the community. So we attracted a bit of attention. Several national magazines like *Seventeen* did stories about us.

Based on my work in rural education, I got a fellowship from the Rosenwald Foundation to take a year out and study at Chicago, Columbia, and the University of Georgia. Then I took a job with Oglethorpe University in Atlanta teaching creative writing, education, and directing the summer institutes for teachers.

I was there until 1948 when, because of a number of things I was involved with, [I] was fired again. Connie was teaching in the public schools and they fired her too. I was being red-baited continually by Ralph McGill in the Atlanta *Constitution,* and the board of the university was afraid my being there would jeopardize some large grants they were aiming for.

I had gotten involved with the Rosalie Ingram Case. That was '48. She was sentenced to the electric chair with her two children because this white man had come to her home and was trying to rape her, and the kids defending their mother got the white man's gun and shot him. One of the kids was only thirteen years old; and all three of them were sentenced to death.

At the same time Henry Wallace was running for President on the Progressive Party ticket and I was state executive secretary for the Georgia Progressive Party. There were two state cochairmen of the party. One was Larkin Marshall, a black editor from Macon, Georgia. The other was a white hill preacher named Charlie Pratt who was the national moderator of the Church of God of the Union Assembly, whose national headquarters was in Dalton, Georgia. That church was centered with the working class in Kentucky, East Tennessee, North Georgia, certain places in Ohio and Texas, and so on. It had a very unique gospel. Part of it was that if you were a member of this church and there was a union in your plant, you had to join it. That was your religious duty. And if there was not a union in the plant, then it was your religious duty to be feeling around to see what you could do to get a union started. The old moderator Pratt preached that the only way the poor people could ever better themselves in this world was through unity.

He was a terrific figure. He couldn't read or write. When he preached, his wife would come up to the pulpit. He'd say, "Come here, woman!" And she'd come up. And he'd say, "Read, woman!" And she would read—she knew what to read. And she would sit down and he would preach on that section of Scripture and when he finished preaching on that, he would look around and say, "Read, woman." And she'd come up and read again. He had great respect for his wife, but he called her "woman," you know, like this. And she sort of helped him to run the operation. An illiterate man but one that had a tremendous understanding of people's psychology. His membership was completely dedicated to him. And the people really supported the church financially too. All the preachers worked as mechanics or cotton mill workers or farmers or whatever made their livings and then preached on Sundays. I was ordained as a minister in that church. The church owned a big supermarket over at Dalton, and a restaurant and furniture store and a number of other businesses. It also had buildings and a lot of property.

And the church was 100 percent in favor of Wallace for President. I organized a meeting in Dalton during the campaign and Wallace came to speak. It was in a church that was almost a block in size that was a remodeled automobile garage or something that had a seating capacity of over five thousand people; the church was packed and they had loudspeakers on the four corners of the church outside and the streets were jammed with people outside. Now, these were poor, white mountain people, working people— cotton mill workers, chenille workers, and this kind of thing. Some of the church members were coal miners that had come down from Harlan County, Kentucky, and different places. There was no other meeting in the South where Wallace spoke to as many white workers as he did right there in Dalton.

So after I was fired at Oglethorpe, Pratt asked me to come up and start and edit a paper for the church, which I did. We called the paper the *Southerner,* and within a year's time we had over five thousand paid subscribers. The *Southerner* was a rather unique church paper, to say the least. We owned our own printing plant. The church bought the presses and everything.

During that time there was an effort made to organize the chenille workers. Dalton, Georgia, was the capital of the chenille industry. It began by women out in the homes being given material and making these tufted bedspreads in their homes, and then some enterprising guy got four or five machines together and got a few women in a room somewhere to doing it and it kept growing and kept growing until it got to be pretty good-sized factories. Of course, they were paying the minimum wage, which was seventy-five cents an hour then. One day, four or five chenille workers came over to my office and said, "Can you organize us into a union?"

And I said, "I'm sorry, boys, but I'm not a union organizer now. I'm a church newspaper publisher/editor."

"Well," they said, "we want to organize a union."

I said, "Maybe I can get you in touch with some union people." So I called up Boyd Payton, who was a United Textile Workers organizer over in North Carolina, and told him what was going on, and he sent three organizers over to Dalton and they began to get out and sign up members. Of course, the companies retaliated by firing every member of the Church of God in every plant in Dalton, Georgia. I had a friend in London who had told me that he had a cut of the Buchenwald ovens. I wrote him a quick letter and said, "Please send me that cut of the Buchenwald ovens." And I used that in an editorial. I called it "The Two-Edged Sword." I pointed out that in Germany, Hitler had singled out for special persecution a particular religious group—the Jews—and had persecuted them because of their religion. In Dalton, Georgia, it just happened to be true that these plant owners were nearly all Jews from New York City. So the Jewish owners of these plants were firing the Union Assembly people because of their religious beliefs, which included the belief that if you are a member of the church, you have to work to build a union.

Well, the editorial stirred up a lot of people and an ugly situation was being created, and so representatives from B'nai B'rith came down from New York and were able to get the Jewish owners to agree not to fire the Church of God people but to put them back to work. That was a very interesting experience.

It still got very hot and vicious, though. Several union people . . . had their cars wrecked. Credit was cut off by the banks to church members and to the church businesses. The windows in our printing plant were smashed and the presses beat up with sledgehammers. Eventually I told Reverend Pratt that I was going to resign and get out and maybe that would take some pressure off him. So I packed up my things in a car and started across Fort Mountain to Ellijay, which was my old home community.

The road was very crooked and narrow, and as I went up the mountain, I noticed out my back window that there was a car behind me that looked like it wanted by. I'm always willing to pull over and let anybody go past me when they want to go faster than I'm going, so I pulled over and the car pulled on up beside me. But it didn't pass me. It just began to edge into my fender, trying to crowd me off the road. I had known about some union organizers in the community being crowded off into the ditch weeks before, and I had put on the seat a .38 pistol that Reverend Pratt had given me. It was loaded, and I just reached over and got the .38 and laid it on the window and emptied it into the front tires of that car; then I stepped on the gas and went on over the mountain.

For the continuation of Don West's interview, see Chapter Four (page 215).

"Highlander Was Like a Little Oasis Down South"
Pete Seeger

Well-known folksinger, songwriter, and social activist Pete Seeger recalls his first visit to Highlander. At the time—the early forties—he considered Monteagle just another stop on a youthful jaunt across America that was led by another folk musician, the now legendary Woody Guthrie.

This pair, strumming banjo and guitar, kept their ears bent to the lyrics of social concern that were expressed in conversations with coal miners, farmers, housewives, and shopkeepers. Subsequently, both Seeger and Guthrie would write songs that pricked at this nation's social consciousness; their art had been born of reality along those back roads.

But unlike Guthrie, Seeger had come from a family where questioning mainstream America was a given. A legacy of liberalism. And with time, Seeger would return to Highlander for more visits. More insights. Like the man himself, Highlander made music with ideas.

. . . My father was deeply involved in radical politics in the early thirties. He didn't make a big thing out of it. He was a musicologist, and Mother was a violinist. I mainly remember him as somebody I used to go on hikes with who had a good sense of humor and liked to tell stories and was highly irreverent. That's how I got into music, and his basic philosophical and ideological approach is what guided me more than anybody else. I remember when I'd put a fancy ending onto a folk song, he'd look at me sternly and say, "Think over what you have just done." It'd be like putting a nylon fringe around a Navajo rug. It just didn't fit!

Both my parents became socialists during World War I when Eugene Debs was running for President and got a million votes. Then in the early thirties the crash came. My father was working with a lot of radical people during 1932, '33, and '34. Then Roosevelt had more success than he had thought possible in trying to repair the capitalist system. My grandmother, who was a fervent Republican, said, "Roosevelt is a traitor to his class!" [*Laughter*] But he saved the damn capitalist system, Roosevelt did, by compromises and taxing the rich to give some money to the poor. My father ended up working for the New Deal—first with the WPA music project, and then later on working for the Pan American Union. Later he went back to teaching again in the last years of his life. But he was the one who got me marching in May Day parades when I was a teenager.

At that time I had a scholarship to a private school. That's the only reason I was there. It was a school full of millionaires and it turned me off on millionaires. Here were kids that were going to step into the presidencies of big corporations and some of them were nudnicks. And I was reading *The New Masses,* a radical publication, way back in 1932 or '33, although by nature I'm a kind of Thoreauvian. If I had my way, I'd really just like to hide off in the woods somewhere.

At the same time, my mother was teaching some Jewish teenagers violin and I was so brash as to say, "The only way you can be honest in this world is to be a hermit. The world is so hypocritical that the more you have to do with it, the more you'll get embroiled in hypocrisy yourself." And the family that my mother was teaching violin to jumped on me like a ton of bricks. They said, "What kind of morality do you call that? You're gonna be pure yourself and let the rest of the world go to hell?" And they posed their traditional Jewish morality against my New England way of looking at things, and I decided they were right, and I've been involved in one way or another ever since.

[When it came time to go to college, I considered a number of options.] Back in the mid-thirties, Highlander Folk School, the Southern Summer School for Workers, Commonwealth College in Arkansas, Brookwood Labor College up in Westchester, and Hudson Shore Labor School up north of here were just a few of the many attempts to start labor schools, which would teach things at that time not being taught at all in public schools, or private schools. I almost went to Commonwealth. I remember my father showing me the brochure and saying, "It might be an interesting place." But one of my private school roommates said, "They look like a lot of older people there. You'd be going in there at sixteen years old and it looks like you'd feel really out of place." I ended up going to Harvard.

I wish I had gone to Commonwealth. I dropped out of Harvard my second year. Back in those days what I wanted to study they weren't teaching. I wanted to study journalism. But I majored in sociology instead, and I soon got disgusted with what I felt was the cynicism and hypocrisy of the professors. I had a sociology professor who wasn't a bad guy as professors go. He was head of the sociology department and he liked to use long words. I once said, "Why do you have to use such complicated words?" He said, "Oh, you have to impress people." He thought he was just cracking a joke but he made me decide to leave Harvard. [*Laughter*] He wasn't the only one. I saw other professors in a rut of long words, and constantly trying to find nice ways of apologizing for the fact that they ignored Marx and Engels. You see, the leading social thinkers of the nineteenth century were radicals, and you couldn't teach them and keep your job.

Then I got interested in the Harvard Student Union, a chapter of the American Student Union which was kind of the equivalent of SDS. It wasn't that radical. It was a bunch of liberals and radicals and pacifists who had a temporary coalition and called themselves the American Student Union. I got so busy learning about *Robert's Rules of Order,* and taking minutes, and putting out newsletters, that I quite forgot to keep my marks up. I lost my scholarship, *and* my family didn't have any money. So my dropping out of Harvard was a combination of getting interested in outside things and losing interest in school and losing money.

Shortly after I dropped out, I went to New York City, and there I met Will Geer, who later became known as Grandpa Walton on the TV show "The Waltons." Will was in New York briefly teaching at a radical theater school. When Will went back to California, he ran into Woody Guthrie, who was singing at fund-raising parties to free Tom Mooney, a radical labor leader who'd been framed and sent to jail. Will writes me a letter and says, "Pete, you gotta meet a fellow named Woody Guthrie; he's the best songmaker I've ever met."

Woody was a dropout of a different kind. His mother was in a mental institution and died, I guess, when he was a teenager. His father had been a small-town oil-boom speculator who made money one week and lost it the next week. He was a John Wayne type, liked to fight, and believed that the world belonged to the strong. Oklahoma had fifty thousand socialists in it around World War I, but Woody's father thought they were just a bunch of nuts, and he even wrote a book called *Komrid* ridiculing the socialists. He had a big library of socialist and antisocialist books. Although he was very much an active, physical man who loved to sing, and loved to drink and brawl, he also read a lot. And so Woody grew up in a house with a lot of intellectual argument going on.

But it seemed to him in the thirties that his father was totally wrong. A lot of good people were broke and a few clever people were too rich, so Woody wrote a song about it. [*Singing*] "As I look around, it's mighty plain to see, this world is such a great and a funny place to be. Gamblin' man is rich and the workin' man is poor, and I ain't got no home in this world anymore." And Woody pulled up stakes and went to California with the Okies, and wrote more songs. [*Singing*] "So long, it's been good to know ya." You ever hear it? It was on the top of the Hit Parade in 1950.

Well, I'm telling you all this about Woody. It's in a new book by Joe Klein called *Woody Guthrie: A Life*. It's a fascinating book, a social history of the times of World War I, and the twenties and thirties.

In the spring of 1940, Woody comes through New York. I'm a very immature twenty years old, but I can pick a banjo. He liked my banjo, although he must have thought me a strange duck. Anyway, he says, "There's a big country out there west of the Hudson River."

I said, "Really?" [*Laughter*] I was a New Englander.

And he says, "I got to go out to the panhandle of Texas. You want to come with me?"

And I say, "Sure, I'd love to." I always loved to travel. So Woody and I teamed up together and I tagged along after him. He was about seven years older than I. We took off and one of the first stops we made was Highlander Folk School. I was fascinated to go down South where so much good music was, and I was also fascinated to see how Southerners were trying to solve the problem of Jim Crow. We only stayed a few days, but a photograph was taken of us there which you may have seen. I have half my back to the camera and I'm facing Woody and we're just singing a song together. Woody is strumming a guitar and I'm strumming a banjo. Me with pimples all over my face—teenage acne. Highlander was like a little oasis down South. There weren't that many places in the South where you could go and find black and white sitting down eating together and drinking together and kidding each other and teasing each other, and dancing together. That was when Highlander was at Monteagle, a little country town, and they regularly had to patrol their grounds because the Klan threatened to burn them out every few months, and finally did.

Woody and I stayed on the road together about a year. Then he went on alone to try once again to get back together with his family, and I hitchhiked on back to New York and got together with Lee Hays, who was a big man from Arkansas who had taught at Commonwealth College. We started a group called the Almanac Singers. Woody joined it in June of 1941 and we went West. That's where we met Studs Terkel and people like Irene Paull, a wonderful woman—a writer who lives out on the West Coast now. Her husband was a labor lawyer up in Duluth, Minnesota, and they put us up.

But I learned from Woody some very important things about living, about people, and ways of working—a kind of directness. He was a direct action person. Once he found himself singing at a cocktail party which was raising funds for some good cause, but no one was listening to him. He stopped in the middle of the third song, didn't say a word, just hitched his guitar on his back, went over to the liquor table and picked up two bottles of whiskey and walked out the door. If they weren't interested in listening to him, he wasn't going to stay there. So he took two bottles of whiskey as pay and left. [*Laughter*]

To get back to Highlander for a minute. Over the years I visited the school several times. That first time I didn't really know what Highlander was about except vaguely that it was a kind of an adult education center, mainly for union people in those days. Along the line, they were also fighting against segregation because you can't really have a good union unless you have both black and white in it. Otherwise, one scabs against the other. If you had all the blacks out on strike, the whites would scab against them. If you had the whites out on strike, the blacks would scab against them. This went on throughout the nineteenth century. I didn't realize until recently how Jim Crow most American unions were. When they didn't want to bring in blacks, they laid themselves wide open. The employer would bring in a trainload of blacks and break the strike, and this contributed to racial antagonism. In fact there were brickyards here on the Hudson. Our neighbor, who's dead now, told me that a whole trainload of Chinee were brought up the Hudson River once to break a brickyard strike. He said, "They brought up a trainload of Chinee, and we dumped them all in the river!" [*Said with much expression*] And people wonder why there's racial violence in this country. It's been fostered for a century or more by employers who found it very handy.

Now at this late date, Washington has realized that racism is America's Achilles' heel, and it's the weak point of many a modern society. It's not easy for races to work together. Not only do we look different, but our culture is different, the words we use are different, our pronunciation is different, even the way we walk. One guy's walking down the street kinda loping along, and somebody looks and says, "Why doesn't he straighten up and walk like a man?" Another person is walking down the street, and his back is straight as a Prussian. The other person says, "Why doesn't he relax? Why does he have to be so stuck-up?" These are just two different ways of walking, but they make people mad to see.

I have a strong suspicion, and this I got from my father, that the lingocentric predicament has caused more grief in the world than most people realize. Charles Abrams called it the tyranny of definitions. You define something, and everything in the world has to fit that definition.

Anthropologists have a term called "the ethnocentric predicament," which means that if you are raised in one culture, you can never 100 percent understand another culture, because you look at it through your own glasses. An African can never completely understand a European, or a European completely understand an

African. They can *try* to. We all better try to! But we have to admit that the way we are raised with our own mother's milk and rhythms and all, teaches us certain values which are different from others'. Well, the lingocentric predicament is that anybody who uses words should sooner or later face up to the fact that nobody has the same definition of those words. . . . People ask me what I think of folk music. I say, "Unless you can successfully define that, I don't want to bother to talk about it." Nobody I know has been able to successfully define it.

It's like drinking beer. Put a glass of American beer in front of a Londoner and he spits it out: "Uhush! That cold, pale, watery stuff!" Put a glass of English beer in front of an American and he spits it out. "Uhush, that warm, frothy stuff!" They're two different drinks. They're both called beer, but they're different. . . .

The word is an astonishing step forward or step backward, depending on how you view human history, in that it is a classification of phenomena. But even the word "house" means a different thing to an Eskimo than a South Sea Islander. In fact, one of our neighbors came up and saw this cabin and said, "That's a house?!" [*Laughter*]

Learning how to get along with each other is not something you learn easily. It can be done, but it sure isn't easy. That's an area where Highlander made some real contributions—especially among blacks and whites who, before integration, never really got together on much of anything.

But Highlander has stuck to its guns, and this is tremendously important. At any one time, Zilphia and Myles must have looked at each other and said, you know, "How are we going to pay our bills this year? Maybe we should just go get a job somewhere. We could reach many more people, perhaps." Myles could have been the head of the sociology department at some university with professors working under him and a million dollars to distribute among the various projects, but they decided this was the most important thing they were ever going to do. And even though they always need money, they never get so desperately low on money that you really think they're really gonna close. You know they're gonna keep on going somehow. They're never gonna quit. . . .

So they've stuck at this, year in, year out; decade in, decade out. And *this,* I think, points up one of the more important lessons that you can mention: that patience may be an overrated virtue. The people of the world are really too patient with corruption, with inefficiency, with laziness, with selfishness. We're *too* patient. But we are not persevering enough. Perseverance is the quality we've got to learn. If we don't make it this year, keep on next year. If we don't make it this half century, keep on the next half century. But we are not going to let go. We are not going to let go. Tennessee is worth saving. Alabama, Georgia, Mississippi, South Carolina, North Carolina—they are all worth saving, and we are going to stay here. You can burn us down, and we are gonna grow right back. You can murder us, you can beat us, and we're gonna come right back. For every one you beat, there's gonna be ten more taking their place. This perseverance is the great lesson to learn from Highlander. And withal, a wonderful sense of humor. I don't think without a sense of humor they could have lasted a day. Cracking jokes, my gosh. Woody used to tell stories all the time. He told the story of two little rabbits who were out enjoying themselves and they heard the hounds. [*Makes barking noises like a hound*] And they ran but they couldn't run faster than those hounds, and they knew they were going to get caught when they saw a hollow log. *Into* that log they went. And the hounds were too big to get in the log. They went sniffing at one end, and sniffing at the other. And the girl rabbit turns to the boy rabbit, and says, "What are we going to do now?" And he says, "Honey, we stay here until we outnumber them!"

That's Highlander. . . .

For the continuation of Pete Seeger's interview, see Chapter Four (page 211).

4

1950–61
When Segregation and the
Self-punishment of a Nation Were
Called "Patriotism"

. . . Man doesn't automatically come with courage. Courage is something that grows on him as he learns how to use it. But he has to learn first what it is to be a human being. The company's job is to see that he doesn't do that. And the company does its job better than the union.

Part of the reason the union doesn't do a better job of making the worker realize he is a human being is that too many unions are more concerned with their institutional problems than they are with the broader aspects that are more philosophical and more political. And they're afraid the unions will get away from them.

The crucial problem in all these situations—and you get this in *Norma Rae*—the crucial problem is to make people feel that they're human beings and that they've got rights. That's really what got me all involved in this in the beginning. How do you make people feel that they have rights?

By the way, this is the thing that Myles Horton and I have so much in common: It's a comprehension of the fact that people not only have rights but they've got *to understand* that they have rights. And you've got to educate them to understand; they've got to understand that there are rights that have to be exercised.

—*RALPH HELSTEIN*

. . . We've grown to be more tolerant in this country in many respects; yet I can point out to you—today, tomorrow, yesterday, and possibly every tomorrow to come—gross injustices that go on not only in our economic system but in our judiciary and our political systems. So you can only fight and hope to live to fight another day.

You can't get discouraged. As each problem comes along, you get a little bite out of each, and if you can hold on, eventually you may have done enough to have done some good.

The one area I *can* become pessimistic about, though, is the fact that people can be built up to hate something—another country, or a race, for example—so much that they are willing to risk the destruction of everything to eliminate it. Nuclear war could actually result from that hatred. The McCarthy era sprang out of that capacity for suspicion and hatred. Highlander was almost ended because of it.

That's the only thing I know of that I'm pessimistic about: the fact that people are so susceptible to being fed a bill of goods and buying it hook, line, and sinker.

—CECIL BRANSTETTER

★

"Wasn't That a Terrible Time?"

Pete Seeger
and Don West

In 1950, U.S. Senator Joseph Raymond McCarthy launched his campaign against the "internal subversion of Communists in America." This govern- ment-run investigation of prominent citizens would last until the Senate in December 1954 voted sixty-seven to twenty-two to condemn the senator's actions. But during his five-year reign of power, it was as though America's disenchantment with its former World War II ally, the Soviet Union, found in "McCarthyism" an expression of national self-punishment.

Pete Seeger, who led the folk music revival during the fifties with his group the Weavers, recalls his appearance before one of McCarthy's hear- ings:

My lawyer made his defense on the basis of the First Amend- ment rather than the Fifth. It's a legal question. The Fifth Amend- ment in effect says, "You have no right to ask me this question." The First Amendment is more like, "Nobody has the right to ask *anybody* such questions." So it's a broader opposition. When I was in the hearing before the committee, I said, "I don't think any American should be forced to answer such questions, especially under the threat of reprisal if he or she gives the wrong answer." And for another three quarters of an hour they kept asking me questions. I said, "Same answer." Finally Congressman Walter said, "Mr. Seeger, I do not consider that a proper answer. Do you realize that you may be in contempt of Congress?'' I think I shrugged.

I did get him mad once. I shouldn't have done it, I suppose; but he showed a picture of me marching in a May Day parade, which was supposed to be a terrible sin. I was in my Army uniform and I carried a large cutout picture of a microphone labelled "The Censored Mike." He said, "Is this you?"

And I thought, "It's kinda like when they asked Jesus was he king of the Jews," and so I said, "Thou sayest it."

He got red-faced and said [*pounding on the table*], "We'll have none of that in here!" [*Laughter*]

Six years later I was sentenced. I got a real lesson in the American legal system, and great admiration for parts of it, although, sadly, it doesn't always work as well as you would like. First of all, it's very expensive to see a trial through. It takes tens of thousands of dollars. And it takes a long while. The mills of justice grind slowly. A year after the hearing, I was cited for contempt of Congress by Congress, and a year after that I was indicted by the Justice Department. Four years later I was finally brought to trial and the judge found me guilty. Actually he literally directed the jury to find me guilty, which they did, and he sentenced me to a year in jail. I said, "I'd like to say a few words," so I said a few words. And I had my banjo with me. Said, "There's a song which kept coming up in the hearings, and I feel it's a good song, and I'd like to sing it."

The judge said [*very deep voice—beating on table*], "You may not!"

The song was, [*singing*] "Wasn't that a time, wasn't that a time, a time to try the soul of man; wasn't that a terrible time?" You know Tom Paine's famous phrase, "These are times to try the soul of man"? It was said during a low point in the American Revolution. The song was written by Lee Hays, who wrote "If I Had a Hammer," and a friend of his, a poet named Walter Lowenfels, who used to live in Peekskill [New York]. He's dead now. The first verse was about Valley Forge; the second verse was about Gettysburg; the third verse was about World War II and the fascists; and the next verse was about contemporary times when people were being thrown in jail. The last verse goes [*singing*], "Our faith cries out, we have no fear; we dare to reach our hand to other neighbors far and near, to friends in every land. Isn't this a time? Isn't this a time, a time to free the soul of man? Isn't this a wonderful time?''

I used to sing it all through the frightened fifties and still sing it occasionally, but now I realize it's all full of men-this, men-that, and I have to apologize to women. If Walter and Lee had been writing it now they would have made up some different verses and changed the chorus.

In retrospect, the big damage that was done by the red scare was not to the occasional radicals, who often could shift for themselves, but to the full soul of America in the same way you can say that slavery as an institution damaged the soul of America, not just Africans, nor the abolitionists who were lynched and beaten when they tried to agitate against slavery. I don't suppose anybody but a really good novelist could bring out this kind of story. You can't do it by writing a history textbook, because you can't get into the psyches of people well enough. I know that friendships were broken up and people stopped doing things they should have done because they were scared. On the other hand, some people thrived. People sometimes say, ''Gee, it must have been hard with the blacklist around.'' But I had it easy. I kept on singing for the kids in schools and colleges. If I'd had a job in Hollywood I couldn't have done that.

Interestingly enough, the thing that saved us from Senator McCarthy is that there is a deep distrust in America of demagogues of all sorts. At various times they rise pretty high, but they often trip themselves up. And this is what happened with Joe McCarthy. While some people were enthusiastic for him, others were increasingly suspicious: ''This guy's out for himself. He's not really against Russia. He's just *for* Joe McCarthy, and he'll use anything he can to get in a position of power.'' When Eisenhower was elected Republican President in 1952, McCarthy had been saying, ''We've had twenty years of treason!'' [*Very dramatically*] Meaning the Democrats had been in power for twenty years. And six months later, when Eisenhower wasn't paying enough attention to Joe McCarthy: ''And perhaps twenty-one years!'' All of a sudden, the Republicans realized, ''This guy won't stop at anything. If we don't knuckle in to him, then *we're* Communists.'' And belatedly they realized they had to chop him down. So it was the Republi-

cans who chopped down Senator Joe McCarthy. It wasn't the radicals; it wasn't the liberals. Partly it was Joseph Welsh, a conservative
Massachusetts attorney in the Army-McCarthy hearings. There was
a young lawyer on Senator Welsh's staff who he knew personally
was innocent, and McCarthy was insinuating that because this man
had once attended a party at some person's house that this young
lawyer was perhaps a communist infiltrator. The guilt-by-associa-
tion trick. Welsh was *outraged* when he saw the kind of innuendos
that McCarthy would go in for. He said, "Senator, I don't think
until now I ever realized quite how evil a person could be." Then
Senator [Ralph E.] Flanders, of Vermont, a Republican, an elderly
man, proposed that McCarthy be impeached.

One way Highlander has always gotten around the guilt-by-
association trick, and the way I've gotten around it, is you shake
hands with everybody. Do you know the story of Ali Baba and the
Forty Thieves? One of the thieves snuck in and found out it was Ali
Baba who had found their gold, and he put an X on Ali's door. He
went back and said, "Okay, tonight we will go and assassinate the
man. We've already put a cross on his door so we know where he
lives." In those days, the streets were no-man's-land, as they are
now in New York. Meanwhile Morgana, the slave girl, going out for
water at the well, noticed the cross on the door and she says,
"What's that there for?" She was suspicious, so she put a cross on
every house in the whole neighborhood, and when the thieves
came that night they found a cross on every door and they didn't
know who to assassinate.

Similarly, the Weavers were singing in Cleveland, Ohio, once
and the local red squad came in. I met an old radical friend and
he pointed out the red squad. "See there? They're taking notes on
you and me too. Watch what I do." And he went around table-
hopping, just like a politician. Went to every table in the whole
room: "Flo, Jo, glad to see you here! Nice evening." Shook hands
all over, even with some bitter enemies, but they were not going to
make a scene, so they shook hands with him. Meanwhile their
local red squad was totally nonplussed. He was shaking hands with
everybody!

Now I joke about the word "communist" because it's like the
word "religion." It means many things to many people. When
somebody asks me if I'm a Communist, I say, "Ever since I was

seven years old and read about the American Indians." The American Indians were Communists. They were. Every anthropologist will tell you they were Communists. No rich, no poor. If somebody needed something the community chipped in. That was the standard way for human beings to live until the agricultural revolution when some smart cookie found out that you could herd sheep or cows, or raise chickens, and you could grow the grain in your own backyard instead of hiking two miles to a distant place to get it; and so society started being farmers instead of hunters and gatherers. The agricultural revolution was the beginning of class society. It's generally agreed on. Friedrich Engels pointed it out in the 1890s, but it's now generally accepted by most sociologists. Once you had agriculture, you had a little money to spare. Some people said, "That's mine, all mine," and the devil take the hindmost. It was also the beginning of male supremacy, really, on a big scale. Man said, "I want *my* crops and *my* herd to go to *my* sons." And so his wife had to watch where she went and who she invited in, and so on. But the word "communism" to the average person means you want Russia to take over America. It's becoming a little confusing now, though. They can't quite figure it out: "Isn't China a communist country? How come Nixon went there?" We take our few allies where we can. . . .

Unlike Seeger, Don and Connie West could not as easily withstand the economic pressures that McCarthyism wielded. In particular, her job as a public school teacher was dependent upon government funds. So Don recalls how his appearances before congressional committees affected the Wests' livelihood, marriage, and family:

. . . In the mid-fifties when the McCarthy thing was very strong and people were being investigated by people like Senator Eastland, [I was] subpoenaed to testify before his committee. I was subpoenaed several times. The first time, I was back on my farm plowing down on that river bottom by the Chattahoochee River and that guy walked out across the field—mired up in the plowed dirt—to give me the subpoena to appear before a committee in Memphis. Later on, quite a few more of us were subpoenaed to New Orleans. Virginia Durr was one of the ones called to testify. Eventually there was a House Un-American Activities Committee and I was summoned before it in Atlanta in 1958. I remember the year because Connie had just been in a very serious automobile wreck in Bowling Green, Kentucky, coming back from the National Teachers Association meeting in Cleveland, and she was at the point of death in the hospital in Louisville. I was there with her, and I got this summons to come to Atlanta. I pled with them to let me stay in Louisville but they wouldn't even listen to it so I had to leave her and go all the way back to Atlanta to be at that damn hearing.

That was a period in which there was a lot of terror and fear. You went around feeling like you would be a coward if you didn't speak out on certain issues, and you knew that if you did, you were not gonna have a job. If you had a family to feed, you can imagine what that meant. It was a period in which people had been squelched. The spirit of the thirties had just completely been beaten down and people were sort of dormant, and a great deal of fear abounded everywhere, it seemed. Even President Eisenhower seemed to be afraid of McCarthy. Nobody seemed to have the courage to stand up to him until eventually he was censored and lost his power after he just became so terribly vicious. It was a time when people were just afraid to talk. There were few people who were willing to take a stand on any kind of controversial issue and if you took a stand, you knew darn well you were sticking your neck out and you were gonna get it. And you just waited, not knowing what time it would come, but knowing darn well it would come. That was terrible. It went on up into the fifties, you know, the silent generation of the fifties. You felt so alone because there was no movement. There was no anything. You were just one person by yourself. It was really a rough time.

And they never did prove anybody was a red or anything else. It was just to discredit people. If you failed to "cooperate" with them, as they called it, then you were put down as a non-cooperative witness, and if you had a job in a university as a professor or teacher somewhere, that just automatically meant that you were out. You were fired.

But I refused to grant those committees credence. I said, "What this committee is doing in my opinion is contrary to and a violation of the Bill of Rights of our Constitution; and if I honor this committee and if I grant that it has these rights, then I am violating in my own conscience the Constitution and the Bill of Rights.'' So I was a very uncooperative witness. And, of course, all this was taken down stenographically and they did everything they could to put in ugly implications and all this. It was all purely to discredit people.

You know, you can get copies of these stenographic reports today, and just since I've been here in West Virginia—just a few years ago—one of these right-wing groups like the Birch Society reproduced the record of one of my hearings and passed it out in this county: *The Investigation of Communism in the Mid-South in the Year 1955: A Record of Donald L. West.* And it was handed out on the street corners and passed out and put in the paper boxes all up and down the road, all over this community, all over this county. I don't know how far [it was distributed elsewhere], but I certainly know that it was here because a friend of mine in Hinton brought me fifty copies. They were giving them out on a street corner. He said to the fellow, ''I'd like to have a lot of these.'' And he got them and brought them on up and gave them to me. So the effect of those committees was awfully negative. A terrible effect it had on people. Their careers were completely destroyed. Of course, we were on the farm then, and I grew vegetables and peddled them in Atlanta. I have always been able to keep my head above water financially, one way or the other, from the time I got into college with a total of $1.65 in my pocket on up to the present time. My youngest daughter, Hedy, and I would be up at four o'clock in the morning and get to Atlanta before daylight to peddle vegetables. We had regular customers and in some of the houses I knew exactly what they wanted, so we would just leave it at the door and collect later. Hedy was a great help with this peddling. She was a good salesman. She would go from door to door. She was just a little tyke then, and she could sell very well. The living was hard, but we managed. But eventually with the kids being attacked at school and the ugly phone calls and threats and all, Connie went down to Florida with the girls and got a job and for three to four years we lived more or less in separation because of that. She could get a job there and we very carefully kept it under cover that she had any connection with me. She was just a schoolteacher. So our kids graduated from schools in Florida.

* * *

But guilt by political association was not the only "offense" that was used to taint some Americans in the fifties. Following the U.S. Supreme Court's Brown v. Board of Education *decision in 1954, civil rights became a volatile issue once again. Some white leaders, providing early support for the efforts of black civil rights leaders, also became targets of discrimination and ostracism. Don West recalls how Aubrey Williams became such a victim, not only in the fifties but extending through the sixties until Williams' death:*

Aubrey was a man who was thoroughly committed to human values. All his life he worked in that spirit. After [working in the] WPA, he was National Youth Administration director under Roosevelt, and then he went with the Farmers Union, and then he ran the *Southern Farmer,* which had a million circulation. But when it came to real issues, he was ready to come to grips with them.

During the Montgomery bus boycott, when the blacks were boycotting the buses [by] walking and carpooling instead, his wife drove a car daily, hauling black people to and from work. He supported it completely. And with that kind of attitude, advertisers boycotted his paper; clients of his printing business, like a Catholic newspaper, withdrew their business; and he was boycotted and pressured until he went bankrupt.

After he went under, he came back to Washington to die of cancer. For a while, he was still able to be active, and he called Lyndon Johnson on the phone one day. Lyndon was then President; Aubrey was the guy who [had] appointed Lyndon to his first important job as NYA director of Texas, and Aubrey had been a great friend of Lyndon's at that time. But Lyndon wouldn't accept the call [at the White House], and it hurt Aubrey terribly.

When he died in Washington, only a handful of people came out. Here was a man who put his life on the line as far as black and poor people were concerned, and there were only two or three blacks there. It was sad. But I had tremendous respect and admiration and regard for him.

For the continuation of Pete Seeger's interview, see Chapter Five (page 275). For the conclusion of Don West's interview, see Chapter Six (page 371).

"It Took Guts to Do These Things"
Edgar Daniel Nixon

Having already been an activist in Alabama for thirty years, E. D. Nixon was solidly prepared in 1955 when a Montgomery policeman arrested Rosa Parks on a segregated bus. History credits Nixon's and other NAACP leaders' responses that December with the launching of the modern civil rights movement.

But, as Nixon recalls, those monumental events were deeply rooted in the trial-and-error methods of earlier activists and in the deep social consciences of other individuals who had demonstrated similar courage in the forties:

If I hadn't had the training from people like Roy Wilkie, A. Philip Randolph, Walter White, Thomas T. Patterson, and B. F. McLaurin, I wouldn't have known what to do. They taught me that the first thing is that you need to have a technique, and your technique has got to be such that people respect you for what you are trying to do. And that you must be honest, maintain your integrity, be on time, and no matter what happens, don't let nobody sway you from the principles you are fighting for. Now they have told me that time after time. And because of that, we were getting some things done twenty years before the bus boycott here in Montgomery. People say the bus boycott was the beginning of the movement, but they just don't know.

[The specific techniques included how to be an effective

speaker in public; how to use the press to draw attention to a cause
and attract public support; and] using the courts as long as you
could. When I was head of the local branch of the NAACP here, I
got a lot of experience with the courts—finding lawyers to go into
court with us to represent people whose cases we had taken on. I
handled a case where a black taxicab driver got beat up by a white
policeman, and a case where two white police assaulted a black
woman, and a case where a black man was charged with raping a
white woman—things like that.

And then we used the courts in behalf of large groups of
people who had been mistreated—times like when the city of Tuskegee gerrymandered all the black people out of the city limits
and the courts finally ruled in *Gomillion v. Lightfoot* that that was
wrong.

[And] once people could vote, you could use politics. In
1954, they had an election for commissioner of police in this city,
and one of the candidates, Dave Birmingham, came to see me and
said, "I need every vote I can get to win the election today."

And I said, "All right, I tell you what. I'll get you elected, but
it's gon' cost you something."

He said, "Well, I don't have a whole lot of money."

"Who said anything about money?" I said. "I want to find a
man whose word I can depend on; then I'm gon' support that
man for what it's worth," I said, "and the price is gon' be Negro
policemen."

All right. Dave Birmingham won, and then about a week after
he won, he called and told me to come down there and said,
"Bring a committee." Said, "Don't be large. About three."

I said, "All right." So I got another man and a woman and
carried them with me down there and we walked in there into the
mayor's office, and the mayor and the number-two commissioner
and Birmingham was in there, and Birmingham said, "Mayor,"
said, "these are my friends." Said, "They helped me get elected
and I promised them that if I got elected I was gon' help them get
Negro policemen." He turned to me and said, "Nixon, you know
three of us make these decisions, and so it'll take two of us to vote
to get you Negro policemen." And he said, "So if you don't get
Negro policemen, you'll know that these two men voted against
me." When they did vote, the mayor voted with him for Negro

policemen, and then for the first time since Reconstruction days we had black police in this town.

So that was another technique. And another one—one I always considered a last resort [but an effective technique]—was to go to the streets. Randolph taught me about mass pressure in 1941 when he went before President Roosevelt trying to make it possible for blacks to work during the war in the defense industry. Roosevelt give him all kind of reasons why he couldn't do this, couldn't do that, and Randolph decided, "There ain't but one thing gon' move the President and that's mass pressure." Said, "I'm going out and organize ten thousand people to march on Washington."

We said, "Well, where you gon' get ten thousand people, Little Chief?" We called him Chief. He said, "Well, we got our porters and their wives, we can start there." In a couple of weeks we was talking about fifty thousand people. And when the President got concerned, and got Walter White to talk to him about it, he was talking about a hundred thousand people. He called Randolph and he said, "Phil, how many people you really gon' march on Washington?"

Randolph say, "A hundred thousand."

To make a long story short, the President issued an executive order, number 8802, drafted by Aubrey Williams, giving blacks the right to work in the war-related industries.

Well, I learned from that, see? When the United States Supreme Court ruled on May 17, 1954, that segregated public schools were unconstitutional, I was the first man anywhere in the United States to lead a group of black children into an all-white school. That was at the William Harrison School—ain't ten minutes' drive from here—out on the bypass. They wouldn't let them stay, but I carried them there. It took guts to do these things.

And at the same time we blacks had to learn that not all whites were against us. I had a whole lot of help from white folks. You'd be surprised that the first person that helped me in Montgomery was a white woman, and she was head of the welfare department. She rode on my Pullman car going to Washington, D.C. She give me her telephone credit card and a telegram to send at Danville, Virginia, and that's how I discovered she was from Montgomery. I looked at her card and saw who she was. When I got back and give her her card, I told her who I was and I said, "You know, I'd really like to talk to you sometime." And she wrote on the back of one of her cards, "Whenever this man comes down to the office, see that he get into my office." When I went in there, they carried me into her office and we talked about things—what I was trying to do—and she and her assistant, Doris Bender, came to meetings where I was trying to do things and told me what I did wrong and what I should do next time. They really helped me. And not only them. There were others from time to time.

When I was head of the NAACP here, one time we had a sixteen-dollar phone bill we couldn't pay, and they threatened to cut my telephone off. And I didn't know where we was going to get the money from, and somebody sent me to see Aubrey Williams, who was head of the Southern Conference Education Fund. I told him who I was and what I was doing and what I was up against, and he paid my telephone bill. And I told him I didn't know when I was going to pay, and he said, "Don't worry about it." A couple of weeks later he called me one day and asked me could I come over there. Jim Dombrowski was in his office. He introduced me to Jim Dombrowski and we started talking about things and he told me about Highlander, and several years later me and Miss Parks went up there for a weekend. I talked about some of the things we were doing, and met Septima Clark. I didn't go but that one time, but I think Miss Parks has been several times since. But Myles and I became friends. You tell him you seen me and he'll light up like a light! And Aubrey Williams and I went on to be friends all of our lives, and of course, Attorney and Mrs. Clifford J. Durr. They handled several of our cases and I relied on them quite often for different things.

[What I'm getting to is 1955. The success of the bus boycott was due to the fact that we took all the lessons about using the press and public speaking and the courts and politics and white friends and mass pressure and all the rest and used it all at the same time. But the boycott was] my idea. Everybody knows that, and I'm not just saying it; everybody in town knows it. If I hadn't decided that there had been a bus boycott, there wouldn't have been one. . . . A whole lot of people don't understand what we wanted from Miss Parks' case here. And a whole lot of people don't know that [our problems with the Montgomery buses went back years and we hadn't been able to get them resolved]. We had one woman who was convicted same as Miss Parks in 1945. She was pulled off a bus downtown on the corner of Dexter Avenue and Lawrance Street, on Saturday evening. She and the bus driver had a run-in and they found her guilty and fined her ten dollars and costs, and we appealed it in the Court of Appeals. At that time, we didn't have no black lawyers here. All right, that was 1945. When Rosa L. Parks was arrested in 1955, ten years later, we still hadn't moved that case to the Court of Appeals.

And a lot of people don't know that three other girls had been arrested that year on the buses in 1955 before Miss Parks. The first was named Winfield, and the second was Claudette Colvin [March 2, 1955], and the third was Mary Louise Smith [October 21, 1955]. Groups like the Women's Political Council tried to handle those cases but they couldn't get nowhere with them either.

Then Miss Parks was arrested and taken to jail. She called her mother, and her mother called home to tell my wife. Mrs. Nixon called me at the office and when she did, she said, "They arrested Miss Parks."

I said, "For what?"

She said, "I don't know, go get her!" Like I could just go down there and get her, see?

And so I called down there to find out what the charge was. Of course, the sergeant on the desk told me it was none of my damn business in no uncertain terms. So then I called Attorney Fred D. Gray, a black lawyer, who was a youngster—just came out of school—but he was out of town. Then I got hold of Clifford Durr, and Durr called down there and found out for me and called me back and said, "They got her charged with violating Alabama segregation law."

I said, "Well, I'm going down and make bond for her."

He said, "Come by here and I'll go with you."

I said, "That's fine." I remember it was Thursday, December 1, 1955. And about time he got out to the car, his wife, Virginia, come running and the three of us went down there. We got down there and 'cause he was white, the desk sergeant figured he was gonna make bond, and he got the papers all ready and carried them to Mr. Durr. Mr. Durr said, "Mr. Nixon's gonna sign the bond." He said, "I don't own no property." But that sergeant was just so sure that because Durr was white he was gonna sign the bond.

We took Miss Parks home and asked about using her case as a test case and she agreed. Then I started calling people the next morning to tell them I thought this was the right time. We should boycott the buses on Monday, the day they were going to try Miss Parks. There was a lot of support, and when I went home Friday night, I said to my wife, I said, "Well, I believe we got what we looking for."

She said, "Like what?"

I said, "Miss Parks' case." I said, "I think we gonna use Miss Parks' case to [change the treatment we've been getting on the buses]."

She said, "How you gonna do that?"

I said, "Well, we gonna ask the people to stay off the buses."

She said, "Man, don't you know them folks ain't gonna stay off the bus, cold as it is!"

I said, "I don't know, but if we can keep 'em off when it's cold, we can keep 'em off when it's hot."

She looked at me and shook her head and she said, "My husband, my husband." She said, "If headaches were selling for a dollar a dozen, you'd be just the man to walk in the drugstore and say, 'Give me a dozen headaches.' "

The next morning I got up at five o'clock and started calling people to get them to come to a meeting that night. I called Ralph D. Abernathy first, then I called Reverend H. H. Hubbard. The Reverend Martin Luther King was number three. [Dr. King, who was twenty-six at the time, had arrived in Montgomery in September 1954, to take up his first pastorate at the Dexter Avenue Baptist Church]. Now Reverend King said to me, "Brother Nixon, let me think about it a while and call me back."

I said, "All right."

So I went on down the line and called eighteen peoples, and every one of them I told to meet at the Dexter Avenue Baptist Church that evening because we needed a strategy meeting to let people know what we were trying to do. When I called Reverend King back, he said, "Brother Nixon, I decided I'm gonna go along with you."

I said, "That's fine. I'm glad to hear you say that 'cause I've told eighteen other people to meet at your church this evening and it would be bad for them to get there and you not be there." And that's the beginning of how the bus boycott got started.

[After that meeting, where we decided to definitely have the boycott and to have a mass meeting Monday night, December 5, to decide what to do next,] I called Joe Abzell [city editor of the Montgomery *Advertiser*] to tell him about the boycott and the mass meeting. I told him, "Joe, you got a chance now to do something decent. If you want to do it, I'll give you a hot lead." He came over and I told him about it, and he wrote the story[2] [which appeared on the front page of the Sunday, December 4 edition of the paper]. His article was the first article ever wrote about the bus boycott.

When his article came out on Sunday, I sat down to the telephone, and I had a list of names of every [black] minister in town, and I called every one. I said, "Have you read the paper this morning?" Some said yeah and some said no. I said, "Read it! Take it to church with you. Tell your people we want two thousand people at Holt Street Baptist Church tomorrow night."

All right. In the morning, which was December 5, Rosa L. Parks was tried and found guilty and fined ten dollars, and the lawyer appealed her case and I went on her appeal bond. When we got outside, something happened that I'd never seen before. I'd been going in and out of the court for almost twenty-five years supporting or helping people with their cases, and I never saw a black man in court unless he was being tried, or some of his close friends or relatives. But *this* morning, December 5, when they found Rosa Parks guilty, there was over five hundred black men up and down the street. It was the first time in the history of my life that I'd seen that many black folks in and around the courthouse.

I put Miss Parks in the car with my wife and I came back to the group that was out there all up and down the street, and I got about halfway in the middle and said, "How many of you all know me out here? Hold your hand up." And it appeared to me as I looked that everybody held their hand up. I said, "Look upstairs.

[2] This sentence, and the preceding quotation, were taken from an interview with E. D. Nixon, conducted by Tom Gardner, that appeared on page fourteen of the Spring 1981 issue of *Southern Exposure*.

See them men upstairs there?'' I said, ''See this man out here with this sawed-off shotgun? Don't give him a chance to use it. Don't give 'em that opportunity.'' I said, ''I'm gonna ask you all to quietly move from around this police station now; Mrs. Parks has been convicted and we have appealed it, and I've put her in the car—you saw me put her in the car with my wife.'' And I said, ''Then as you move, don't even throw a cigarette butt, or don't spit on the sidewalk or nothing.'' I said, ''Don't give these men a chance to use these guns.'' I said, ''But one thing you can do.'' I said, ''Go home and if you really want to do something, get in the streets and tell people we're gon' have a meeting at the Holt Street Baptist Church tonight where we gon' talk about bus boycott.'' I said, ''Tell all of your friends and relatives and everybody to be there.'' I said, ''Don't let me down.'' I said, ''I got to have two thousand people in that church tonight.''

That afternoon at three o'clock, we had a meeting to plan for that night meeting. [That's when we formed the Montgomery Improvement Association, and Reverend King was elected president, Reverend L. Roy Bennett, vice president, I was elected treasurer, and Mrs. Erna Dungel, financial secretary. She] was secretary for the Mount Zion AME Church, and she had asked if she could sit in on the meeting and I said, ''Yeah, you can be a part of this meeting.'' There weren't no other women in the meeting at that time but her, and from then on she helped us keep up with the finances.

Four hours later we walked into the Holt Street meeting. I had wanted two thousand people there. The *Advertiser* had a headline the next morning that said, ''4,500 HYMN-SINGING NEGROES MET AT THE HOLT STREET BAPTIST CHURCH.'' I'm here to tell you if it wasn't seventy-five hundred in and around the church, there wasn't a soul there. If we don't do nothing but think about the mass of people that turned out to that meeting—that first meeting that night—it [still would have] made history. But at that meeting, [since they had found Miss Parks guilty and wouldn't change the seating laws, we decided to keep the boycott going].

But you see, if I hadn't been a member of the Brotherhood of Sleeping Car Porters, there wouldn't have been no bus boycott. But you tell people that across the country, they'd think you're crazy. I was trained by them, and I could call on them for help and advice. And because of that when the bus boycott started, I told Randolph what we was up against and he passed a memorandum throughout the country and almost everywhere I went people knew me. We had to go out and raise the money, and from the middle of December to the last of March, I raised ninety-seven thousand dollars. I got thirty-five thousand in one evening at a banquet in Detroit sponsored by the United Automobile Workers Number 212.

And the press played a big part. They built the bus boycott into what it was by playing it up. People all across the country got to reading about it. "Let's go down to Montgomery and see what them black folks doing down there." But if the press had kept still about the Montgomery bus boycott, and radio and television had kept quiet about it like they'd done on a whole lot of other issues, it couldn't have survived. They built it. You could have had a dozen Kings, but if the press had kept silent about it, it probably wouldn't have worked.

But a lot of things happened from that. Six to eight months after the Montgomery bus boycott, the Southern Christian Leadership Conference (SCLS) was formed out of the Montgomery Improvement Association, and Reverend King was elected president, and of course, that gave him a wider range to do what he was doing. But if I hadn't known A. Philip Randolph, the greatest black leader in the last hundred years, you [might] never have known Martin Luther King.

Just like a woman told me about Reverend King, "Well, Mr. Nixon, you know Reverend King was educated."

I said, "He shore was." He was highly educated in the field of religion. He didn't know nothing about organized labor because he never had a job; he didn't know nothing about poverty because he'd never been hungry; he knew nothing about politics because he had never started voting. You see what I'm talking about? But I knew something about all those things. Surely, I couldn't argue with Reverend King about no religion, see what I mean? I couldn't hardly argue with him about the Bible as far as that's concerned. But I could argue with him all day about the Brotherhood and about organized labor. I would argue with him about welfare. He didn't know a thing in the world about it.

Like I had a visitor up here last year and at that time the walls were covered with plaques and pictures and things. He looked around there and he said, "Mr. Nixon, you don't have a picture of Dr. King."

I said, "No, I don't have one."

"Do you mean to tell me after all Dr. King did for the people of Montgomery, you don't have a picture of him?"

I said, "Dr. King haven't did anything for the people of Montgomery." He thought I was crazy. I said, "The people of Montgomery did something for Reverend King." I said, "Now, Reverend King owed everybody in Montgomery something. Nobody in Montgomery owe Reverend King anything. We paid him."

Several places I have spoken away from here, and I'll mention someone like Mrs. Erna Dungel, and someone will say, "Mr. Nixon, I ain't never heard her name before." Well, it's because of the fact we've forgot about the contributions other people made besides King. And it's sad. My contention is this, that somewhere along the road, we ought to get together somewhere and bring all the people together who really contributed something to building the Montgomery Improvement Association or the bus boycott. That would include the women who were arrested before Miss Parks because they were a big part of our Supreme Court case too. But they're forgotten. There are a whole lot of places I go that nobody never heard of me. Right here in Montgomery, we celebrated the twenty-fifth anniversary of the Montgomery bus boycott and I wasn't even invited to be on the program.

For the conclusion of Edgar Daniel Nixon's interview, see Chapter Six (page 375).

★

"The Back of the Bus Was Already Crowded"
Rosa Parks

Even though this Montgomery woman committed one of the most dramatic acts of civil disobedience in the twentieth century, at the time, she considered refusing to give up her bus seat to be nothing more than a logical reaction to the illogical demands of a solitary white man.

With clarity and directness, Rosa Parks recalls the NAACP and Highlander events that preceded the 1955 bus boycott precipitated by her singular act. And she explains why she subsequently declined to participate in other civil rights activities.

There was one thing I did with NAACP that looked like it might go somewhere. After I had been there a while, Johnnie [Carr] and I were interested in getting the youth organized. She had children, and so her children, of course, could be members. I didn't, but there were a few others, and we finally got a youth council started and received a charter from the NAACP national office, but after her children grew up, and the other children found other interests and finished school and married, we lost the charter because we didn't keep the membership up. That is, it just became inactive. But finally after a couple of years—I guess in about 1954—somebody got another group of youngsters interested in joining and we reactivated the charter. One of the things I did like about the second organization of young people in the Youth Council was that they started right in to write letters to

Washington. The older people in their meetings would argue points and discuss how motions are put, or whether somebody had made the right motion or worded it right [*laughing*], so that is as far as we got at times. But the young people, as soon as their meeting was adjourned, would have a letter-writing session to the senators and representatives in Washington. I can recall a reply Alabama Senator John Sparkman sent. He wrote back something like, "Of course there will never be any desegregation. There will always be segregation of the races. I will never be for any change in that." [*Laughing*] I was sorry I didn't save that letter.

Some of the young people would actively challenge the racial segregation. For instance, they would request books from the library. There was one main public library near downtown, and on the west side of town, a residential house had been set up as a branch library for colored. They would go to the main library to request a book, and they were always told that they couldn't get it there, but on a certain date, they could go crosstown to the colored library and pick it up. [*Laugh*] And the young people were, of course, saying things like, "Well, I need it right now, and I feel that I should have it," but they never did make any case of it. Then some of the young boys would tell me in the meeting, "Miss Parks, I sat in the front of the bus last night, and the driver didn't say anything." But I guess the reason the driver didn't say anything was he didn't know what these youngsters would do. I always asked them if they felt like what we wanted to do was to do what we could to break down racial segregation. Then I'd tell them that if they found themselves running into an arrest, make certain that they knew how to conduct themselves in a way that they couldn't be accused of disorderly conduct or resisting arrest. So they were pretty active, but there still wasn't much progress.

For me, personally, the first little bit of encouragement came with the United States Supreme Court decision of 1954 to outlaw racial segregation in the public schools. I felt enough encouragement that hopefully the young people would have an opportunity to have an equal education. That was the very first time that I can think of seeing some hope. At least there was a federal law now.

In the summer of 1955, they were having a workshop at Highlander on public school desegregation, and the principal of Oak Ridge (Tennessee) High School was at Highlander, and several other people who were interested in implementing the decision. And Oak Ridge, I believe, was the first school in the South to move toward desegregation because it was on federal government property and they could not afford to continue racial segregation. As far as I remember, the principal didn't seem to know exactly how he was gonna cope with it there! [*Laughing*] That was the first workshop like that in the South. It was in July. That's when I first met Septima Clark; in fact, when I first met everybody at Highlander. [*Laughing*] They raised some money in the community for my transportation to get there, and I wasn't even aware of what it was like until I came. I had heard there was such a place, but I hadn't been there.

MYLES HORTON: My impression is that neither Septima nor Rosa or anybody really thought of Highlander as being a place where we were violating the law and a place of civil disobedience. They just thought of Highlander as a place where people were decent.

ROSA PARKS: Oh, yeah, and could just enjoy the relaxing atmosphere without having to have color lines drawn anywhere. I remember that statement you gave the press when they wanted to know, how did you get white and black people to eat together? You told them you just put the food on the table and rang the dinner bell and that was it! [*Laughing*]

ELIOT WIGGINTON: It's amazing to think now, in 1981, about the fact that with that simple gesture of having blacks and whites eating together, you were breaking the law.

M.H.: Well, it's true. Although we weren't encouraging the black people we worked with then to break laws themselves at home, but to work instead within the law for change, we had decided ourselves by 1932 that we were going to refuse to abide by a law we thought was immoral and take the consequences. I would write every incoming governor and say, "Highlander is violating a federal law, and a state law, and we're going to continue to violate that law. We think this is not only immoral, but unconstitutional. We wish you would use us as a test case." They never answered my letters. When you came to Highlander, Rosa, it was the one place in the South that was openly, proudly violating an evil law. I've always been curious. Were you aware of that when you came to Highlander?

R.P.:   I wasn't aware of anything that Highlander was about at all the first time I came.

E.W.:   After that first meeting you attended, then you went back to Montgomery and continued your volunteer work with NAACP?

R.P.:   Right. In March of 1955 is when Claudette Colvin was arrested, and I was doing some work with that. I typed some letters regarding the incident. And then she joined the Youth Council too. She was just fifteen at the time. We also formed a committee to call on the officials regarding that incident because they brought more than one charge against her. Instead of just charging her with violating the segregation laws, they charged her with disorderly conduct, resisting arrest, and assault and battery. There were three policemen who put her in handcuffs and took her off the bus. Then Mary Louise Smith was arrested in October, and then I was the third person arrested [for a bus violation] in Montgomery on December 1, 1955.

But none of this had been planned in advance. No one had planned for them to get arrested, just like no one had planned for *me* to get arrested, including myself. [*Laughing*]

M.H.:   Well, it was a supreme act of civil disobedience, which is a great American tradition of ours which gets lost when people don't realize that most of the changes that happen have happened because people have been willing to violate unjust laws. That's why I'm stressing this point. But were you thinking about that when you decided you weren't going to get up?

R.P.:   Well, first of all, at the time when I refused to move from this seat and stand up, I didn't feel that I was breaking any law, because the ordinances, as far as I could recall, didn't say a driver had the right to make a person who was already seated leave a seat and stand. They could rearrange the seating in order to maintain segregation, but in my incident, when I was ordered by the driver to leave my seat, there was nothing I could do but either stand up and get off of the bus, or stand up over this same seat that I had vacated, because there was nowhere even to move. The back of the bus was already crowded with passengers. People were standing in the aisle up to where I was sitting. So I didn't feel I was even violating the segregation law. The only thing I did was just refuse to obey the driver when he said, "Stand up." See, there were four black people involved: a man in the seat with me who was next to the window, myself, and two women in the seat across the aisle. So that meant four of us would have to stand for one white person to occupy that row of seats. That would leave three vacancies, unless another white person got on, because the white man we were supposed to clear that section for was the only white person standing. When he got on, I had already been in my seat through two stops. The other people in my row got up, but I just didn't see there was anything there that I should obey. There was this very popular phrase saying, "In order to stay out of trouble, you have to stay in your place." [Obey everything the whites say, and] that way you won't get your feelings hurt. You won't be insulted. But when you did that, you were *still* insulted and mistreated if they saw fit to do so. About twelve years before this, about 1942, this same driver had evicted me from his bus for refusing to hand him my fare and then get off of the bus and go around and try to find my way back in the bus by the rear door. Because I refused to do that, he evicted me from the bus. He didn't call the policemen that time. He just told me I couldn't ride his bus. I told him I was already on the bus, and I didn't see any need of getting off and going around to the back door to try to get in, but that was one of the things he demanded. It was the very same driver, because I never did forget his face from that time on. I don't *think* he remembered me at the time I was arrested. It just happened to be that he felt like he wanted to throw his weight around or exercise his power beyond just enforcing the segregation law. Now, all drivers did not go this far. There were times when I'd be on the bus and if what they called the "white section" or the "white reserved seats" were occupied and any white people were standing, they would just stand. But this one, I suppose he just didn't want to see a white person stand as long as there were any available seats he could get black people out of.

He wasn't the only driver I had problems with, but the other times, it just didn't create the kind of incident where they'd get off the bus and call the police and have you arrested and taken to jail. There was another driver who told me to get off the bus after I paid my fare and board from the rear, and when I told him I didn't want to, he said, "If you think you're too important to go to the back door, don't ride my bus." And so from then on I never did ride the bus that he was driving unless I just happened to get on with a group, and then he wouldn't say a thing about it. But if I was alone and he saw me about to board, he would shut the bus door very quickly and drive on.

E.W.:   After you got arrested, it seems as though you were used as a magnet to pull people together.

R.P.:   Well, after I was arrested, people just pulled themselves together on the first day of the protest, which was December 5, the day of my trial. They just decided themselves that they wouldn't ride the bus that day, but the first day of protest was so successful they kept it going. That is when they had their big mass meeting at the Holt Street Baptist Church. Dr. King was speaking. Many people spoke: Abernathy, King, Mr. Nixon. I think everyone on the pulpit spoke except me.

E.W.:   You'd already said your piece.

R.P.:   That's what they said! [*Laughing*] I didn't have any remarks.

E.W.:   But you were like the rallying cry almost. I was just wondering how it felt to be in that kind of a situation, to be flapped back and forth on the end of a flagpole. [*Laughter*]

R.P.:   I didn't have any feelings about it so long as people had come alive and awake to the realization that they had to take direct action in order to get some results.

After the boycott started, I myself really became less active, in a way. I didn't continue as secretary of the NAACP, in order to not say or have it said that the bus protest was organized by "outside agitators," and organizations from the North. In fact, the NAACP was completely outlawed, and we couldn't even meet under the name of NAACP for quite a while. I remember thinking before the bus boycott that we had a fairly growing branch of NAACP. In 1955 I believe we had somewhere around four hundred members, and we thought we were sort of moving along then. [*Chuckle*] But after the boycott started, there was one meeting when Congressman Charles Diggs spoke where there were more than a thousand new memberships paid at this *one* meeting. Memberships were coming in after this bus incident faster than they could handle them. So what the state of Alabama did was to declare the NAACP an illegal organization and outlaw it. But the people did remain together anyway. In Montgomery they formed the Montgomery Improvement Association, which was organized on the date of my trial. In Birmingham, they started the Alabama Christian Movement for Human Rights with the Reverend [Fred] Shuttlesworth. Then there was the Tuskegee Civic Association in Tuskegee. People just set up local organizations to keep the movement going in spite of the fact that they had declared the NAACP activities illegal in the state of Alabama. So then we were together for the first time.

e.w.: What ought to be going on now, today?

r.p.: I think individuals can make up their own minds on what they can do to solve or help solve whatever problems are confronting them. It's very difficult for me to tell somebody else what they ought to do. I feel like each person should think and be aware of and learn as much as they can about what has occurred and the results, and realize that whatever is going on did not just begin with them. That's what I would say to young people. There's no such thing as "having it made." By the time you make some gains or feel like you're accomplishing something or making a breakthrough, there are always forces at work to destroy what gains have been made, and if you rest and relax and think, "We're going to enjoy a good time because we no longer have that type of oppression," or take too much time out to just sit down and not do anything, those gains will soon be reversed. So I think everybody should be involved if they want to see better opportunities. I don't think anybody should be eliminated from doing what they can to bring about whatever is necessary for full and complete freedom.

★

"Finding Your Way Back Home"
Septima Clark
and Bernice Robinson

When Septima Clark returned in 1947 to Charleston, South Carolina, her work with the YWCA unwittingly led to workshops at Highlander. And from these Monteagle gatherings, she and Rosa Parks and Esau Jenkins, among others, returned to their home communities across the South with a new impetus: Citizens must first understand their rights in order to exercise them.

Almost immediately, other daring and remarkable events followed the example of the 1955 bus boycott in Montgomery—including Clark's Citizenship Schools. But these new defiances against unjust systems were different because these activists "educated themselves." They learned their rights and determined how to work the system of segregation to integration's advantage. In the process, they exposed segregation for what it was; and that exposure to the nation simultaneously revealed both the integrity of the oppressed and the indefensible stances of their oppressors.

But in effecting this exposure, black leaders also set an example. They affirmed for the nation as a whole that constitutional rights possess meaning only when each citizen knows about, understands, and is willing to act in defense of these rights whenever they are jeopardized. The way Septima Clark did.

. . . [In 1947] I was asked to be chairman of a health committee for the public health people. We were working on venereal diseases, and on getting the children on the islands immunized for diphtheria.

The next year, 1948, the National YWCA was establishing a committee for the interracial relationships of the Y. It was one of the very few organizations actively trying to figure out ways for all races to work together. In Charleston, neither Jewish women nor black women could work as clerks in stores, and when some of the women in the Y began to visit the stores to talk about this problem, I became involved too.

That same year I invited Mrs. Waring, Judge J. Waties Waring's second wife, to speak to our annual meeting of the black branch of the YWCA. The women of the central branch, who were all white, hated her—despite the fact that she was white too—and they didn't want her to speak at all. It caused quite a controversy. . . .

Judge Waring had been married to a wealthy Charleston woman for thirty years. He eventually became a great friend of the blacks, however, and I think this first wife just couldn't go along with his change of heart, and so they were divorced. He didn't see how he could live with her after he had changed, given the fact that she refused to go along with any of his feelings on integration. I once heard him say that he went to bed one night thinking about all he had seen. He said, "I saw white men come into my courtroom, and I knew that they were bums, but they were considered gentlemen. And I saw well-dressed black men with good character come in, and they were all considered bums. And I didn't feel as if I could support that any longer." He said, "You know, a judge has to live with his conscience."

So he divorced his first wife, and later married a wealthy woman from the North who didn't have that much knowledge of the life of blacks, but who loved him and supported him. Then he became a great champion of our cause. It was Judge Waring, for example, who ruled that blacks should be allowed to vote in the primary elections—one of the most important decisions made in our behalf.

They were a very unpopular family with most of white Charleston. I don't know what the whites hated worst about them —the things they stood for, or the fact that the judge had married a Yankee. I think most everybody in Charleston felt that if he had gone next door and taken a Charlestonian, it might have been all right. [*Laughter*] But to take a Yankee woman! You know, that was all over the South. Everybody knew about it.

We certainly had some strange times. In January of 1968, when the judge was buried, there were two hundred blacks and about twelve whites at the funeral. A man who had done so much . . . In 1968, the whites were still that angry. He had even left a scholarship to the College of Charleston in his will to send a black boy to the college each year for four years. And when Mrs. Waring's body was buried in November, there weren't but nine of us at that funeral. . . . The hostility goes on, stays, and passes down into the young. But that's why the white women of the Y didn't want her to speak to the black branch. I think they were afraid that the controversy it would cause might undo much of the interracial cooperation they were trying to foster. And she was good at making the Charleston aristocracy squirm. Once she gave an integrated dinner and had *Collier's* magazine come in and take pictures!

Anyway, she spoke to our group. I sat with Mrs. Waring up on the stand, and the place was packed. She was real nervous. She thought somebody might shoot her through the window, there was so much controversy. But we had placed some men by the light switches so that if anybody came, I could get them to turn off the lights and get her out. And she gave her speech. She really went after the whites, and called them decadent and lowdown. My mother was there that night, and she got so nervous and upset she lost the use of her legs and we had to carry her out bodily after it was over. It was all too much even for her, with her courage.

Right after all that I was elected to the central board of the YWCA. [I was the first black on that board,] and we got some good things accomplished. We had been having some problems at the YWCA with boys coming over to use the phones and upsetting the girls. The woman in charge was afraid to tell them they couldn't come in. So some of us had a meeting with Mayor Wehman. We went in, and when he saw me, he sat down and turned his back to me. He didn't want to deal with a black woman at all. The white women felt terrible about it, but I didn't say a word. I just took ahold of a chair and sat down behind him at the table. I said to myself, "Whatever I have to say will penetrate his back." And sure enough, when we started talking I did get a chance to speak. I said to him, "The only reason why these boys are difficult around here is because the city has no place for boys to go. If you would provide a place for the boys, you wouldn't have this difficulty with the girls. I think you need to get a branch started of the YMCA for the boys." He thought about that, and it wasn't too long after that that he sent to New York to find a man to come and work with the boys. They got a little club started they called the Boys' Club, and from that they got a YMCA. . . .

One of our YWCA workers, Mrs. Anna Kelly, went to Washington to a childhood education meeting in 1952, and while there she met George Mitchell of the Southern Regional Council. She was wondering where blacks and whites could meet together to talk about some of the problems that we had, and he told her about the Highlander Folk School. She went the summer of '53 and while she was up there, since I was on vacation from teaching school, I volunteered to sit at her desk until she got back. When she came back she said, "It's a place where you don't have to spend a nickel! You go, and you eat, and they pay your way there and everything. And you meet Southern whites and Northern whites, Southern blacks and Northern blacks, all talking together." And, gee, that was so surprising.

So then she wanted me to go. The summer of '54, when the Supreme Court decision came through ruling racial segregation in public schools unconstitutional, I went up. And I found that what she said was true. I was really surprised to find out that a white woman would sleep in the same room that I slept in, or eat at the same table. We just didn't do that in Charleston.

After I came back, I wanted Myles to come down to Charleston and talk with the teachers and get them to believe in blacks and whites meeting together, and he did. Myles and Zilphia and Betty and Henry Shippard came down. The teachers were having a hard time getting bank loans so they could continue on to college and get their master's degrees, so they wanted a credit union. I set up a big meeting in one of the schools, and we laid the groundwork for that credit union, which still exists today. At the same time, we showed a movie about Highlander and its work. We even went over on the islands and talked with the people who were gathering cabbages at that time, and working in the cornfields and cotton fields. All that helped them believe that there were some whites who didn't mind talking to them and who were interested in them.

The principal was fired for letting us have that credit union meeting in one of the public schools because we were talking about blacks and whites meeting and working together, but at least we opened the door.

The next summer I got ahold of my sister's old Chevrolet and made three separate trips to Highlander with people from Charleston and the islands. The first group I took up there knew that white people were going to be there, and they couldn't believe they were going to be able to eat there, so they cooked up a lot of chicken and stuff and carried it with them, just in case. Myles said, "Just let them get hungry and they'll come on down," but it took them until Wednesday to get up the nerve. After the workshop, they were so astounded that they managed to live through eating and sleeping with whites that they told the others on the islands and we had to make two more trips just so the others could see this thing and believe in it. We hadn't even started the Citizenship Schools yet. We were just getting them acquainted with sitting together and talking together and sleeping together and letting them know that there were some whites in the world who had a warm spot in their hearts for black people, and this was the type of thing that we did that summer.

Rosa Parks was at one of those workshops during 1955. She was very timid because she wasn't sure the whites were going to accept her, and she wouldn't talk at all in the workshop for two or three days—wouldn't tell at all about how hard it was in Montgomery. There was another person there from Montgomery—a black teacher—and she hadn't even told her people at home that she was going to Highlander for a workshop. She told them she was going some other place in Tennessee because she was afraid she might lose her job if anyone at home found out.

When they ended that workshop, Myles always did a thing called "Finding Your Way Back Home." He wanted to know what they were going to do when they got back. Esau Jenkins, who was there, says, "I want to teach my people, that's what I want to do. I want them to be able to vote, and I want them to make me one of the school board members." But Rosa wouldn't say what she expected to do, she just went on back home. She was nervous about riding on that Greyhound bus, and I had to go with her down to Atlanta where she had to change. She thought some of those bus people might know her and would be mean to her.

It was December of that same year she got arrested, and after that she couldn't make a living in Montgomery anymore. That's why she moved up North where she lives now.

The latter part of that summer of '55, Myles asked me if I would direct a workshop, which I did. It was with middle-class blacks from Chattanooga and Nashville and those places who didn't believe there was any such place as Highlander. We recruited about fifty of them through the YWCA and various churches, and we paid their way up there and back and took care of their food and everything. Even though they were middle-class, they still couldn't vote and they still had to go in the side door of the moving picture houses and sit in the balcony, and they still had to sit in the back of the bus.

But I wasn't able to accomplish anything with them. They didn't have to learn to read and write. They needed to learn how to work with other people, but I wasn't able to get them to do that. I don't know whether they were afraid to try to teach others, or if they had some highfalutin idea that poor people were so far beneath them that they wouldn't fool with them. Many middle-class blacks were extremely hostile and prejudiced one to the other. That's the way they were. And so going to Highlander with them, we had a hard time. We got them to see what conditions they were living under, but we couldn't get them to do any of the work in their community to help others to change. Couldn't get them to do that.

That's the one big reason why, when we started the Citizenship Schools, I felt it would be best not to try to use middle-class blacks as teachers. It would be better to use people from the community in which they lived who could just read well aloud and write legible, rather than trying to use the others. That's why we got Bernice [Robinson] to run the first school that we set up on Johns Island in 1957. She was the first teacher we had for the whole South and after we had a success with Bernice in that school, then we could get others. . . .

At the end of that summer, I went back to teaching. It was

during that school year that the law was passed by the state legislature that no city or state employee could be a member of the
NAACP. That meant none of the teachers could be members, and
there were 726 of us black teachers who were. And I said to myself,
"The KKK is an organization, and the White Citizens' Council is
an organization, and they can belong to those. Why can't I belong
to NAACP?" Then I thought, "If we just admit it, surely they can't
throw out all of us. There are too many." I got in touch with them
all, but only forty-two would admit to being members—eleven
from Charleston and thirty-one from the county. Twenty-six of us
met to plan to see the superintendent, and when the day came to
go see him, eleven showed up; and when it was the hour to go,
only five of us went. All forty-two who admitted being members
were dismissed, and I've never been able to teach in South Carolina since.

We had a three-judge court trial. The state had three lawyers,
and an NAACP lawyer from New York named Greenburg represented the teachers. The judge finally said, "We don't know all of
the facts, so we'll dismiss this court for thirty days so the lawyers
can bring us in new briefs." The next day the legislature was called
in, and they changed the wording from "No city or state employee
can be a member of the NAACP" to "List your affiliations." The
very next year, one of the teachers listed her affiliations, which
included NAACP, and she was dismissed too, but she didn't push
her case. If people listed NAACP, they were fired right on.

And we never heard any more from that case. The papers we
sent to the national office just caught dust. They claimed there
wasn't enough pressure from the state office. The head of the state
NAACP said they were busy integrating a golf course across here,
and he said when they got through with the golf course, they were
going to take up the teachers' case, but they never did get to it.
The same thing with the NEA. We had a local branch, and I was a
member and I went to Columbia, and they claimed that the national office said that they didn't have any push from the local,
nor from the state, and so their hands were tied. That's the way
they said it. But you know that's not true. That's just what they
said.

[I never went back to public school teaching.] That whole
thing was a real hardship to me—especially when only 42 of 726

teachers answered my letters. That was a real disappointment. So I decided to carry on the work in other ways. Myles offered me a job with Highlander, and I went. I didn't know how I was going to stay up there during their winters, but I did go. I had several other offers, but none of them sounded like what I wanted. One organization said that I would be good, but I would not be able to go out and make any speeches and I would have to be careful how I talked about integration. "Well," I said, "that's not the place for me." So I went to Highlander first as director of workshops and then as director of education.

In 1957, the first Citizenship School opened. Myles and I had been to an NEA meeting in Cincinnati, and on the way back on the plane, we started talking about how to set up the first school. That night, back at Highlander, I sat down and started writing out "Education for Citizenship." Alice Cobb was there, and when I'd finish a piece, Alice would type it and then Myles would come in and we'd consider it. Finally it was finished, and the question was, "Where are we going to start?" I said, "If we don't have one little success, we won't be any good." That's when we decided on Johns Island. We got Bernice as the first teacher, and we found a building. It was an old abandoned schoolhouse—a three-room thing—and it was run way down. We asked the county board about buying it, but they sold it to a white man for a thousand dollars. Wouldn't sell it to us. It wasn't hardly a week after that when that white man sold it to Esau for fifteen hundred dollars.

The two back rooms were the ones that we taught in and we purposely took those two back rooms to keep people from looking in from the road and seeing what we were doing. It took a whole lot of chicanery to get that work done on the island.

Esau had a bus, so we had a bus that could go around and pick the adults up in the nights and bring them to the school. People who had babies and little children they couldn't leave brought them and we put them down on pallets on the floor. The big girls that came along to help with those babies, we taught them how to crochet.

We learned a lot with that first school. We soon found out that you don't tell people what to do. You let them tell you what they want done. Then you have to have in your mind certain things that you feel they need to do, and so you get their thoughts and wind your thoughts around them. Over on Johns Island, the people didn't have stores, and when Bernice went over there, they wanted to learn how to make out money orders and how to send out money orders and application blanks to mail-order houses. That's the way they got their things. And so the first thing she had to do was to get a blank money order. I had a nephew here working at the post office, and he got her some of those forms and had them [copied] and she taught from those. Those were the things they wanted. Later, we taught them how to read the election laws—used them for reading lessons—and the women taught the same things to the men. We also used the book that tells what taxes you pay in South Carolina, and what laws and rights you have in the state.

I had asked Myles not to come down to the islands when the schools were just getting started because I was worried the pupils might be frightened away by a white man being there. After our first success getting people registered to vote, and after several schools had been started, I read an article in the newspaper where a man was saying, "There are schools on those islands that not a single White Citizens' Council man knows about. What should we do about that? Those niggers are learning to read and write." I went right over there when I read that page, and I found a black fellow from one of the plantations standing on the porch of a store *reading* to the people, and the people didn't run. And I said, "Now this is good." And he made the statement, "Any time somebody wants to help you learn, you are going to find that you have criticism from these white overseers and these white planters." I said, "That's good; we've got it made." So I went then from one of those places to another where we had the schools, and I found out that the black people weren't afraid anymore.

Then I knew it was all right for people like Myles to come. I knew the idea had taken hold and couldn't be scared off. That's about the time the Marshall Field Foundation became convinced they should help us spread the idea through Highlander. [And I was arrested.]

We saw it coming. We had already been designated a communist outfit. Because blacks and whites were able to live together and to work together at Highlander, the people of the South had a feeling—in fact, it came out in the McCarthy era—that they were

bound to have been Communists. . . . And since we were working in violation of the segregation laws of Tennessee, Myles knew
that eventually they would close down the school.

In fact, he had already talked to Dr. King about taking the
Citizenship School program, and as soon as the state officers padlocked the Highlander doors, he started sending me down to Atlanta to begin working with Wyatt Tee Walker, who was Dr. King's
assistant at SCLC at the time. The same time Nixon was being
stoned with tomatoes and eggs in South America, they had my
picture in the paper for being arrested in Tennessee.

*By the early fifties, Bernice Robinson's involvement with the NAACP
had already turned her Charleston beauty shop into a political outpost.
And from there, she contributed solidly to the fight against segregation.*

*Then her aunt Septima took the ingenious beautician to Highlander
and thereafter encouraged her to focus beneath the hairdos and into the
minds of the black community in the Charleston area. The result? A natural teacher emerged. On Johns Island, Bernice Robinson's first lessons were
about everyday skills, but her ultimate goal for these students was full
citizenship.*

In 1951 or '52, Joe Brown took over the NAACP, and that's
when we really started making something out of the Charleston
branch. We raised the membership from three hundred to way
over a thousand. It got to the point where we were working so
hard getting people to register to vote that I would leave people
under the dryer to take others down to the registration office to
get them registered. [*Laughing*] I would say, "If you get too hot
under there, just cut her off and come out!" I had good customers. They would call and they would say, "Do you think that you
would have time to do my hair today?" [*Laughing*] And I didn't
have to worry about losing my job or anything because I wasn't a
schoolteacher or a caseworker with the Department of Social Services or connected with anything I might be fired from. I had my
own business, supplied by black supply houses, so I didn't have to
worry. Many people did. I used to encourage my customers to join
the NAACP, and there were many of them that were teachers and
nurses and that sort of thing who would have their membership
cards come to my house so that their mailman, who often was

white, would not even see any literature or anything coming to them from the NAACP. They had to be very careful. That was one of the reasons Septima lost her job as a teacher. She was so active in all these things that they just came right down on her. That's the way it was all over the South. The whites would chop you down in a minute if you were dependent on any of them for your job. We had a man, named L. A. Blackman, who was a black contractor, and he lost just about everything dealing with NAACP. He used to do all this work for white people, you know, and they refused to give him any more work. Although he was his own boss, they cut back on him like anything. He had a rough time of it. He is the guy that went to a Ku Klux Klan rally, and they were talking about him, and he stood up in his pickup truck and said, "Here I am. If you want to do anything to me, I'm here. You don't have to look for me."

Then there was Reverend Parker who was moved out of South Carolina because of his participation in the NAACP. He wound up heading a church in a little subdivision out of Detroit.

The NAACP was important for me, though, because through it I began to make contacts with people in other parts of the South, and I began to find out what was happening with blacks in other areas. We'd have state conferences, which meant that you would meet people from all over the state who were involved in NAACP, and then we'd have regional conferences, where people from all over the South would come together, and we'd have national conferences. At all these conferences we'd have workshops on things like how to organize people, or how to get people to register, or how to encourage our young people to stay in school and get an education since they'd have to be three times as good as a white guy to get a job.

Then we always had great speakers like Bayard Rustin or A. Philip Randolph or Walter White or Roy Wilkins or Whitney Young. I remember, particularly, in 1957 in Detroit, we had Hubert Humphrey. He was *exceptionally* good and his encouragement was for us to move on into politics and to fight to get to become elected politicians so that we could get in on the policy-making. He was dynamic. He took a chance then. It wasn't an easy thing for him to come and speak to an NAACP convention in 1957.

ELIOT WIGGINTON: So as early as 1947, you were pretty heavily involved in NAACP and voter registration; and by the early fifties, your beauty shop was a center for all sorts of subversive activity. [*Laughing*] You were making contacts all over the region. Esau Jenkins was helping the workers on his bus memorize a piece of the Constitution so they could fool the white registrars and get registered to vote. All kinds of craziness was already going on, but on top of all that, you also decided to take on the Citizenship Schools. Right? How did all that happen?

BERNICE ROBINSON: . . . In 1955, [Septima] asked me to go to Highlander with her. I have often wondered why she asked me. I guess partly because we're kin to each other. Her mother and my mother were sisters. And, of course, Septima was also on the board of the Executive Committee of the NAACP, and at that time, I was secretary and membership chairman. So we did have close contact. Anyway, Septima said, "I want you to go to a workshop with me in Tennessee," and she told me what week.

I said, "Well, you know, the week before that I'm going to be in Mission School at Camden, so I have to close my shop that week. If I go with you, that means I'll have to close the shop *again.*" [*Laughs*] I was the only one operating my shop so there wasn't any money coming in when I wasn't there.

She said, "Well, it won't cost you anything. I will take care of the expenses and all." Well, she convinced me that I should come. She also convinced Esau [Jenkins] to come with us. He had never been to Highlander either.

The workshop we went to was a United Nations workshop run by a man named Auram Mezrick. Rosa Parks was at that workshop. She was an Alabamian. And some people from Columbia, South Carolina, were there. There was a cross section of people from all over the South. And you know who else was there? Mrs. Lamont. She was my roommate. I never will forget that because I had no idea that she was a millionaire. [*Laughs*] A rich, white woman, you know. That's the way we met at Highlander. You're Sue, I'm Bernice, you're Eliot. I don't know that you teach school. I don't know what degree you've got. You don't know whether I've got one or not. This is the way we came together at Highlander. That was Highlander's success, really, because nobody was intimidated by anybody else. You never knew what another person was really doing unless you just got in a personal conversation. I might say, "Well, what do you do, Eliot?" You know. Or you might say, "Well, what do you do, Bernice?" But it was real funny. Mrs. Lamont wore these shorts, and every morning she got up real early with these shorts and these rusty shoes and went walking around, you know, taking her exercise that way. And we got very close talking back and forth. I didn't know she had any money. I didn't know anything about her. But we became friends and we kept in touch for years.

Anyhow, we talked about the United Nations all that week and what they did, and we looked at all the films of the World Health Organization. At the end of the workshop, they asked us what could we do to promote the United Nations in our particular communities when we went back. Esau Jenkins said, "Well, I don't know about the promoting of the United Nations, but I'll tell you what I'm interested in," and then he started in. "I need to get my people registered to vote. They got to read a part of the Constitution and they don't know how to read and I'd like a school set up." He went on to tell them how he was trying to teach them in the bus going back and forth to work. "Some people memorizes it," he said, "but that ain't gonna work at all with everybody." Then he gave the story about Mrs. [Alice] Wine and how she memorized it so well that when she was standing in line to get registered, and people ahead of her would miss a word, she would tell them what it was. When she got up to the counter, they didn't even bother to make her read. They just figured she knew it so well, there wasn't any need. They just went on and gave her hers. [*Laughing*] That woman wouldn't have known one word if they'd switched the words on her. She wouldn't have known a thing! Then Esau said, "This is not going to happen with everybody, and it's important for us to get our people registered. I need a school. I need somebody to help me. Tell me *how* I can get a school going to teach my people."

Well, you know, it's like you say, blacks and whites just accepted a lot of things as a way of life. I knew that there was a lot of illiteracy all around me, but I accepted that as a fact. That was gonna be there, you know, and there was nothing anybody could do about it. But when Esau started talking, I thought, "Yeah, that *is* something to think about. People can't read." He turned the whole workshop around. [*Laughs*] Everybody became interested in this, and that's all we talked about the last couple of days. What are we going to do about this situation on Johns Island?

So Myles said, "Well, let me see if I can find some money for you to set up a school. You try to find a place and we'll see where we go from there."

Esau went back, and the first thing he did was run for school board. He lost, but there were three vacancies, and he came in fourth. He used that as a stepping-stone to tell people, "See, if you were registered to vote, I could have made it."

From that he started to look for a building. It was a hard thing to find a place. Our church had a community center on Johns Island that we were just certain we could use, but the minister that was in charge of the churches on the island was afraid, and he said we couldn't have anything like that going on in the center.

Sometime before all this, Esau and the people on the island had set up a little organization called the Progressive Club where they paid little dues and stuff to bail people out of jail when they were arrested for minor charges. They found this dilapidated old school building and came up with the idea of buying it if Myles could find a way for them to borrow the money and then repay it. They worked that out and they acquired the place.

By the time they got it all set up, it was the end of 1956. That's when they approached me about being the teacher. "You know," I said, "I never been no teacher and I'm not going to be a teacher. I told you up there at Highlander that I would help you all in any way that I could, and I would even help a teacher *with* the school, but I ain't no teacher!"

Well, they just laid the law down to me. "There is nobody else to do it. We don't want a certified teacher because they are accustomed to working by a straitlaced curriculum. They wouldn't be able to bend, to give. We need a community worker to do it who cares for the people, who understands the people, who can communicate with the people, and someone who has been to Highlander who knows Highlander's philosophy, so there's nobody to do it but you. Either you do it or we don't have the school. You know a program is needed. You know there is no way you can get out of it at this point." [*Laughing*]

So I said, "Okay."

It was a pretty big job, but the thing that made it a little bit easier was that we could only have classes three months out of the year since December, January, and February were the only months the people weren't planting and digging in the fields. That was what they called their "laying by" season, and that was the only time you could have classes because the other months they worked in the fields until dark and they'd be too tired to come. Well, it was already December, so that meant the first school could only run for two months—January and February of 1957. Then we could start up again in December.

Another thing that made it a little easier was that we decided, for the first school, to meet only two nights a week from seven o'clock to nine. But even so, I was working in the beauty shop, and my mother was ill too, to the point where I couldn't—wouldn't—leave her alone at night. So I had to get somebody to sit with her. On school nights, it meant that I cut short my work in the beauty shop in order to finish up, get my mother a light supper, get myself together, and get one of my brothers to drive me over there by seven o'clock. My sewing and stuff I would have to do the nights that I wasn't over there, and the nights I wasn't over there I was trying to plan some lessons to see where I could reach them.

And then I had to do all the recruiting. I went around to all the churches to explain what the adults who came would learn how to do, and to tell them that the school would be free, and all that. Luckily, I had been to NAACP meetings on the island and various workshops, so I really knew the people. I also knew that many of them had enrolled in public school adult classes every year and that they'd start filtering out in about a month and the classes would have to close because they didn't fill these people's needs—so I knew this first school would have to be different. I didn't really know exactly *how,* and I didn't really know where I was going with it because I had nobody to show me anything about how to teach a school, and so I was quite nervous. In fact, that first night I guess I was *more* nervous than the people. They came in that night and I told them, "I'm not going to be the teacher. We're going to learn together. You're going to teach me some things, and maybe there are a few things I might be able to teach you, but I don't consider myself a teacher. I just feel that I'm here to learn with you. We'll learn things together." I think that sorta settled the folks down, you know?

I started them out with some materials I brought that two of my sisters-in-law who taught elementary school used to teach kids how to read and write. But then something hit me while I was talking, and I realized then that I had no kind of materials to deal with *adults*. I would *have* to put them on a different level. So then I asked them what *they* would like to learn. They told me that they wanted to read a newspaper, they wanted to read the Bible, they wanted to know how to fill out an application blank you had to fill out at that time to get a money order so they could order things by catalog. They didn't understand those things. I just made notes of all the things they said they wanted to learn, and I just threw out the material I had brought with me because it was too juvenile. I just had to reach them on their level.

We got along well after that. I was able to get a book out of the post office that had real money orders and forms in it. Let's not put in print how I got it [*laughing*], but that book had to be back in the post office by seven o'clock the next morning, so I worked all night on that one night tracing those forms off on onionskin paper. Then I'd copy them up on the blackboard and teach them how to fill them in.

Then I used newspaper ads like the specials from the grocery store as arithmetic. "If two pounds of beans are forty-nine cents, and you want four pounds of beans, how much will it be?" That sort of thing. Lots of this produce they were growing themselves, so it was meeting them where they were. For the men, I used problems like, "How many gallons of gas would it take you to go from here to Charleston?" If they wanted to measure to put up a fence, we'd work out the math for that.

They also opened up a little co-op store in the front of the building, and the same Alice Wine that memorized that piece of the Constitution worked the store, and she had problems counting out change. She used to have to count on her fingers. So I used toothpicks and matchsticks and tutored her with subtraction until she got to the place where she could count without those sticks, and she worked beautifully in the store after that. Another guy was interested in learning how to drive and he brought the driver's manual to the class. I used all that *trying* to meet them where they were, and they were a very enthusiastic group. The parents had to bring their teenage kids with them because they weren't going to leave them at home when they came to class, and I had to do something with them, so I taught them how to crochet and how to sew.

Then I worked with them on public speaking. Myles was always sending down boxes of materials, thinking that maybe there would be some that I could use in the class. Here comes this box of material on public speaking and on how you should stand and everything. I looked at this material and I said, "Well, I can't use this with my adults." Then I thought, *"Ahhhhh,* those young people! They have been snickering when some of the older ones try to read and they miss a word. I'm going to turn the tables on them. I'm going to have them read this little exercise through and study how to present themselves as public speakers, and then I'm going to give them each a little thing to read and have them stand up before the class and give a little talk." I did that with them. We had a good time with those young people. Some of them would get up there and put their hands in front of their mouths, and they would swing from side to side, and they would finger with their hair, and we would just laugh at them and kid them and say, "See how it feels now when you're not doing something right? You don't want nobody to laugh at you, so let's not laugh at the others." At the same time, I got them out of that habit of twisting and turning and putting their hands over their mouths and fingering with their hair. I'd say, "People can't hear what you're saying" or "People are attracted to what you are doing and they're not listening to what you're saying." I worked with them and they enjoyed it. It was something else I could offer to the younger people that made it a little more interesting. They would also read stories about people like Mrs. Roosevelt that the older ones couldn't read yet, and then give the whole group a synopsis.

I became so involved with those people that nothing else really mattered. Just to see a sixty-five-year-old woman finally recognize her name meant something to me. It really meant something. I can never explain or express how I felt when I put the names of all the students up on the board and I said to this sixty-five-year-old woman, "Now, can you find your name up there on that board?"

"Yes, ma'am, I sure can." She took the ruler out of my hand.

"That's my name there, Annie, A-n-n-i-e; and that's my other name down there, Vastine, V-a-s-t-i-n-e." I had goose pimples all over me. That woman could not read or write when she came in that class.

But, like I said, they presented me with what they wanted to learn and I taught them that, and we really had a good time with it. That same curriculum went *all* the way through the Citizenship Schools.

At the end of five months, all fourteen of the pupils that I started with had received their registration certificates, they could read and write their own names, and they could do arithmetic.

After that, it just grew like crazy. People started registering on the island as an outgrowth of the class. When students got their registration certificates, they would be at school ahead of me, and as soon as I walked in the door, they were waving them in my face. *"I got it! I got it!"* And their enthusiasm bubbled on out into the community to people they knew who could go and register who hadn't before. Everybody wanted to know, "What's happening? Why are the Johns Island people getting registered so fast?"

So then they wanted a class down on Wadmalaw Island. The class on Wadmalaw started at the end of '58, and it was run by Esau's daughter, Ethel, and one of her in-laws named Miss Grimble, who could teach sewing. We had taken both of them to Highlander by then, so they opened the second school.

Then Edisto Island wanted a class. Then another one opened in Marylee Davis' beauty shop in north Charleston. Pretty soon they needed a supervisor, and so *every* night I was gone then, recruiting teachers to be trained at Highlander, taking them to Highlander for workshops, opening new schools, supervising old ones. It was really a busy time. That's when Maxwell Hahn came down from the Field Foundation and ran around with me and Esau for a week going to the various classes. Myles had warned me about him. He said, "Don't pay any attention to how he looks because he wears a stony face and you will never know whether he approves or disapproves of anything." On the last night, Septima and Esau and all of us were out there at an oyster roast on Johns Island, and when Maxwell Hahn was getting ready to leave, he came and put his arms around me and said, "Bernice, you are doing a *beautiful* job." A good thing he had his arms around me, because I would have fallen. Shortly after that, the Field Foundation funded the staff salaries, materials, and everything for the Citizenship Schools, and they funded them for about ten years— right on through 1970 or '71.

For the continuation of Septima Clark's interview, see Chapter Five (page 302). Bernice Robinson's interview is continued in this chapter (page 264).

Watching the Unions Bow Down to Pressures

Ralph Helstein
and Lucille Thornburgh

Though McCarthy's actions were condemned by his Senate colleagues, Mc-Carthyism took on a life of its own. Across America, many union organizers and civil rights leaders alike were branded as "Communists" in unabashed efforts to turn back the cultural clock. Ralph Helstein, then president of the Packinghouse Workers Union of America, recalls how such pressures specifically affected Myles Horton and Highlander as well as Dr. Martin Luther King, Jr., and the Southern Christian Leadership Conference.

After I had known Myles a long time, we got Myles to agree to take over our educational programs, and he became the educational director of the Packinghouse Workers Union at a time when we must have had close to two hundred thousand members. The purpose of the job was to carry on educational programs that would make the members more meaningful union members and people and citizens—help make people aware of what their problems are and make them want to do something about them.

He did that until it shook things up too much politically for some of the directors and they began complaining like hell. I said to Myles, "Go right ahead. So let them complain."

And he said, "Well, look, it's going to get you into trouble."

And I said, "That kind of trouble I can take care of. It's not that serious."

Well, he felt it was for him. What happened was, they made it harder and harder for him to work. He wasn't really able to do the things that he had said he wanted to do in the union.

We went through all kinds of situations together. At one time Myles was ostracized by the CIO because they felt he was too radical. I must say in this connection, Paul Christopher, who was the CIO director for Tennessee, stood by Highlander and remained on the board of Highlander, even though it took great courage. He was under tremendous pressure to get off of it, but he stuck with it. That was when we increased our support of Highlander. We used to contribute more money and get more of our people going there; but we did that because Highlander and Myles represented the same things that we believed in. We knew he wasn't a Communist. It was perfectly *ridiculous* to call someone who was as independent as Myles a Communist, just as he realized that it was ridiculous to call us Communists. The end result was that we had this community of feeling that transcended the ordinary relationships.

I was at the twenty-fifth anniversary party [in 1957], for example, when Martin Luther King, Jr., spoke. That's when that guy [Marvin] Griffin, the governor of Georgia, put out those photographs taken at the celebration saying that King was affiliated with a communist training school and all that stuff. One of the photographs was supposed to have me in it—that's what the caption said—it was a complete lie. In a hearing before the Illinois Senate for confirmation as a gubernatorial appointee to the Illinois Civil Rights Commission, I had the great satisfaction of refuting it. I knew I wasn't going to be confirmed anyway. It was perfectly clear they were going to dump me.

But I see this guy—this little cheap tinhorn McCarthy kind of character—sitting there with that paper Griffin put out with those photographs in it, and I said to him, "I see you've got a document there that looks familiar. Would you pass it down?" I knew that he wasn't going to let it out of his hand. So I said, "Well, don't bother, I'll come get it." This was one of those amphitheater kind of arrangements and he was sitting at the top row, and I simply got up from my witness chair at the very bottom and I walked up and I took it out of his hand before he knew what was happening. And I said, "Oh, yeah, sure, that's the thing that this jerk Griffin put out;

you know, the man who said he was governor of Georgia. Maybe he is, but I don't think you would have voted for him."

And I said, "You were going to ask me about this picture, weren't you?"

He said, "Well, I-I-I-I had been given this." This was a very cool customer and all, but this was something he couldn't deal with and he began stammering around.

I said, "Come on now, tell me and tell your colleagues you were going to ask me about this and if I hadn't come up here you would have done it and you would have made something out of it —or tried to. Is that my picture? Look at it."

So he said, "Well, I didn't think it looked like you."

And I said, "Don't tell me you didn't think it looked like me. You *know* it doesn't look like me. You *know* that's not my picture, don't you?"

He said, "Yeah, well, I—it isn't your picture; I agree that it's mistaken."

I said, "Pass it around and show it to the rest of your colleagues and show them the kind of stuff you were going to use in order to further your aims. I think you ought to expose yourself so that people understand where you're coming from."

And so I started passing this around to the other legislators on the Senate Committee. He just sat there nonplussed. It didn't do any good; they didn't approve me. I knew they weren't going to anyway.

But this thing followed me around the country. Every place we had an election, that paper showed up and they'd say, "This is a communist union. Look, there's a picture of the president of the union along with Abner Smith," or whatever his name was, who was supposed to be a Communist from New York.

But there was no way of answering it unless you were confronted with it and had the chance to do what I did with this character in the Illinois Senate. There was no way of answering it. How do you answer the goddamn thing?

But that's the kind of cheap stuff that went on. At any rate, I did meet Martin at that anniversary party and we became very good friends. In fact, Martin Luther King organized the Southern Christian Leadership Conference [in 1957] with seed money that he got from the Packinghouse Workers. He didn't have any money. We gave him a check publicly at the Morrison Hotel in a meeting with hundreds of people present for eleven thousand dollars to use to organize the Southern Christian Leadership Conference.

Then I was on his research committee, and we used to meet monthly with him in New York to discuss strategy and tactics. Andy Young and I used to have some problems, because Andy, I felt, lived in an unreal world during that period. Andy used to say, "All we have to do is go out and preach." This was when they were coming to Chicago. And I kept saying to him, "Look Andy, Dick Daley is not Sheriff Jim Clark. He isn't going to hit you over the head. He isn't going to commit any violence on you. He's just going to embrace you, and when he embraces you, he's going to choke you to death. Now there is no answer to this but careful organization."

And Andy kept arguing with me, "All you got to do is to go out and preach," and I'd say to him, "Preaching isn't going to do it in Chicago. Preaching might do it in Birmingham; might do it in Georgia; might do it in other places; but in Chicago, you better organize those blacks." And I told Martin after the first couple of marches that Rachel and my daughters went on, and he came back and they told me that over half the marchers were white, I said, "You better find a way out of this, because it can't work. If you can't get blacks organized and out, the whites alone can't carry it and they aren't going to because there aren't enough of them that want to."

But anyway, that's how Myles and I got so close. When my wife gave me a birthday party for my seventieth birthday, who came up from Tennessee to attend it but Myles! [*Laughter*] And you know, it was just right; that's the way it should have been. That was just right in the same way that it was just right that Myles came right here to my house in Chicago to prepare his statement when he had been subpoenaed to appear before that Senate Internal Security Committee of Eastland's. It was written right upstairs with the help of Gene Cotton, our lawyer, who was a close friend of Cliff Durr's. Myles made it clear, "By God, I'm gonna take that First Amendment and they can go to hell. I'm not gonna tell them nothing. I'm gonna tell them whatever they want to know about me, but not about anything else."

I'm saying, "Go ahead."

But I'll show you the table upstairs where that was written.

But there are very few things that go on in the world of real concern that Myles and I didn't agree on as to the solution. And I say that without even having to ask him. We were always on the same side of all issues.

As a union organizer, Lucille Thornburgh saw firsthand how the threat of being labeled a Communist affected not only her union job but also her status in the community. By 1958, she would be forced to choose between affiliation with Highlander and her pensioned position with the union. In a sense, that choice was a harbinger of Highlander's prospects as well.

. . . After the merger of the AFL and the CIO in 1956 we began getting more women delegates in the Central Labor Council, but even then they could only serve as secretary or treasurer, never president. The only reason was that the president had always been a man. That central body was formed in 1888 and to this day they still have not had a woman president. It's only in the last two years that the AFL-CIO has had a woman on the national executive board.

All the time I worked for the *Labor News,* I stayed active in organizing and assisting the small local unions with whatever had to be done: typing contracts, distributing leaflets, picketing, etc. In 1958 when the ILGWU put on an organizing drive at Standard Knitting Mills, I wrote and directed a weekly fifteen-minute television program during prime time. We held mock elections, sang union songs, and urged the workers to join the organizing drive. However, we lost the election and the Standard is still nonunion.

We didn't have copying machines at the labor temple and I would type as many as a hundred copies of a contract. Hard work. I was a notary public and notarized papers for all the people in the movement, and for many outsiders too, because I didn't charge the usual one dollar. . . .

Being a woman was an obstacle [as a union organizer]. The men organizers would make their contacts in the taverns, but in these small Southern towns, it was not socially acceptable for a woman to do so. The fact that they were buying six-packs at the grocery store and drinking at home was not a consideration. But I did eventually go to the taverns, and I think I paved the way for other women who said, "If she can do it, we can too."

Then once we got them into the union and got a contract signed taking care of the bread-and-butter issues, we could discuss political and community activities with them. The contract had to come first. It is useless to talk to a person about electing a friendly senator or serving on the board of a charitable agency when his wages are not adequate and his working conditions are bad. Even in the sixties when the civil rights movement was at its height, we didn't try to talk about integration until the basic issues were settled. You can't fight on all fronts at the same time. . . .

We would talk to the workers individually until we got enough of them together to hold a meeting. We would rent a motel room because we didn't want to jeopardize their jobs by meeting in a home. Hopefully, at this initial meeting we would sign up all those present, then we would have "inside organizers."

When we won an election, I stayed in town until they elected their officers and I had shown them how to conduct a meeting. Then I would call in a negotiator to help them draw up their contract and negotiate it with the employer. I was not a negotiator.

It was amazing how little some of these groups knew about handling their own affairs. They had never had an occasion to learn parliamentary law and these first meetings would sometimes turn into an unruly mass. I insisted on the officers studying *Robert's Rules of Order*. The president of one local union I visited made all the motions!

I remember one of our organizers telling me about a group of very low-paid workers he had organized. I asked him about their contract.

"Contract, hell," he said. "First I have to teach them to read." And he did just that, with blackboard and chalk at the labor temple. Today they have a good union. This situation was duplicated many times.

[But] we always had opposition. I know the modern-day organizers try to get the community on their side. I didn't even try. I knew the churches, businessmen, and the newspapers were against us and I didn't waste time trying to convince them otherwise. I spent my time with the workers. Our strongest opposition, of course, came from the employers. They would tell the workers that the first thing a union does is call a strike and they'd be out of a job. If that was not enough they would use the time-worn bit about moving the mill out of town.

In those days the church was our second biggest opposition. You can't make people do something they think is wrong and they were not going to join a union when the preachers were telling them it was sinful to join. So we had to combat that. Another thing we had to overcome was when we began organizing, some of the companies, to avoid the union, would give the workers a small pay increase, a decent rest room, a water fountain, and occasionally a paid holiday. Of course, after we gave up on a plant like this management would take back the benefits. Many workers got onto this and learned that being a "free rider" was not so free after all. Then we'd go back and organize the place.

And remember too, at that time all active union members and especially the organizers were accused of being Communists. I went to a home in Rome, Georgia, and the father of the girl I went to see met me at the door and told me in no uncertain terms, "We don't want no old Russian reds here. Git out." Being alone, I got! But before leaving I did tell him that I was not Russian, that I was born in Tennessee, and I was not red, I was white! Silly. Time wasted.

But we had to face this all the time. "We don't need no foreigners coming in here to get our people riled up" was another favorite saying. If I could get the women off to themselves I could usually convince them that I was not red nor Russian, just a hillbilly cotton mill hand who had come in to help them get better conditions.

Then we had people who said all unions were corrupt. Of course, the unions had isolated cases of embezzlement, but our opposition blew these cases all out of proportion. Our answer to this was that there were more bank officials in prison than there were union officials, and we had figures to prove it.

I never condoned corruption of any kind in the labor movement. I agreed with William Green, then AFL president, who told us, "Just because a bank official steals a million dollars from his depositors you [union officials] are not justified in stealing a three-cent postage stamp. The members have entrusted their hard-earned money with you and you should protect it." Green was not a strong, progressive leader, but he was strictly honest and did his utmost to make his whole organization honest.

We had many obstacles. Many times wives would discourage their husbands from joining for fear there would be a strike and their income would be cut off. My job was to convince these women that their family's income would be higher, through union wages, and even if they had to strike, they would be better off financially in the long run. I tried to organize auxiliaries. Sometimes I was successful, many times I was not.

At one time, I was assigned to organize office workers in Atlanta. An impossible job at that time. The employers had convinced them that as white-collar workers they were not in the class with carpenters, textile workers, etc. I would point out the wage differential and ask them if they got a discount at the meat market because they were white-collar workers. I had been told years before that "no organizing is ever wasted." I thought whoever said that just hadn't tried to organize office workers in Atlanta. But I was wrong. Three years after I left Atlanta, a large insurance office that I had tried to organize did become unionized and today has a good contract. When their wages remained low and their working conditions didn't improve they remembered what I had told them. I had sown the seed!

. . . I learned about Highlander through Franz Daniel and Zilla Hawes, organizers for Amalgamated Clothing Workers who came to Knoxville to help with our strike. They were active at Highlander and, I think, helped set up the school at Monteagle. Later, Myles and Zilphia Horton came in to help with the organization of a shirt factory.

In 1958 I served on the Highlander board for a short period. My term was short-lived because I was working for the Central Labor Council and they neither endorsed nor supported Highlander. In fact, the council delegates generally felt about Highlander like the rest of the community did—"a communist school that catered to 'niggers.' " My job was in jeopardy and I had home responsibilities that would not permit me to lose it. Being blacklisted and an active union member, I didn't think I could easily find another job, so I resigned from the Highlander board.

I have always kept in touch with Highlander, both at Monteagle and in Knoxville. I attended workshops there and remember meeting Martin Luther King, Jr., there. Some of the international unions held workshops there but the top leadership of the AFL never endorsed Highlander. To me, this was sad. At Highlander they had a golden opportunity to send members for leadership training, and goodness knows we needed trained leaders, but they passed it up. Even though I could not be as active at Highlander as I would have liked to have been, it was always comforting to know the school was there—the one bright, liberal light in East Tennessee!

And the People Bought It, "Hook, Line, and Sinker"

Bernice Robinson
and May Justus

Bernice Robinson was at Highlander in July 1959 when Tennessee officials raided the school, searched both the institutional buildings as well as Myles Horton's private residence, and then made arrests. These are her memories of what happened.

. . . The raid on Highlander at Monteagle in 1959 was nothing new. They had been trying to get Highlander on something so they could close it down. They wanted that school off that hill. There had been a real increase in civil rights activities, and an increase in the number of people coming to the workshops. That night they came we had fifty-some-odd people there for a workshop on voter registration.

The night they came, I was sitting out on the lawn. We were showing this film called *The Face of the South*. This film had to do with the difference in how the land was portioned out after slavery. I wasn't in there looking at it because I had seen it several times, you know. We showed it at all the workshops. I was out on the lawn and this same young lady that had been traveling with me to Boston and everywhere else was out there with me. Esau Jenkins and a couple of guys were sitting under a tree, and I thought I saw headlights of a car coming up. Then all of a sudden you wouldn't see them anymore. So you'd keep talking and lights kept flashing, and I thought I saw movement, but I wasn't really conscious of what was happening. Finally it dawned on me that I had seen headlights more than once and I had seen movements more than once. What they were doing was coming up and dropping out these people who they had deputized all of a sudden all over the grounds at different places. And I said to Gertrude, "Something's happening here."

I got up to go around to the side of the building to come into the kitchen, and at that time some of the men came in on the grounds and they caught Gertrude. One of them grabbed her and took her on into the house. I came on into the back and these men were all in there. They had Septima [Clark] by the arm. They had grabbed Guy [Carawan]. And Septima's granddaughter, Yvonne, ran out and hollered, "What are they doing with my grandmommie?" And I grabbed her to quiet her down and that was the only thing that saved me from being arrested because I wanted to know what they were doing with Septima. But they had covered the whole grounds in that time. I remembered seeing the flashes of light and suddenly the light wasn't there, you know, and I'd see movement, and suddenly the movement wasn't there. And all this time they were spreading their guys all over the place. They had gone in there and the movie was still going on, and they said, "Cut the damn thing off!" Nobody moved, and they didn't know how to cut it off themselves, so they finally yanked the plug out and everybody started singing the freedom songs. That's when the verse "I am not afraid" was added to "We Shall Overcome." It was really hectic. They went through everything. They took people's money, which wasn't in line with what they were supposed to be doing. They went through all the drawers and everybody's belongings upstairs and all through the house. . . .

[They were looking for] liquor. They found a little bit. I think it all came to about a jigger of whiskey over in Myles' house. Septima said one of the men came to her and asked her if she was in charge and she said yes. And they arrested her for being in charge of running a school with alcohol on the premises in a dry county. Of course, they dropped the charges on her. There was this big headline, SEPTIMA CLARK ARRESTED FOR POSSESSION OF WHISKEY, and everybody that knew Septima knew that she didn't even drink coffee. [*Laughing*] Guy was supposed to be drunk, and all Guy had had was orange juice because at that time Guy wouldn't drink anything but milk and orange juice because he didn't want to hurt his voice. And this other fellow they accused, Mac Sturgis, was the fourth person that they arrested. Mac was real upset about it because Mac said the little bit of liquor they did find in Myles' house, he put there. He had brought it and he was real upset because he said they wouldn't have found anything if it wasn't for him. But it wasn't enough to make a legitimate legal case, because you are allowed to have at least a quart in your home even in a dry county, and what *was* found was not even found on the school grounds. It was found in Myles' house. It wasn't anything. We didn't even have cooking sherry in the school building. But even though all that was proven they intended to get Highlander. They had been trying for years to get Highlander and to put it out of business. And they succeeded that time. They padlocked the place and sold it at public auction.

The raid on Highlander became the focus of a three-year legal battle in the Tennessee courts. When Highlander lost its charter, Cecil Branstetter, Highlander's lawyer, immediately made application for a new charter for the Highlander Research and Education Center. The charter was granted and Myles Horton moved the school to a large house in downtown Knoxville.

May Justus had known Myles Horton and most of the people associated with the Highlander Folk School since its inception. She had also established herself as a woman of considerable accomplishments. Five of her books that had been published in the forties and fifties were selections of the Literary Guild, and she had received a fellowship that enabled her to write two more: Dixie Decides *and* Cabin on Kettle Creek.

With these successes, and the complications of a heart ailment, she had also retired from teaching in order to concentrate full-time on her writing. But the community persistently sought her help, so May Justus began a private school and taught a total of seventeen pupils in her home over a span of nearly ten years.

Similarly, when criticism against Highlander resurfaced, May Justus also responded.

. . . I had grown up in a mountain community where there were no black people at all. I never met any black people except very casually until I met the black people who came to Highlander. Septima Clark was the first black person I ever knew intimately. I heard the stories of injustice and persecution from people who came there and that certainly influenced my thinking to feel that I would do or say anything I could toward the defense of Highlander's policy about black people, even though some of the people in our community had grave misgivings about Highlander's new work.

And then I experienced some of that injustice firsthand. Septima Clark was the educational director at Highlander. The State Department at times had students come from foreign countries and visit certain sections of the United States to learn about our country firsthand. We had a dozen or more French students visiting at Highlander one time. Septima and I, and I don't remember who else, took them down to Nashville to meet there at the Andrew Jackson Hotel. Somebody from one of the television stations was going to meet with them, so we met in the room there and they had this interchange. After it was over and we started to leave, Septima and I started down the hall and we came to an elevator. The elevator boy stopped us, and looking at her, said, "You'll have to go down to the other end of the hall. The colored people do not go down on this elevator."

"Well," I said to Septima, "we'll both go down on the other elevator."

So we went to the other elevator. She couldn't go down on what we'd call "my" elevator, so I went down on "hers." I may have to suffer fools gladly sometimes, for politeness' sake, but I'm not going to suffer wrongdoing gladly. So when I got home, I wrote the manager of the hotel and told him exactly what had happened. I said, "Now, I don't blame the elevator boy because I realize that he was simply carrying out the policy of the hotel, which *you* are responsible for." And I said, "I hope the time will come when this policy will change, and the sooner, the better, that we can all go down from one floor to the other on the same elevator without having to look to see who's black and who's white."

Well, I never did hear from him. Never did hear from him and I don't know whether that did him a bit of good in the world or not, or changed the policy at all, but it did me good to express

my feeling and I just thought in time that manager might consider
that.

Meanwhile, some of the local people continued to be upset
over blacks being at Highlander. They got to telling stories and
would call it that "terrible communist school." It wasn't the first
time it had happened. I felt that they considered it a communist
school long before they turned against Highlander for having
black people there. People would say that Highlander had a short
line to Russia and all these wild things. They used to say when
Highlander was having labor classes over there, that the school
held Russia up as a model of government and all that sort of thing.
I wasn't present at any of those meetings if they did that. When
they spoke out for integration, though, Vera and I both felt that
they were doing the right thing.

So the first thing I did actively to get involved in Highlander's
defense was when they began to have black people over there. I
began to write letters to the newspapers all over Tennessee saying
that I had been there and the black people that I knew at Highlander were as truly American as any of the white people that I
had known, and all that I had met were Christian ladies and gentlemen and that I had never seen anything un-American on the
part of the black people at all. Of course, that was what turned
some of the people in Tracy City against Vera and me. I believe a
lot like Lowell, who said:

> *They are slaves who do not speak for the fallen and the weak.*
> *They are slaves who will not choose hatred, scoffing and abuse*
> *rather than in silence shrink from the truth they needs must think.*

That was my feeling about it. I was going to stand up and say what I
thought was right.

In the late fifties, Vera got caught in the backlash against
Highlander. Vera's trouble all came about because she went over
to Highlander to hear Mrs. Eleanor Roosevelt. The pictures that
came out in the newspaper showed Vera and Mrs. Roosevelt with
some black people. Mrs. Roosevelt afterward wrote a letter saying
that she was so sorry that a picture of the two of them together
had been published and had caused her this trouble. If there was
anything that she could possibly do, she would be happy to do it.

But there was nothing she could do. Soon after that, Vera lost her job—about a year before she would have retired. I was irate over the injustice of it. She should have been allowed to teach on till her time was up. She was acknowledged to be a good teacher. But all the notice she had was a letter that said, "The Board of Education voted to send you a letter notifying you that you might not be re-elected to your position in the school system for the next school year."

Vera wrote a letter outlining her position, and without replying to that, the superintendent simply informed her that she would not be reappointed. These were her *friends*. The American Legion went on record as opposing Vera McCampbell because of her association with the Highlander Folk School. She was summoned before the board of education to explain her position, but she lost her job in the end.

It wasn't that we couldn't live [on my income], because by that time I had a number of publishers and even very meager royalties. We lived simply so we weren't in danger of starving, because what I had I shared with her, and she did have a small retirement pay. [But they did not pay her pension because she lost her job before she became eligible for that.] Then we had a garden and we canned things and we got along all right. It worked a hardship because any injustice works a hardship, but we got along nicely in spite of it.

And the letters we received helped. [One, from a Walter Mitchell, a retired bishop in Arizona, read:

My dear Miss McCampbell:

It made my blood boil to read just now, in the last issue of the *Southern Patriot*, of your enforced retirement and beg to express the hope that the matter will not end there, but that you will either be re-employed or offered proper place elsewhere. It just might be that I know the fathers of some of the members of the school board. . . . I'm not a prophet or the son of a prophet, but it did not take that to foresee what would happen. When J. H. McGrath was Attorney-General, I happened to sit next to him at a luncheon, discussing McCarthyism. I predicted that if he and the others kept on, before long they would be after such organizations as the FOR

[Fellowship of Reconciliation], the American Civil Liberties Union, and World Federation Union, all of which I was and am a member. That is after finishing with the communists, they would have to attack the next to the left and on and on toward the center. Not long afterwards, two employees of the public schools out here were dismissed because they belonged to the ACLU. I've long since become used to being called a communist. When it is complained that I am too radical, my reply is that my only fear is that I am not radical enough to please our Lord for He was the most radical person ever to walk the earth. He too, you remember, was charged with subverting the people, and if allowed to go on, would destroy our place and nation. We are in good company! More power to you.]

In 1959, the school was raided by agents of the state of Tennessee and closed down. Septima was arrested and taken to jail, along with several of the men. We went to the jail that night that they took Septima and got her out by paying the five-hundred-dollar bail, but they wouldn't let us get the young men because they accused them of being drunk. . . .

I had never been to a trial in my life. You know, someone has said that the reason there is so much trouble in the world is because nobody [on the side of good speaks out]. Those on the side of evil are wrong and they're very vociferous about expressing themselves. I've always felt that we should speak out [on how we feel about things happening around us]. I used to tell my children in Sunday school class that early in life you form traits and you either side with the right or the wrong. It may be a very small thing, but you'll always have it in you to decide. Nobody makes you choose the wrong thing any more than anybody picks you up by the ear and pulls you over the threshold of heaven. You choose yourself. I told them, "The sooner you get in the habit of doing what you know is right in your heart, the better it will be."

At that trial, I felt that I was on the side of the angels and [I was doing the right thing]. One of the lawyers said, "Miss Justus, we know your good name in this community. Aren't you afraid of hurting it?"

That ought to be beneath anybody who practices law to ask a

person a thing like that. Of course, the people who were prejudiced against Highlander and its principles and the policy of integration weren't going to applaud me. That would be the betraying of their side. I could understand that, but yet I was conscientious about how *I* felt. That's why I did it. I couldn't have chosen any other thing.

There were no personal threats or retributions made against me after the trial, but of course you must remember that I had been here many, many years, and I had taught Sunday school here all those fifty years. And I was a neighbor and friend. I had made bread for my neighbors and baked cookies for their children. And although my neighbors did not exactly approve of my stand or applaud me, they gave me credit, I think, for being honest in what I was. They were my children and my children's children. It was quite different from being in a place where you're not known and where you have not befriended people too. They couldn't look upon me as anything but a friend.

I don't know what they think among themselves [even today]. You're really on dangerous ground when you try to interpret other people's inner feelings. There was never any physical manifestation or personal reproach against me. I knew that the people in my [Presbyterian] church did not approve. They didn't side with Highlander and they certainly didn't approve of one of their oldest members siding that way. I knew the church was afraid of what might be said like, "Oh, if Miss Justus just hadn't sided with that awful school," so I went to one of the elders of the church and said, "Now, Mr. McDonald, if my belonging to this church is going to cause an embarrassment to the church and members, I am perfectly willing to withdraw my membership. However, I don't want to leave the impression that I think that what I am doing is wrong and that by leaving the church, I am leaving the kingdom of God." I said, "That's a place I don't want to resign from."

So he looked at me and he laid his hand on my shoulder and said, "I'm an old man. I think I've lived long enough to know a lady and a Christian when I see one. You stay right in this church."

And so I did. And nobody else said anything about it. I mean, action was never taken. So I'm still in that church.

You can't always have happiness in your heart over something you do, but you can always have peace. I knew I was doing what my conscience told me to. It never occurred to me to do anything else. I never really worried that I would lose friends over my actions. I don't think that I lost any friends that were worth having. . . .

For the continuation of Bernice Robinson's interview, see Chapter Five (page 297). For the conclusion of May Justus' interview, also see Chapter Five (page 334).

5

1960–70
Highlander's Influence on a New
Generation of Revolutionary Leaders

. . . I remember those highway billboards that said, "MARTIN LU-
THER KING ATTENDING COMMUNIST TRAINING SCHOOL." Now actually, the
photograph on that billboard was taken at the twenty-fifth anniversary celebration of Highlander, which I was present at [in
1957]. King and Rosa Parks and several hundred others were
there. That was the first time I met Rosa Parks.

People are all the time scratching their heads: "Now, how
can we get something started around here?" I think Rosa Parks
demonstrated that you get things started by first of all having a
certain amount of courage, [and using it on] a battle you think
you can win. You don't pick a battle you think you're gonna lose.
You want to demonstrate to them that they can win, not demonstrate that they can lose; that's been demonstrated too many
times.

One of the ways you win is you don't pick something too big.
It taught me a real lesson in tactics and strategy when the civil
rights movement got off to a flying start by winning the bus boycott. For a hundred years black people had been trying this and
trying that and writing great theses and asking questions like,
"How are we going to get rid of Jim Crow and segregation, and
get the right to vote?" And who would say that sitting in the front
seat of a bus was that important? My heavens, that's way down the
list of priorities. Voting's important, schooling, health, housing,
jobs, *but* they couldn't win on those right away—not in Montgom-

ery, Alabama. But they were able to win on this ridiculous issue of sitting in the front seat of a bus.

You see, they demonstrated a fundamental principle: You can get something done if you stick together. . . . And if that lesson can get hammered home, my, then all sorts of things start happening and people just move from success to success.

I didn't know for sure whether . . . they were going to succeed or not. But the coalition held till finally, when King was assassinated, it broke up, and the radical youth and the conservative oldsters and the Southern and Northern blacks and all the educated and uneducated blacks no longer could stick together as well.

—PETE SEEGER

The Same Piano Beat as "Heart and Soul"

Pete Seeger

If any song characterized the radical changes that the civil rights movement made in American life, it is "We Shall Overcome." Pete Seeger, Guy Carawan, Frank Hamilton and Zilphia Horton are listed as the song's arrangers, and here Pete Seeger explains how the song was created over time by African-Americans. He also recalls how Guy taught it to students thirteen years later in 1960 during the historic sit-ins at Greensboro, North Carolina.

As a result of those sit-ins, the Student Nonviolent Coordinating Committee (SNCC) was formed, a new generation's protest movement began, and "We Shall Overcome" became its soul song. All royalties from the song go to the "We Shall Overcome" Fund. Highlander administers that fund in order to provide small grants, mostly to black musicians. But Seeger also describes how protest songs like this one generated more than revenues; indeed, they often symbolized a spiritual dimension to the movement's acts of courage and determination.

While King was still alive, I remember writing down to the Montgomery Improvement Association, saying, "I understand you have some songs you made up. Could you possibly send me the words?" And it was E. D. Nixon who sent me the words [*singing*], "We are movin' on to vict'ry, we are movin' on to vict'ry, we are movin' on to vict'ry, and I know the time ain't long." I'd heard songs like that on and off. The poetry of it! One said, "My feet is sore but my heart is light."

[Then there was the song "We Shall Overcome."] Zilphia Horton had a beautiful voice. She didn't need any guitar or any accompaniment. You just loved to hear her voice. When Zilphia sang a song in that rich alto voice, she knew how to decorate the melody in the wonderful old traditional ways. She didn't just sing the notes out straight, but gave them all nice little bends and twists like a good singer does. She was also a good song leader. She could stand up before a crowd of union people and teach them a union song and get them all singing out well on the chorus. And Zilphia was always looking for a good song, as every song leader is. You're never quite satisfied. You say, "If I only had exactly the right song." On one of her many trips around South, she visited a tobacco workers' strike, and there were the pickets keeping their spirits up singing songs, and they'd taken the old hymn "I Will Overcome" and just changed it to first person plural instead of first person singular—which incidently has been done with other songs. Decades earlier another song was made by black workers who changed "Jesus is my captain, I will not be moved" to "The union is behind us, we shall not be moved." Only one of the really old spirituals uses the plural: "We Are Climbing Jacob's Ladder." This is one of the tactical disagreements between Christians and class-struggle types. One is saying, "I will be saved," and the other, *"We* will be saved." This use of the first person plural was very important and Zilphia realized that. She wrote down the words and in 1947, I think at Highlander, she taught it to me. I tried to sing it, but I didn't sing it particularly well. I tried adding some new verses to it like, "We'll walk hand in hand" and "The whole wide world around." Zilphia added some verses too, I'm sure. "Black and white together" and "We are not afraid." One never is quite sure where which verse came from.

Guy Carawan added verses and taught it to students in 1960 who were sitting down asking for a cup of coffee in places where black people had never been served before. The students latched right on it and gave it a slow rock beat. Each step it changed slightly from an earlier song. No one knows who improvised the new melody from Rev. Charles Tindley's 1903 song "I'll Overcome Someday" but in 1990 I learned from Bernice Reagan that it was

Lucille Simmons, a member of the Food and Tobacco Workers Union, who changed it from "I" to "We" and liked to sing it very slowly, "long meter" style. It was during a strike at the American Tobacco Company in Charleston, South Carolina, 1946. Zilphia also sang it very slowly. I didn't have the voice to sing it that way, so I gave it an oom-chinka oom-chinka banjo rhythm. I taught it to Guy Carawan in California, 1951.

In Tennessee in 1960 Guy taught it to black students. They didn't hesitate an instant. They gave it the "Motown Beat." The same beat that "Heart and Soul" has on the piano, or any other slow rock. You give three short beats to every one of the main beats. You have four main beats [*beats out a rhythm*]. One, two, three, four—one, two, three, four—but it's very important that you break those up into threes: ta, ta, ta—ta, ta, ta. It's a technical matter, but it's interesting that the song as we know it now is a combination work of white and black musicians and songwriters in the North and South. My name is on the copyright of the song simply because the publisher says, "We cannot tie down the copyright of this song unless somebody will claim to have done something to this song." I said, "All I did was add 'the whole wide world around,' one of the verses." "That's enough." The copyright law says you can copyright an arrangement of an old song, but if there is no arrangement you want to claim, it's thrown open and now any bastard can copyright it too. This has happened with songs. They take some rather nice songs and massacre them. I've heard lousy versions of "Down by the Riverside."

[Sometimes songs are also created out of prose, like] "Turn, Turn, Turn." I was leafing through the Bible once. I like to leaf through it. I've never read the whole thing through, although I've often intended to, but I'm fascinated by the concepts and the language. And, lo and behold, in this hard-bitten section, it starts off with this beautiful little thing. Ecclesiastes is a very hard-bitten section of the Bible. That's where he says, "Vanity of vanities, all is vanity." He's literally saying there is no hope, the end of the world is coming, and all your dreams are going to crumble. It's a very pessimistic section, but it starts off with this little chant, and I realized late in life that that was Hebrew poetry: a time for this, a time for that, a time ta ta, a time ta ta. And all I did was rearrange the lines so they rhymed and add one couplet, "A time for peace, I swear it's not too late." I don't know if Ecclesiastes would have approved that. [*Laughter*]

I turned down about fifty thousand dollars several years ago because there was a company that wanted to make a commercial out of it. I decided it wasn't worth it. . . .

I used to think I was irreligious until I found out I was having a lot of fun meeting and talking with a lot of religious people. I had sung with Catholics and Protestants and Jews and Moslems and Buddhists all around the world, and I found out we had a lot in common, so I can't call myself irreligious anymore. . . .

I confess if somebody asked me what's my religion, I'd say I don't know. But I do put a last verse on [my version of "Gimme That Old-time Religion"]: [*singing*]: "I will arise at early morning, when my Lord gives me the warning, that the solar age is dawning, and that's good enough for me. Give me that old time religion." I guess that's my religion. I walk out of here and I feel like yodeling when I see the sun come up.

So if people want to call me religious, I won't argue with them. I even use the word "spiritual" often. Paul Robeson used to use the word "spiritual" because he sang what were called Negro spirituals in those days. And he said, "Europe and America are going to have to learn something of the spirituality that Africa and Afro-Americans have." I understand when I've been in a church where everybody is singing and everybody in that room is just caught up in the rhythm and the melody and the ideals and the present exaltation there, their pulses all going, and their feet tapping together, and somebody says, "The Spirit of God was in this room." I won't argue with them. But if someone doesn't like that and wants to have a more technical analysis of what was in the room, I won't argue with them, either.

For the conclusion of Pete Seeger's interview, see Chapter Six (page 400).

★

"A Watershed Period in American History"
Andrew Young

Most recently he has served as mayor of Atlanta, Georgia, but over the last three decades, Andrew Young's career has ranged widely in the areas of diplomacy, politics, civil rights, and the ministry. In 1977, under President Jimmy Carter, Young became the chief U.S. delegate to the United Nations. Earlier, he was elected to Congress in 1972 as the first black representative from Georgia since Reconstruction.

More specifically, however, Young's public career had its roots in the civil rights movement. Throughout the early sixties, he served under Dr. Martin Luther King, Jr., as executive director of the Southern Christian Leadership Conference (SCLC). After assuming that post in 1961, Young is credited with having influenced major civil rights legislation and with marching beside King in nonviolent protests across the South.

Thus, this United Church of Christ minister who became a political activist provides, as few can, a succinct overview of the era, the personalities, and the underlying beliefs that made the SCLC such a vibrant force for social change.

I grew up in New Orleans in a neighborhood that was predominantly white. It was a poor neighborhood that was mostly Irish, Italians, Polish, and Cajuns who came in from rural areas, and my brother and I were the only black children in the neighborhood. So all of our early childhood playmates were white, and yet we went to segregated schools—we couldn't go to school with them. We were bused out of our neighborhood to go to an all-black school, and so it was almost like I grew up in two worlds. The society was segregated but we never accepted it. But neither did we resent it. I mean, my parents taught me that this was not something to hate. They taught me that these were people that just didn't know any better and that even though we were all God's children, they just didn't believe that. They [simply] thought that white people were better than black people. But the Bible clearly says that "God is no respecter of persons." And so, I shouldn't let them get me upset because they didn't realize that I was God's child too. They just didn't know any better. So you had to help them to learn that.

So I went to a segregated public grammar school and to the Methodist High School. Our schools always had a strong Negro history component, and there was a lot of motivation to make the world a better place. We didn't think of it too much in terms of desegregation in those days. We thought of it in terms of being able to compete equally. We were taught that the world is structured against you because you are black and so you've got to work a lot harder than anybody white to succeed, but nobody ever thought of changing the situation. They just said, "In order to survive in the situation, you've got to be strong to put up with all you're going to have to put up with."

[But my attitude changed when I started] a pastorate in Thomasville, Georgia, in 1954–55. In '55 Maynard Jackson's grandfather came down and asked if we would try and run a voter registration drive. And I saw that as part of my religious commitment. If you say the Lord's Prayer—"Thy kingdom come on earth"—in our society, the coming of the kingdom is in some sense a political process. If people live together more harmoniously, it's because governments work out the terms of their living together more justly. And so I came to believe that religious commitment often required political expression.

Then I went to New York for a while with the National Council of Churches. My job was to try and help young black and white people in the South to get to know each other. We had a series of conferences all over the country, but we concentrated in the South just to give black and white teenagers a chance to get to know each other. At that time the society was strictly segregated and most white kids would grow up not knowing anybody black; and most black kids would grow up not knowing anybody white—except maybe the policeman, you know. We [held those conferences] in every Southern state except Mississippi. In Alabama they were held under the auspices of the Episcopal Church.

It was in the course of that work that Chuck Boyles, one of the young men who was working with us at the National Council of Churches, went to work at Highlander and in the winter of 1961, he invited me to a student conference at Highlander to lead Bible study for a weekend. That was a conference of students who had been active in the sit-in movement, and basically they were talking about ways of following up the sit-ins—ways to get the movement off the college campuses and into the communities. It was not long after that meeting that the Freedom Rides occurred, and I contend that being together there at Highlander and talking about long-range goals and strategies [was partly responsible for that] core group of people who were committed to doing something like the Freedom Rides.

I led worship there that weekend and I met Septima Clark for the first time. And Myles Horton.

When I got back, Myles and Chuck wrote me about coming to work at Highlander. Well, I had always said I wanted to be in the South. I had been offered a job by Martin Luther King and I turned it down, in part because I wanted to write about the movement and be a little more removed from the action, and I frankly didn't think that I was able to measure up to the standards and needs that Martin demanded. He wanted me to be his administrative assistant and I just didn't think I was ready to do that yet. But I and my family were ready to go back South. So I told Myles that I was ready to come back to Highlander to work.

In the meantime the suit against Highlander came about and the property was auctioned off. Meanwhile I had sold my house in New York, I had resigned my job, and I didn't have anywhere to go. So I went to the United Church of Christ Board for Homeland Ministries, explained to them what had happened, and asked them if they would assume the sponsorship of Highlander's Citizenship Training Program with SCLC and make available one of our church conference centers—Dorchester Center—down in Liberty County, Georgia. They said they'd be glad to if I would come on as the administrator. So the church put me on the church's payroll to be the administrator of this program. We were to train neighborhood leaders as teachers and as voter registration organizers. And from the period of 1961 to about 1966, we trained almost ten thousand teachers. Now, those were not public school teachers. What we used to look for was the person with the Ph.D. mind in a community who had not had an opportunity to get a formal education, but who was respected by everybody as one of the wise leaders of their community. And we recruited people like Fannie Lou Hamer in Mississippi; Uneeda Blackwell. The two guys who were the sheriff and the probate judge in Greene County, Alabama—Gilmore and Branch—were recruits; Hosea Williams started out with us as a Citizenship School supervisor. So Septima and Dorothy Cotton and I ran this program. Septima was the educational director. And actually we ran it as a team and we worked together as a family basically and we drove around the South together recruiting people and then we went once a month down to Dorchester Center to conduct these training sessions.

And from one end of the South to the other, if you look at the black elected officials and the people who are the political leaders across the South now, the list is full of people who had their first involvement in civil rights in that Citizenship Training Program.

[You can look back now and see all sorts of consequences of all that activity.] I think of the period in the late fifties and sixties as being a watershed period in American history. We underwent a *tremendous* upheaval of change and we did it without destroying any person and very little property. In fact, the movement itself destroyed no property or person. It was essentially nonviolent. Now that's exactly what needed to happen in Ireland and Lebanon. This is one of the few places where people have learned this —have demonstrated that very difficult and explosive problems can be solved without killing anybody, or without taking something from anybody. And so it's important for me that high school students particularly, maybe even junior high, understand that the way to solve problems in today's world is creatively rather than destructively. I think all of the messages I got as a kid were that you killed your enemies. I grew up during the Second World War and all we played was war games as kids, you know. And that trains you to destroy your enemy. That contributes to a very destructive, military-oriented society. I think it brings a great deal of tension into race relations, into class relations; it even brings a great deal of tension into the relations between husbands and wives and between parents and children. So whenever the child has ideas of his own that are different from his father's, his father's [impulse] is, "I oughta knock the hell out of that kid!" And that's not the way the world is supposed to be. What we tried to demonstrate in the civil rights movement, and what I tried to do later on in politics and at the UN, was to demonstrate that the most difficult problems can be solved without destroying either persons or property. . . .

[So why is it that nobody talks about it?] I think they still don't understand it. Part of the blame I take is that I'm one of the few people that really knew what was going on and understood this philosophically as well as tactically, and I haven't written anything. And I'm trying to remedy that now. But there are other cases in the world too [that we can look at]. The situation that is going on today in Poland, for example. Poland has got the Soviet Union really held at bay. The national consciousness is not in the hands of the Russians or the Communist Party; it is in the hands of the church and the people. And they have had a revolution in a communist state and nobody has broken a windowpane. And it is far more successful than what you see going on in Lebanon or in Northern Ireland, or in Britain. And in Poland, everybody is winning. In the U.S. everybody won. But in England and Ireland and in Lebanon, everybody loses. [When I was in the UN, I tried to apply some of those lessons. It may have been a case of] "fools rushing in where angels fear to tread," but my experience has been that when you get people together—in the UN we got the Patriotic Front together with the white Rhodesians. I had no problem going to meet with white South Africans or black South Africans. I really felt that people in the Middle East have to live together so they ought to talk to each other. All of those things were very controversial. And I finally had to resign my job, simply for trying to get people to talk to each other. [*Laughter*]

But the message that needs to be taught is we all lose when there is violence, and we all win if we can find a way to resolve our differences without being destructive. I think the civil rights movement very consciously demonstrated that.

★

"We Didn't Realize What We Were In"

Dorothy Cotton

"Like the Good Friday that Dr. King went to jail . . ."

In 1960, Dorothy Cotton assisted the Reverend Wyatt Tee Walker and Dr. Martin Luther King, Jr., during the development of the SCLC in Atlanta, Georgia. Then in 1961, after a workshop at Highlander, she helped Andrew Young incorporate Septima Clark's "Citizenship School" concept into SCLC's voter registration drives among blacks in the South.

"Like the Good Friday that Dr. King went to jail . . ."

Because Dorothy Cotton was there, and working, when these organizations for social change began, she is now able to provide vivid glimpses into the SCLC's early working methods. And her insights into the uniqueness and charisma of such civil rights leaders as Young and King seem pure, as if unimpaired by time and tragedy. Hers are poignant recollections from within the inner circle.

"Like the Good Friday that Dr. King went to jail . . ."

There was a preacher in our town, his name was Wyatt Tee Walker. Wyatt was the Baptist preacher at the Gilfield Baptist Church in Petersburg, Virginia, and I was a member of his church. I was in college there at Virginia State College, and a lot of us flocked to his church. You know, he was this young, handsome, dynamic preacher; and in those days everybody got all dressed up to go to church, you know, hats and gloves. You know how we used to do. [*Laughter*]

. . . So we went to hear Wyatt preach and got really involved in the church. But Wyatt was also the head of the NAACP local chapter there. Black folk could not use the public library—if you can believe that—because the public library was housed in some building that had been given by some family, and the excuse the town fathers gave (and it probably literally was the town fathers in that day) was that in the will it was left for the white folks.

Well, Wyatt was one of those preachers who dared to take the gospel to the streets. Most don't do it. In other words, to live it, and—I need to recall that passage, but I think it is in Matthew somewhere—"to set at liberty those that are oppressed." Dr. King took that quite literally, as did quite a lot of other preachers. That was how they saw the gospel coming alive for people. Some felt it and some didn't. For some it was only the Sunday morning hour.

So Wyatt looked at this library situation and said, "We cannot have that." And he asked the national NAACP to help us make a case and take it through the courts. They had so many cases at that time, they couldn't take that on. So Wyatt, being the renegade or whatever he was, said, "We will protest here locally." He formed the Petersburg Improvement Association, which was a takeoff on the Montgomery Improvement Association, which was the group which sprang up out of Rosa Parks' action in Montgomery.

This was in the late fifties, and I was out of college by now, but I was still very active in the church. Wyatt used to say I was kind of his right arm, you know, so I was secretary to the Petersburg Improvement Association.

Anyway, we began some activity around trying to integrate the public library. Then we moved from the library to the dimestore, where they had a lunch counter for whites only. I don't think I really knew consciously what I was getting into because I remember walking with a picket sign one day at the dimestore, and I remember this elderly black man who said, "Why don't you stop all this mess out here in the street?" You know, we were like six or seven folk who were picketing and the folk up on the hill were wishing we would stop all that "foolishness in the street." And then this man said to me, "Lady, ain't you got a table at home [where you can eat]?" I remember at that time putting my picket sign down and going to talk to this man. And I realize now I was convincing myself: "Look, mister, if your wife were down here shopping and she wanted to have a cup of coffee at this lunch counter, do you realize she would have to go all the way home? Don't you feel she has the right to have a cup of coffee here also?" So I'm convincing this black man on the sidewalk who's telling me to get off the street with all this "foolishness," and I was really convincing myself that the cause was right. [*Laughter*]

So we were doing some interesting things in Petersburg. Then Reverend Walker met Dr. King somewhere in his travels and invited Dr. King to come to Petersburg to speak. And I remember the first time I saw Dr. King, he was sitting at a table in Wyatt Walker's house, where we had a little supper for him after he spoke at one of our mass meetings. You know, the mass meeting was a vehicle that got to be quite popular through which we organized and did things; but Dr. King liked what Wyatt was doing with us in the movement and he asked Wyatt to come to Atlanta to help him formulate the Southern Christian Leadership Conference.

He had not even moved to Atlanta from Montgomery then. In fact, the reason he was invited to speak to us was because of his activity there in Montgomery with the Montgomery bus boycott. But Wyatt said, "I will come if I can bring the two folk who helped me most here." And that was a fellow named Jim Wood, who is dead now, and myself. I was working during the summers to finish my master's in speech therapy, if you will, at Boston University, but I said to Wyatt, "Well, I'll go down for about six months"—and that was twenty years ago. [*Laughter*]

So I came to Atlanta to work with Dr. King and Wyatt Walker. At that time we were about five folk: Wyatt, Jim, myself, and then Ernestine Brown and Lillie Hunter, who were the clerical support people. Of course, we grew into the hundreds as the various campaigns happened. I tell you one thing, when we came in 1960 to Atlanta, we certainly didn't know the movement would take the turn that it took. There was no way we could have known then of its eventual scope, size, importance. Even those of us who were so intimately involved with Dr. King, I think, didn't realize what we were in. If we had, we would have had tape recorders and when we were driving along on people-to-people tours, we called them, with Dr. King in the car when he was having these great and fun philosophical discussions, and arguing with Andy Young on some theological point, if I had only had sense enough, I could have had ten books filled with just fantastic discussions. His *humor* in all of it, and the way that he could recall all of the philosophers and theologians and how they counterpointed. I was just really enthralled by it all. Really, absolutely wonderful, powerful experience!

But about all that was going on in those early days of SCLC was the Montgomery bus boycott, and a Citizenship Training Program that Highlander had that we had heard about. In fact, early in 1961 I went to a workshop at Highlander when it was at Monteagle—my first visit—and that was the first time I met Septima Clark, who was on the Highlander staff. Myles [Horton] knew Highlander's "demise"—at least in Monteagle—was imminent, but the Field Foundation was still willing to fund the Citizenship Schools, so there needed to be another place for that program to go and for the funds to go.

And so we—SCLC—got the program from Highlander, and the funds were actually given by Field to us through the United Church of Christ [for which Andy Young was working]. Of course, the United Church, they don't like to be called a conduit for the funds, but that's what they were. [*Whispered, smiling*]

So we got the program from Highlander, but what we did was to spread that program around all of the Southern and border states. Luckily we were able to get the people who were with it initially, who were Septima and Bernice Robinson. They came on the SCLC staff. So Andy and Septima and I drove all over the South recruiting people and telling them about that program. Andy was the director and I was called the educational consultant and Septima was a teaching specialist. I heard Andy say one time that the Citizenship Schools really were the base upon which the whole civil rights movement was built. And that's probably very much true. I can hardly think of an area of the South from which we did not bring a group of folk—I mean busloads of folk, sometimes seventy people—who would live together for five days and we, like, *did* it! We had fantastic sessions.

We worked out of the Atlanta office, but we would go to Dorchester Center [operated by the United Church of Christ] every month for five days. Then we'd leave Dorchester, come back to the office, and then hit the road to recruit again. Once in a while we would go over to Penn Community Center, but most of the time we were at Dorchester Center. For five days we'd work with people we had recruited, some of whom were just off the farms. Like Fannie Lou Hamer, who stood up and said, "I live on Mr. Marlowe's plantation." And talked about how Pap, her husband, had to take her to the next county because they were going to beat up Pap and her if she didn't stop that voter registration talk. You know, she stood up and talked about that in the first workshop where she came and taught us the old songs that they sang in the meetings to keep their spirits up. You know, we sang a *lot* in the workshops then. Maybe it's *true* that black folk do sing, huh? We sang a lot! [*Laughter*]

[But the main thrust of the Citizenship Schools, after they went to SCLC, was still teaching people how to read, voter registration and basic skills of that sort.] And, of course, we learned that from Septima and Bernice, and the Highlander folk. We kept that same model, and probably expanded it some. I remember a session that I did on "How to Teach," because we were trying to make teachers out of these people who could barely read and write. But they could teach, you know. They could teach. If they could read at all, we could teach them that c-o-n-s-t-i-t-u-t-i-o-n spells "constitution." And we'd have a grand discussion all morning about what the Constitution was. You were never telling anybody. We used a very nondirective approach. You know, "What is it?" And after an hour's discussion, we would finally come to a consensus that it was the supreme law of the land. And then we'd start talking about parts of that document. And, of course, we'd get very quickly to the "Fourteenth a-m-e-n-d-m-e-n-t spells 'amendment,' and the Fourteenth one says what? And what makes you a citizen?" And then we would really get into the Fourteenth Amendment. People would say, "You are a child of God," you know, because we come from the Bible Belt, right? Or people would say things like, "If you register to vote, you are a citizen." But before the session was over we would know that all persons born or naturalized in the United States are citizens, and they would learn that, and we'd write that. That's what they were learning to read and write.

And the right of the people peaceably to assemble, and the fact that no state can take away your privileges. And then we would have to translate that into this grand discussion [about the fact that Alabama Governor George] Wallace cannot tell you that you cannot march down Highway 80, or whatever.

People learned those kinds of things in the workshops. We'd have our outline for the week and first I'd ask them, "What's _____," and use some other word than "citizen." I remember using the term "habeas corpus" in one session. (And, of course, I hoped that nobody would know because otherwise they would blow my whole design!) And then I'd tell them what that was. Then I'd ask them what "citizen" was. And we'd have a two-hour discussion, and when it was over everybody knew what a citizen was because we had talked about it for two hours. Rather than telling them, we talked about it. In the first instance we'd give them the answer, but with "citizen" we wouldn't. And then, of course, we would say, "Well, you see when you go home, rather than just throw out answers or speeches to people, discuss with them what it is they need to know."

So then it was the folks who left Dorchester who went home and worked in voter registration drives and who went down to demonstrate. You know, it was Miss Topsy Eubanks—I quote her all the time—who said in a workshop in Dorchester, "I feel like I've been born again!" And she was probably sixty years old then. She went back to Macon and was seen sitting in the courthouse as a poll watcher. She'd never thought of herself as being that before. But demonstrations grew up around peoples. The enlightenment that happened for them there in Dorchester became a flowing out from that experience. . . .

One woman told me she had argued with her son who was involved in the demonstrations, trying to get him out of that "mess in the street." And he started asking her questions, like, "Do you feel it's right for you to be treated the way you're treated, and for black folk to only get jobs pushing brooms?" And, "Do you feel it's right just to be a second-class citizen and have to sit in the back of the bus?" And she said, "And the cobwebs commenced a'movin' from my brain!" [*Laughter*] So the cobwebs "commenced a'movin' " from a whole lot of folk's brains. And they went home on Friday, and they didn't take it anymore. They started their little citizenship classes discussing the issues and problems in their own towns. "How come the pavement stops where the black-folk section begins?" Asking questions like that, and knowing then whom to go talk to about that, or where to protest it.

Eventually, in later years, the so-called black militants—you know, the guys who were black power with the fists and the berets and the jackets and the boots—they started coming to Dorchester also. And I well remember a group who came late—we already had our little circle in the middle of the floor and were into our discussions about change and all that—and these guys walked in and saw our table of materials and saw copies of the U.S. Constitution, and they took copies of the Constitution, and one guy tore one in half and threw it on the floor, and said, "You folk are against the"—I won't use the expletive—"revolution." We have some photographs from that workshop, and a girl who was working as our secretary then said, "Dorothy, you looked scared." And I told her, "I probably was!" [*Laughter*] But by the end of that week those guys were one of us, and we were all kind of loving each other the way it often happens when folk really come together. But we had some hard work to do. They came in cussin' us out, telling us we were against the f—g revolution, and if you want a new school system burn down the f—g building and "off" the superintendent. And we somehow, thank you, Father, had sense enough to say things like, "Well, if you gonna burn down a school, do you know how to build one?" And, of course, they didn't have any answer to that. "If you gonna blow up the bridge, which one of you is an engineer? Do you know how to build one back? If you gonna burn down that factory, you better first talk to Miss Lucy over here. Her husband works there, and that income is their livelihood. Now if you burn down the factory, Miss Lucy will kill you." [*Laughter*] And we finally got them to do some of the activities like the trust walks, and all of that. And we said, "You take Miss Lucy on a walk through the grounds out here, and when you come back, you tell us what she said." And, of course, we had to do that more than once 'cause they came back not telling us what *she* said, but what *they* said to her. "But did you listen to what *she* said and what *she* wanted?" If you want to have change, of course, the bottom line is that the folk for whom the change is meant must be involved in it. And they learned their lesson. I mean, you know the story. . . .

[Some people only remember Andy Young as Ambassador to

the United Nations, and they can't picture him in blue jeans and running a program like that, but] the amazing thing about Andy is that if anybody lives that description of "one who can dine with kings but never lose the common touch," it is Andrew Young. . . . And when Septima Clark and Andy and I traveled around the South, we used to go into little churches that had potbellied stoves. We also used to go into little joints—you know what I mean —that had little potbellied stoves. And I have seen Andy talk to guys with a bottle of wine in their pockets in some joint down the road about his life and voter registration and that kind of thing with his jeans on, and fly up the next week and speak at Riverside Church, and he was at home at both places—and still is! You know, any dance that they could do, Andy could do it too. . . . [*Laughter*] He's a great dancer. . . . That's the genius of Andy Young. And he genuinely cares about people. I learned a lot from watching Andy. He's a great teacher.

And whatever needed to be done, Andy would do it. He wasn't too proud to do anything. He would do any of it. He would do any of the work. I just thought of something Andy did in one of those little joints, so at home with everybody. A couple of guys got into a fight in one of those—you can't call it a bar, I mean, it's really a joint, you know, out on some little country road. And you know how everybody runs to try and stop the fight, holding tightly onto somebody who's pretending he's going to do somebody in? I remember Andy so gently saying, "Turn him aloose. Turn him aloose. He's not going to hit anybody." 'Cause what was really making the fight happen was the fact that everybody was holding this guy [*Laughter*], and Andy just cut right through it and they turned the guy loose and of course, he didn't hit anybody. The other folk were really making the fight by holding on to him.

Eventually, of course, he felt he no longer needed to come to the workshops at Dorchester, and I remember the feeling, the break as he was being pulled in other directions. We *had* had him to ourselves, you know, as just a great force in the midst of our workshops. But Dr. King was pulling him into other places with him. Dr. King hardly moved without Andy's counsel, and Andy became the executive of SCLC and started to come less and less to the workshops. But, of course, the workshops continued. They were really solidly fixed and established by that time. . . .

Dr. King relied on his staff a great deal, and I've never known another situation where people worked with someone who was at one time the "boss" and who was also their "friend" and someone they genuinely loved being with. I realized this after the fact, and it almost makes me a little bit sad to realize how little I knew about just what a fantastic human being Dr. King was; that he could sort of *hang out* with us the way that he did, and the wonderful way that he gave of himself with us and how he enjoyed us as people. And yet we got the work done. You know, the movement happened. [We were relaxed and casual, and yet] we could go into some serious, heavy sessions. Like the Good Friday that Dr. King went to jail. I'll never forget. We were sitting in Room 30 at the A. G. Gaston Motel in Birmingham, Alabama. We must have sat in that room for what seemed like twenty-four hours debating what we should do next. The demonstrations were at their height with the dogs and the fire hoses in Kelly Ingram Park and all of the marches, and we were all strategizing and figuring out ways we could get downtown, you know, through side streets. And some of the little middle-class ladies were hiding away in a corner making picket signs for us and driving us in their fancy cars through back ways to get us downtown onto the main streets. I mean, the whole town was really kind of at a standstill and the momentum was just great. And so many people had been arrested. There must have been three thousand students in jail. I'm not sure of the numbers, but the schools were virtually closed down because so many students were locked up.

And the question was who should lead the next march because the leaders, of course, were the first to go to jail. And we sat in that room debating the question as to whether Dr. King should now lead the next march, because surely he would be arrested. We debated notions like, "Dr. King should stay out of jail because we need him to travel around the country now to raise bail bond money for the other folk who are in jail." The jails were so full that they had started putting people out into some closed-in place. I remember this big wire fence around the fairgrounds or something because there was no space left in the jail.

But the question was, "Should Dr. King lead the next march?" We debated that question back and forth in Room 30, and Dr. King eventually stood up and put on his overall jacket and didn't say a word. But we knew that the decision was made and that he was going to go. *[Dorothy begins to cry and there is a long silence.]* I don't know why I'm doing this. Anyway, he led that march. We made a circle in the room and sang "We Shall Overcome" *[crying]* and he just went upstairs and he didn't say anything *[whispering]*. That's how decisions got made, I guess. He listened to all the deliberations, you know. He listened to all the deliberations. *[Long silence]*

. . . How does one define or describe charisma; and yet charisma isn't really it, because I know people who have charisma who are not leaders of people. I don't know. It's so elusive. What made . . . ? Was it the times? Was it the situation? Was it the fact that he inspired hope in people who had no hope, and he knew that they needed that most at that time? Was it that he defined the issues so clearly for people? Was it that he articulated so well the issues and the goals? Maybe deep down in ourselves we knew that we needed to change things, but he *said* it—he articulated it. You know, when Rosa Parks wouldn't get up from her seat, he could interpret that for people, and then people quietly within themselves could say, "Oh, yes *[spoken softly]*, I ain't gonna take this no more," and start to feel that they *wouldn't* take it and therefore would walk [instead of riding the buses], as they did for more than three hundred days in Montgomery. But people around the country started to feel they didn't have to take it, because he articulated [their frustrations] for them.

And he projected where we could go with the movement. He kept saying, "My people will get there." And we felt that he had a vision of where "there" was. "I may not get there with you, but my people will get there."

There were also times when we all felt really down, you know, and depressed—Dr. King included. He, most of all, knew when people needed a victory. To keep going the people needed victories. So in some of the long deliberations I told you about, there were many times when we knew we had to pick a strategy that would lead to a victory for the people. Sometimes the goals were big, like the time when we were arguing about whether it was time now to raise the issue of the right to vote. Finally folk were convinced that clearly we had to win that one, and Dr. King was convinced that that was one we ought to tackle, but there was a big staff discussion before we moved to the point of saying that we ought to raise *that* issue. And then, of course, we had to figure out the strategies. Even with small marches and demonstrations, the same kind of discussion would ensue around those. Shall we have a big rally, or shall we go down and try to negotiate with the powers that be, or shall we take folk to the courthouse? [And each move would dictate our next. Like] when C. T. Vivian takes a bunch of folk down to the courthouse to register and they hit him in the mouth with a billy club. When people saw that kind of violence, we would come back, regroup, and talk about what happened, and we would know after a moment like that when we didn't get in to register to vote that we had to do something else. Dr. King called on a lot of folk around the country for advice and counsel. He knew how to work with people and to dialogue about a strategy and a next move [to keep the momentum going].

Interestingly enough, the city officials or whoever made the decisions to allow a march, for example, or not to allow it played a great role in the escalation of the movement because every time they said, "No, you can't register to vote!" or "No, you can't march down this street!" it clearly gave impetus and momentum to the movement. It just enhanced our work and our determination. And no town learned from the other town, you know? We could win the battle of Birmingham and get public accommodations open, and then go to New Orleans and they'd close the doors in our faces, not having learned a *thing*—nothing from the prior movement activity. In every city we had the same battles to fight all over again.

I remember in St. Augustine, we were having a wade-in because they had said black folk could not use the beach. It was my duty one day to drive some children to the beach, so I drove a group of them there and I left them off at the entrance, and I went back to the "freedom house" where we were gathering and having a meeting and working to get another load to bring back for the wade-in. When I got back, some of the children met me at the entrance saying, "Miss Cotton, there's some men over there who's saying if we come any closer to that beach, they gonna kill us." I jumped out of the car and slammed the door and took two of the children by hand and walked straight through to the beach and that's the only time I ever got hit by some men during the movement. I think inside me I must've thought, "They will not keep me from walking on this beach," and I took the children by hand and I went. One little girl's nose was broken, and I got some blows on the side of my head. But I had to do it. I did it because I had to.

[White students also headed South to become involved in the movement, and] I think certainly they made a real contribution, and I think we learned a lot and they learned a lot. Some of the lessons were very painful, and in SCLC, sometimes there were real confrontations. But they played a very helpful role. But there came a time when we discussed what role they *should* play, because there came a time when we felt like we really had to do it for ourselves. I think we could make the analogy of children growing up. Your parents may know how to do it better, but you've got to learn to flap your wings yourself. And even though you are glad to have your parents there when you need the rent paid, there comes a time when you know you must pay your own.

[The real problems were caused by those] whites who came in with the kind of attitude that "we will do it for you." Others came in who knew how to do it more *with* than *for.* And, of course, that was a more healthy relationship. But, of course, we've all grown. I guarantee you, though, that most of the white students who came down here learned certainly as much as we learned. They learned about themselves and how you interact with people and how you work with people and how you don't work with people. Those lessons were to be learned. People working with people. That whole area is kind of a challenge for all of us, and we still don't know how to do that yet.

So it's not just a matter of color. Color is an artificial barrier. My brown skin is not what makes me. It's the totality of my experience that makes me. *Ideally,* I would never refer to you as white and me as black. Ideally. I believe ultimately when the Kingdom comes we will all have learned how to live together and work together on common problems and issues that we see. The superficial divisions will disappear. I don't know when that will come, but I think ultimately it has to come. Things just can't be based on what color anybody is. I mean, I think in the *ideal* world, that just can't be important. I think that just divides people and ultimately that gets to be what wars are fought over. Even movements, if you

will, will have to learn that we are all made in the same image—
that when we were all created, the Creator said, "That's good."
It's all good.

For the conclusion of Dorothy Cotton's interview, see Chapter Six (page 388).

Alone, and Working "Them Little Old Chitt'ling-Switch Towns"

Bernice Robinson

National news headlines in May 1961 focused on the Congress of Racial Equality (CORE) and the Freedom Riders that it sponsored. Violence attracted the photographers' eyes, because angry whites in Alabama and Mississippi used beatings and arson and legal harassment to resist the Freedom Riders' test of desegregation practices.

That same year, but with little publicity, the SCLC, the SNCC, and CORE cooperated in another endeavor: the Citizenship Schools. Bernice Robinson, who had been the first Citizenship School teacher, was employed by both Highlander and the SCLC to set up voter-education workshops in communities across the racially tense South. As such, she made no news headlines, but neither was she immune from threats or danger. The legacy of the Freedom Riders was certain: Once fear had been set loose in Dixie, few civil rights workers were safe.

By 1961, my mother had died. In January of that year, Septima [Clark], who was working full-time with Highlander fund-raising all over the country, had a heart attack and everyone was nervous about her health and felt that she was overworked and needed help. So Myles [Horton] offered me a job and I came on full-time with Highlander in that same year helping to train Citizenship School teachers, who were being sent to Highlander from all over.

Of course, Highlander was under litigation by the state ever since the raid in 1959. And when the Field Foundation decided to fund the schools, they couldn't do business with Highlander since its nonprofit status was in question. That's where Andy Young really came in. He had come down in early 1961 with the intention of working for Highlander, but everything was getting kind of shaky legally, so Andy's church, the United Church of Christ Board for Homeland Ministries, accepted the Field Foundation funds, SCLC took over the Citizenship School program, Andy and Septima went over to SCLC to run the program, and Dorothy Cotton hooked up with them soon after.

I stayed with Highlander and did political education workshops all across the South. Bob Moses organized a lot of them through SNCC and CORE in Mississippi, and Charles Sherrod did the same in Georgia. Other people set them up in Alabama and Louisiana and the other states. They would ask Myles to let me come in, and they would do the recruiting and get the people to the workshops, and then I would set up the workshops as far as getting consultants and working on the subject matter they wanted to discuss: how to get people together, how to get voter turnout, how to get money to finance schooling—all that. I brought Esau [Jenkins] out of Charleston many times to help me. And I would consult with people like Medgar Evers.

In fact, the morning that Medgar Evers got killed [June 12, 1963], I was supposed to have a meeting with him and Aaron Henry and Dave Dennis and Annelle Ponder there in Greenwood, Mississippi. As I was having my coffee and getting ready to catch my flight out early that morning, it came across the radio that he had been shot and killed, and I dropped the coffee pot, the cup, and everything. I went on anyway, and we met and planned what we were going to do, but that was really a shock. . . .

[Many of us, with hindsight, ask why and how we endured, and] part of it's the way you're raised. I mean, it's like in my life a lot of things from my childhood worked within me, I guess, that I was not aware of being there. I just did things because I felt I should and then you wonder, "Why am I here? What am I doing here?" You don't realize that there has been a series of events that brought you to that point of action.

And then, I think, really you don't realize to what extent you're getting into something in the beginning. I know I did not know what all I would be up against. I wasn't even looking that far down the road. You start somewhere with something that you want to do, and you get pulled along. You start out with the voter registration fight. That was just a matter of getting people registered to vote. Then you've got to get them out to the polls. Then you come to Highlander and it becomes a matter of teaching people to read and write. Like I say, I can't explain the feeling I had when that sixty-five-year-old woman who had never read in her life could recognize her name. And if you have any sensitivity at all to people around you, and you have any caring within you, you find yourself saying, "I gotta do more. I gotta do more of this. Gee whiz, people have been in darkness all their lives, and I brought light to that one woman. I brought light to that woman. Oh, I want to do more of that." And you look at it from that angle and you keep moving in, and moving in, and it keeps getting more dangerous, and more dangerous. But you aren't aware of the danger. I don't think that the men in the armed services really realize the extent of the danger until after they come back. I rode all through Alabama, Mississippi, all them little old chitt'ling-switch towns in Georgia, by myself. I was stopped and asked, "You still live in South Carolina?" Well, I know what they were trying to tell me. They see the South Carolina tag on my car, and they're telling me I better get back on home. I'm in the wrong country. Every day I was stopped in Mississippi, and I laughed about it then, you know, to myself. I knew what they were going to ask before they said a word. [*Laughing*] After all that was over with and I came out of it, I'd say, "You know, I must have been crazy."

And I've thought about the many times I talked to the law in Alabama or Mississippi and never said, "Yes, sir." I always said, "What's the trouble, officer?" when they'd stop me. And I thought, "You know, those fools could have killed me, and I didn't even realize the danger I was in." You're in there, you are trying to survive, and you think of ways and means to survive, and also do the job. And you realize the danger after you get out of it. I think if you thought about the danger when you went into it, you wouldn't go. But it's hard to say.

And Myles was right out there to keep you straight too. You might say, "Well, I'll tell you what's wrong with Charleston. This is what's wrong with Charleston. This is what we ought to do."

He'd say, "No, that isn't what you ought to do. Better take it to the people first. Find out what *they* see the problem as being." He was always able to bring you back to that.

And that lesson should be learned by anyone who tries to help bring about positive change anywhere. If you come to help in Charleston, I know you mean well when you come in. You may feel that a certain situation is bad and you need to change that overnight. But the way you might want to go about it might not be the way the *people* want to go. And the situation you want to change might not be one they think *needs* changing. You are going to have to work with people. You are going to have to find out what they feel is *their* greatest need in any particular area. When you find what their greatest need is, then you work with them on *that* need.

Now, you might see something that would benefit them more. But if you are going to get them interested in working with you and having confidence in you, you'd better work with them on what *they* say their need is first and win their confidence, and then you can begin to suggest other things: "Well, what about this? Don't you think we ought to work in this area too?" And they say, "Yeah. Right." And you're getting somewhere.

People who come in and try to change things the other way don't last too long. They ship out pretty soon. Their problem was they didn't *listen*. They went in *telling*. And you don't get very far that way. I may be walking down the road with my feet tied in burlap, and it's freezing out, and you say, "That poor girl. She needs a pair of shoes. I'm going to get her a pair of shoes." But you know, that might be the least of my worries. I might rather have a good meal, or maybe I feel that if I had a warm coat, my feet wouldn't be so cold. If you are going to interest me in those shoes, you are going to have to find out what it is *I* want first. You might just insult me if you give me those shoes. And that's just the way the world is, you know. What people see as their need is more important than what you see. Now what you see might be of more value in the end, and have the greatest good, but you can't bring them around to seeing that unless you start where they are.

We knew, we *knew* that to get black people registered to vote would create a challenge to the white community, and we knew it was important to get that done, but we also knew that for many of those people who weren't registered, the most important thing to *them* was often something different. Causing political change through voting was too intangible at first. They wanted to be able to order something out of a catalog, or read a letter from one of their children from out of town without having to take it to a neighbor or their white madam. That meant more to them than a registration certificate at that moment. They just couldn't see that far down the road. So you dealt with them on that level. You had to. Then the rest followed. That's why those schools worked.

Bernice Robinson left the SCLC in 1970 and was hired by the South Carolina Commission for Farm Workers (SCCFW), under whose auspices she supervised VISTA volunteers in her native Charleston. In 1972, she made an unsuccessful bid for public office, then returned to the SCCFW and worked with migrants until 1977. For the conclusion of her interview, see Chapter Six (page 368).

★

"I Paid My Own Way over to Oslo"
Septima Clark

Septima Clark was the grandam of the civil rights movement—at the time, her threescore-plus years far outdistancing the ages of most of the college students and youthful ministers who filled its ranks. But she lived long enough to see her vision for Johns Island's blacks grow into a powerful political tool across the South. From 1961 through 1964, tens of thousands of Southern blacks were registered to vote as a result of her concept for the Citizenship Schools. And this massive voter registration effort by the SCLC, combined with a steadfast belief in nonviolent civil disobedience, helped convince Norwegian officials in 1964 to name thirty-five-year-old Dr. Martin Luther King, Jr., as the youngest recipient of the Nobel Peace Prize.

These accomplishments, however, stood in sharp contrast to the era's violence. Every summer from 1961 to 1966 the South became the setting for bloody, deadly retaliation: Klansmen against blacks, Southern whites against Northern whites, and law enforcement officials combating all the groups. In the midst of these tragic scenarios, Septima Clark recalls witnessing Dr. King practice the nonviolence that he preached.

[In the beginning days of the SCLC involvement with the schools, Wyatt Tee Walker, Dorothy Cotton, Andy Young, Ernestine Brown, Lillie Hunter, and I worked out of the Atlanta office.] Wyatt handled the business part of it, seeing about the grant and setting up the salaries and getting the contracts signed. Then most of the actual workshops were held in Liberty County, Georgia, at

Dorchester Center, which we got access to through Andy Young and his church.

The very first month, Andy and Dorothy and I traveled meeting people and getting ready. Then, when we got things started, we'd hold a workshop once or twice a month for people we had recruited as potential teachers from communities all over the South. And the rest of the time we'd either be in Atlanta or on the road either recruiting more teachers or helping out in various communities with whatever was going on. The bulk of the workshops were held at the center, unless a group of people just couldn't get there, in which case we'd take the workshop to them. And under Andy's regime, the organization grew until there were something like fifteen women working to coordinate everything out of Atlanta. At one time there were 195 classes going on in the eleven Deep South states, and those women worked mimeographing teaching materials and keeping track of students and all that. So it branched out into a big thing. The strategy, as always, was to get people to read and write so they could register to vote, but since each state had different requirements, in each state we had to do different things.

[But the actual structure of the workshops stayed basically the same from state to state.] I wrote out the day-by-day program that I took with me to the Southern Christian Leadership Conference. The expenses were all paid for the people we recruited to come to the workshops, because many of them could not have come otherwise. In return, they had to promise that they would go back to their community and open up a school, and they were supposed to teach two nights a week, two hours each night and we'd pay them thirty dollars a month for that. We had some teaching materials prepared for them, and then we'd also help them come up with their own depending on their people's needs. We'd help them see how they could teach arithmetic by helping people figure the amount of fertilizer and seed their farms would use and how much they would pay for it—things like that. And, of course, reading was partly taught through looking at each state's election laws.

But the format of the workshops was pretty standard. We worked out a whole plan. The first night, the people would give you their input—telling you their names, where they came from, what kind of work they were engaged in, and how they were re-

ceived in their community. And then we would decide that night
how we would share the work that we were going to do as we lived
there together during that whole week—the dishes and so on.

The next morning somebody would be assigned to the introduction of Highlander and the kinds of things we hoped to get
through the whole week, then the teaching sessions would start.
Each session would start with music, and that was the thing that
really got them going. When they got through singing, we would
go into our work. There were sessions morning, afternoon, and
night on the second, third, and fourth days. Then, on the fifth
day, we usually took them to see some historical place, depending
on where we were. If we were in Savannah, we would carry them
down to see a fort or something, and then to the beach if it was
summer.

At the end of each workshop on Friday night, the people had
to demonstrate what they could do back home. Sometimes they
put on plays built on teaching people how to read and write.
Sometimes they'd demonstrate how to decorate and set a table
using whatever they had in their community and not buying flowers and things of that type.

Overall, it was a real success. The first part of Georgia that we
worked through is a good example. We started with Savannah because Hosea Williams was there and he was a dynamic leader. In
Georgia, in order to register, you had to be able to answer at least
twenty-four of thirty questions they would ask you, and in the
workshops, Hosea would have a session where he would drill into
people those thirty questions, and he really did a good job doing
that.

When we were successful in Savannah, then Hosea found
eighteen counties in the southeastern part of Georgia, and we
started schools in those eighteen counties through bringing people to the center and training them. In three weeks' time, with the
help of the SNCC boys and SCLC's staff, we put nine thousand
black registered voters on the books in 1961.

Then in between workshops, like I said, we'd go to various
places and help out. I went to Albany, Georgia, for example, during their registration drive, and I stood at the courthouse door I
guess for eight or ten days, from morning until late afternoon,

telling the black people as they came up, "Go ahead and register."

The white man would say to them, "You can't vote in this election. It's too late. It's no use for you to register."

And I would say to them, "Registration is permanent in Georgia, so you go ahead and register now. If you can't vote in this election, you *can* vote later on. Go ahead and register." I stayed by that door in Albany from nine o'clock every morning, when the registration books opened, till five o'clock in the afternoon, just leaving for lunch and going right back.

[But] we had lots of opposition. Andy Young was badly beaten in Tallahassee, Florida, going down there to try to recruit the people. That was in the latter part of '61. Dorothy Cotton was along.

Because of that kind of thing, we were always a little nervous. One time we were going from Mississippi into New Orleans, Louisiana, and Andy, Dorothy Cotton, and I were in that car, and we saw a white fellow on the road. He'd run out of gas. And Andy being a preacher, he said, "You know, I just can't let him stand there." He said, "Y'all get in the back and I'll put him in the front with me." So he did. But all the time we were thinking, if he starts any trouble, we'll all have to jump on him together. [*Laughter*] But he really needed help and we were glad that we could take him to a filling station so he could get some gas to put in his car. He must have been surprised, though, for these blacks to give him a lift. [*Laughing*]

Sometimes it wasn't so funny. Five members of our group got beaten for going into the white side of a bus station in Tupelo, Mississippi. It came to trial in Oxford, and everyone was so frightened that when we had recess, not even the black restaurant would sell us a meal. We had to go into the Woolworth store and buy some candy or cookies and a drink and then come back to the courthouse. I couldn't stay anywhere around there. A black beautician finally took me in in Clarksdale. Beauticians could usually take you in because they made their money off their own people and weren't dependent on white customers. But every morning I'd have to drive those forty-six miles to that courthouse.

A man was there from the Justice Department to make sure the trial was fair, but as soon as he was finished that afternoon, he had a car waiting to get him out of there and back to Washington. He knew he'd better because even though he was white, those Mississippi whites would have killed him. That was the kind of thing that we had all the time.

Those people in Mississippi were something. In Grenada, a white fellow took a fifteen-year-old boy that was working with me and threw him on the ground and broke his leg in three places. We had to carry him all the way to Clarksdale to a hospital.

That Sunday afternoon in the same town, we had a meeting in a church, and when we finished, we'd just been out of that church five minutes when the whole thing went up in flames. Every section of that church went at once. All we could do was stand out in the middle of the street and look at it.

Then in Natchez, I went down there to recruit and to establish schools. While I was down there, one night in a Baptist church, the Ku Klux Klan surrounded us. They had planned to come into the church, but the police there sent them away because they knew they'd have quite a number of deaths.

The same thing happened in Selma, Alabama, probably because we had managed to register a large number of people to vote. I had called Washington to get protection for us through the Attorney General after one of our boys had been kicked by a White Citizens' Council man, and Washington called the chief of police there and had him to see who had done this thing and to do something about it. That night we were at church, and the Klan surrounded that church with their faces all hooded and everything. I thought sure they were going to kill us that night, but the chief of police came—his name was Robinson—and he took his horn and he told the Klan, "Go back. Go back. We don't want to have a Watts here." He said, "Go back. Go back." And then he asked all the colored people to go into the church and stay in there until the Klan had gotten out of the way. Charles Evers was arrested that night, and at two o'clock that morning I was walking on that street, going to the jailhouse to get Charles out, and I didn't know what to expect. Luckily nothing happened, but you never knew.

Sometimes our own people would resist the schools. That happened to us at first in Selma. Dr. King sent six of us in to teach the people how to write their names in cursive writing so they could register when the federal man came down in August. A number of the black preachers didn't want us to teach the people how to write their names, and the five people that had come with me couldn't take the foolishness from those preachers and they left. I stayed on alone, walking around until I could find someone who would listen, and when I found one person, I asked him to get some of his friends. And when they brought their friends, I fed them. I found out that that was a good way. I carried them somewhere and had lunch. And while they were eating, I'd talk to them about registering and voting and what it would mean to them, and then I could have a meeting at night.

Finally, at the end of that second week, a man called me in and said, "Who's going to pay for this?"

I said, "Why, we'll pay for everything that we need."

"What about your publicity?"

I said, "Well, we'll get all that out." And everything he would ask me I would let him know that we had money to do this.

"Whose teachers are you going to use?"

"Why, your teachers, of course, we wouldn't bring in any new teachers. We'll pay them the going rate." At that time it was $1.25 an hour. And so the teachers of Selma worked in their kitchens and various places two hours a week for five mornings teaching people. We had some ninety-one years of age learning to write their names, and in August, 7,002 persons were registered. But that happened because I knew I had to be patient enough to wait until the people decided within themselves that they wanted to do this. I knew I couldn't get angry and leave. Nothing gets accomplished that way.

[But some in the movement couldn't resist lashing back.] In early 1963, C. T. Vivian had a fistfight on the street outside the courthouse in Birmingham. He started beating up a white man and we had to grab him and take him inside.

It was a constant struggle. I remember one time a group of seminarians from Union [Theological] Seminary in New York had been down all one summer working with children in Albany, Georgia, and when we had the children over to McIntosh, Georgia, for a workshop, low and behold they were throwing bricks at the cars of the white people passing by. I called that university and let the man there know that his seminarians were teaching these children the wrong kinds of things. I said, "These children are going to have to stay here when your people go home, and they're going to be the ones that will suffer." And he called them back to New York. They could have been the cause of some murders.

Dr. King was a great example, though. Whenever he got the executive group together, he would lecture to them about being nonviolent. "You can't win," he said. "You can't win if you're going to fight back."

I remember him having Stokely Carmichael to come to his house to dinner to tell Stokely, "You can't win if you're going to send the boys up and down the street to knock out the window glasses of the stores along Auburn Avenue."

There are times when I can tell you that I did not feel the same way. I've never been a person to fight, but when Fannie Lou Hamer was being tried in Oxford, Mississippi, in 1964, because she and some others went into the front part of a bus station, I wanted to fight then. They threw them all in jail, and she is a crippled woman, and they beat her terribly. When I heard those men testifying at that trial, I wished that a chandelier would drop on their heads and kill them. My mind wasn't nonviolent. And I don't think that I've gotten to the place today where my mind is quite nonviolent, because I still have feelings at times that I'd like to do something violent to stop people.

But Dr. King insisted on nonviolence, and he meant what he said, and most of us followed his example. He didn't just preach it, either. Coming from Albany, Georgia, one night, we were riding in a car, and some white fellows came up behind us and finally cut across in front of us. Dr. King was in the car, and the young man who was driving got out and went into the trunk of his car and took out a pistol, and the white fellows went on. And Dr. King said, "Frank, do you think I wanted you to do that? No, Frank, that's not the way to do it."

Then one night we were coming from Montgomery to Atlanta on a little Southern plane in the early part of '64. A fellow jumped up and said to him, "You're reading about yourself, aren't you?" —he was reading the paper—and then he hit him. And Dr. King just moved right over and didn't say a word. The steward got him and put him back in his seat. In a few minutes he jumped up again and drew back to hit him, and that steward got him and tied him down in the seat until we reached Atlanta. But Dr. King would never strike back.

In Birmingham at the Gaston Motel in 1963, before those little girls were killed, we were having a workshop down there. And numbers of men were talking, and Dr. King was introducing a fellow from California. A white fellow came up with his collar wide open, and we wondered if this was the man he was introducing. When he got up there he hit Dr. King in the face twice, and Dr. King dropped his hands like that of a newborn baby. I was sitting to the front, and I said, "Don't hit him! Don't hit him!" I knew that he'd just had some trouble with that heart where that woman stuck that knife or scissors or dagger in him right across from his heart. The other men jumped up—old men eighty years of age and all—and they had sticks. They were about to attack this man. And Dr. King said, "Don't touch him. Don't touch him. We have to pray for him." But somebody called the policeman, and the policeman came and took this white guy away. They wanted Dr. King to come up and put charges against him, which he refused. They said he would have to do it, and that afternoon we all prepared to march up to that courthouse. But he decided that he would not prefer the charges against the man. We found out later that it was that guy, George Lincoln Rockwell, that was killed by one of his own men in Virginia. He was the leader of that Nazi party who was killed a couple of years later by one of his own men.

But Dr. King wouldn't do one thing to him. Mrs. Parks was in that meeting, and she went out and got a bottle of Coca-Cola. She wanted Dr. King to have some Coca-Cola and some aspirins because she knew that his head must have been hurting at that time.

Then in 1963—it was Good Friday—we saw those guys roughing him up to take him to jail because he had planned the march to get the stores and things opened uptown. At the same time, we were working with young people, telling them if they couldn't march without being violent, then we'd have to take them off the line. Well, when I saw him throwing his hands down when somebody hit him, I didn't know if we could control them or not.

But we managed. But he would not strike back. He was absolutely nonviolent. Some people had a hard time following his example, but we know now that he was right.

[The SCLC also had some organizational problems. For example,] when we had the march from Selma to Montgomery in '64, so much money came in that one of our people felt that he had to help himself to some. He did that, and somehow or other the alarm went off and he was arrested. Dr. King refused to prosecute him, and he said, "The unemployment for young blacks is so great that I'll keep him and rehabilitate him." He did that too. That man became a great spirit in the movement even to this day.

Another time, we had a group of fifteen people coming to a workshop from Alabama, and we sent the woman who was bringing them four hundred and some dollars to pay for their bus tickets and their meals. She had never seen that much money before, and she took it and paid most of her debts [*laughing*] and didn't pay for a single bus fare or meal for those people. So we had that. You have to work with people.

Then we had some kind of a fund that came in for the SNCC boys. It came to us because SNCC was organized out of SCLC. Dr. King felt that they should have some workshops and settle down gradually to working in the various towns, but they wanted all their money at once. They knew about the grant, and they wanted everything then. They argued with him, and lots of the men didn't want to give it over, but Dr. King said, "Let them have it. It was gotten for them. Let them have it, and let them do whatever they want to do with it." Sure enough, some of them went to Mexico. They went all around. And of course, it wasn't too long before they didn't have any money, and they had to come back to us to ask us to give them some more.

But most of those incidents were the kinds of things you had to expect from people who had never had anything before and who just had to learn. When I got mad was when people who were supposed to know better abused the situation. Like we had a white social worker who came to work with us, and she had the feeling that these poverty-stricken people coming out of Alabama and Mississippi were just so far beneath her that she couldn't be of service to them. She was very haughty. One time she missed her regular plane and chartered a plane to come to Liberty County for a workshop, but she failed to send any money to the people coming into the workshop from Mississippi, and there they came, all the way from Mississippi, starving.

I was really angry with her about that, and I talked to her in no uncertain terms. I said, "Here you are. You charter a plane and sit in an airport in Savannah and eat a good dinner and ride out here in a rented car, and you wouldn't send these people six dollars apiece to eat on, and then you want them to go back in there and work." I said, "You feel that they're all beneath you, and that's your big trouble. You should have the feeling that they are human beings, and that they need your help. And, after all, you're not spending your money anyway. You're spending the money of the foundation people who gave us this." I told her if it weren't for those people, she wouldn't have bread and butter on her table. She and I argued about that quite a bit. I disliked her attitude greatly. She didn't stay long.

Some of our own people had a few problems at first adjusting to working with people who were so poor, but they made this adjustment because they cared so much. Andy Young, for example. When Andy came to us he had been working with middle-class students who could go to Europe, and he went with them to Europe most of the time. One of the early groups that came into Dorchester came from eastern Texas, and we took them to the ocean for our recreation one Friday afternoon. And those women wanted to bring back some water and bottles of sand to let people know that they had been to the Atlantic Ocean. They even took the place mats off their table in the Howard Johnson's so their children could see that they had been able to eat in a Howard Johnson's restaurant. And Andy said to me, "You know, I never thought anything of things like that." He said, "If I hadn't come on this trip with you, I would not have realized just how little of my experiences other people have. I'm glad I have the chance to work with you." And he grew.

Down at Penn Center we had a big workshop right after the voting rights bill. We had a large number of people, and he and Dorothy were singing a song that says, "I love everybody," and both of them had their eyes closed. And I saw a young woman who was really crying, and her face was so distorted. She had come from that part of Georgia where Koinonea is, and a policeman had arrested her at Koinonea, and when they arrested her they put her on the square. They called her a mulatto, and they wanted to make her ashamed. They put her on the square and they put cattle prods to her heels to see her jump up and down. And so she couldn't sing, "I love everybody." She said, "I just can't sing it."

So I talked to Andy and Dorothy. I said, "You've got to open your eyes and see what's happening to this young woman. She can't sing that song. She can't love everybody when the people treated her so mean." Anyway, Andy and I had some words about that [*laughter*], and he told me that I must have been a saint. I said, "Well, there are all kinds of saints. I don't know who you're talking about, but I want you to keep your eyes about you and see what's happening, because you can't expect people like this young woman to sing that until they can feel more comfortable."

He learned, and SCLC had its greatest growth and success under Andy's leadership.

It was funny to me, but most of the educated men seemed to have that trouble relating. They didn't have the patience at first to work in small towns or listen to the poor people who came in. As dedicated as he is, even Myles Horton had trouble sitting and listening to the people from places like Thomasville, Georgia, tell about the happenings there. It was hard for him to sit and listen to them say, "Now this happened the night that that cow had its calf on such-and-such a moon." He wanted them to come right to the point, and they wouldn't do it. [*Laughing*] I found that true with most of the men.

[And yet the men got most of the credit for the success of the civil rights movement.] [*Laughing*] The women were raised to work behind the scenes and not speak out. They didn't really start speaking out until the movement was into its tenth year or so. If you watch the movie, *From Montgomery to Memphis,* you'll notice that they don't mention one woman going through there. Not one. You almost never see their role put down in any of the reports about the movement. You just get "Dr. So-and-so from Alabama State College did such-and-such," but they don't give the women any of the glory at all. It's just starting to come now. Women just weren't as visible as the men. Even Mrs. King's role was stifled until her husband died, and he's one of the few who really recognized our contribution. I can remember Reverend Abernathy asking many times, "Why is Septima Clark on the executive board of the Southern Christian Leadership Conference?" And Dr. King would always say, "She was the one who proposed this citizenship education, which is bringing to us not only money but a lot of people who will register and vote." But it was hard for [Reverend Abernathy] to see a woman on that executive body.

I think that's one of the reasons why Ella Baker had left SCLC by the time I got there. She was very smart and dedicated, and she was concerned about the women not being recognized in a man-made world. It really didn't bother me that much—it really didn't —but she didn't see why a brochure should have sixteen pictures of Dr. King, or why the sign over the door where we met should say "Dr. King and Reverend Abernathy," and not acknowledge anyone else. I felt she had a real point, but nobody was going to listen to her at that time.

They didn't really listen to me, either. I remember at one point feeling that Dr. King was dominating the movement too much. I never felt that he *wanted* to. It was just that others had gotten to the place where they felt everything had to be done by him. I always felt that if you were going to develop other people, you don't talk for them. You train them to do their own talking. This is what I would do, but he couldn't see it. I would not have ever been able to work in Mississippi and Alabama and all those places if I had done all the talking. And when I worked with the college students, I would say to them, "Don't go and cash the check for this woman at the A & P. Let her do it. You can go with her and give her that much courage, but make her cash her check and do her own talking so that she can have the feeling that she *can.*"

I talked to Dr. King about all that several times. The last letter I sent him I said that I felt he had disciples in Memphis who could lead a march. He didn't have to lead them all. He read the letter to the executive group, and there was a secretary sitting there and two other women. I had spoken to them earlier about this, too. But not a one of them said one word. Neither did a young man who was in our office. Not a one of them supported me in that at all. And he went to Memphis [where he was killed].

He was a great leader, though. When he received the Nobel Peace Prize in Oslo, Norway, he said, "I'm on the mountaintop now, but I have to think about those people down in the valley who placed me here. This money is not mine. I must give it to the NAACP, to the Southern Christian Leadership Conference, to the

Urban League, and to CORE." And he did. I paid my own way over to Oslo to see him get the prize. I felt when a Southern black man could win a Nobel Peace Prize, I wanted to be there. And when we came back to New York, we went up to the Armory that night and had a big program, and he had the checks made out and he gave that fifty-four thousand dollars to those organizations right there.

For the conclusion of Septima Clark's interview, see Chapter Six (page 396).

"The Students Won the Victory and the Adults Negotiated the Truce"

Julian Bond

At Chicago's chaotic Democratic National Convention in 1968, this Pennsylvania native became the first black to have his name entered into nomination as a U.S. vice-presidential candidate. During the convention tallies, however, he was defeated by Maine's Senator Edmund S. Muskie. Nonetheless, Julian Bond achieved a milestone in the process: His convention-floor nomination symbolized the reality that after eight years of voter registration drives in the South, blacks had at least established themselves as a national political entity.

Despite this accomplishment, the black vote in the South had little direct impact on the election's November outcome. Outspoken segregationist George Wallace, running as an independent presidential candidate, won an overwhelming Southern majority—garnering forty-six electoral votes from Arkansas, Louisiana, Mississippi, Alabama, Georgia, and North Carolina—while Republican Richard M. Nixon, who gleaned virtually no black support, narrowly defeated both Wallace and Democrat Hubert H. Humphrey.

In the wake of this racially controversial campaign, the civil rights movement seemed adrift. The assassination of Dr. Martin Luther King, Jr., in April of that year had already left a leadership vacuum that no single individual seemed able to fill. Then to be confronted seven months later by the stamp of approval for Wallace's antiblack sentiments that his Southern victory confirmed—well, the protest movement seemed defeated. At the end of an era. The dream faded.

Recalling events that led up to this political low point for blacks,

Bond describes the rise of the SNCC as an organization that was, from its inception, in concert with, but also divergent from, King's SCLC leadership. And Bond provides some perspective on why, after King's death, the two civil rights groups broke ranks altogether—leaving their voter registration gains singularly lacking momentum during the 1968 campaign.

Both of my parents were well educated—middle class. My mother was from Nashville, and her stepfather was the chaplain at Fisk. She went to Fisk and then got her master's in library science from Atlanta University.

My father's family was from Kentucky. He was the son of a minister who had been a fundraiser for Berea College in Berea, Kentucky. His parents pushed him to get an education, and he went away to Lincoln University in Pennsylvania in his early teens. Lincoln was then a private black college—the oldest in the country as a matter of fact. He graduated from Lincoln and went on to Chicago and got his Ph.D. and then worked around at a variety of black colleges. In 1945 he became president of Lincoln and stayed there until 1957 when he became dean of education at Atlanta University.

Being in black higher education, he provided a setting in which I saw lots of examples of people who were doing various things that made them worth emulating. He was very good friends with W. E. B. Dubois, for example, and I have a picture of Dr. Dubois and E. Franklin Frazier and myself taken when I was four years old, and it has the three of us in academic regalia. Then I have another picture of me sitting on Paul Robeson's lap. And I remember seeing Walter White, who was then Executive Secretary of the NAACP. I doubt that there were twenty people in the United States at that time whose full-time concern was civil rights for black people, but Walter White was one, and my father made sure we knew it. There was a real sense that the educated black person had a responsibility greater than just getting the education. You had a responsibility for sharing your training and skills with others—particularly those less fortunate.

Now this was a period predating the physical resistance, with one or two exceptions. While we were living at Lincoln, for example, some students had a sit-in at a local movie theater that was segregated, but that was really viewed in the community at large as a radical, strange act, possibly run by wild men from New York and Philadelphia. They did not understand these things in rural Pennsylvania.

My father would sign ads, though, and join certain organizations he thought should be supported. I'll tell you a bad thing that happened to him when he felt he was deceived. He was president of an organization called the American Society for African Culture —AMSAC—which, it later turned out, was funded by a CIA conduit in New York. This was in the late 1950s. He was very much put out by that.

But he wasn't involved in the kind of activism that would get your name in the newspapers. He just set an example of responsibility, and I watched that. And I watched the way he dealt with institutions and the way pressures came down on him—pressures that nearly crushed him. See, Lincoln University was a serious academic institution that concentrated on training black leadership for the United States, and it turned out well-educated people who went on to be doctors and lawyers and ministers and so on. And though the school had always been integrated, it had never had more than two or three white students at a time. As president, he got into a dispute with the trustees who wanted it to be more aggressive in recruiting students from the local community, which was overwhelmingly white, and he didn't want to do it. He wanted it to remain a national institution for the education of young black men, and they wanted it to be a kind of local parochial Pennsylvania school—which is exactly what it is today.

Anyway, my father lost his job over that, and that's why we moved to Atlanta. I was seventeen.

It was very different. Where we lived in Pennsylvania was rural. I had never lived in a city. And it was a really frightening move to me because my impressions of the South in 1957 were formed largely by black newspapers, and whenever any particularly vicious incidents of brutality took place in the South, they were front-page news for weeks. I can still remember one incident of a black Korean vet being beaten blind in a bus station in some Southern city, and I said, "Hey, no! They're lynching people and putting people's eyes out down there. I don't want to move there!" I thought those kinds of things happened daily and that you were literally taking your life in your hands to walk into downtown Atlanta. It's funny. The whole world wants to come here now! [*Laughing*]

Anyway, I entered Morehouse [College], and I stayed close to campus for the first few years. I had classmates who'd come to school on the bus every day and I'd say, "Gee. How'd they *do* that?" [*Laughing*] I didn't want to do it. I didn't want to be out there. I wanted to be in a safe place. Eventually I got to where I'd go to the segregated Fox Theatre downtown with friends. You had to buy your ticket at a little window around the side, and then you had to walk these outside stairs up to a balcony and go in. That was one of the few times I would go downtown, though. Basically I had no desire to go.

But going to Morehouse was a radically different experience for me, partly because it was the first time I discovered that there was this *national* community of black academics whose children all knew each other because our parents knew each other and were involved in the same life. If you taught at Tuskegee, there were so few of your type in the countryside around there that socially you gravitated toward Atlanta, and your mother would say, "I want you to meet Dr. Jones' daughter. He teaches at Tuskegee." So if your father taught at Tuskegee and somebody else's father taught at Fisk, and somebody else's father taught at Morehouse and somebody else's father taught at Albany State, you all knew each other. Chances were you all went to the same prep school—Mount Herman was the favorite school for Southern blacks to send their kids to—and if you were really heavy, you went to Harvard together. And even if you didn't go to school together, you'd know lots of people in common because of that national network of common interests.

Another great shock to me was meeting students from a completely different class structure for the first time, and actually having to compete with them for grades. Morehouse was a single-sex institution, which I think was good for me because otherwise I would have been playing all the time. And it had an early admissions policy, and an active scholarship program, and so there were all these fifteen- and sixteen-year-old boys who had left high school after the eleventh grade and had come from the worst kind of poverty in rural Georgia, and who had maybe interrupted their high school education to pick cotton or peaches or something, but for whom an education was the most precious thing in the world. Here I was, with this great facility for testing, and scoring at the top of the freshman class in the entrance exams, and by the end of the year, these students who would work at the Piedmont Driving Club as waiters until one o'clock in the morning and then go home, study the rest of the night, sleep for an hour, go to class in the morning, and then go back to work—these students had just swept me aside and left me down around the middle third of the class. I was really attracted to them because they weren't your classic grinds who just study all the time, but they were obviously bright and they were very well-rounded people. They were good people. I was very much attracted to many of them.

Not all of them came from rural poverty—Maynard Jackson went there when he was fourteen, and Dr. King went there—but many of them did. You can go on the campus now and find that still true. I don't know how Morehouse finds them, but they get in there at fifteen years old and whip on through and get their Ph.D.s at Harvard. We had a guy who had just come back to Morehouse to teach who left Harvard over a dispute with his teacher over the answer to a question on a test. The student was right and the teacher was wrong, and the student left and finished his work at the University of California at Berkeley. He knew he was right, and he wouldn't go back into class and say he was wrong. But that is the kind of person Morehouse often produces.

[When I dropped out of Morehouse to go to work for the civil rights movement, it was] a trauma for my father—and not because of the work I was doing, but because I had dropped out of school. He was very much put out at that, but he didn't say, "Stop that and go back to school." But I could tell he was very displeased. He believed in that education.

[But for me,] it was nothing. I mean literally nothing. It was nothing, that is, in terms of what I wanted to do with my life at that time. Even now I can't imagine doing a job for which I've got to present my B.A. in order to qualify! [*Laughing*] I just can't imagine it. I finally went back and got my B.A. ten years after I was supposed to get it, but I don't need it to be a politician. . . .

[Lonnie King drew me into the movement in the first place.] He's one of those students I was talking about who had not come from a middle-class background. He had left Morehouse to join

the Navy because of the Korean War, and had come back to finish
up. Of course, he was older than most of us, but he was very much
a big man on campus. Football hero. Earlier in the year I had seen
the woman who ran the campus post office give him a cake for
running a touchdown, so I knew he was a big guy! But we didn't
know each other.

Anyway, it was about February 3, 1960—I was twenty years old
—and I was sitting in the Yates and Milton Drugstore on the corner, and he came up to me with this copy of the Atlanta *Daily
World* that had an article in it about the Greensboro students who
were in the second or third day of their sit-in. It was a big thing.
We later discovered the same thing had happened in Oklahoma
City two or three years before, but at that time it was the first we
knew of that technique, and of course Greensboro became our
blueprint.

But he showed me this newspaper and he said, "Have you
seen this?"

And I said, "Yeah, I've seen it."

He said, "What do you think about it?"

I said, "It's okay."

He said, "Don't you think someone ought to do it here?"

I said, "They will."

He said, "Let's *us* do it here. You take this side of the drugstore and I'll take the other, and let's get everybody in here to
come to a meeting at noon."

I was intimidated by him, really, and so I agreed. He was a
hard guy to say no to. And I don't know why he asked me and not
somebody else. I hadn't exhibited any leadership potential. I
wasn't in student government, wasn't in a fraternity, wasn't a
BMOC. I was active in a little literary magazine we had revived on
campus, but I wasn't in the school paper. I just sat in the drugstore
between classes and then went home, so I guess it was just fortu-
itous that he grabbed me.

But he did, and that's how it began. [The people in the drugstore agreed to get involved;] that was the easy part. You got almost universal acceptance. Almost everyone said, "Sure, great,
wonderful." See, that was a funny thing. You had people there like
John Lewis who saw all these contradictions of segregation when
he was in high school. and in '55 when the Montgomery bus boy-

cott started, as a high school student, he had gone to Montgomery to see Reverend [Fred] Shuttlesworth and Dr. King to see if they would help him file a suit against segregated high schools in Pike County. They encouraged him not to—thought he would be killed. And a number of the other students had been active in high school NAACPs, so they already had some exposure to civil rights. And so when this sit-in thing sprang up, they were already in place, waiting, poised, and ready to jump in.

On top of that, the cause was right and the approach was right. Nonviolence, for example, was morally right, and it held up a standard of decency and goodness and honesty to your opponents who were so obviously *not* that. That appealed to people like Charles Jones and John Lewis and all the rest who were preministerial students. And we thought we were legally right and economically right—we spent this money and we should be allowed to sit here. We were right in every way.

So first, we formed this student committee that went to see the Atlanta University presidents, and the Atlanta University presidents—Dr. Rufus Clement, in particular—told us that the AU Center had always been different from all the other black schools all over the country and that it wasn't sufficient just for us to sit in. I think they were trying to buy some time. They said, "No one will understand what you are doing." Of course, people *would* understand what we were doing, but we said, "Yes, you are right, no one will understand why we are sitting in." So they encouraged us to issue a statement of principles before we did anything else.

A group of students began to draw that up. They based their information on a booklet called *A Second Look at Atlanta,* which had been published by a group of largely university-based professional people who had formed a committee called Atlanta Citizens for Constructive Action—ACCA. This booklet, written by Whitney Young—who was then dean of the School of Social Work—and Carl Holman—an English teacher at Clark—and some others, documented inequities such as the fact that black people were 32 percent of the population but lived on 8 percent of the land, and couldn't eat anyplace downtown or work at certain places, and so on.

So we took our information out of that and drew up what we called "An Appeal for Human Rights" that listed about a dozen

things that we thought were wrong. It was signed by the presidents
of all the student bodies of the schools, and it concluded with,
"We pledge our hearts and minds to do whatever is necessary"—
which was strong language then—"to see that these rights are
granted us."

Dr. Clement helped us find the money to publish this in a
full-page ad in the Atlanta papers, and that caused a little storm. I
remember the governor saying, "This thing sounds like it was written in Moscow or Peking," and the mayor—who liked to think of
Atlanta as a liberal city—saying, "Of course this was not written in
Moscow or Peking; this was written by our own students, whose
demands are entirely legitimate," and so forth and so on. This was
before any action at all.

And then the following week, Lonnie and myself and somebody else went downtown to survey our lunch counters, and really
made the store people nervous because we went in with yellow
pads and pencils and said, "Now let me see, there are fifteen
people at this lunch counter," and so on; and you could see the
store detectives just about to faint. They knew something was happening.

Then on March 15, 1960, there we went. Student groups
targeted restaurants in three different areas: every dime store and
bus station in town; the cafeterias for state and federal employees
in the state capitol and the federal building; and the City Hall
cafeteria. All served only whites. I was the leader of the group that
went to the City Hall cafeteria, which is still there. It had a big sign
saying, "CITY HALL CAFETERIA: PUBLIC IS WELCOME," but again, it was only
for white city employees and the white public. We went in, and the
woman said, "We can't serve you here," and we said, "We'll wait
until you can," and she said, "I'm going to call the police," and
she did, and the policeman came, and said, "I'm going to read
you the Georgia antitrespass law and give you the opportunity to
leave, and we said, "We choose not to leave." So they backed the
paddy wagon up to the door where the mayor parks his car now,
and we filed out one by one and got in and they took us to what
was called "Big Rock," which was the old jail before it was torn
down. That was one strange thing. All the people arrested on state
property were taken to the county jail, and everyone else was taken
to the city jail. We were very afraid for those taken to the county

jail because they were in state hands and we had no control what-soever over those who fell victim to the state government. But they were treated about the same way we were.

I told our group that we would only be in jail an hour, and the hours ticked by, and they said, "What's happening, Bond? You told us we would only be in here an hour. I've got a class this afternoon."

I said, "Ah, don't worry about it." It wasn't until about six that evening, though, that we got everybody out. Some of the adult property owners signed our bonds, and we were later in-dicted by a grand jury and charged with conspiracy and restraint of trade. If we had been convicted, we could have had maximum sentences of about ninety-nine years each, but I don't think any-body was ever actually tried on those charges. Everybody just kept getting bound over. I finally got my charges dropped last year. The D.A. came to me about a little matter—wanted an extra attorney in his office that the state had to provide for him—and I said, "You know, I've often wondered about these charges the state has against me."

He said, "Don't worry about it, we'll see they're taken care of." So I assume they have been dropped.

The night we were released, we all went to Paschal's for din-ner and a celebration—Mr. Paschal gave us all a free meal—and then we got together and decided to engage in hit-and-run sit-ins where you'd sit in a place, but leave just before the police arrived. That's when the stores began to adopt a policy of just closing down their lunch counters completely. That's when, on the advice of the lawyers for the NAACP Legal Redress Committee, we decided to focus on Rich's, which the NAACP thought would make a better legal case than a Woolworth's, for example, which was a national chain and took its orders from New York. There was enough pres-sure on them anyway because they were being picketed at the time in probably a hundred Southern cities, and CORE people were negotiating with their New York headquarters—as well as those of the W. T. Grant stores and the Kresge stores—and we felt we needed to do something *here*. Well, Rich's occupied a unique posi-tion in Atlanta in that it provided real leadership in Atlanta's mer-cantile business. All the local managers looked to Rich's for guidance, and if Rich's didn't break, nobody would break. If Rich's buckled, everybody else would too.

You have to remember the position Rich's held in the public mind to understand that decision. See, this store occupied a mythical position in black people's minds. It doesn't now because you've got every other store. But if you were a woman—black or white—interested in fashion in the slightest little bit, this was your store. This was where you bought all your kids' clothes; this was where you bought *everything*. And it was a place where you could take anything back. You could buy a formal dress, wear it that night, and take it back the next day. [*Laughter*] And many people did. They put on a show every year—kind of a fashion show—with singing and dancing, and one year the song was about a woman who wanted to take her husband back [*laughter*] and everybody just laughed and laughed—"Can't take your husband back to Rich's!" [*Laughter in his voice*] The paradox was that if you were black, you could do anything whites could do at Rich's—except eat in the dining room.

At the same time we knew Rich's had to fall, we also knew it was vulnerable, because we had had a meeting with Mr. Richard Rich, and he had said, "I don't care if another Negro ever comes in my store." We knew we had him then.

We set up our base of operations in the basement of the Flipper Temple AME Church in the middle of a public housing project, and the first thing we started doing was collecting Rich's credit cards. I don't know how many we collected, but we collected quite a few. The best one we ever got was John Wesley Dobbs' because he had such a big family. We got all their cards, and they must have spent thousands and thousands of dollars a year there by themselves.

Next we had a boycott of the *entire* downtown area, stretching from Rich's all the way up to Davison's. At one point we put a picket around the whole downtown area with fourteen hundred or so people. It was almost exclusively students. If there were adults, they were public housing people. Occasionally we would have "Ministers' Day," or "Doctors' Day," and you would get some of these guys to picket, but most of them said, "I'm too busy. Here's a hundred dollars." We had about five thousand dollars in the bank at one time if I remember.

During the picketing phase, we had two-way radios; we had a succession of volunteer cars coming every day. We had women from the community who brought food in at lunchtime for the picketers; we had heavy jackets that football players wear that we had gotten from the athletic departments at Morehouse to protect the girls from blowguns and spit; we had all-weather laminated picket signs painted with real paint rather than just poster paint—heavy-duty signs that you could use day after day after day. You know your typical picket sign is no good after a day's work, but ours were forever!

We even got Dr. King arrested down there. We went to him and said, "Listen. You're from Atlanta, and these are Atlanta students—many of them from your alma mater—and you aren't doing anything to help. Come and get in with us." And he did, even though he was primarily interested in national issues then and not local agendas like ours.

In the midst of it, we had a meeting down at the police station with the chief, Lonnie, myself, Mr. Rich, and several others, and Rich said, "Why ya'll picking on me? I give five hundred dollars every year to the United Negro College Fund." But we knew we had him, and we pushed him and we pushed him, and we boycotted him and the trade just went down, down, down. You could read the Federal Reserve reports published every Sunday morning in the *Constitution,* "Retail sales down in Atlanta for fifth week," and you knew something was happening. Either that or there was a recession in the country, and I don't think that was it.

We finally got an agreement, but it was a terrible agreement the way it first came out. What happened, actually, was the students won the victory and the adults negotiated the truce. The first part of it had to do with ending the boycott. Then there was a section about a staggered integration policy of the dining room. Mr. Rich wouldn't admit that he had had to give in, so he wanted to do it on his own timetable and under his own steam. We wanted it immediately because we wanted to demonstrate this cause-effect relationship, but we didn't get it. And third, somehow or another, the white merchants managed to tag on a section declaring that if there was any violence over the upcoming integration of the public schools, the store lunch counters wouldn't integrate at all. There was absolutely no connection—one had nothing to do with the other—and we felt this was somebody else's delaying tactic to slow down what we'd put a lot of hard work and effort into, and we were really steamed—but I guess the two issues were connected in the merchants' minds somehow. If you had trouble at the schools, you'd have trouble at the lunch counters. But there really was no connection. Anyway, we had a mass meeting across the street from Mount Moriah Baptist Church and on the podium were Lonnie and Hershel and Daddy King, Sr., and the NAACP lawyers, and Martin Luther King, Jr., and some others, and the crowd was incensed. It repudiated Lonnie. It repudiated Hershel. Almost had Lonnie and Hershel in tears. People called Daddy King an Uncle Tom. I don't think he had ever been called an Uncle Tom in his life before. It was an angry crowd of people, many of whom had been boycotting this favorite store for months and months, and now they were being told by their adult leaders that they should end the boycott and go back and shop without being able to eat at the lunch counters. I can remember this nurse in her uniform storming up the center of the church yelling, "You mean to tell me . . . I tore up my credit card!" [*Laughter*] "I didn't give up shopping at Rich's a year for *this!*"

But *then* Martin made a speech and I have never heard such a masterful speech. It was on leadership, and it said, in effect, that you have to trust your leaders. They are not always going to do what you think they ought to, and sometimes they will do the opposite, and sometimes they will do bad things, but you have to stick with them. He really played the audience like a violin and lifted them up and let them down, lifted them up and let them down, and lifted them up and let them down, and the last time he was through; and the stores *did* integrate on a fairly regular schedule. I can remember when Rich's integrated. They had wanted us to send testing teams—selected groups of people to be the first—and when the word went out that Rich's was going to integrate, some matrons in this community who had never lifted a finger to help us wanted to be among the first there. They turned out in furs, hats. And I mean just to go to Rich's to eat lunch and be there for the occasion!

And I remember some friends of mine going in during the time we were sending testing teams, and the guy at the door saying, "Oh, you're early. You're not on the list till next week." They said, "What list? We just want something to eat." Eventually the scheduling just broke down, and people just started going. . . .

Right after that initial period in February and March of 1960, I began to take a secondary role. Lonnie and Ben and Charles Black were the upfront people, and I became the publicist, sending out press releases all over the country to the black press and keeping in touch with the local offices of publications like *Time* and *Newsweek* and the New York *Times* and the Washington *Post*. I don't remember if I volunteered for the job, or Lonnie volunteered me for it, but I could write things that were clear—that other people could understand—and I liked doing it. And it was really important. We knew people would support us locally if they knew what we were doing, but because the larger local papers were basically silent, no one knew what we were doing except people that passed a picket line or something, so we needed control over *some* media to get the community support we needed. We couldn't even get coverage in black newspapers like the Atlanta *World* because they were so conservative. I remember at one point we got all the real estate men to withhold their ads from the *World* for a week to put pressure on them to cover us, but they still resisted.

So at that time, in order to get the news of our activities out, we were publishing a newsletter. I wrote most of it, and we printed it on K. C. Hill's offset press at Hill's Church and Office Supply on Auburn Avenue. We'd stay up late every Saturday night printing thousands and thousands of these things, and then John Gibson and Ruby Doris Smith and Mary Anne Smith and I would go around in cars early Sunday morning dropping it off at the churches to be distributed. It was really going places. I was hot to show how we were winning, so we had news about the boycotts, and those Federal Reserve reports I mentioned earlier, and all that. At the same time, Connie Curry was running the NSA [National Student Association] office at 41 Exchange Place, and she made it possible for us to have access to a mimeograph machine there in the evenings to run off press releases. I used to write the press release, type the stencil, get the paper and the stencil, and carry it up to Connie's office. The janitor would let me in, and I'd run it all off, clean up the machine, bring the stencils and the releases back down to our office, fold them on our folding machine, stuff them, stamp them, and take them to the post office.

We still hadn't been able to get any coverage in the *World*. About this time, even though the Rich's thing was still going on, we began to move on to job targets rather than lunch counters. One of them was an A & P on the corner of Hunter and Ashby. So we were picketing the A & P, and it was one of the biggest advertisers in the Atlanta *World*, and it put pressure on the *World* which then began to attack us. This was sort of like the final straw, and so with a group of sympathetic businessmen, we formed the Atlanta *Inquirer*, which was a regular newspaper, but open to news about all that was happening with the movement both here and nationally. I was very much caught up in that, and when the Student Nonviolent Coordinating Committee (SNCC) set up an office in Atlanta, James Forman, who headed the office, looked through the files and saw that I had done this publicity work for the local committee. He needed somebody to do it for SNCC, and he called me up, and I gave up the work with the *Inquirer* and went to work with SNCC full-time doing publicity. By that time I knew all the journalists and national magazine people and wire service people and so forth, and they got to know me, and I became the guy they called if they wanted to know something. . . . I didn't think I would want to do this forever. . . . But I was glad to be doing that kind of work at the time because I thought we were doing something really important and it was ego-fulfilling to be right there on the cutting edge.

[I was also at the April 1960 conference in Raleigh when SNCC was formed.] It was called by SCLC—by Ella Baker, really, as sort of her last act before being succeeded by Wyatt Tee Walker. It was a good conference. About five hundred students from all over the South as well as Northern student observers. All the student movements were there; and representatives of NAACP and SCLC and CORE and all these groups were lobbying us to become their youth affiliates. But Mrs. Baker and Marion Barry and a number of others felt strongly that we should be independent. Most of us didn't want any adult affiliation at all. We were very suspicious of CORE because it was a Northern group, and we were suspicious of SCLC because it really wasn't involved in what we were doing with sit-ins and boycotts. It was primarily the adult organization and hadn't really supported the student movement, and here were students like Ed King who had been beaten and still had his bloody shirt in his suitcase—very much like Mrs. Kennedy and her bloody dress—and now these older people were very obviously wanting to capitalize on what we were doing. So there was this general feeling that students had done a certain amount already, alone, and we didn't need these older people telling us what to do. We didn't have to wait for leadership figures to [certify our idea or plan our strategies for us]. There was also some evidence that money intended for the student movement—checks addressed to "Southern students c/o Dr. Martin Luther King"—was never being forwarded. Many of us felt that in terms of real movement and activity, we were doing all the work and they were getting all the money.

So we decided to form a temporary Student Nonviolent Coordinating Committee and hold another conference in Atlanta in October of that year to make it a permanent SNCC. After that conference, they set up an office here which was first run by Jane Stembridge and then Ed King and then by James Forman, which is when I got involved. At that time there were four of us in the office—myself, Forman, Norma Collins, and John Hardy—and Charlie Jones and James Bevel and some others in the field. Bob Moses. He had come down from the North to work for SCLC. He had seen these students' faces in a picture of some kind of rally or demonstration or something, and he said it was the faces that drew him down here. Of course, the thing that he connected with immediately was SCLC, as everybody did. SCLC to most people *was* the Southern civil rights movement. Nobody knew about us— something that was quickly ended due to my marvelous P.R. work! [*Laughing*] But he came down here to work for them, and I don't know what he expected to find. I think he thought that hundreds and hundreds of students would be out in the streets, picketing, marching, sitting in like crazy all the time, and he came in the summer when there was no student population on the campus, and the only work SCLC gave him was stuffing envelopes, but that wasn't very challenging to him so he gravitated toward our office. We thought he was a Communist because he was from New York. What we really thought was that he would capture our minds and lead us to Moscow! [*Laughing*] He had to be a Communist. Why else would he come down here from New York? He was sort of a strange person anyway. Quiet. Couldn't dance. Liked folk music—

that was a giveaway right there! So we shunned him for a little while. But he had one thing going. We had this picket line going around the A & P at the corner of Edgewood Avenue and Butler Street, and we hated picketing. I did anyway. It's hard to get people to picket; it was in the hot sun and people driving by would sometimes stop and get out of their cars and push you or hit you— nothing really serious, but it was thought to be kind of dangerous. You never knew when a car was going to come up on the sidewalk. But Bob would picket like a champ. All day long. So we used him that way until we got used to him and found out he wasn't subversive or something. Shows what we knew about Communists! That's one of the reasons we were confused when people red-baited us. If we had ever met a real Communist, we didn't know it. If we had been twenty years older and had been in the ACLU fight to expel the Communists or had been in the trade union movement and had fought against the CP it might have been different, but none of us had had any of that experience. This was brand-new stuff to us. We had a sort of storybook idea of what a Communist was—this bearded, burly man with an Eastern European accent and a raincoat—but we didn't know any such people and knew they weren't behind what we were doing. When we decided to sit in at lunch counters or do the Freedom Rides or go into Mississippi, those were *our* decisions. This was *us*. This was not Communists.

Besides, looking back, I think many of those charges were diversionary and intended to make us say, "Let's stop all our work and answer this." Forman, I think, was the guiding spirit in this regard. He was the guy who said, "Let's just ignore this and go on." And we just went on.

[Once we established SNCC, we were never close with the SCLC.] But we used to go in the bank, Forman and I, and see Wyatt Tee Walker in there in his pressed blue jeans depositing sacks of checks—I mean real bags of checks—while we were depositing two dollars or five dollars and so on. It was irritative as the devil. Forman finally got King to agree to give us a subsidy of about five hundred dollars a month, and that probably kept us going, but we never got close. In retrospect, I think the tension could have been handled better if we could have overcome our organizational identities and if Wyatt or Ella had convinced the powers that be in SCLC that we were worthwhile cooperating with and that we were, even though young, capable of doing adult work. A lot of it could have been muted. It couldn't have been absolutely overcome because there was too great a gulf between styles and between methods of operation. It could have been diminished an awful lot, though, but I don't think they were interested in diminishing it. We were.

[The SCLC's method was] the swoop into town, the series of demonstrations which may stretch over several months, but then leave—the crisis method of operation—and ours was the slow steady drive toward building a local movement infrastructure and eventually at some point pulling out and letting *that* run the show. And those two styles just weren't compatible. They could have melded together, I think, and to a certain extent in hindsight they did. SNCC would go in two years earlier and sort of warm up the town. SNCC was to SCLC as Ed McMahon is to Johnny Carson. [*Laughter*] But we just operated differently. The funny thing was that the national perception was of us as the radicals and the irresponsible ones and SCLC as the moderates when, in many ways, exactly the opposite was the truth.

[At any rate, in my opinion, what finally caused SNCC's demise] was its failure to realize the need to build on and establish that tradition that made us different from the others—that tradition that came out of our ability to say, "The reason we exist is because NAACP and SCLC are doing things their way because of *their* tradition, and we do things our way because of *ours*, which is to meld in with the people, to live in the community in which we work, to develop local leadership, to build up an infrastructure that can carry on the work, and then to move on. That, by the way, is why I always thought the Citizenship Schools program was an ideal program. But we didn't establish that approach as our *tradition*, I think. And because we had no tradition, we failed. "When there is no vision, the people perish."

In the early days, that was not true. As new people were brought in, the organization trained them and indoctrinated them. It said, "Here's the way we do it. If you don't like this way, there are other groups who do it differently, but this is the way we do it." And those who stayed were brought into the family. At later periods, new people came in who didn't ease their way in—who weren't brought in—they just *came* in, and the mix of people got bigger and bigger and you had these enormous ideological clashes and personality clashes and lifestyle clashes, and the tradition was not well enough established to withstand them. That, plus as the organization got older, people were hired. It was almost like having a job. Not to say that it was mundane or any less dangerous or anything like that, but the experience was very different for the later arrivals than it was for the earlier ones; and the later ones never understood what it had been for the earlier ones, or what the tradition was that made SNCC special.

Of course, in those later days—the late sixties—the movement was coming apart anyway. It was getting away from the mass demonstrations—and I don't mean the local picket line or the march on city hall, but mass demonstrations like the Selma-to-Montgomery march. In fact, the last big, big demonstration the movement had was in 1963. Then, when you get into '66 and '67, the movement's most famous spokesman, Martin Luther King, was beginning to be subject to internal movement criticism. In '68, with his death, SCLC suffered an immediate boost in contributions, but after that it began to decline too, and the professional, full-time civil rights worker became a rarity. People left in their local communities were left to their own devices, some of them able to carry on by themselves, some of them not. But none of them able to make the kind of national connection they had once made. They didn't have Dr. King and Dr. Abernathy coming to town and being followed by NBC and ABC and the New York *Times*. At the same time the antiwar movement grew up as a competing force in terms of public attention, so that in 1968 you were in the middle of this process and by 1970 you were at the end of it. That is, it was an accomplished fact. What movement there was in the South was largely carried on by people who were indigenous to the area in which the movement occurred—the local people. The "War on Poverty" in the late sixties sustained a number of activities, but it was federally funded, and the Nixon cutbacks and the shift to revenue sharing ended that. So all that caused a decline. Of course, certain goals had been won that had an effect on the momentum too. A lot of the people who had been marching on the courthouse were now sitting *in* the courthouse. That made a difference. [But the momentum needed to tackle the remaining problems wasn't there anymore.]

With SNCC specifically, one blow came after '64 with the withdrawal of all the summer people, who were essentially three-month people. And then at the end of the year after the convention in Atlantic City, a lot of people became discouraged and pulled away. Then in '65 we took a principled position on the Vietnam War and issued an antiwar pronouncement that had a real negative effect on contributions. Then a sector in the organization issued an anti-Israeli statement about the Arab-Israeli War that was seen as anti-Semitic and the contributions just vanished. The antiwar movement sucked away the last of the money and support, but that was a factor almost outside our control. We had never created that national ongoing support that would sustain us over a period of years. So it ended. And it was like the dissolution of a family, because this group had become family for enormous numbers of these people. These were people you saw every day, and you worked with and slept with and ate with, did everything with, shared everything with; and it just came to an abrupt end. It was just awfully traumatic, and particularly traumatic for young people. If we had been twenty years older, we wouldn't have been doing these things, but had we been twenty years older and doing these things, it wouldn't have been quite as traumatic. We would have had a little more life experience. But this way it just was a family breakup. It was chaotic. It was like a divorce—the parents scattered, the children scattered. Suddenly you lose your roots and you're cast adrift in a hostile sea. . . .

For the conclusion of Julian Bond's interview, see Chapter Six (page 359).

★

"The World Marches Inch by Inch"
May Justus

Looking back two decades, we can see that many basic ideals of both Highlander and the civil rights movement have clearly survived, while many activists of the sixties are dead, or they have at least aged and changed. America has changed as well. And Highlander itself is no longer in Grundy County, Tennessee, though it remains open and functioning in a new location elsewhere in the state. The adage seems affirmed once again: That which was lasting—the wheat and not the chaff—has endured, either in presence or in abiding influence.

The wisdom of a May Justus also lingers. From her Grundy County home, she watched most of the people in this book come and go. As a good teacher and writer, she gleaned from them—drawing upon the strength of their ideas while gradually discarding concepts that time and experience proved to be weak. A white Southern woman lacking early relationships with blacks, she solidly embraced integration in her final novels. And a Grundy County resident, she embodied Highlander's spirit long after the institution moved elsewhere.

In a sense, then, May Justus was the type of person that Myles Horton and Ralph Tefferteller, E. D. Nixon and Septima Clark, Andrew Young and Dr. Martin Luther King, Jr., all sought after: one whose mind could conquer prejudice, whose heart could embrace humanness, and whose actions could demonstrate a greater fairness. So the conclusion of her interview also functions as a retrospective on social change in America, from the thirties through the sixties.

. . . When they started integrating white schools [a tragic thing happened]. They started integration in Nashville with a little black girl attending the previously all-white Hattie Cotton School. The school was promptly bombed, and that distressed me very much—to think that that thing could be. I wanted to do something. I thought, "Well, I can't demonstrate or do anything to show that I disapprove of the school being bombed, or about the violence happening that way."

So I thought and thought about it, and I decided that I'd write a book. *New Boy in School* [1963] is derived from that incident. This child is the only black child in a white school and it's a very simple little story, but it had a wonderful reception. The Conference of Christians and Jews made it a Brotherhood Book and People of the English Speaking Union chose it as an Ambassador Book. No other book on integration had come out for children under twelve [at that time]. There were books for older children on the subject of integration, but none for younger ones, and it was well received.

Later on, integrated neighborhoods became a big issue. I heard so much about the property values going down when a Negro family moved into a [white]community, and so that became a great thing. Then a little later I thought I'd write a book about housing, about a Negro family who doesn't have a decent house to live in. That was *A New Home for Billy* (1966) and these two books became companion volumes. Hastings House published them.

But I would probably never have written *New Boy in School* if I had not heard teachers and ministers talk about their problems and the black children's problems. Highlander's racial policy certainly did influence me. If people who are prejudiced were exposed more to those they are prejudiced against, that might change them. I know people who have been prejudiced but they've changed. I've had people tell me that. They didn't get it by listening to sermons and they didn't get it by reading pamphlets on toleration. They got it by meeting somebody, as I met the people over there at Highlander. They met somebody like Septima Clark or Ralph Abernathy or Dean B. R. Brazeal of Morehouse College. That's how. They met them and they talked to them. They recognized quality. Only the blindest, most prejudiced person could refute evidence as strong as that. There's nothing in the world like personal contact. Nothing. Nothing. And the people who influence you most in your life are not the people who preach to you, but the people who live with you and the people you see in their daily lives. "What you are speaks so loud I cannot hear what you say." That's an old axiom and it's just as true now as it was when the first person uttered it.

That's why I think the thing for black people to do now is to go on doing what they've been doing and are doing right now. And that is to prove their ability and their worth and good character by being and doing the best that they are capable of. There is something that cannot be denied, and that is quality. Quality doesn't need to be defended. It speaks for itself. If you get a teacher in school who is black and she teaches English or she teaches arithmetic or whatever not only as well as but maybe better than her predecessor, that speaks for itself. She doesn't need to get up and say, "Now, children, I hope you will both love and respect me in spite of my black skin." Her quality speaks for itself. I would hate to think that my children would have to wait till I've died and some preacher stands over my grave and says, "We're burying Miss Justus today. Let me tell you what kind of a person she was."

The world doesn't march on seven-league boots. It marches inch by inch. These people who are prejudiced [against blacks] are not totally to blame, because they have inherited a tradition that they did not create. It was handed on down to them. They are not entirely to blame, because they have inherited it and they were schooled in it. You say you are different. You don't have these prejudices against blacks. You will marry someday and you will have children. Your children will inherit what you are and that's how progress is made. The ones with prejudices will die off.

Many things are better now, but it wouldn't have been that way if people had kept on saying "yes, yes, yes" instead of "no, no, no." You have to speak out. But generally, as I say, the world doesn't march on seven-league boots. It marches very, very slowly. But march it does. One measure of the change in attitudes now is the fact that now it seems strange that Highlander's programs, dedicated to the uplift of American citizens, should have been so bitterly opposed. It seems incredible that Highlander's educational aims were so feared and resented. The fact that Highlander's program has been faithfully supported by so many people for half a century speaks for itself. This program goes on and will go on as long as it is needed. When we have no second-class citizens, when all Americans have equal rights and opportunities, when no one is turned away from a church or a school because of the color of his skin, then Highlander's great goal will have been reached, and many will start to seek another goal beyond the horizon of another frontier.

I wish that everybody who wants to do good in the world would help other people who want to do good, and that they would join hands and not allow church differences and political differences to affect their attitudes. We all differ in some ways, but those are minor political or religious preferences compared to serving God. That is the main thing and anybody who contributes to that is my brother or my sister. If all could just feel that way about it—well, to me, it seems that would save the world. I helped at Highlander in every way that I could, and if people misunderstood that, I can't help it, because Jesus said, "He that is not with us is against us."

I'm an old woman and whatever wisdom I have, I've garnered over the years, and I've met many people of different faiths and some of the dearest friends I have ever had are certainly different from me in religious viewpoints. I'm not very strong on doctrine. If people want to make a great deal of that and it makes them happier, fine. I once knew the catechism by heart and taught it. The one thing [in the catechism] that comes to my mind is: "What is man's chief end? Man's chief end is to glorify God and enjoy Him forever." And to glorify in my mind is to serve Him. I'm glad it was a part of the foundation of my life and earlier instruction, but that's not the big thing that matters to me anymore. The big thing is service.

Through my life, I've had two things—a deep sense of religion and a wonderful sense of humor. The two together have really taken me through a lot of hard places. Someone asked me recently, "How do your neighbors and the people of this community treat you now? Have they resumed their friendships with you?

Do they ever bring it up? Have they apologized for their attitudes at that time?"

I said, "No, it's never mentioned." You know, it's just exactly as it used to be back when I was growing up. A girl in the community had an illegitimate baby and she was from a very good family and all. The neighbors would all talk it over and they'd say, "Well, now, her family is a nice family and they're good people. This is the only mistake she's ever made and I think as Christians, we should all rally around."

When the folks would all get together, they'd talk about the weather or they would talk about the sewing society or some project they had or how Uncle So-and-so was, but if she was among them, this unfortunate young lady, they would just ignore her "condition." When she would come to church the first time after the baby was born, everybody would rush up to her and tell her how glad they were to have her back. She was a lost lamb from the fold returning. The preacher would have a good sermon on "Let the angels rejoice." Now that's the attitude the people around here had toward Miss Justus. They probably said, "Well, she's been here all these years and she still shares her garden with us and she still makes us bread and asks the children in and is nice to them. I think we should just ignore her misdeeds of the past, and besides she's getting old and a little childish and not entirely responsible, and she's always been good-hearted and she was sorry for those people." They've just decided to let bygones be bygones.

I think my books have done more than I have because they've reached more people. I live in a little pocket here in Summerfield, but the books, of course, have gone out all over the world.

Thoreau once said, "I have traveled extensively—in Concord." He never got out of Concord, and that's how it is with me. I have traveled extensively—in Summerfield. Here I've stayed all these years. [I have traveled very little.] I went to Chicago as a young woman and I've been to New Orleans once, but I've never been to Philadelphia or any other large cities. I've never belonged to any of these literary things, not even the authors' league, and I've never gone to an authors' workshop.

I've stayed right here, living in this little old hundred-year-old house [all these years]. The only improvements we put in were electricity, running water, and a thumb-size bathroom. But it suits me. I'm not as much of a recluse as Emily Dickinson was. I like for people to come see me. I suppose people from every state in the union have been here—people on vacation traveling through the country say, "Why, that's where Miss Justus' house is. Let's stop and see her." I went to the back door one day and there stood a man and his two little boys. He said, "Oh, I'm so sorry to bother you, but we're from Nova Scotia and we're on our way to Florida. As we got up here, Bobby said, 'Daddy, that says Tracy City and that's where that lady lives that writes those books we've got in the library. Let's stop and see her.' " And that's the way it happened—just that way. They don't always start out to see me, but they stop by—many, many people. So I have a lot of contact with the world that way, right here in my own little kingdom.

When I was a little girl, and people would ask me what I wanted to do when I grew up, I'd say, "I'm going to marry as soon as possible and have twelve children just like my great-grand-mother did." But you see, it developed differently. I had decided by the time we moved here that I would probably never marry, so I felt that I'd like to [settle permanently] here in Summerfield. I've said the Lord never gave me a husband and proper children of my own as I had hoped when I was little, and one day in school I was telling my children about that. It was a very cold, bad day and only twelve of them had come. We were all sitting around the fire, and one of my little boys said, "Well, Miss Justus, I wouldn't feel bad about it because you've got twelve of *us*. You've got one, two, three, four, five, six, seven, eight, nine, ten, eleven, twelve!" I thought that was quite nice. But the children I've taught over the past fifty-four years still come to see me and I feel as close to them and their children as I would if they were my very own.

I'm reminded of a young girl I taught at Huntsville, Tennessee, before I entered the mission field in Kentucky, a girl I taught more than fifty-eight years ago. I had lost complete track of her until not too many years ago when she was chosen Tennessee teacher of the year. She was asked, "Mrs. McClothian, how did you ever come to be a teacher?"

She said, "When I was a little girl in the seventh and eighth grades, I went to a lady named Miss May Justus and she made me want to become a teacher." Well, there had been fifty-eight years between that time and the time that she got the plaque. When that information came out in the paper, I wrote her. She was surprised to learn I was still alive. She said, "I thought you had died and gone to heaven long ago." But since then, she comes to see me every year, once in the spring and once in the fall.

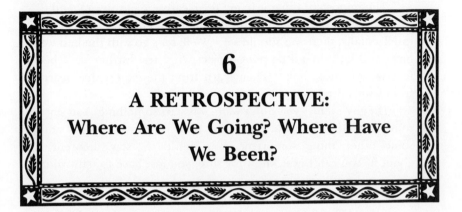

6

A RETROSPECTIVE:
Where Are We Going? Where Have
We Been?

To think that history provides blueprints is a mistake, but to think that history provides no insights is an even worse mistake. It does.

[The challenge, however, is] to invent the application *of history. . . . What went on in Athens and Greece can read like some of the descriptions of New York City and Chicago today. In that sense, you know certain things* happen when you get a lot of people together in a metropolitan situation, so you can learn things like that. But you can't learn the exact way to deal with the problems of New York today; there are special problems now that have to be looked at in terms of new, specific facts. . . . So I think you have to reinvent the actual application of history to [new] situations.

Information [and] facts are not just some all-truth-for-all-times sorts of things. When you have a new situation, you've got to get new facts and new information that are tailored for that situation. You can't say, "We're going to accumulate a lot of knowledge and a lot of information, and then pick it up and have another social movement, [but] use only old information. . . ."

[Granted,] it helps to know that our Founding Fathers struggled . . . , [or that] certain things happened in Philadelphia. Those things are part of our traditions and part of who we are, and they . . . shouldn't be ignored. But I don't think you can save time that way. I don't think you need to look to history for saving time. What you need to do is to learn how you could not make as many false starts and as many mistakes as you make, and how you could qualitatively improve . . . your programs and your activities. Not by imitating; not by transferring some specific strategy from one period to another, but by getting insights that you might apply now . . .

The important thing is to get the clearest idea you can; and if you take the responsibility of thinking it through as far as you can, intellectually, then you should say, "Well, let's go with the best we have, and let's do a little pilot project, . . . test further . . . before we go whole hog." Then learn from the experience, learn from your mistakes and successes.

[In any event,] you don't wait. You start something. You start something now. You find something that you can start today and some other thing tomorrow. You don't . . . stay theoretical about it. You can't ever know for sure; you just have to trust your ability to improvise. . . .

I used to think I had to figure out all those things . . . in my own head. [Then] I had some learning experiences where I found that just by talking it over with people and getting advice [from] other people, a lot of help came, and [I] didn't need to do it alone.

[So] that's really the basis of my thinking about education at Highlander. . . . It's knowledge and people that we don't credit. We don't credit the experiences of people for being something that can be learned from. Experiences don't educate; analyzing experiences educates.

—*MYLES HORTON*

★

Is "Self-Censorship" The National Lobotomy?

Studs Terkel

Symbolized by having spent most of his life in Chicago, this interviewer and author possesses a heartlander's grasp of the history and the ideals that imbue today's American culture with diversity. Born in 1912, he is old enough not only for World War I to have affected his boyhood but also for the Great Depression and World War II to have shaped his early manhood. His memories and sensibilities span the twentieth century. But it is Studs Terkel's gift for listening, and for responding to what he hears, that makes his eclectic career contribute to our journey toward the next century.

Though he has earned credits in the theater as well as radio and television broadcasting, Studs Terkel is most widely known as an author and an oral historian. His books, the first published in 1956, include Hard Times *(1970),* Working *(1974) and* American Dreams: Lost and Found *(1980). In 1985, he was awarded the Pulitzer Prize for an oral history of World War II entitled* The Good War*. Indeed, his oral histories often contain the modern equivalent of an ancient oracle's sayings: The wisdom of others speaks through.*

In a similar way, his reflections on "Where Are We Going? Where Have We Been?" span the range of this book's interviews. He targets what we can learn from both the labor movement of the thirties and the civil rights movement of the fifties and sixties. And he cautions what we may expect if we fail to remember both this century's particular lessons and the far richer history of humanity that continues to engender the present way of life on this planet.

During the Depression my mother had a men's hotel here in Chicago. It played a tremendous role in my life. These were skilled craftsmen who later on in the Depression didn't work. They were self-taught, self-educated. They had little Halderman Julius blue books. They were nickel blue books of Voltaire, Tom Paine, Bob Ingersoll, all that; and so they'd argue a lot. And that was kind of a good college for me. But then I joined this theater group. It was called the Labor Theater group, and we did plays about a strike called *Waiting for Lefty,* and then we'd entertain on picket lines as well. What they would call straight theater today. We called it mobile theater. We were at the tavern the day after the Republic Steel massacre here on the South Side of Chicago, Memorial Day, 1937, doing sketches for the guys. At that time the Almanac Singers were traveling around the country, playing at unions and in the picket lines, and it was Pete Seeger and Woody Guthrie and Lee Hays and a guy named Millard Lampell. I'd just married recently—we had two and a half rooms—and when they were in Chicago, they slept on our floor. They didn't want to be separated. Lee Hays did the cooking and so he had the couch. And Pete was just a pimply-faced young guy of eighteen, nineteen. Had that Adam's apple bobbing up and down. And Woody would go to the taverns at night and come back home and I'd hear him typing away on my typewriter. He'd be typing out this stuff about experiences at the tavern, and it was like James Joyce and Thomas Wolfe, and then he'd throw it away.

And I was on the WPA Writers Project then. The New Deal had some good things to it there. I learned to write on the Writers Project. That's how I became a writer. Aside from the roads that were built and the electrification and the dams, there was the Federal Arts Project [under which came that]Writers Project along with Theater Project, Music Project, Dance Project, Graphic Arts, Paintings, Sculptures; and then there were the photographers in the Farm Security Administration. You'd see these great works of Walker Evans and Margaret Bourke-White and Dorothea Lange and Ben Shahn. But the Writers Project was what also gave us guides—every state has a guide. These guides are great. You look at them. They are witty and informative. Then the Theater Project had plays. They invented new kinds of theater called "Living Newspaper," which today you'd call mixed media. One called *One*

Third of a Nation got its name from a phrase from Roosevelt's 1936 inaugural speech: "I see one third of a nation ill-fed, ill-housed, ill-clothed"; and it was about housing. Another one was called *Spirochete* about the fight against syphilis; another one called *Triple A Plowed Under;* another one called *Power.* The House Un-American Activities Committee killed all that. Said it was dangerous, you know. There was a play by Christopher Marlowe that was performed, and the HUAC guys wanted to know of what communist cell was he a member. Christopher Marlowe! The ignorance of the guys! Anyway, Hallie Flanagan, the head of the Theater Project, had these traveling troupes doing plays, and they even did Shakespeare in little rural communities. At first the actors were disappointed because the audience didn't applaud. They discovered later on that people had never seen flesh-and-blood actors before. They were so entranced that they just sat there. It was the highest compliment they could have been paid. . . .

[And that demonstrates the importance of the arts.] A problem with American labor unions is that they have only one thing in mind: wages, hours, and nothing else. European labor unions have a thing called labor temples where they have books, different things. But here it's wages and hours—what's called pork-chop issues—and nothing else, you see. That's not gonna cut it either. There's a story told by Hosea Glacios in *Hard Times.* He's a writer, Spanish descent, and he's talking about his mother and father, who were cigar makers in Ebor City, a Spanish-speaking suburb of Tampa, during the thirties. And they had a reader's strike. In other words, these Spanish people and Italian people would hire an actor—Spanish-speaking or Italian-speaking depending upon the workers there—and then, in one large room, they'd roll cigars. Each one contributed fifty cents a week for this actor, put him on a platform, and he'd read to them while they worked. And he read what they chose. It might be *Three Musketeers* or *Les Misérables* or something political. But he'd read. The owners didn't pay a cent, but they thought something was dangerous here, so they destroyed the platform, and there was a strike and the workers lost the strike.

But it was the Europeans who connected literature, writings, music—all of their lives—as well as wages and hours. And working conditions. Because labor didn't do its job here, we had to have an

OSHA finally, and OSHA now is being knocked off by Reagan, you see.

But about the arts, you know, the famous textile strike in Lawrence, Massachusetts, in 1912 involved immigrant women and guys, and they had a slogan: "Bread and Roses, Too." Judy Collins took part in a Woody [Guthrie] concert that I emceed for public television some time ago, and she sang the song called "Bread and Roses," which was right from that period. Think about the concept—bread and roses, roses, of course, being beauty.

In public schools, they often think of it as the frills, whereas dancing and song and expressing yourself is marvelous. It gives you a sense of beauty, because life is also beauty. There's *always* a quest of this beauty. I never will forget going through this mining country in eastern Kentucky, and I was in a flower shop. And I said, "What the hell is a flower shop doing here?" It's amazing, you know.

I've always been involved in the arts in some way. For a while I emceed a program called "I Come for to Sing" at a nightclub here in Chicago called the Blue Note. A friend of mine, Wen Stracke, would sing frontier songs. And Big Bill Broonzy would sing all kinds of traditional blues, some of which he made up. He was one of the great blues singers of our time. I wish he had lived during the civil rights movement. He died in '58. Big Bill was a man who came out of the South. He worked as a sharecropper starting at the age of five and six, and he remembered all this, and musically too. Came out of Scott, Mississippi, and later on Little Rock, Arkansas. And he came to Chicago in the thirties and helped a lot of younger musicians all the way through to preserve the blues. He's the one who sang that song, "If you're white, you're right; if you're brown, stick around; if you're black, oh, brother, get back, get back, get back."

And one night at the Blue Note, Zilphia Horton showed up, and we had her onstage. Zilphia sang "We Shall Overcome." That was the first time I heard it, I think. And it became the anthem of the civil rights movement. You know, unfortunately, I've never been to Highlander. . . .

My knowledge of Highlander is through all the people I've met who went and in one sense or another affected my life. [And through] Myles, of course, having met him a number of times.

And so the name "Highlander" and its meaning is quite important to me. When I think of Highlander, [for example,] I think of a certain gathering in Montgomery at the home of Virginia and Clifford Durr during the Selma-to-Montgomery march. The Durrs are what you call premature integrationists. They're of a distinguished Alabama family and have always stuck their necks out. And, of course, they and Myles have been close. At that gathering, there they were—Myles was there; E. D. Nixon was there. That was the first time I met Nixon. John Beecher, the Southern poet, was covering the march for the San Francisco *Chronicle*. A number of others. Word came that Viola Liutzzo had been killed, and everybody was stunned. And I remember Myles' comment to E. D. Nixon—everybody was going home now—"This is old stuff to you, isn't it, E.D.?" said Myles.

And I think of Rosa Parks. She had worked for Virginia Durr. She also worked for E. D. Nixon. And she had attended Highlander. Had Rosa Parks not attended Highlander . . . It's one of those conjectural matters, you know—the role of Highlander in the psyche, the mind, the will, the gallantry, the deed of Rosa Parks. [But there was probably some influence there.] And multiply this by the thousands who have attended [over the years].

The thing I like about Myles' approach, he's probably one of the country's great *educators*—and I use that word deliberately. We hear about schools and, you know, the difficulties schools have—I don't mean simply as far as race—I mean schools, the quality of what we're taught. You watch a TV commercial for education. You see a ghetto black kid there and he's told, "You go to school because you'll get somewhere if you do. You'll make out!" That's not what education is about. Education is to enrich the life of a person, to make him more contributory to a community because he's richer. This is, of course, what Myles has done through the years. Myles says, "I look at a person, man or woman, with two eyes. One eye tells me what he is; my other eye tells me what he can be." It's what he *can be*! Myles always deals in the potentialities in humans. We use that word human "potentiality" because all these phony groups use it—est and the others, you know, these make-out groups. But Myles *really* does it! Myles has that second eye that shows you what a person *can be*.

I first heard of Highlander when it was at Monteagle, Tennessee, and was burned out by the Klan. And yet Myles does not write off the Klan. That's the point! He doesn't write off a Klansman, I should say. In *American Dreams,* I have a man named C. P. Ellis, ex-cyclops of the Klan, Durham, North Carolina, who became a remarkable person because of an event. He didn't go to Highlander but could well have. Myles had a number of Klansmen attending Highlander through the years. Guys who were labor organizers. But one day, this one guy is playing poker with this black guy. He had never sat down at a table with a black man before, and the black guy beat him at poker. He shouts, "Damn, I never dreamed a 'nigger' could beat me at poker!" And it opened his eyes. He always thought of these guys as being an inferior species. But Myles says it doesn't matter what the *way* is—the *way* someone is changed. [What's important is that] the guy has become a different sort of person. So Myles does not write off people. Coming back to that idea, you take a person as he or she *is,* that's not gonna do it.

That's one quarrel I've got with the media. You got the press, you got the media, you got the banality that is shoved at people every day. We elect Reagan, we go along, he's popular, we're told. Well, day after day after day we're fed this bullshit, you know. The banality. You know, Hannah Arendt, the German observer, wrote of "the banality of evil" in describing Nazis. I reverse that. Right now I say we're experiencing the evil of banality, because banality is what we get every day. Banality stunts the imagination. Stunts what distinguishes the human being from other species—the ability to think. To think! To *imagine* too. To imagine what something *can* be. To think the unthinkable in the good sense. We use "think the unthinkable" in the obscene sense in thinking about a nuclear war that people can survive. Well, that's the *unspeakable.* But I'm talking about thinking the unthinkable in an affirmative way, you see. And Myles does that. He cuts through the banality in the daily lives of people and sees the possibilities.

I also remember hearing of Myles as the first guy to tell off John Edgar Hoover. [*Laughter*] No one ever told off John Edgar Hoover. No one ever tells off the saint, the sacred cop. You know, he was the hero. He had a volunteer public relations man named Walter Winchell, the most widely influential columnist in America, who was a hysterical bastard and phony as a three-dollar bill, you

know. Every day [he broadcast] things about the great John Edgar
Hoover and G-men in action, and Myles comes along and chal-
lenges this phony, you see. *Now* we *know* Hoover was a brutish
phony, but no one ever dared say it then. Myles did. So we need
now to talk of Myles' courage, which was always there. Even in that
mountain community that seemingly would be hostile—I imagine
it must have been—it wasn't a question of just speeches and lec-
tures about integration and equality. It was simply daily living together. Just like that Klansman playing poker with that black
guy. . . .

[But the fact that it often takes one or two people to break the
ice before others will follow] is the old story. You know, Myles tells
this one about that time of the Selma-Montgomery march. He
says, "You know, as I took part in that march"—remember there
were thousands—"and I [realized I] didn't know very many people there and they didn't know me, I felt good." And he talks of
the early ones, the very individuals we're talking about. Those
indeed who were pilloried, you know, if not physically beaten or
threatened. Certainly pilloried as far as reputation. They were always the few, and Myles was among those few; and they all knew
one another, those fifty people or twenty-five people who marched
as hostile crowds lined the sidewalks and threw things at them, or
threatened them, or defamed them. And *then* came the hundreds
of thousands, you see.

And so, this has been ever so. This raises a question about
minority opinion and thought. During the thirties there were hunger marchers and there were marchers for things as pinko and
commie as Social Security and unemployment compensation.
They were called subversive pieces of legislation. Today it's part of
the very lives we live—although Reagan is trying his best to knock
that off. But, you see, it's always been so. There's a play by Henrik
Ibsen called *An Enemy of the People,* and it is a marvelous play because it deals with someone who may be in the minority but who's
right. It's about a certain town in Norway, the latter part of the
nineteenth century. And the town is a spa and the people come
there for their vacations and the people of the town prosper. Now
the honored figure in the community is a Dr. Stockman; and one
day he discovers the spa is poisoned. And so he says, "We've got to
close it." The respectable people, including his brother, the

mayor, are furious with him because they want it kept secret. Think about pollution today and what's happening, and radiation. Think of the parallels. And they want to stone this guy, you know, because it would take away their money, even though life may be endangered. And so they stone his house and he makes a speech to these people. "I know you're a majority, but since when has the majority always been right? Was there a majority who backed Christ that day at Calvary?" You see? "Was it a majority . . . ?" And he goes down through history to show that often it is the minority of one, two, five, ten, twenty. "A Gideon's Army" is a phrase that was used during the Henry Wallace campaign. . . .

Think about the American Revolution, if you want to go right down to it. It wasn't a majority that were for the American Revolution. The majority sat by. It was a minority. It was Sam Adams causing trouble. Sam Adams was a rabble-rouser. Let's face it. Sam Adams was a troublemaker, as Myles is a troublemaker. Sam Adams was rougher than Myles. We were a colony, and there was an imperialist named George, and Sam and the boys were telling this guy to go screw himself. Well, today he's honored [even though] some don't like him. But it was a minority. The property owners who were thinking of their own skins didn't like him. It's always been so. . . .

I have a fantasy. I got this tape recorder, right? I wish I had this tape recorder at the foot of Calvary on Good Friday, you see? Now, what would have been the case? There you are, a man up there is going to be crucified, nailed to the cross. Who was this guy? He's part of an underground, subversive organization called the Christians that is challenging the Roman establishment. And around there you got the guards. You got some young soldiers— Roman soldiers—what are they thinking of as they see this guy carrying that cross up the hill? You've got informers around and about, and you've got these people who are scared stiff and say, "I don't know him. I don't know the guy. No, I don't." Think about that now. Wouldn't it be good to have had a tape recorder then, you see? What was life like? We know about 1588 and the Spanish Armada. Francis Drake, that's all we know. Now Bertolt Brecht wrote a poem and one of the lines is, "We read that King Phillip wept"—the king of Spain wept when the Armada sank—"Were there no other tears?" What about some of those sailors on that ship and the widows and the others, you see? "Were there no other tears?" He goes on further. "When Caesar conquered Gaul, was there not even a cook in the army?" You see? And when the Chinese Wall was built, where did the masons go for lunch? Or in 1066, when William the Conqueror beat the Saxons, how did that affect the life of a Saxon peasant? I'd like to have had a tape recorder and gone home with that Saxon peasant. Did that affect their lives in any way? Was the one overseer simply supplanting another? How did it affect their lives? You see, that's what we're talking about.

[The thing is that now we *can* get that kind of information— information that can be the source of future wisdom and strength —and we don't take advantage of it.] I think one of the things that disturbs me most today is the elimination of the past. Look at our attempt now in El Salvador to put down what is a natural and indigenous feeling of discontent, and to give aid to the brutes, as we've done throughout, so soon after Vietnam. And the President says, "This is a noble cause," as though [there was] no history. Ford as President said, "Put Vietnam behind us." If you put some- thing behind you, it means forget it, it never happened. [It may also mean] that you do it again. Or when, during the Iranian hostage crisis, when a reporter got up and asked Carter, who was then President, "Do you have any second thoughts, any regrets, about inviting the Shah here, or about 1953?" which, of course, is when the CIA helped overthrow the legally elected government in Iran. "Any regrets about it?" And do you know what Carter's reply was? I remember it. "That is ancient history." He was dismissing the question. Ancient history! Well, if 1953 is ancient history, there is no history. And so, here we go again. Let the big boys do it again as though there were no Depression in the thirties. The big boys did that and fell right on their fannies, right? But here we go again. And so to me that sense of history and past . . . is vital. And Myles, of course, has old and young there [at workshops]. There is a past [represented there to learn from], you see? And if we don't learn from the past, we don't learn. We speak of the kids having no sense of history. They've been taught *not* to have any sense of history. You know what some kids said to me? I did the book *Hard Times,* which is a gathering of people's thoughts about the Depression and the thirties. Many of the kids said, "I never knew there was such a time." The only thing they knew about it was as a bawling out, "You never had it so good."

They were never told about the fears, the humiliations; the early ones who organized labor, or hunger marchers who got their heads battered and bloodied. There are a bunch of kids today who are antilabor, antiunion, 'cause all they know about unions is the name George Meany or Jimmy Hoffa or Frank Fitzsimmons. That's all they know. They don't even know about those unknown ones who got their heads battered and bloodied. Some of those very ones who went to Highlander Folk School. They don't even know where they got the minimum wage. They think they got the minimum wage by magic or [because] their boss was nice and gave it to them. That's what lack of history does.

[And the public schools, for example, never address this fact.] Coming back to the history book. What about the thirties? [Students] are taught that Franklin Roosevelt was President, was elected four times, and they are taught there came a war, and that's about it. They are told maybe [there were] sixteen million unemployed. They aren't told what it was like in the Depression. What the movements were that came into being; the attempts to put them down, the battles, the gallantries of the anonymous groups. Even a spirit of camaraderie too. There was that there too, you see. *But* in the midst of adversity. But this is what they're not taught. Some of the black kids of SNCC never knew there was a group of sharecroppers who marched to Washington in the thirties led by a Southern preacher, a black man, named Owen Whitfield.

It touches every aspect of our lives. Even in the field of the arts, and popular arts. I was on a bus the other day, and it was very funny. A bunch of white blue-collar kids are going to a rock concert. There's a ballroom near where I live that has rock concerts. And I said, "Where you going?" I talked to them, you know. They said, "We're going to see a group called Chicago." And so I say, "What ever happened to Bob Dylan?" And these kids say, "Bob who?"

And so, there is no history. Not that I'm in love with Bob Dylan, but he did write some good songs. But a lot of kids have heard of Woody Guthrie. Would there have been a Bob Dylan without a Woody, you see? And so this is what I'm talking about too. Then jazz. They never heard of early jazzmen. They think it began with Miles Davis or somebody. I mean, this concerns every aspect of our lives. [It's almost like there's some kind of censorship going on.] We know certain governments employ heavy censorship. We *don't* have government censorship, but we've got something else far more subtle. It's a self-censorship. Through the years, you get conditioning. Certain questions are never asked by commentators when they quiz a person on the air. Even on the better shows they often never ask any questions that mean anything. . . . And self-censorship can be even more corrosive than governmental censorship.

Once in a while you have a fairly good program that comes on, but that doesn't have any effect, because day after day after day you get the other, you see? It's a daily thing you get. Let's say the hostages in Iran, that's on my mind. When they came back, I thought a couple of them would be saying they were badly treated and it's a terrible thing; and whoever took them was stupid and rotten. But you would think that *some* of them would also have come back saying, "You know, we did a terrible thing there that caused them to feel that way." Not a word about that at all. Not a word of what we did to them.

There was an item that appeared in the New York *Times,* by a man named Prini Goupta, who is one of our correspondents who covered a moment of grief in Iran. Here's the scene I'm setting. It's a classic case of how the media and experts determine how we see the rest of the world. Four hundred and something days, and we had ABC in Tehran, CBS and NBC as well as PBS, MacNeil, Lehrer. So you got network guys in Tehran for four-hundred days, and every day we saw what? Hate-filled faces, death to Carter, down with the Americans. Okay. Blindfolded hostages. Did we once ever see something called Iranian grief? Well, there's this story where this guy Prini Goupta [covers] a gathering. It's not too far off from Tehran. And don't tell me these high-priced correspondents didn't know about it. Scores of thousands of Iranians gathered to memorialize the dead, mostly young, who were killed by SAVAK, the Shah's secret police. And at the cemetery they have the pictures on the gravestones of the young guys: "So and so, young cobbler, shot on the way to work by SAVAK!" "This guy tortured, killed." "Student carrying a book here." And you got the parents grieving and their fruit and flowers on the grave as is the custom, and one old woman is crying, "Don't look at me that way, my son; don't look that way in the dark." And the old man is digging into the dirt and people are walking back and forth. And this woman stops a young boy, a young mourner, and says, "Will you be my son for a minute?" And the boy starts crying, and she comforts the boy. And this thing is multiplied by thousands. Now, did you see that on TV? And did you see an Iranian mother on TV crying? Now, you have for four-hundred-odd days, ABC, NBC, and CBS, high-priced correspondents—they didn't know about this event? If they did know, they didn't cover it. It was not important. "It's a goddamn Iranian, for Christ's sake." "It's a gook!" You got a Vietnamese gook, you got an Iranian gook. And so we come back to it. Not only is it absence of history, it's even absence of contemporary truth as well, you see. . . .

What I'm afraid of is a national lobotomy. When Swift wrote *Gulliver's Travels,* he had little Houyhnhnms—the horses with more brains. Well, I speak of the "lobos"—a "lobo society"—"lobo" being short for "lobotomized." We can't become a land of lobos—a word I want to coin right now.

When these clowns on TV speak of the volatility of the American voter, that's a stupid word. Doesn't mean anything. What you mean is that we have no sense of past, so therefore we go one way or the other depending upon the wind or the whim or what you see on TV. The guy's got a good smile and he's nice, and the other guy was tense, you know. Or the handsome Jack Kennedy beat the guy with the scowl and dark beard. That's a hell of a reason to vote for a guy, isn't it?

[There's also a flip side to the argument that we need to learn from history. There's a group that says we *need* to constantly reinvent the wheel.]

Well, [technology sometimes changes the wisdom of that. Remember that] each time a new piece of weaponry comes into being, it's far more devastating than the others; so now, if we have to reinvent the wheel [in terms of the causes and prevention of war], we're not gonna make it to the year 2000, you see, because now, for the first time, the human race can destroy itself totally, completely. It's no longer the bow and arrow, it's no longer the cannon, it's no longer the machine gun, it's no longer the tank, it's no longer the strafing plane. Now it's not even the man. It's a coil of wire. As Norman Karwin said in a marvelous play, *A Note of Triumph,* "It's a coil of wire to replace the fighting heart. . . ." Even the soldier has been replaced now. We'll all die civilians because now you have the nuclear missile. And you see the reason these scientists feel so despairing is because they say that all weapons that were invented have always been used. And now with more and more countries getting these weapons, now it's more desperate than ever. . . .

A school should be to make you aware of yourself as a person who is part of a community. See, we're taught about the individual rights—and, of course, an individual should have his rights—but we've been taught through the years to make it, by God, for me and my family. "I can do it on my own." The old frontier philosophy. It never was true; but assume it was. There was a geographic frontier, true, so a guy could go West. He could head out like Huck Finn for the Territory. Okay, maybe he built a cabin, maybe he got along. Some few did, many did not. There is no such illusion today. There is no such frontier today. What there are are *communities.* And so the person's individual rights should be respected, but he doesn't live in a vacuum! This is the thing that Myles teaches also, the need for communal feeling. It's part of an old tradition. There were many so-called utopian communities that failed, but there were hundreds of them. So it indicates there was that feeling among many Americans, you see. And there was a strong populist movement once in the Southwest, of all places, the Sunbelt, that today is called the center of reaction. The Sunbelt then (Oklahoma, I'm talking about) had more American and indigenous socialists than New York City. There was a populace. But through the years, that communal strain has been muted, you see, and Myles represents that strain in American history and American impulse.

It's a muted strain, but it's still there. You know, there are three or four hundred groups in the country [focused on] one subject only [such as]stopping the expressway through their town? They won the fight to stop it in Chicago. Now, [each is centered around] a local issue, but there's something important about those groups: they can be coalesced. That's the thing. Even though it's a local issue, for some people out of that organization the windows have been opened and they see that the same kind of people that want that expressway through—the cement lobby and the insurance companies and the bankers—are the same ones who make the wars; are the same ones who wave the flag. Not that we shouldn't wave the flag, but I feel bad about giving the other side all these symbols. And so, that *is* happening. And the fact is single issues can be taken and made multiple issues.

[The potential] is all there. Now the neighborhood groups are planting a big row, if they can be coalesced. Blue-collar people are learning how the tax laws are misused. The realtor gets the breaks, the bungalow owner pays through the nose. There's ACORN in Arkansas. National Land for People in Fresno, California, with Jessie Delacruz, a Chicano woman. George Ballast fighting agribusiness and winning a fight or two now and then, representing the small family farm. And there are new unions too. You remember police are being organized, firemen being organized, public service employees being organized. Never were before, you see.

I'm gonna give the negative side now. There is also a new kind of young. I don't remember [them] from the past, though maybe they've always been there with *The Wall Street Journal* under their arms. They're what I call the new Stockmanites. These kids are cool, and they've been taught to make it no matter what. "Me, myself and I."

But another hopeful thing—I want to bring this up because I'm looking for hopes. Now, I'm looking for those slender reeds—and that is that in every community you find [people who are really concerned]. There's always one person or two in the community who comes up after I speak to say, "I thought I was alone." That's the thing, "I thought I was alone, and it's good to hear someone say what I've been feeling."

You see, there's something that hasn't been touched yet. There's an innate decency. I'm not saying people are basically saints. They're not. There's saint and devil in all of us. [But what predominates] depends on what the society most values: the cooperative nature or the aggressive. Now, anthropologists always have this dispute. Robert Audrey popularized the idea that man is basically aggressive. There is an aggressive, but there is also a cooperative, nature. We know this from the anthropoid animals. Ashley

Montague would point this out, you see. So, it's both. It depends [on what the society rewards]: "On my own, by God, and to hell with the rest," or, "I'm part of a community." This is what [Albert] Einstein talked about. Einstein was quite marvelous, and you know one of the things he mentioned I used as an epigraph in *American Dreams:*

> The individual has become more conscious than ever of his dependence upon society. He does not experience this dependence as a positive asset, but rather as a threat to his natural rights. All human beings, whatever their position in society, are suffering from this process of deterioration. Unknowingly prisoners of their own egotism, they feel insecure, lonely, and deprived of the naive, simple, and unsophisticated enjoyment of life. Man can find meaning in life, short and perilous as it is, only through devoting himself to society.

[And sometimes, in order to set wrongs right, that devotion to society has to take the form of collective action that is more forceful than simply writing letters to representatives in government. In 1954, for example, when the Supreme Court ruled that public schools must be desegregated, the South went on with separate schools as though there had been no such ruling at all.] The point is, had Eisenhower taken that kid by the hand in Little Rock, had there been a feeling that government would *enforce* the law, schools would have been desegregated and there would have been no problems. But the racists knew, deep down, that upstairs they weren't serious. [And so blacks were forced to take more direct action. That's the history of the civil rights movement.]

Coming back to possibilities in people; I'm not particularly religious, but the word "god" with a small *g,* I would say, is in everybody. In short, the possibility to transcend his present self. This is what Myles talks about. Possibilities. In that sense it's religious in that within people is a potentiality not yet tapped. And that's what Highlander taps. . . .

I don't think you call upon anybody across the great blue yonder. No, it's here. It's us. If it's going to be fixed at all. . . .

And so Highlander, in a sense, is symbolic; but more than that it is representing, you might say, as a school, all those disparate forces of positive change. That's why Myles always lends a note of history [to any occasion]. Always when I'm in the company of Myles, I know something's cookin'. Something's cookin'.

"Keeping People in Motion"
Julian Bond

In contrast to Studs Terkel's expansive and historic perspectives, many leaders of the civil rights movement openly denounced history as meaningless for the sixties. Instead, young men like Julian Bond made history in such a fervent way that for a while at least, they lived as if America's calendar had reverted to the Year One.

After nearly three decades, however, the experience of time's passing has given Julian Bond a more objective view. His responses to "Where Are We Going? Where Have We Been?" trace the aftermath of the civil rights movement from 1968 through the early eighties. And his twenty-five years in the Georgia legislature provide an insider's perspective of how politics, rather than protesting, can effect change today.

. . . People never really regrouped in major ways. We lost the ability to sustain. We didn't push hard enough, didn't keep at it enough, didn't drive enough, didn't organize well enough—just didn't do as much as we could have. We, myself included, and the voters and the leaders, were consciously diverted into other things. We lost the ability to sustain.

But groups like [the Student Nonviolent Coordinating Committee] at least provided some models in their earlier days for getting the work done. One of the most important things SNCC did, for example, was to provide a funnel through which the activist young person could pour himself or herself and come out at the bottom directed towards something they could do that was useful to the movement. If you were a student at the University of Minnesota, you knew you could jump into this thing and come out at the bottom pointed in some useful direction. It was this wide open space you could drop yourself into and be spat out in some other place where after some indoctrination and training, immediately you were "hands-on" to the problem of the moment. And for many people these skills are still what they do for a living. Wilson Brown, for example, who came to SNCC and was trained as a printer, used that skill then not for his own advantage but for the advantage of the larger movement; and now he's a printer with his own print shop earning a living doing that. Or Bobby Fletcher, a photographer today, who first enlarged and used that skill for the benefit of the movement.

But there's not much like that you can jump into now. What can you jump into? That funnel doesn't really exist anymore. Some groups try. The NAACP can do it in a limited kind of way, as can the Institute for Southern Studies. I'm trying to be a funnel in some ways but I'm limited mostly by my financial resources and my inability to spend a lot of time on this. Funnel people into the voting rights protest, for example. So there are limited versions of it, but nothing as encompassing. And partly because of that, you have all these students who just get up, go to school, and come home at the end of the day—just function from day to day—and they aren't provided an alternative that not only accommodates their daily lives but also provides them with some social-political outlet. That funnel has to be provided, to show them how they can jump right in and be part of something. For the first five or six years I was in office, I never had any student volunteers coming over here to work. I thought they'd just come naturally, you know, and I couldn't understand why they didn't. It really made me feel bad. There they were, just a block away across the street. Why weren't they here in droves being turned away: "Sorry, I can't use you today"? Finally I began to solicit them for the first time, and it wasn't until I began soliciting them that they began to come. The interest was there. People wanted to do not only very involved and intellectual things, but also just little jobs like half an hour's typing or arranging cards and so on. They were willing and eager to do everything, but they didn't have this feeling that they could cut in and be useful. Maybe they thought they'd have to first go through some rigid ideological identification, or prove themselves in some way first before they could jump in. Maybe they didn't feel they could contribute to what I was doing. Maybe they felt it didn't have anything to do with them. Or maybe they didn't feel such work would be assigned any value outside of the normal value of a paycheck—that it wouldn't have any currency among their peers and people they respected. But once I went and got them, that began to change. [They have to have that entry point, though, and where is that for the mass of them today?]

[In my view, in the South, the movement is localized.] You go to towns and you find the NAACP doing something here or SCLC or some neighborhood group doing something there; but it's fragmented, which doesn't mean that it works at cross-purposes but that it doesn't work under any one umbrella.

And what focus there is is largely political and economic. Political in the sense that it's interested in electing, first, black candidates, and secondly, influencing the election of white candidates for public office; and economic in the sense that it is trying to create a mercantile class of small businessmen, shopping-center owners and so forth. But it's largely a jobs-oriented movement. Sadly enough, it's not a job-*creating* movement, but a job-*winning* movement. Too many people just want to get the jobs that are there already—have them equitably shared between black and white and men and women—rather than creating brand-new nonexistent jobs. I shouldn't have to compete for one job with some guy who just graduated from the University of Mississippi. There ought to be a job for each of us. And the problem is not that the economy can't finance that. It's that the economy as it is run *now* can't finance it.

But the point I'm trying to make is that the movement now is scattered—there's not that same sense of connection and community there used to be. We've all gone in different ways. We've all matured in the sense that we have staked out something and said, "This is it for me. This is my life now. This is my primary interest." We've become family people. We have psychological investments in certain lifestyles. [We've moved on to other things and nothing has taken the place of the goals of the sixties for the students who have come on behind us.]

But all of us who went through that, even though we've scattered, are still in one way or another movement people. That is, we bring a movement perspective to the work we do today. A reporter I know brings a movement perspective to his work that makes him a different kind of reporter because of the experiences he had then and what he did. Marion Barry is just a regular politician, as all politicians, in one sense, but in another sense he's a movement politician. . . .

What made me a good [political] candidate was, first, I lived in the district and so I was legally the only person on the [SNCC] staff who could run. The others lived outside the district. Secondly, I was one of the few people on the staff who could say to people, "Remember when you had this picket line around the A & P at the corner of Ashby and Hunter in 1961? I was on that picket line and now black people are working there. I was a part of that. And remember when we had a voter registration drive in the summer of '61? I was a part of that drive. You remember me from that." I was one of the few people who could say, "I've been laboring away at all this for a number of years, and now I'd like to try to do it in another way. Put me on the city council or the county commission or in the state legislature. I've been able to do certain things in one form. Now let me try to do them in another."

Well, the SNCC people realized all this, and when they approached me in 1965 about running, I was interested. I had worked in other people's political campaigns and I was fascinated by the technical aspects of the thing: how you turn out voters; how you organize a campaign. And I was fascinated by the idea of being in the legislature because I thought it was a forum where you could do something. I never had any grandiose ideas about accomplishing a great, great deal, but it was a way to communicate with the public at large as well as a way to energize the voters in the district to broaden their political consciousness and concerns. Because of the situation in the South, it had been impossible for someone like me to run before, but now that it was possible, I decided to try it.

Well, I got elected to the state House of Representatives. In fact, there were seven of us from various districts around the city that got elected about the same time. Up until then, there had been no blacks in the House, and those first years were miserable years. There are three groups in the House: the way outsiders, the peripherals, and the insiders. I was obviously an unpopular person. There were 205 members, and many of them wouldn't speak. Those who would speak spoke in odd ways. I was a strange person to them—definitely outside. So they weren't happy years. It's hard as hell to get on the inside.

Since I wasn't inside, I had this time to just sit and watch. I had the chance to see and learn. The legislative process is complicated. In some ways it's like a personality contest. That doesn't mean that you want to be a nice guy so other people will like you and will vote for your bills. It doesn't work that way. But you have to learn that this person is chairman of a committee, and he has a personality, and you appeal to his personality in one way and someone else's personality in another. You have to learn who is powerful and who is not. Often the person who is the chairman of a committee is not the powerful person. Someone else is. You have to learn how the whole thing works. You have to learn the rules. There are both written and unwritten rules, and you have to learn both. And by rules I don't mean rules in a bad sense. I don't even mean the rules that say, "Don't speak till you're spoken to" or "Freshmen legislators don't make speeches or introduce bills," or rules that say, "Don't talk about economic interests or concentration of power." I'm not talking about those kinds of rules. I'm talking about the natural flow of a body like the Georgia State Legislature or the Congress of the United States. It has its own rules, and they are not rules that anyone of conscience would object to follow. They are partly rules of courtesy, of honesty. A member of the body who lies to his fellows, for example, is very quickly ostracized. It happened to a fellow who's a friend of mine, and it was as though he had died. He just was outside the pale. He served for another year and then left to run for another office because he knew he would never get anywhere otherwise. There's a tremendous amount of integrity among politicians in interpersonal and interpolitical relationships—a tremendous ethical standard among representatives. And almost everyone meets it. Now some people slip from this standard, and their slipping is tolerated a little bit. But if you stray too widely, you're out. This guy told a lie to all of us and I mean it was *literally* as though he had died. A lot of people who've come upon the scene rather lately like to pretend that they don't play by the rules, but everyone plays by the rules. Everyone plays by the rules, or they lose the game.

I spent several years in the House, and then I was elected to the Georgia Senate, which I've grown to enjoy a great deal. It's a smaller, more intimate place. And I really take political office seriously. It sounds like the Fourth of July or a bicentennial speech to say so, but I really think it is a sacred trust. These people have gotten together and made a choice here and entrusted me and several hundred others with their lives in a certain sense. They've given me a trust. I'm their representative. That's serious business. You can't fool around with people's trust.

Now nine out of ten things people ask me to help them with have nothing at all to do with the strict definition of my job as a state representative. That is, they are not state concerns. I'm asked to act generally as an ombudsman between them and their government—and most usually their city or federal government, not state. But they see me—and the others like me in this situation—as people who will help them, and most things they call you about you can help them with. Often it's simply a matter of referral.

But even at that level, the job is important. And to people who say electoral politics is not important in their lives, I say that's not true. Hubert Humphrey could have been President in '68. Just the black vote alone could have elected him if we had turned out in larger numbers. We had six years of Richard Nixon instead. So it's obvious to me on the face of it that this is a very important process and has an awful lot to say about all of us. And those people who don't register to vote because they think it doesn't make any difference who's President are simply wrong.

Look at the Reagan presidency, for example. In a very short time, his administration has managed to erase an enormous amount of the civil rights law written over the last twenty-five years. It almost completely eliminated affirmative action. Protection of women in college athletics and against sexual harassment is being cut back. Contractors are once again being allowed to use federal funds to buy memberships for their employees in segregated private clubs. The Voting Rights Act is in danger. And on and on. I don't think Reagan's mean. I think he's just the figurehead for a group of people who have seized control of the government—

clever technocrats who like to think of themselves as self-made men and women and think that government's main purpose ought to be to protect and enhance their wealth. They are contemptuous of poor people. They are racists. Some of their politics border on the fascist. They are a frightening phenomenon. And the ones closest to Reagan—who, by the way, strikes me as utterly and absolutely out of touch with the United States in the latter part of the twentieth century—have formed this kitchen cabinet immune to any public accountability because they don't hold public offices.

But what we have to remember is that there is an enormous power in the American body politic that can be properly funneled and channeled to change policies that are clearly wrong. It can be done. It's been done twice in my lifetime—once on the question of race and once on the question of war—and it can be done again. It can be done with this conservative tide, but it takes hard work and it takes a combination of political pressures. It takes formal political pressures such as letter-writing campaigns and visiting representatives and organizing voters to say, "If you don't change, we're going to vote for candidate B." And it takes the informal political pressures we've abandoned over the last fifteen years that have got to be revived again: demonstrations, picket lines, and street protests around your local courthouse and your local federal buildings. You've got to find ways to hold these guys' feet to the fire and, if necessary, defeat them. Target them for real defeat and teach them a lesson. They've got to change or they've got to go.

One of the big problems we're facing is that many of these issues are hard to get voters worked up about. Nevertheless, they have to be looked at. They are moral issues—questions of simple right and wrong—and you have to make that moral appeal and combine it with a renewed push for voter registration, voter organization, and voter education. Look at the question of South Africa, for example. That's complicated and hard to articulate to people, but Reagan has rescinded the Carter-era prohibition against supplying assistance to the South African military and police. We allow South African Coast Guardsmen to train at the Coast Guard Academy. Now, in South Africa the coast guard is a military function. Here it's a civilian function. In South Africa it's like a subnavy. It's hard to explain that to people. I've written to my congressman to ask him to do something about it, but it's not an excitable issue. It's not something that people get real up on. But that is a moral issue. When South Africa uses its military strength to invade Angola, that is a moral issue. We organized a march of three thousand people here in Atlanta against that invasion, and about thirty people spoke, including the presidents of four of the five black colleges here, and there was not one word of coverage in Atlanta's two daily newspapers. The only coverage in the newspaper was a photograph of the car to which two speakers were affixed being ticketed by a policeman. It's pathetic, but that's what we're up against.

Of course, other issues are easier to get people mobilized around, and we need to be doing more of it. We need to mobilize teach-ins about the Voting Rights Act on college campuses in Georgia. We need to have more people concerned about the quality of public schools. Generally, I think they're awful. I have three children in the public schools, and I don't think the public schools are demanding enough or strict enough. They've got into this whole system of social promotions which is just awful for the child, and teachers aren't held to a high enough standard of teacher competency. They resent teacher competency tests, but when I get notes from teachers that I can barely read, I say, "Hey, how can these people teach my kids how to read and write if they can't do it themselves?" Pay them more—they have a justifiable complaint there—but demand competence.

We need to have more people organized around economic issues. These are issues that increasingly go beyond simple questions of race too, although disproportionate numbers of the victims tend to be black. These are issues that involve poor whites and Hispanics and Vietnamese—class issues that demand that we seek out allies and friends and other people who are in the same condition.

Educational institutions like Highlander and the Institute for Southern Studies have to continue doing what they've always done: citizenship training, getting people involved in community work, showing people how it's done, really empowering people to take control of their own lives. No one does that that I know of. SCLC doesn't do it. The modern-day civil rights movement seems to be conference-oriented. People come to a central spot and hear a succession of speakers and go home. That's great for me because I'm the speaker, you know; but it's not so hot for the people, I think. People are told what's wrong but they are not told what to do about it. They are not *shown* what to do about it. And somebody needs to do that.

I think the thrust needs to be on energizing people and getting them out in any of a variety of ways. Getting them out to the polls, getting them out to protest, spreading information among them and agitating them and riling them up and sticking pins in them. Getting them to do things they wouldn't do ordinarily, ranging from writing letters to their elected officials to descending on the state capitol when the budgets are discussed. . . .

And in addition to all these other things, I think you have to continue trying to create your own vision of what the world ought to be in a variety of little ways. Ways in which we find the means to pay for ourselves without government help—self-sufficient organizations among low-income people, for example, that provide employment for people who don't have it, training for people who don't have it, money for people who don't have it, food for people who don't have it.

That's part of what I'm interested in: keeping people in motion. . . .

★

But How Do We Pass the Torch?

Bernice Robinson

Like those of Julian Bond, Bernice Robinson's accomplishments during the sixties defined her as a pure activist. Through the Citizenship Schools, she served as a frontline soldier for the movement, and those experiences peppered her thoughts with action verbs.

Understandably, then, she is troubled by the comparative passiveness of the average American today. So her reflections on "Where Are We Going? Where Have We Been?" pose more questions than answers. "We need to get together and find out what's happening to us," she affirms. "But how?"

Of course, there's still a lot of illiteracy on the islands. We need more Citizenship Schools now. We didn't scratch the surface, so it would seem that there is no point. But I will tell you a little story about Horace Mann, who founded a school. And it seems like an awful lot of money had been spent towards the buildings and things, and when he was questioned about that, he said, "If one child is helped because of all this expensive outlay, it's worth it."

So his companion said to him, "Isn't that stretching it a little bit, to say that one child, one boy, is worth all this expensive outlay?"

He said, "No, that's not stretching it. Not if he were *my* boy." Look at problems as being what it takes to save one boy, one girl, or one mother or one father. If it were my mother or my father or my boy or my brother it would be worth the effort. You can't say that all is lost.

Although we haven't scratched the surface as far as literacy is concerned, we have had an influence. We've changed the way some public schools run their adult education classes, for example. At least they no longer teach about Tom and Jerry, and they finally became aware of the fact that you have to meet an adult in an adult world. So some progress has been made, even though it may be minute when you look at the overall picture.

And some changes have been made in important areas. In the first eight years after the Voting Rights Act was passed, over 876 blacks were elected to office in the South. Now that figure has probably quadrupled.

So *that* progress has been made, but we're sitting on a time bomb in this period. We have to protect that progress and hold it or else we'll be right back in the same boat we were in right after Reconstruction when everything was going fine until the troops were pulled out of the South and we lost almost everything again. At the SCLC convention in Birmingham in 1966 or '67, Andy Young reminded everyone of that. It was a good warning at the time, and it's still good. I don't know who else may remember that he said that. He may not even remember that he said it himself. But he did, and he was right. That was a great insight.

He also said we had to use the expertise and know-how we gained during our long fight, and use it to maintain that momentum and progress. But what's happened? We were so busy doing what we had to do that we never passed all that knowledge and expertise on, and when we tell kids now what we went through, and how we used to have to sit in the back of the bus and how we used to not be allowed to try on clothes in department stores in Charleston, they think it's a joke! That has opened my eyes to the fact that a lot of what we've done is lost. People who were born in 1960 and later don't know *nothing*. They don't know anything about what had to happen so they could enjoy things they enjoy today. In fact, they think nothing is happening now. They don't understand that we are still just about on the second rung of the ladder and we've got about fifty-six more rungs to go. But how are you going to convince them?

This is what bothers me, because I see too much complacency. You get accustomed to the good life, and you don't want to give it up. Too many people have two, three cars, they have homes, they are in debt over their heads, and they can't think about anything else. It's hard to get people to move now. Back then, it wasn't so hard. Of course, it was easier to see the problems then. I'd give anything to have the insight that Myles always seemed to have. He could always see twenty years down the road and know where you should be going. Where you should be heading in planning your strategy, your workshops. It's pretty hard. Especially when people are so busy trying to keep their heads above water that they are not interested in what's going on outside. Not realizing that the neighbor next door is having the same problem, and the one across the street is having it too, and the one across town is having it too, and the one in the next city is in the same shape too. We *need* to get together and find out what's happening to us. But how? That's the big question.

I don't know how we can maintain the momentum. I don't know how we can work together again. We come so far, and we make so many inroads, and then we see Reagan elected and get our hopes dashed.

And we see a trend where the KKK is coming back up strong again, and where the rednecks are going to take over again. They are in worse shape than *we* are in, and they don't have enough sense to see that they need to join arms *with* us and really get something going that's strong and will last.

Now what about that?

★

"Be Different in Ways that Make a Difference"

Don West

While many left Highlander to create social change in mainstream America, the cofounder of Highlander Folk School ultimately focused his efforts on Appalachia. Following political persecution during the McCarthy era, Don West was awarded a two-year research grant to study Appalachian history at the Library of Congress and the National Archives. Concurrently, his wife, Connie, was employed by the Baltimore County public schools. He also taught at Baltimore's Orthodox Jewish Rabbinical Training Institute and at the University of Maryland.

Once they were financially secure, however, the couple dedicated their work in Maryland to living on only one salary while saving the other. After ten years, they accumulated enough money to purchase a three-hundred acre farm in Pipestem, West Virginia. There they established the Folklife Center, and once again, the couple was positioned to make a difference.

But since Don West's experiences have, for the most part, run counter to those of others whom Highlander influenced, his reflections on "Where Are We Going? Where Have We Been?" also differ. Ironically, this lifelong educator contends, "I have never felt that education per se is enough."

. . . Every summer, groups of Appalachian kids come here to the center to live with us and learn about their history and culture, and they learn in a good atmosphere. I think education must take place in a congenial atmosphere with love and understanding being shown by the adults toward the young people, and a willingness to be considerate toward the many crazy things that a kid may do, and the student must be encouraged to take every bit of responsibility that he or she is capable of taking from decision making to carrying out decisions. The first thing we always do when we get a group together is to let them know right off that we are not going to tell them what to do, or what they should think, or what they should believe. But we hope that they may be stimulated to think a little and that they may be stimulated to be committed to some value that is worthwhile. I have never felt that education per se is enough. Germany used to be a mecca for scholars—even W. E. B. Du Bois had to go there—but that didn't keep Hitler from taking Germany in. Education of that kind just didn't have any morality. I think education has to have some morality, and I think kids must be stimulated to be committed to some moral values. They have to discuss and see what values are worthy of their being committed to. I don't mind telling kids what I believe, and I believe very strongly in things. Now, this doesn't mean that you have to accept that, but I believe certain things and they can believe them too or they can question them. I always encourage them to question. I think the questioning approach to education is basic. (But there are certain values it would be irresponsible not to incorporate into any decent kind of education.) I've seen individuals who were racists become people who accepted all groups and who understood how ridiculous their former position had been. I've seen a complete change in their values and the way they looked at things. Hopefully I have helped some of them to do that.

And hopefully I've helped some people see that human welfare is indivisible, and that as long as there are people who lack security, nobody can really have it. That's what the Wobblies taught. They had this slogan, you know: "One for all and all for one." And Jesus taught that over and over again. I think that's what Jesus was saying in the parable of the Good Samaritan, and what he was teaching there is the same thing I say the Wobblies taught: As long as there are human needs neglected anywhere, nobody has security. Human welfare is indeed indivisible.

I was very impressed as a child by an old mountain preacher, Larkin Chastain, who was a close personal friend of my Grandpa Kim. He preached a tremendously human kind of ethical Christianity. We didn't have this condemning vengeful God that was going to burn people in brimstone, but a God that was concerned for human welfare. That influenced me a lot. And that led me to my concept of Jesus as a true revolutionary. I've always felt that. And by revolutionary, I don't mean somebody with a bomb in his pocket and a butcher knife between his teeth looking to stab and kill and blow up. My revolutionary is one who wants to change ugly conditions to more positive humane conditions and to have a turnover from the kind of regime that may be rotten and corrupt to one that is more humane. So I see Jesus as a revolutionary on the side of the poor people. Not only that, he was a very realistic person. As I see him, he was the kind of teacher who didn't want to be different from other people just for the sake of being different. He was so like the people in at least two instances I can think of that he managed to escape possible death because he lost himself among the people. Where they were going to stone him in Nazareth, and another time when they were going to throw him over a bluff to his destruction, he lost himself in the midst of the people. And even when they came to arrest him in the garden, they had to have a Judas to go along and point out who this dangerous character was because he was so much like everybody else that nothing stood out that made him look different.

Understanding Jesus this way influenced my own attitudes tremendously. I have never wanted to be different just for the sake of being different. I want to be just as much like the common ordinary person as it is possible for me to be, because if you're going to communicate with people, and understand them, you've got to be as much like them as it's possible to be. And if you're going to be different, it should be in a way that makes a difference. To me it was rather infantile the way some of the movement people in the sixties tried to be different. It was not in a way that made a difference, but in a way that tended to put a barrier between them and communication with common people. Many of them—not being common people—became the fiery revolutionaries wearing the revolution on their sleeves and sowed their radical wild oats for a while and went back to rich Papa. That's why I have always had very deep feelings that the most responsible and the most dependable element is the working class, and I have considerable question about the stability of a lot of people who don't come from the working class.

Another problem I had with a number of those movement people was their lack of understanding of the work that had gone on before them. I remember hearing one of these super radicals back in the sixties say, "To hell with the thirties," because someone was speaking about what came out of the thirties. But look at that decade. Just to mention a few things, there did come a pretty considerable organized labor movement. There came old age insurance, old age pensions, unemployment insurance, Social Security, workmen's compensation, welfare itself—we were fighting for it under the name of direct relief. All of these things came out of the thirties, and some of them were called communist ideas when they were being advocated. They were supposed to be communist, and now we have them! And nobody, except maybe some of the extreme right wing, would like to do away with them. Few people seriously talk about eliminating Social Security, unemployment insurance, old age pensions, or any of those things.

At any rate, I've always believed, as I was saying, that human welfare is indivisible [and that even if one's goals along those lines are never fully realized] I personally think that there's never been a battle for decency or for justice or for the rights of people that has been a total loss. And those beliefs have never changed. When I was a student at Vanderbilt, some of the more conservative students used to say, "Just wait till you get out and get a family, and then you're gonna change your whole philosophy." Well, I guess the family has suffered a good bit, but the philosophy has never really changed. It's still the same because, as far as I'm concerned, that's the only thing that's viable. That's the only thing that's real.

★

Recognize The Value of Experience
Edgar Daniel Nixon

To this civil rights activist, the question of "Where Are We Going?" relates best to "Where Have We Been?" when the context is essential and practical. As a boy, barred from most educational opportunities because he was black, E. D. Nixon studied everyday life as his library. The influence of people became his books, and trial-and-error experiences his lessons.

Maybe that's why he differs with Studs Terkel's emphasis that knowing history is essential. Or does he? Nixon describes "something that happened back in 1870" as "not worth a dime," if students can't also learn the history in their midst. He encourages people who would effect social change to study living *books: the elders, the survivors of recent repressions—those whose actions have already accomplished more than the rhetoric that pervades our nation today.*

. . . The children ought to know the truth. When you talk about Black History Week, somebody ought to know the truth about it. A couple of weeks ago, a church down here had Black History Week, and there was some boy and girl played the role of so-and-so, and something that happened back in 1870. [Okay. But that's] not worth a dime [unless they also are] able to talk to people who done something this year, and last year, and ten years ago, that's still alive. You ought to recognize those people because if the children knew them, it would give them something to stand up for. These children want something to hang on to just like I wanted something to hang on to with A. Philip Randolph. And that hasn't happened.

They need to know about those people who stood up when everyone else was afraid. We had to fight two wars. We had to fight the white people for the gains, and then we had to go around and fight the black folks to make them accept the gains. All these black folks hollerin' about, "Old E. D. Nixon gonna get everybody killed" or "Old Nixon gonna get everybody run out of town" or "Old Nixon gonna get everybody put in jail!" Then finally they come out and holler, "Look what we done." They's a whole lot of people that all along through life have never done anything because of fear. And we got a whole lot of peoples afraid now. We have peoples today who will blow off about this or that. When you look around, that person haven't done anything. Like we had Dick Gregory here one night, right after the civil rights law passed, in the Holiday Inn up there. One of our local professors here said, "Brother Nixon, I didn't ever dream that we could ever sit down in a Holiday Inn motel and eat a juicy steak without being humiliated."

I said, "You ought to keep your mouth shut!" I said, "You ain't done nothin' to help bring it about." I said, "You ain't done nothing but listen at Bull Connor sic dogs on the children in Birmingham, or Jim Clark turn water hoses onto the demonstrators. You ain't done nothing but set down and listen to that on the radio." I said, "But if you had got out there with a whole lot of the rest of the folks, you and a whole lot of them who sat down and watched it on TV, it would have made the job a whole lot easier for us who was out there."

A lot of us put our lives on the chopping block, but here was a job that needed to be done. Somebody *had* to do it. And you had to be prepared that you were gon' do it or die. Randolph said if anything wasn't worth dying for, it wasn't worth fighting for. And I stuck to that principle.

At our first meeting about the boycott, I said, "This is a problem we have had for a number of years." I said, "You who are afraid, better get your hat and coat and go home. This will be a long drawn-out affair." This is the first meeting we had, that Monday night, December 5. I said, "Before it's over with, somebody gonna die." I said, "It may be me for all I know." But I said, "If it's not worth dying for, it ain't worth fighting for."

And they tried to scare us off and make us give up lots of times. I remember when they burned my house. I was on the train, and a red cap run up and brought me a paper and said, "Brother Nixon, they burned your house last night. Nobody got hurt. Here's a paper, you can read it for yourself." Just like that. When I got to Birmingham, I called my wife and said, "I just got the paper and found out what happened there."

She said, "You know what they're tryin' to do. They're tryin' to make you quit." She said, "Don't do it."

I had letters from the Ku Klux Klan with caskets on them. Time after time I was called and threatened and told to get out of town. A guy called and woke me up one morning and said, "You the guy that wrote that article in the paper this morning?"

I said, "Yes, I did."

"All right, we coming out there and get you now and drag you all over the street."

I said, "All right, you done said yours, now let me tell you mine." I said, "They tell me the road from here to hell is awful lonesome," and I cussed and I said, "and I ain't going by myself."

Another time they threw a bomb on the porch roof and it rolled down in the driveway. One time they called and told me they were coming out there and bomb my house, and I told my wife, I said, "You got time to catch a train. I can send you home to your daddy." And I said, "If I'm alive in the morning, I'll call you."

She said, "I ain't going nowhere." She said, "I don't believe they coming." She said, "If they come, I'd rather be the widow of a man who had the courage to fight than to be the wife of a coward." She said, "I ain't going nowhere."

But see, I went through a lot of things a whole lot of people never knew about. And I kept on doing it, not because I wanted to be a big man. I done it because I thought it needed doing.

[So should high school teachers also be helping kids learn what they can do to help make a better world?] . . . If the teacher isn't able to help students figure out a way to solve these problems, what good is the teacher? I think a teacher ought to be able to help a student solve any kind of problem, whether it's teaching them how to use the courts or whatever. That's what he go to school to learn and that's part of learning. And if *I* know that, mister, it look like folks who done spent years and years in school and come up through college and master's degrees and all that—*they* ought to know that. . . .

The first thing I would tell children—like I had to tell some adults the other day—is that right now we have outlived the useful-ness of what we call marching. We got the civil rights law. We ought to use the courts. If we just put pressure on a man—say me and a group of children don't trade with this man and he give in just to get our business back—he may change again [as soon as the pressure's off]. But if we use the courts and win [the change may be more permanent]. So they have to learn how to use the courts. Let's us use the law to win our grievances.

But even before that, *number one*, I'd tell them to be honest with themselves and be honest in dealing with peoples and pre-pare themselves, whatever they intend to do in life, learn to do it well. Be on time. Earn respect. My life in Montgomery has been such that I get the highest respect from both white and black in this town. Some of them may not want to do it, but they have to do it because I don't give them the opportunity for no other alterna-tive. And whether it's a woman or a man, if there's something I want done, I don't know an office in this town I can't get in. The governor's office, anywhere. I had an appointment with George Wallace at three o'clock yesterday evening. But you earn that. So it's those kinds of things we have to talk about now.

I go in schools all the time. I got a list in my car of every school we've got in the city—we've got fifty-two. I can be driving down the street and decide I want to go in a school and pull out my list and say, "Oh, Miss So-and-so is the principal here." Go on in . . . And some of what I see I don't like. This present genera-tion is gon' have to learn that we got to be trained to be part of this society. They have to get educated. You can go downtown right now and you can find seventy-five or a hundred boys running all over the street downtown. We aren't gonna make it that way.

I was in a schoolroom here some time ago, and here's a black child sitting right here with a pile of spitballs on the corner of his desk, big rubber band where he could shoot them across the schoolroom; had on a pair of sunglasses, hat up on top of his hair.

White teacher. I says to her, "You let that boy sit in the class like that?"

She said, "Mr. Nixon, if I say anything to him, he'd eat me up."

So I walked to him and I said, "All right, son, take your hat and your glasses and go put them in your locker. That's where they belong." He looked at me like . . . and I said, "I mean do it *now*." So he got up and put them in his locker.

Then when he came back, I stopped him at the door outside before he come inside, and I said to him, I said, "Young man, you see the white boy sitting beside you?"

He said, "Yeah!" Real gruff.

I said, "How do you know his father don't own a business in this town?" And I said, "When he gets grown, old enough, he might come in possession of that business or come to be personnel manager or something of that business and come to the point where he's gonna hire help." And I said, "You go walk up there looking for a job, he won't hire you." I said, "He *know* you don't know nothing because he sat right in class with you and he *know* you don't know nothing." I said, "Who the loser?" I said, "You the loser, not him. You the loser." I said, "If I were you, I'd go back in my desk and clean all that mess off my desk, and I would challenge that white guy sitting next to me. If he could learn his lesson, I could learn mine."

Here we got 210 million other people against 26 million of blacks. We 26 million ought to try to amalgamate ourselves in with these other races of people because we aren't going to get anything anymore just preaching about we blacks. We need to start talking about education and jobs and stop talking about being black, because you may pressure a man into hiring you, but there ain't no law to make him keep you. You have to earn that.

All black people don't agree with me. I know that. But I'm for what I think is right. Do you know I'll be eighty-two years old Sunday? All right, I'm sitting here holding down a job at the age of eighty-two. You can say what you will, but a white man is responsible for me having this job. All right. Then I ought to have sense enough to realize that all the man would have to do would be to say, "Naw, we ain't gonna work you on this job anymore. You're too old." There ain't a black man in town would give me a job at this age. So, for that reason, I have to see both sides of the coin. I don't just see one side as white over here and that's all I see. I try to make sense out of all these things.

My point is now we have got to learn to get people together so we can work both white and black together. You see, I don't see a black problem or a white problem. I see problems. And if I can make a contribution in solving those problems, I want to do that. The days of you against me got to be over.

And then I tell these children that along with education, you got to have some common sense. I don't care how much schooling you got, if you ain't got no common sense, number one, you ain't gon' have no money, 'cause ain't nobody gon' have no money ain't got no common sense.

You see, we, as blacks, spend almost a fifth of our earnings on carrying charges. We can't afford it. The last seven automobiles I had I paid cash for them because I couldn't afford to pay carrying charges. So what my philosophy is is it's not how bad you want a thing. The question is how long can you do without it? You don't have to spend money just 'cause you got it.

A whole lot of people don't see that, but if you really want to be independent where you gonna stand on your feet, you're gonna have to learn how to spend money. Not how to save it, but how to spend it. We got thousands of people in this town who are saving money every day—Christmas Saving Club, all that kind of thing—and January 1, 1982, will be broke. You know why? Because they haven't learned how to spend money! If they'd learned how to spend it, they'd had some of it.

You can't be independent and broke. As long as you broke, you got to stay on your knees.

And then I tell children that even if you can't get a good education, you can *still* use common sense and plan your strategy. I've held out my hand 214 times for citations—that includes books, magazines, tokens, cups, medallions, degrees. Mayor of Los Angeles give me a metal key to the city. Lieutenant Governor of Alabama stopped the Senate in session on the nineteenth of July and introduced me to the Senate. But I only had sixteen months in school. I refused to be handicapped for the lack of formal school training. We got plenty of people that think just because they spent more time in school than me that they are my superior, but with my years of experience in organized labor and with the NAACP and with other organizations, I was able to see a whole lot further than professional men who only stayed right here in school and didn't get those experiences.

Just because a man spent a whole lot of time in college . . . I keep telling people we need to pool our resources regardless of academic training. And let me tell you something. The day will never come when just book learning alone will be superior over travel and observation. It's hard for some people to see that. Now a whole lot of my professional friends here had read about Stone Mountain or read about Pikes Peak, for instance, but I've had my hand on it. I've had my hand on it. There's a difference when you've laid your hand on it.

★

Young People Effect Most Social Changes
Andrew Young

"We never could have gotten adults to do what they did," according to the man who has been mayor of Atlanta, Georgia, since 1982. In fact, it is Andrew Young's clear memory that much of what became the modern civil rights movement was initiated by daring people who, at the time, were still in high school or college.

So to Young, asking "Where Have We Been?" also involves examining the role of public schools, then and now, in terms of the type of citizens such schools produce. If the public schools of the fifties shaped young minds in ways that enabled some students to "invent" sit-ins, boycotts, and protest marches, is the absence of such inventiveness among today's youth also related to the education they receive? And what does such an education portend about the question "Where Are We Going?"

ELIOT WIGGINTON: There were a lot of people during the civil rights movement—yourself included—who put themselves on the line for things that they believed in, knowing that it was dangerous. I'm trying to figure out where that courage comes from.

ANDREW YOUNG: [Partly] it's religious. It's also a certain foolhardiness. We never felt like our work was dangerous. It was fun. And when it did become dangerous, you were already into it and your very manhood wouldn't let you back out. But also I was taught by my father to confront danger rationally. You didn't run from a dog. You didn't run from somebody that was picking on you. You talked to them. He traveled around the state of Louisiana as a dentist, and historically we were taught to stand up to the system, but to do it in a nonviolent way. He would always speak to people and call them by name when he knew them. He didn't lay back and act afraid. He was aggressive toward people who he knew might be hostile to him. And I learned that that's the way you deal with people.

E.W.: But I think of all the people who deliberately put themselves into situations knowing they would probably be arrested or beaten or scorned, and I still wonder . . .

A.Y.: It's hard to know. It's hard to know. Partly, it's circumstances. But I really do think that families and church have a lot of credit for that. There are leaders of various kinds in almost every community, and if you look at a Martin Luther King, there are three or four generations of leaders who were courageous in their own way. I don't know Rosa Parks, or I don't know much about Septima [Clark's] family background, but you can bet that there was somebody there that taught her as a child to stand up for what's right. Unfortunately, in the public schools, you are not taught to stand up for what's right. You are taught to conform to what is. And the kids who get in trouble are the ones who stand up for what they believe in. My daughter almost got put out of school in fourth grade because she thought that the girls ought to have a right to play touch football too. And she started organizing the girls. [*Laughter*] So they finally said, "If you bring your own football, then the girls can play football." So I bought her a football, see, and they started playing football. Then she was beginning to be an organizer. So then she said, "The teachers take a coffee break and they go out of the class two or three times a day to smoke. Why can't we chew gum?" So she organized petitions for the students to get their parents' permission to be able to chew gum in class, but with a code of conduct about how you chew gum: you can't pop it, you can't take it out of your mouth, you can't blow bubbles, but if you chew gum quietly, you ought to be able to chew gum in class. The principal and teachers said, "No," and discouraged that effort and branded her as a troublemaker.

So the danger in public schools—and maybe the only danger from the administrative side—is that too often they breed conformity. Now from the other side, when they are integrated along class and race lines, they also create the social mix that actually does stir up the pot. So I'm a believer in public schools, and I think as bad as they are, and as much as they try to breed conformity, they actually produce more leaders than private schools do. I mean, you don't find many courageous leaders coming out of private schools.

E.W.:   Do you think that public school teachers ought to be actively involved in dialoguing with students about issues and about strategies for positive change and about leadership?

A.Y.:   I think there is no education without values. And there is no education without motivation. And what you're talking about is motivation and values. Now, we have traditionally grouped that under religion and prayer, and we've tried to make learning objective and pristine and secular. Most school people are uncomfortable with concepts like commitment or values. Our training in the civil rights movement was very practical. We said, "If somebody asked you to give your hand—said that they were going to chop off your hand for what you believed in—you'd say, 'No!' But if somebody said, 'Would you give your life for what you believe in?" you are much more likely to say 'Yes.' " So we never asked people for a partial commitment. We said, "If this is something you believe in, you've got to be willing to die for it. And you shouldn't take it lightly." Dr. King always said, "If a man hasn't found something that he's willing to die for, he's not fit to live." And just in terms of standing up for the truth, I think we don't reward people for being truthful in our society. You are almost punished for being truthful. And so those concepts—truth, commitment, value, meaning in life—that's got to be a part of education.

Now the anxieties at the high school level about life and death and meaning and value are very, very great. And how can we find an educational system that addresses those? Public schools say, "That's for the church," but the church is not doing it. Or they say, "That's for the family," and the family's not doing it. I think it's for us all.

[There is no question in my mind about the fact that young people can get committed, can learn from that commitment, and can make a difference.] The leaders in the civil rights period were not the mayor, not the President. It was four college freshmen that started the sit-in movement. It was actually high school kids who got upset because their parents couldn't register to vote that got the Voting Rights Act. It was high school kids that closed down the entire economy in Birmingham because it was segregated. Now, we helped them, but we never could have gotten adults to do what they did. In all of my lifetime, social change has come from the young, often while they were still in school.

[And they'll set aside material concerns, in the right environment, in favor of greater goals.] I think one thing that young people are hungry for, and one thing that's more important to them than material things, is that they have an association with somebody that *believes* in something positive. I mean, because we believe in something, our children grow up wanting to believe in something too. In fact, the thing that worries me sometimes is that they get in over their heads. I mean, I worry about them going too far. And then you have to kind of trust them and trust God to see them through.

But it doesn't worry me [when young people are materialistic] because I think that there is a maturation process which carries them through the materialistic phase. I would not try to stop them. I would try to get them to go through it as rapidly as possible. One of the ways I think it happened to me was my family always had enough of everything, but my mother was very proud that she didn't have a fur coat, for instance, because it was more important for her to save money for my education. And I saw her friends who had fur coats and who had big cars and who tried to outdo each other in building their homes, and I could see that they were concerned about the big cars and the big homes, but they didn't spend as much time with their children as my parents spent with me. So I guess I saw in my own life that there were some material things that you could get along without—particularly material things in excess—but that you couldn't get along without the personal, spiritual things.

In families that are totally materialistic, introducing a concept of values and sacrifice [to the children is harder because] there is no frame of reference for understanding. I'm a firm believer, though, that a meaningful life is a life lived for others, and I got that from my grandparents. It's very much a part of the black community. I am my brother's keeper. In the Scripture it says,

"Inasmuch as you have done it unto one of the least of these, you have done it unto Me."

E.W.:   A lot of times when I talk to people about trying to make a difference, especially in a city, they say, "Yeah, but the problems are so huge. It's just too big for any of us." What do you say to those people?

A.Y.:   I quote a hymn, which was Ghandi's favorite hymn, "Lead Kindly Light":

> *Lead Kindly Light amid the encircling gloom;*
> *Lead Thou me on.*
> *The path is dark and I am far from home;*
> *Lead Thou me on.*
> *Guide Thou my feet. I do not ask to see the distant scene.*
> *One step is enough for me.*

And so, you have to ask yourself, and you have to insist, not that you solve the problem, but [that you determine] what is the step in the right direction that you should take at this moment. And when you get to preaching on that, in the black community, there is a whole folklore that comes into play. The Lord says, "You take one step, I'll take two." I mean, when Rosa Parks sat down in the bus, she did not know it was going to eventually be desegregated. When Martin Luther King came to that first [bus boycott] meeting, the leaders had no idea that they were dealing with desegregation. They called the bus boycott to try to get courteous treatment, and they never raised the question of desegregation in the beginning. And yet one step led to another. And so [an answer to] solving the problems is not an answer you know in advance. It's a process you enter into. And the strength, I think, of Highlander, and Myles Horton particularly, was that he never offered any answers but he believed in the process of people getting together; and he believed that if people would get together and think things through together, they would come up with their own answers to their own questions. People accused him of planting all these subversive ideas, but I never heard Myles make a speech about anything. He very seldom even participated in the discussions except to ask questions to keep things moving. But when you get people together to face a situation which is unjust or compromising or confusing, they find ways to get out of it; and that's what produces leaders.

My training in the civil rights movement [has led me to a point where] I just don't believe that there is such a thing as a problem that can't be solved.

"You take one step, I'll take two."

"Make Students Feel What We Went Through"

Dorothy Cotton

Motivated by one aimless black youth who lived next door to her in the early eighties, Dorothy Cotton applies "Where Are We Going? Where Have We Been?" to that young man's point of view. In so doing, she echoes Andrew Young's concern that values are not being taught in public schools. She concurs with E. D. Nixon's belief that young people can be inspired by face-to-face encounters with survivors of this era's civil rights struggles. But she also demonstrates a powerful tool: how students can be made to feel *history in their midst.*

Partly because of what I've been involved in, these last fifteen to twenty years, I'm very much interested in what's happening with youngsters in school now. But also because I had a conversation with a thirteen-year-old boy who lives next door to me about two weeks ago. He dropped out of school and it took him about two weeks before he could admit to me that he had dropped out of school. I had been challenging him since his mother died to like— "Hey, John, you might be the next mayor of this town." I just felt like he needed some encouragement. But he said something that made me feel so sad: "Well, you can't be nobody if you ain't already somebody." When he said that to me I really kind of stood there. I gave him a spiel, and yet I walked on up my driveway feeling really helpless, you know, in terms of a way to help him. But I started asking myself, "What happens in the classroom?" I knew that he was bored with school for a long time. He'd drop over sometimes, and sometimes he'd come over with a suit that looked almost like a tuxedo—you know, emphasizing all these extraneous, outward kinds of things; and I just kind of felt that he was lost because of where he was putting his emphasis. And nobody in the house seemed to be motivating him. He was turned off about school. But when he said you can't look forward to being somebody if you ain't already somebody, I thought just really how sad.

And that caused me to reflect on what happened to me. I lived in what we called a shotgun house—a shack, you know—where you looked in the front door right out the back with the outhouse in back and all of that. I don't remember any books in my house or even a newspaper, and there was nobody in my family or on my block that I knew about that had gone to college; but somehow I *knew* I was going to college. As I reflect on what made that happen, I know there was a teacher that helped to motivate me and inspire me, and I really will never forget Miss Rosa Gray, who was the high school English teacher and drama coach. Maybe that's why I majored in English in college. One day I had to do something in class—some speech or performance—and she said, as I finished, "There's your ready girl." And I still remember when Miss Gray said that. It gave me something to start to live up to. Then, somehow I got to be the lead person in all of the plays in high school and I just felt really close to her. I guess I was just her protégée all the way through. She made me believe that I could go to college, and she also facilitated helping me get there. Like she talked to people at Shaw University about me working, because I never remember anybody sending me a dime to help me go to college. But I felt like a leader with her and because of her. It occurs to me now as I reflect on it that I then sort of played that role, and right on through college I got into leadership positions.

The closeness [was the key, though]. We don't have that now. I felt close to Rosa Gray. She was very special to me. Who is special to that thirteen-year-old next to me? What teacher became special to him? I think with both parents and teachers there's such a big cop-out going on. It's like we're scared of kids. Parents are scared of their own children. Teachers are afraid of them. You know how far we've gotten away from being close? Who is close to anybody?

We have gotten afraid of it. I mean it's a phenomenon in the
society to be close, and to touch, either physically or to touch in
some of those other ways that teachers can touch a child. They
need the touching physically and mentally and emotionally and
spiritually. Uplifting them, inspiring them, taking an interest in
them. I think that's a real lack, and we need to learn how to do
that again.

There's so many newfangled contraptions in this day and
time. Maybe folks felt like this during the beginning of the Industrial Revolution. It's like everything's out of control now! You
think of every area of your life and you tend to feel like somebody
else or something else controls it and has the power over it. Not
you! Your health care, your education . . . You know, that boy
who is my neighbor feels that he can't do anything. He feels helpless. He doesn't feel any sense of power, himself. He doesn't feel
like he's anybody. And he feels no ability to change his situation. I
think the schools could facilitate that happening by helping him
first learn how to observe the situation in which he finds himself,
and then to know that he does have some power. I think schools
really ought to teach that. I think that that's what's missing, that
the youngsters in school today don't feel like they can achieve.
They are competing with so much, I guess. Perhaps we didn't have
quite so much to compete with. They are being bombarded with
what brand of sneakers they should wear, or what brand of T-shirt,
you know, and all of that becomes the focus.

I've thought about getting [my neighbor] involved in a special church I know, and I've said, "Gosh, I wish he were going to
one of those kinds of churches," because they tell you, "Hey, you
can, you can, you can!" when the others are saying, "You sinner,
you sinner, you sinner!" And he doesn't need to hear, "You sinner, you sinner, you sinner." He needs to hear that power indwells
you, which is what those other churches teach. I'll keep working
on that, perhaps, because I think that maybe if he can't get it in
the schools, maybe he can get it someplace else. . . .

I'm really interested in this whole business of how we help.
I'm glad we're starting to talk about that. How do we help? What
have we learned in the last few years about how we help? I'm
willing to admit now that maybe we have not done everything

right, and we've got to be willing to look at that honestly. How do we help? I don't know that I have the answer.

I do know that lots of students don't know much about how things work. It's almost like we need to do Citizenship Schools everywhere because that kind of thing is what we learn: who the mayor is, what his duties and powers are, how he got there in the first place, and learning that you have something to say about who he or she is. You have something to say about that, and you have something to say about your livelihood, your lifestyle, public policy. I learned more about civics when I was teaching and running the Citizenship Schools than I ever did in any civics class in school. But today young people don't know anything of how all that happened.

How can they know? How should they know? Maybe we are to blame for that. As a matter of fact I feel that we are greatly to blame, because I have even seen some youngsters who think they are patterning their behavior after "the movement," and what they end up doing is stealing. I've heard kids talk about how, if you need a coat, you "liberate" the coat. I think that they think they are doing what the movement people did. And the reason I think we are at fault is because we didn't *teach* them what we did. We didn't teach them how Dr. King made a decision to take an action. We have not described those actions to them. You know, we didn't just jump out into the streets and march. I mean a lot of things happened before we marched, sometimes sitting up, not only all night, but for *days* in retreats agonizing over an issue before we went into Alabama to get into the activities that led to the Selma march, for example.

Now, I have gotten invited to speak on some college campuses. Last February, for example, was so-called Black History Month. Again, when the Kingdom comes I think we won't have to have any particular month [*laugh*] for any of that. But when I have gone to speak on campuses during Black History Month, folks want to know about my work with Martin Luther King. They want to know, and they don't know. I don't know why they want to know, except, I could guess at this point, that they themselves feel troubled and have some concerns. But I've spoken on campuses where the black students have been in the minority on the majority white campuses. They have black student unions on the campus, and I've seen a lot that's unhealthy in that because they really pull themselves apart for what I think are some unhealthy reasons. If, in the dining hall, there's a black table, and [you, as a white student won't] come sit at the "black table," what if I want to talk with you about some film or tape or book you're writing, and it's got nothin' to do with what color you are? Then I've got to decide whether I sit with you or not based on what color you are. To me that's a bunch of junk, and it perpetuates that which is unhealthy. What I'm saying is there are some problems in our relating now, and because there are some problems, maybe that's the reason that youngsters are interested in what we went through. They hear the names "Martin Luther King" or "Andrew Young" or "Jesse Jackson" and they feel some problems themselves, and therefore there is a curiosity about what we went through. They want to know. They have a lot of questions about it. . . .

I ask myself, "How can I make them feel, *feel* what we went through?" and I know that some of them *can* really get with me. I mean, I can sing an old song like, "I've been in the storm so long, I've been in the storm so long, children, I've been in the storm so long, Give me a little time to pray." And I look up, and they're crying, and so am I. I tell 'em what the storm was, that they had to pick the cotton before the sun went down or go back to slavery, and I always intersperse some of the old songs with the talking about it. And I know now I do that to help them *feel* rather than be intellectual about it—to feel what it was then, which enhances their need to know and experience what we went through. I consciously came upon that as I struggled through the years to talk to them. How can I make them *feel* when they never saw any "white only" signs or lynchings? I could sing a song like, "Southern trees bear strange fruit, Blood on the leaves and blood at the root," and because I can really feel that, they can relate to that. They *want* to know. They can relate to it because I think they have already had a confrontation with some injustices that they want to change.

Now one problem becomes to help them see what has to be done next. I don't even think they even have clear goals, and I don't think kids know how to analyze the problems and to see what issues there are. I think we haven't helped them to see what the next issues are. . . .

In a way, what we need is simple. It may be so simple that we cannot grasp it, because we are so used to complicated issues. First of all, I'd probably help young people focus on what kind of world they want to live in. I could play with that a lot. What kind of world do you want to live in? What's the ideal situation for you? . . .

For example, I think after I got a television in every room, I'd probably decide I didn't even want them on most of the time. I don't think it takes a long time to learn that. An overinvolvement with material consumption is not fulfilling, and I really think people learn that after—maybe *after* they get it. I guess I really had to have a fur coat to know that it's okay if I don't have it. But I guess I had to have it to come to that point.

But what are things? I mean, I'd like to talk to folk about getting what they want to get in terms of material things, but that first, "Seek ye first the Kingdom," if that means anything to you, because even after you get the *things*, you will find an emptiness there. . . .

Seeking first the Kingdom really is important, and that means for me knowing that life itself is a gift. That it is an invitation, and there is an RSVP. Can you respond to that invitation to life? . . . That you will find the greatest sense of fulfillment in serving in the world.

I think we are not even used to looking at what life is all about. I don't really mean to be so philosophical, but I think we don't know what life ought to be about or what the good life really is. I don't know if anybody asked John, my neighbor, "What is the good life?" I'm not sure people know. If we focused on that, then we could start to look at what causes it to happen. I really think that we are searching for something, which we wouldn't even recognize if we found it, because we haven't taken time to think about it.

[But] it really is knowing why I am here in the universe at all. I think I know. Would you believe it? I think I know. I have at this point a feeling and interpretation and understanding, if you will, of what God is; and I'm so glad that I have come to know that it is not some little man sitting up in the sky keeping a record, but that there is a spiritual force in the universe. That's what God is to me. A spiritual force in the universe, and somehow I am a manifestation of that force—as I think we all are—and we are here to fulfill the purpose of that great spirit. What we have to do is simply relax and be open to the flow of that spirit within us. Does that make sense to you? To be open to it? I think if we are, then we start to feel attuned to all growing things and to life itself. When I started really to reflect on this, I could pass a tree and somehow feel akin because I had started to feel that, hey, all life is one. Life is a force that flows and connects all of us. . . .

Number one, [this knowledge] *is* pleasurable, because one does start to feel peaceful and that's a pleasurable feeling. Also one does impact other lives because people feel that kinship and that at-one-ment, if you will. They simply feel it. You start to relate to people in a different way, and in that way you impact other people's lives in a very positive kind of way. I could go back to the Scriptures at this point, and talk about the "peace that passes understanding." It's not even something that one knows intellectually, I don't think, but you just know that one can be peaceful about life, and then you start to fulfill whatever the divine plan is *for* your life. And you make all kinds of things happen. And if everybody knows this, then the whole world is better. I don't have to create war. I can get into my art or singing or writing or teaching or fulfilling some other grand and noble purpose. When you are in the flow of the power and the force that runs the universe, beautiful things happen.

It just doesn't seem right to me that we spend our whole lives struggling. Somewhere we need to get it right: the way we structure societies, the way we interact with each other. We need to get it right. Some of my best friends say, "Life is a struggle," and I've always wanted to argue with them because I don't think it *should* be a struggle, but maybe *I've* been wrong. Maybe it *is* a struggle. Maybe we always have to "watchdog," for want of a better word. Watch what's happening. Monitor what's happening. Because we do know that mankind is capable of all manner of evil; and yet even as I say that, I think if we taught some things right that we could greatly lessen that evil that sometimes comes out. If we taught people right in the schools and could help students like John know he *is* somebody, and to really *know* that . . . But, see? Nobody told John he could be more, doggone it. And so he dropped out of school. If we taught and pushed and showed that man is capable of fantastic good, if we really *showed* that, then that other side of man might not manifest itself—not half as much. Maybe not at all . . .

People can be turned around. That's one of the fantastic lessons I've learned in my life. We can all learn. It's fantastic to really ponder the fact that we can *grow*. No matter what I do I think I will always look back on those years with the Southern Christian Leadership Conference as the richest, most dramatic, and most dynamic and powerful years of my life. You know, it's like when I pass off the scene, you know it's okay, don't cry, just say, "She had a groovy life and was involved in something meaningful and real." But even as I say that, I'm looking forward also to continuing to unfold into the divine plan for my life. I do think there is something else for me to do. . . .

And John can be more. Every youngster in high school and elementary school, and every adult, can be more. *We all* can be more. If we were pulled into our quiet place like [a] caterpillar into [a] cocoon, we could start to grow wings. I just think that's so apropos. But we've got to learn each stage of that lesson, because if we broke open that cocoon and said, "We're gonna let that creature out of there," before it was ready, then we'd destroy it. That doesn't mean that we can't have some help along the way. Hopefully, that's what Highlander's about, and the King Center and some other places. It would be wonderful if the school system were about that: helping people understand that you can be more; that when you're ready, and your wings are strong, you can fly out and soar to great heights. That really says something to me. We can all be more.

★

Teach How Change Comes About
Septima Clark

In one of the strangest turnabouts to occur after the turbulent sixties, Septima Clark—once fired as a public school teacher in Charleston, South Carolina—ultimately became a member of that city's school board. As the discriminated-against employee turned employer, she acquired the power once denied every black person in the South.

But in this new position, was she able to assure that the school system's classrooms also taught students about people like Dr. Martin Luther King, Jr., Rosa Parks, or herself? Or were policy decisions in a public system like Charleston's more difficult to alter than when she worked within the private organizations of Highlander and the Southern Christian Leadership Conference on behalf of the Citizenship Schools?

We still have a long way to go, and I really feel determined that we've got to do a better job. We do some things, though. On January 15, we celebrate Dr. King's birthday, and I went around to school every day last January for one whole week talking about King. Then in February, it was Afro-American Month, and I went to a number of schools talking about the various blacks like Sojourner Truth. In one of the schools, they even sort of talked about me at that time. They know who I am. But we need to do more of that. And I'm not only asking them to do just that. Whenever they speak about a black in America, I think they need to find a white who does somewhat similar. The problem is it's usually all white, even now. Just recently a booklet about American government was passed around in a school board meeting so we could see if we wanted to use it in the schools, and you know there wasn't one black in that book? Not one black. I wanted to know who the black children would have to look up to in that book. I felt it was wrong to place that book in the hands of teachers. There was nothing in there that would help black children to feel that they had a right to the tree of life. And I know how important that is. I didn't feel as if I could ever do anything worthwhile when I was living in North Carolina until Mary McLeod Bethune came down and spoke. And there she was, a real black woman sitting in Roosevelt's ["kitchen"] cabinet, and she said, "I'm just a fly in that bowl of milk, but I'm certainly there." And that gave me a great feeling, that a black woman could be sitting in Roosevelt's cabinet. And I think this is what it would do for our children too. They need to know about such people.

They also need to know how change comes about. You have to develop them to do their own thinking and not accept unjust things but break through those things and change them. I once felt I had to accept things as they were. I rode on the bus and I sat in the section of the bus where black people were supposed to sit and I would get up and give my seat to any white man because I knew it was the law, and I did it without feeling angry. Not until I got to Highlander [*laughter*] did I learn that I should defy laws like that that are unjust.

[But today, teachers say, "If I start talking to my kids about things they ought to change, I'm going to get fired."] And we got that case right now. There is a young woman who has been talking to her children about standing up for their rights, and her name is on the list to be terminated. I don't want to miss that meeting Monday, because I'm going to vote on her to stay in that school. And the only reason they want to fire her is because she will speak out. And she has been an excellent teacher. They're going to try to fire her, but I'm going to fight them.

[I tell teachers and students,] "Stand up for your rights, regardless." You have to stand up and take the consequences. It's not going to be easy. It's not going to be pleasant. After I was fired, I went to Highlander, and for three long months I couldn't sleep. Then at the end of that time, it seemed to me as if my mind cleared up and I decided then that I must have been right. I really didn't find out for sure that I *was* right until Governor Edwards, in 1976, said, "You were unjustly fired," and sent me a check for the pension I was owed. And that made me realize that I was right all the time. But I had to wait until I was eighty years of age to find out. I went all those years knowing that the people thought I was wrong—even my own people. My brother said to me, "Why did you tell them that you were a member of the NAACP?"

I said, "I couldn't live with myself otherwise." So you have to be strong. You have to tell the truth and take the consequences. And it's not going to be easy. It's not going to be pleasant.

[Say you were one of those teachers, for example, and you said to me, "Septima, I can't talk to my white kids in class about the KKK because these kids love their parents and the parents are members of the KKK. Now I know the organization is wrong, but I'm afraid I'll hurt those kids."] I would have to tell you that regardless of what happens, you are going to have to let those kids know the very truth about the KKK, because when you see the kinds of things that they have done, you will know that those things are not right. They might burn your house down. I couldn't tell you that they won't. I have had a lot of things to happen to me and I had to live through it. I've had policemen sent to my door looking for the fight. Just harassment. I've had firemen sent to my door looking for the fire. Pure harassment. I've had people call and curse me over the telephone, and I would just say, "Thank you, call again." I'd put the phone down and here would come another call. There were nights when I couldn't sleep for that kind of thing. People were even afraid of me. Thought I was a Communist.

But now that's changed. I have honorary degrees. The housing authority has named a day care center for me. A highway has been named for me. I've been on television. Not long ago I was interviewed five times in one day. I've even had visitors from Spain. So you live through the bad times. You have to have faith.

[Today] you don't have those unjust laws that we had to work on, but when [young people] look long enough, they'll see that it's more subtle things that they have to work on. I say to them, "You have to look at your administrative groups and see if any of you are sitting there helping to make the laws. What about your legislature? What about your city council? What about your county delegation? Do you see any blacks sitting there? What about your school board? Do you see any blacks? I'm the only black on our school board, and when I get off next year I wonder if there will be another one who will come on. What about stores and banks? You can find black clerks and cashiers, but what about the administrative groups? Can you find any there? What about the pollution off our coast? Do you know this is where you get your food to eat, and now this source is going to be denied you if you don't grow up and vote against things like that? And what about the inadequate health screening for our first graders? What about aides for the handicapped children? We need to have special money for handicapped kids and it's coming out in the papers every day. People are voting against those things. We need to have physical education, art, and music in first grade, and Reagan wants to cut these out. Now we've got to stand up in arms against those cuts. Don't sit down and accept them. Instead of accepting them, stand up and vote against them.

And if they get discouraged, I tell them that there were times when I felt discouraged, too, but I felt I had to go on. I could not do anything by quitting. A quitter receives nothing.

But they are going to do more. Right now I have a feeling that now that we have been able to open doors for them, they should go through those doors and get all the education that they can and then come up and be the administrators. I know I'm not going to live to see a black President, but I do hope in times to come there will be one.

[So political action and education are still the keys to a better future.] I really felt that the great turning point for us was the Voting Rights bill in August of '65. That had a great effect on the American people. That opened the doors for us for both political action and education. They both go together. I'll always remember when one of the fellows we were teaching in Anamanee, Alabama, went up to the bank in Camden to cash a check, and the white man took out his pen and said, "I'll make the *X*."

He said, "You don't have to make the *X* for me because I can write my own name."

The white guy says, "My God, them niggers done learned to write."

★

Refuse to Be Silenced: Sing the Unimagined
Pete Seeger

In some ways, the free-spirited folk singer offers the most pessimistic of responses to the question "Where Are We Going?" After having dedicated his life to music that provoked social change, he questions the meaning of societal reform in the face of potential doom for the planet itself.

But in the vein of his 1961 folk song, "Where Have All the Flowers Gone?" which became a rally anthem for Vietnam War protestors, there is a beauty in Seeger's grim perspective, a hope that persistently blooms forth. He sprinkles wisdom from such diverse men as T. S. Eliot and Will Rogers to shore up his forecast that contemporary societies will redirect *energies and resources.*

I'm not as optimistic as some people think I am. I think there is only a slim chance for the human race to survive. I'm unwilling to say there's no hope. Some people do say that. They'll say, "Look at the statistics." Just as we can say the sun has five billion years to go, we can say that at the rate the present trends are going, the human race has a hundred or two hundred years to go, maybe less. If it isn't the nukes that get us, it will be the toxic chemicals or the population explosion—something. And I have to confess the figures are on their side. Look at all the poisons we've generated. A lot more than they realize. PCB is just the tip of the iceberg. Cadmium, mercury, lead, DDT, 2-4-D: a lot of fancy words which I don't know and only a chemist could untangle, but some attack the bone, some attack the liver, some attack the brain. Few of them kill you right away. Only after years and years. When you finally die, you don't know whether it's due to what got in the water or what got in the air, or something you ate in the local potato chips.

It's the dominant religion of every modern country that the unlimited accumulation of fact and knowledge—even in a computer bank—is a good thing. My father would say, "It's an act of faith. It's a belief held with no proof, and so you can say it's a religious belief." But my father, who died at age ninety-two, also felt that most scientists haven't faced up to the fact that the unlimited accumulation of knowledge is not necessarily a good thing. Perhaps Galileo was wrong. You never can tell. The human race is now trembling on the brink of annihilation because we know so much. You get the wrong information in the hands of an insane person and the whole world may be blown up. Or someone may make a mistake. Could happen tomorrow. You know, you read about the near accidents when the computer said that we were being attacked and found it was a mistake.

On the other hand, I rather suspect that if we do fail to make it, T. S. Eliot may be right. Remember when he wrote: "This is the way the world will end. / This is the way the world will end. / This is the way the world will end. / Not with a bang but a whimper." [*Chanted*] You know when we're all choking [*Seeger coughs*] and we ask, "Why is there no air left?" "Well, it's what they did fifty years ago. They had a chance to stop it then, but now it's too late. Now you have to wear gas masks to live."

I'm a banjo picker, and I've seen an audience of thousands turn their heads 180 degrees in two hours from being a group of dispirited individuals to ones feeling that life was worth living. And if an audience can do this right before my eyes, why can't the whole world do it? This whole world could straighten up and fly right and quit wasting money on bombs and poisons and spend it on education and jobs and health and skills and understanding of all sorts.

What's it going to take? That's the question. We know we need some big changes, but how are we going to get them? I think what constitutes a revolution is going to be worth discussing in the years ahead. Now there's no need to come with blood and violence. I think it was Kennedy who said, "The people who make bloody revolutions inevitable are those who make peaceful change impossible." Beautiful phrase. John Kennedy had a fine grasp of English. . . . And this is what Somoza made impossible in Nicaragua so that Ernesto Cardenal, a really wonderful Catholic priest and poet and writer, came to the conclusion that the Catholic Church must support the young Sandanistas with their rifles.

I think it's also going to take the courage of people who refuse to stand silently by and watch. Scientists are like priests in the Soviet Union. I went out to Lake Baikal to see how they were saving it. It was a scientist and a poet who saved it, really. The poet started off by writing a poem, "Sacred Baikal, you will never be the same again." They had put a pulp plant on it. It's an extraordinary lake, four hundred miles long, fifty miles wide, and one mile deep. It's so deep it has more water in it than all our Great Lakes combined. The water is so clear you can see a hundred feet down. No fooling. And so a pulp mill was put in. Well, the scientist then stood up and said, "This poet is right and unless strong measures are taken, this lake will be ruined for millions of years." The commissars came out from Moscow and said, "Now, Doctor Galasy, don't hold up progress." But he stuck to his guns and in Irkutsk, a young radio reporter who interviewed me said, "Dr. Galasy is our hero. He refused to be silenced." Now, he was a loyal Communist, but he knew that within the communist system you had to keep arguing or else the wrong forces would win out.

It's also going to take a tremendous change in the way we educate our populations. You know Einstein used to say that the important thing in any problem is to learn the right questions to ask. Once you've found the right question to ask, then you're on your way home and pointed in the right direction. Trying to find the right question to ask, though, is darn difficult. Right from the beginning I think every teacher should realize that the most valuable quality to inculcate in any human being is the willingness to spend the thought and time to figure out the right question to ask. When kids are very young we take the easy way. We say, "Do this," and it annoys us when they say, "Why, why, why?" all the time. Yet that quality is vital. During the sixties I was delighted to see classes asking questions. I'd often go to speak or sing at classes of junior high or high school students, and I noticed young people really starting to ask questions in the sixties. By gosh, in the seventies they had all clammed up again. The main thing they had learned out of school was, "Stay out of trouble and keep your mouth shut!" They weren't going to open up to me. I say, "What do you think of this?" Dead silence. I was, and am still, terribly distressed when I face a crowd of young people and I say some outrageous statement and they won't question it at all. They've learned that you don't stick your neck out unless you have to. Even with one's close friends, you pick the time and place to argue. You don't argue at the wrong time and place. And you often preface your contradictory ideas with something that lets them know that you're a friend.

The tyranny of the majority is really what people were scared of when they founded America. The majority lays down a rule: "We've decided this, there's no more discussion." "Abortion is murder, so there is no more discussion of this." Or it could be just the opposite. And yet the ability to discuss some of these things is really what civilization is all about. Public schools should be debating the major questions of the day instead of leaving them for history, but usually it isn't until you get into college that you really get into this. And even in colleges, it's often only an extracurricular activity.

Courage. Education. Did you ever hear of Ammon Hennacy? He was a great old anarchist who had a fine mind. He said, "Courage alone is foolhardiness as in the average soldier. Wisdom alone is cowardice as in the average intellectual. Love alone is sentimentality as in the average churchgoer." He says, "You need all three —love, wisdom, and courage."

I'd be wrong to say there aren't some hopeful signs, though. Here's one example. A century and a half ago, small towns of America were ferments of ideas. The women's suffrage movement didn't start in Boston or New York; it started in small towns. A hundred and fifty years ago, Concord, Massachusetts, and probably Fishkill, New York, here, were full of people willing to debate slavery, and willing to debate temperance, and women's suffrage. . . . But the opening of the American West and the jobs in the city with better pay drained off the brighter, ambitious people, and this ended the intellectual freedom, and small towns just got more and more conformist.

Now, in the post–World War II era, I see this turning back. I see the television age changing the whole thing. If you see something on television, you can talk about it with your neighbor over the bar: "Hey, did you see what that person said last night, wow! They're gonna be on again tomorrow, you better catch it." And so all sorts of things are breaking through the crust.

I used to joke: "They once said the pen is mightier than the sword," and I said, "Maybe the guitar will be mightier than the bomb." But I have a feeling that maybe the camera might be the tool which will save the human race, because it leaps the language barrier—leaps right over it. And we're just at the beginning of learning the different ways a camera can be used.

There's different ways that pictures can be used that haven't even been tried yet. Different kinds of paper and print; different kinds of screens; different kinds of exhibits. Most people don't have any idea of the different ways you can exhibit pictures on a wall. "The Family of Man" exhibit was put on in a series of rooms in the Museum of Modern Art in New York, and some of the pictures were on the ceiling because the camera was looking up a tree at a man standing there chopping it down. The camera was looking up, and so you have to look up.

And in one place, you turn a corner and it gets darker and darker and you find yourself in a dark alley. You're not expecting it. All you think is, "What's going on here? It's getting darker!" Then it's pitch-black, and you turn the corner, and you suddenly see this big transparency of the hydrogen bomb just staring you in the face. Close! About three feet away from you. The picture is about five feet high and you're only three feet away, and you suddenly turn the corner and there it is. You're *right in it*! And then you walk out and you see that beautiful picture by Gene Smith of the two little children walking under the bush through the shadows out into the sunlight. You've seen the book *The Family of Man*? Well, the book's good, but it's *nothing* compared to the way it was set up in that museum. That was a triumph! I suppose [Edward] Steichen did it. He was a genius. From the moment you walk in until an hour later when you walk out, it's as exciting as a good thriller. It has humor in it; it has horror; it has all sorts of things familiar and strange and exotic.

Gene Smith, who took that last picture, is dead now. He did

the book *Minamata,* the story of the town in Japan whose people were poisoned by mercury from a chemical plant. One of his great pictures shows a Japanese woman in a big tub, and in her arms is her teenage daughter, all crippled [*at this point Pete chokes with emotion and there is a long pause*] but this mother is bathing her daughter and she will have to all her life and she knows, "When I die, who will take care of my daughter?" But the mother ate the mercury-poisoned fish while she was pregnant. The company knew that it was mercury. The doctor of the company had it on his conscience when he died that he, to keep his job, stayed silent about it. He knew that it was mercury that was killing people.

Smith followed these people, and for three years he lived with them and he ate the mercury fish too. He knew he and his wife just had to be with them completely to tell the story.

At one point there was a batch of local fishermen camped out on the sidewalk in Tokyo in front of the headquarters of the chemical company that was responsible, and they said, "We will not leave here till we can speak with the president of the company." The company sent down all sorts of representatives. "No, we will speak to the president and no one but!" They were camped out on the sidewalk in tents, I think. Finally the president of the company says, "We've got to get rid of these people. They're getting so much publicity that the whole of Japan is hearing that we refused to speak to them. I'll talk to them."

There's the president surrounded by his lawyers on all sides watching him like a hawk. They don't want him to say anything that will get him in dutch. And the president says, "I realize now that the evidence is in, that it *was* the mercury from our plant which caused this; but you are asking for so much money in compensation, it will put this company out of business. The company can't exist if we pay out all the money you are asking for."

At which point, one of the fishermen cried, "I can't go on any longer, I can't live. You see, my hands are shaking. I can't live any longer!" And he smashes a glass ashtray on the side of a table and cuts his wrists. Blood, all over the place.

The president says, "All right, we'll pay, we'll pay!" At which point the lawyers just pounce on him to shut him up, but the words are out.

And the company did pay, millions and millions. They finally had to get the government to help them pay in order to stay in business, because they had poisoned thousands of people irreparably. This is all in Gene Smith's book *Minamata*. It's a great book.

The only trouble with it, though, is it's so grim. This is my only criticism of the Bible. It's so grim. I'm convinced that we're going to learn the truth more through a laugh, a shout of discovery, than a sigh.

Woody Guthrie's hero was Will Rogers. He named one of his boys Will Rogers Guthrie. Will once said, "The voters of Oklahoma will vote dry as long as they can stagger to the polls!" [*Laughter*]

Once he was giving a speech to a big corporation and he says, "I've heard a lot about the service you do. Your company gives service to the American people, and I was wondering what do you mean by this? Then I remembered that when I was a boy on the farm I heard that our cow was going to be serviced by the neighbor's bull, and I went down to watch, and now I know what you do." [*Laughter*]

And I'd say, what gives one strength in these times is a combination of having family and friends that support you . . . , and also a knowledge of history. As Lee Hays said at the Weavers' reunion, "Just a few notes on the recent unpleasantness at the polls to remind you all that 'this too shall pass.' I've had gallstones and I know."

There are hopeful signs. In fact, this is the greatest thing about America. I meet people in the television industry, and I say, "Why is it that television has been ignoring what to my mind is the great story of the decade?"

"What's the great story of the decade? Isn't this decade full of apathy?"

"Nope," I say. "There may have been a decline in some ways, but there has been a buildup in other ways."

"What's the buildup?"

I say, "I don't think in any previous period of American history have there been so many community efforts going on as now." In every state of the union that I visit, in every city, village, suburb, there's more organizations than people can attend. Meetings, meetings, all sorts of things. Posters on the local walls, fundraisings, and everybody scratching their heads: "What is it that hasn't ever been tried before?" We're having so many interesting things going on. In fact, I say this all so many times that my wife can repeat it verbatim. But I'm convinced that if there is a human race five hundred years from now, they'll look back to the twentieth century and they'll have a name for the crises that we faced, just as we look back and say there was a thing called the "Renaissance," or there was a thing called the "Colonial Era." I don't know what name they'll give us. It may be a Chinese name, or an African name, or a Spanish or French or Russian or German name. Who knows? Somewhere, somebody's gonna get a name for what's going on now. Just like the Renaissance started off with the two letters, *r-e,* I have a feeling it may be an *re* word. Something like "rediscovery," perhaps. A rediscovery of ourselves and our communities. Or a "redirection." That may be the name for it. Not rediscovery, but redirection. All sorts of people who had been headed in this direction said, "Wait, this is not exactly right. That may be the right direction."

Woody and Myles know the great art of storytelling is to pull the right story out at the right time so that it's not just a story, it's a lesson. People in politics are always accused of changing their tactics and strategies: "You're not *consistent.*" The same man who went shaking hands in Cleveland told a story which Woody loved, and Woody told it everywhere: A man died, and his wife gave him a good funeral. A year or two later she died and she found herself up before St. Peter. "I want to find my husband." "Well, ma'am, what was his name? I'll look him up." "John Smith." "Well, ma'am, we've got lots of John Smiths. Middle name?" "No middle name." "Well, any particular work? We got a butcher John Smith; we got a printer John Smith; we got a painter John Smith; we got a bricklayer John Smith. What?" "No, no, no, my husband was really very average. He wasn't anything in particular." "Well, you must have *some way* you can identify him." "Well," she said, "when he died he says, 'Mary, if you ever look at another man, I'll roll over in my grave.'" "Oh, you mean *whirling* John Smith!" [*Very loud and dramatic*] [*Laughter*]

Well, this, to my mind, is a beautiful way of explaining that when the world situation changes, you change your tactics. When I'm down sailing on the river and the wind changes, I change tack and go in a different direction. I can even sail back and forth

across the prevailing winds and move forward against them. Someone looking from here says, "Why, that person's zigzagging all the
time. Can't he make up his mind?!"

But this is the art of redirection when the situation demands
it. If I'm sailing at one angle, the wind can cause me a lot of
trouble, whereas if I'm at another angle, I'm just set to *use* it.

During the age of exploration, Columbus and the others were
discovering other continents. But now we've almost reached a
dead end there. It is as though the ultimate in reaching out into
space made us realize more the need for reaching in. There's that
picture of that little jewel there. People have written poems about
it and songs about it and made speeches about it. This little oasis
in space, this little blue planet, the water planet, so beautiful—and
there's nothing like it so far as they can find for billions or trillions
of miles.

It's all we've got. So I refuse to say there's no hope, but I do
believe it's a real slim chance, in which case, by God, you give all
the energy you have. I say, if you've got any energy, use it, wherever you are, wherever you think you can be effective. City or
country, family or community, do whatever you can do.

Everything has an effect.

Afterword

Carrying It On
John Gaventa, Director, Highlander Research and Education Center

Highlander can't be described as an organization because it isn't departmentalized and mechanistically conceived. It's a mosaic or a piece of weaving. Back in 1932, if you used colors, it would be a certain type of color that dominated. Later on, another color came in and merged with that, and as Highlander changes, the series of colors changes, but there's always some of the old and some of the new. Now two colors may be blended, and always hopefully something new is introduced, so the weaving is still being made. Highlander is a weaving of *many* colors, some blend and some clash, but at least you know it's alive.

Myles Horton in *We Make the Road by Walking: Conversations on Education and Social Change with Paulo Freire* (1990)

For sixty years now the Highlander Center has carried out its unique mission of education for social change from its rural center in the mountains of eastern Tennessee. Throughout its history, Highlander has held to a central principle: For social change to be effective, solutions must come from the people who experience a problem and who will be directly affected by an action taken. Grassroots leadership must be developed through an educational process that allows people to analyze their problems, test their ideas, learn from the experience of others, and strengthen their organizations.

The stories found in this book give strong testimony to the enduring power of that philosophy. The people whose voices are found in this book have all been associated in one way or another with the Highlander Center's work. But as their stories weave in and out of their association with Highlander, they also weave a much larger story, one of how ordinary people have come to shape social change in twentieth-century America, especially in the labor and civil rights movements.

The stories in this book were gathered as part of a larger project—conceived by Eliot Wigginton, then a Highlander board member, and by Sue Thrasher, a Highlander staff member—to record the oral histories of citizens who had made a difference in the South. For space and editorial reasons, only a few of the oral histories which were collected could be published here. Many others are on record at Highlander Center's library and archives in New Market, Tennessee.

Every year in our workshops at Highlander we are also privileged to hear the stories of hundreds of other grassroots citizens, who come to share and learn with others about how to act on key problems that affect their communities. The participants today are often less known than some of those whose stories are found in this book. But they are part of the rich tradition of social change these voices represent; they are inspired by it, and they are weaving the tapestry of change into future decades of American history.

Highlander is perhaps best known for various "periods" of work: as a labor school of the late thirties and early forties, a civil rights school of the fifties and sixties, and an Appalachian school in the seventies and early eighties. Much of this work occurred during what Myles Horton, Highlander's founder, often called the "peak" periods—times in which social movements provided clear focus and attention to Highlander's work.

But these periods have been relatively brief and illusive in America's social history. Consequently, much of Highlander's sixty-year history has also been spent working in the "valleys"— times in which there was not a clear movement that unified social action. Though less known, the programs of these periods are also important. These were the times for experimentation with new issues, for developing grassroots leadership and organizations as building blocks for social change, for trying out new educational approaches. They help to provide the threads of continuity and strength as well as the new colors in the weaving.

The 1980s were such a period. Highlander broadened its programs from the focus on Appalachia to again include other cultural and geographic parts of the South. New programs were developed in the areas of toxics, economic education, youth leadership, and participatory research. Residential workshops and cultural programs continued on new topics and themes.

In the beginning of the nineties, we have already seen the emergence of new fervor within the region and around the world. Before he died in 1990, as he heard the news of the Pittston miners strike, the changes in eastern Europe and South Africa, and the growing grassroots toxics movement, Myles had the hunch that we were maybe climbing towards another peak period in our history. As Larry Wilson, our environmental coordinator, describes the new energy, "We don't yet see a single movement, but we see a lot of people moving."

The "moving" is felt at Highlander today. 1990 was the busiest year at the Center in the fifteen years since I've been around; over sixty workshops and gatherings were led by our staff and by other groups, involving some two thousand people from forty states and a dozen countries.

Perhaps the greatest movement is witnessed in the growth of the grassroots environmental justice movement. In the last few years we've held dozens of environmental or STP (Stop the Poisoning) schools, in which hundreds of people directly affected by the poisoning chain have been brought together to learn from one another about their local struggles and build a more broad-based and racially diverse movement. In this effort we've deliberately recalled the role Highlander's Citizenship Schools played in the fifties, helping to build the consciousness and local leadership that later became building blocks of the civil rights movement.

"Moving" is also seen among workers and low-income communities who are feeling the pinch of global economic restructuring that brings them closed plants, new but worse jobs, abandoned communities, and attacks on workers' rights. This economic crisis is high on our agenda; we hold economy schools at Highlander and in communities around the region, run an Environmental-Economic Program that helps poor communities overcome environmental "jobmail," and help to support organizing work on plant closings in the region.

Perhaps no segment of society is hit harder by environmental degradation and economic restructuring than the young, especially those from African-American and poor rural communities. Begun in the 1980s, today our youth program actively works with young people from across communities in Appalachia and the South through "youth citizenship schools," a summer institute, and community internships. This last year we also held a series of workshops intended to pull together grassroots communities organizing around the educational systems that disempower young people.

Grassroots leadership development has always been a part of Highlander's work. This thread of the weaving is a vivid part of Highlander today, through the Southern and Appalachian Leadership Training program, now some fifteen years old. While the program was started for Appalachia, it now works with African-American, Native American, and poor white rural communities across the South, adding a great deal to our multicultural work.

While the program and issue areas remain broad at Highlander, we are also convinced that we must try both to weave together the various aspects of our own work within Appalachia and the South, and to strengthen the links between our regional work and similar efforts in other parts of the nation and the world. We are now working with other groups to spread the STP workshops to other states, and are building community exchanges between Appalachia and the South and other poor regions of the country.

Myles Horton spent much of his last years helping Highlander develop working partnerships with similar popular education centers in other parts of the world. We've used these networks to help develop educational exchanges between communities affected by Union Carbide toxic chemicals in West Virginia and Bhopal; between women textile workers in Tennessee and in the maquiladora zone in Mexico; between popular educators in Appalachia and Nicaragua; and between human rights activists in the South and Latin America.

At this point in history, we don't believe that we can choose just a single issue or constituency or place to work. We see the need to link the issues, groups, and places, to find and build common ground among them, and to help extend a multi-issue, multicultural, multiregional tapestry of social change through the nineties and beyond. We hope that in the process we are strengthening the voices of people like those whose stories have been told in this book, and that they in turn will continue to write the history of grassroots social activism for twenty-first-century America.

Biographical Profiles

Septima Clark, at the time of her death in 1987, was recognized as a pioneer teacher in the Citizenship School program, which had a large impact on the civil rights movement of the early 1960s. She came to work at Highlander when she was fired from her job as a teacher in South Carolina in 1955. At the time it was not possible in South Carolina to belong to the NAACP and teach in the public schools. Later she would work with Dr. Martin Luther King, Jr. at the Southern Christian Leadership Conference and travel with him to Oslo to receive the Nobel Peace Prize.

E. D. Nixon was instrumental in the campaign that became the Montgomery bus boycott in the early 1950s. Long active in his native Alabama, he served as president of both the Brotherhood of Sleeping Car Porters and the Montgomery chapter of the NAACP. He recruited Mrs. Rosa Parks into the organization, and helped shape the strategy under which she became the test case against segregation on the public buses. His wisdom about church politics in Montgomery also led him to involve the newly arrived Dr. Martin Luther King, Jr. in a leadership role in the bus boycott. He died in 1987.

May Justus served for many years as the Highlander librarian in Monteagle. A schoolteacher who had come to the Cumberland Plateau from her home in the Smokey Mountains, she was the author of many children's books—approximately one per year over a fifty year history. May showed great courage in standing up for Highlander when it came under attack and was closed by the state in 1961. Her status in the local community suffered and she was even expelled from her church, but she steadfastly maintained her support of the school and kept in contact with its staff even after it moved across the state. She died in 1989.

Ralph Tefferteller was one of the early cultural staff members at Highlander. He grew up in eastern Tennessee and was a caller of regional dances. He was on the Highlander staff from 1934 through 1938, working with bugwood cutters and farmers, miners, and union activists. He returned to Highlander in the mid-1970s for a tour of mountain communities, teaching dances and playing party games, and maintained an interest in the school until his death in 1988.

Don West was a cofounder with Myles Horton of the Highlander Folk School in 1932. Growing up in northern Georgia, he became a poet, a preacher, an educator, a union organizer, and finally the director for many years of the Appalachian Folklife Center in Pipestem, West Virginia. During the 1940s, his books of poetry were distributed and read widely in the South. He currently lives in West Virginia.

Zilla Hawes Daniel was another early staff member at Highlander. She came to the school fresh from Vassar College, inspired by what she knew of the European folk schools. She quickly took to union education, and organized the first Amalgamated Clothing Workers' local in the South. She left the Highlander staff in 1937, returning for the 50th anniversary celebration in 1982. She now lives in Oregon.

Lucille Thornburgh has long been a supporter and board member of Highlander. Growing up very close to Highlander's current location, she became a union activist while very young. She edited the *East Tennessee Labor News* for many years. In recent years she has been an activist for the issues of the elderly and a tireless worker in local community organizations. She lives in Knoxville, Tennessee.

Ralph Helstein was a life-long labor leader, bringing his connection with the CIO to Highlander in the early 1940s. In 1946 he became president of the United Packinghouse Workers of America and subsequently recruited Myles Horton as the educational director for the union. Helstein maintained his support for Horton and for Highlander long after the CIO withdrew its support in the years of red-baiting and fear of communism in the 1950s. He died in 1985.

Rosa Parks is best known for her central role in the Montgomery bus boycott of 1955. She was an active member of the NAACP, and had been to Highlander shortly before refusing to give up her seat on the bus. She credits Septima Clark and Myles Horton with helping her understand that there can be harmony and progress between the races in the United States. She has worked for many years in the office of Senator John Conyers in Detroit, where she currently lives.

Bernice Robinson was the first teacher in the Citizenship Education program developed by Highlander in South Carolina in the late 1950s. She had been a beautician in Charleston and a social activist in the segregated community where she grew up. The curriculum and approach to adult education that she developed, along with Septima Clark, would eventually be used widely throughout the South during the 1960s in the effort to register large numbers of African-American voters. She is still active in Charleston, South Carolina.

Pete Seeger is known to all as a folksinger and popular historian of people's movements in the United States. He visited Highlander in the 1940s with Oklahoma songwriter Woody Guthrie. He formed a life-long interest in the school during that visit, and has given support in many ways ever since. It was Pete Seeger who took the song "We Shall Overcome" north in his concerts after learning it from Zilphia Horton on his initial visit to Highlander. He and his wife, Toshi, live in Beacon, New York.

Andrew Young is well known as the recent mayor of Atlanta and the former ambassador to the United Nations. He was closely associated with Highlander in the early 1960s, when he directed the

Citizenship School program inherited from Highlander by the Southern Christian Leadership Conference. He has had a long career in politics, diplomacy, civil rights, and the ministry. Many of his ideas and values grew out of his work in the civil rights movement of the 1960s.

Dorothy Cotton is another veteran of the civil rights movement. Along with Andrew Young, she conducted Citizenship School classes for the Southern Christian Leadership Conference. She worked closely with the SCLC staff on many other projects and has maintained a close connection with the King Center in Atlanta. She has also been on the Highlander Board of Directors for a number of years. She served as Director of Student Activities at Cornell University, and is a dynamic speaker and singer invited to college campuses across the nation. She resides in Ithaca, New York.

Julian Bond is currently teaching history at the University of Virginia and hosting a national television program on contemporary issues. He joined the civil rights movement as a college student in 1960, and was the director of communications for the Student Non-violent Coordinating Committee (SNCC). He came to Highlander during that period for workshops of youthful civil rights activists. In the mid 1960s he was elected to the Georgia State Legislature, and in 1966 was refused his seat because of his opposition to the Vietnam war. A year later the Supreme Court ordered that he be seated.

Studs Terkel is a well-known author and documentor of American stories—particularly those of working people. He has published a number of remarkable books, winning the Pulitzer Prize in 1985 for an oral history of World War II, *The Good War*. He has also hosted a radio program from Chicago for many years. His interest in Highlander began years ago and continues to the present.

John Gaventa is the current director of the Highlander Research and Education Center. He has been a Highlander staff member since 1975. People desiring more information on Highlander's work should contact the center at 1959 Highlander Way, New Market, Tennessee 37820, (615) 933-3443.

Index

A

Abernathy, Ralph D., 224, 234, 312–13, 335
Abrams, Charles, 205
Abzell, Joe, 225
Alabama
  NAACP in, 234–35
Alabama Christian Movement for Human Rights, 235
Alcoa, Tennessee, 55–56
Almanac Singers, 204, 344
Aluminum Company of America, 55
American Federation of Labor (AFL), 126–27
  and Highlander, 263
  textile workers, 122–23
  See also United Textile Workers of America
American Federation of Labor-Congress of Industrial Organizations (AFL-CIO)
  women in, 259
American Plan, 73
American Society for African Culture, 317
American Student Union, 202

Anderson, C. P., 147, 148–49
Appalachia, 371
Armour Company, 152–53
Atlanta Citizens for Constructive Action, 321
Atlanta *Inquirer*, 328
Autoworkers, 147
Avery School, 13–14, 17

B

Baker, Ella, 313, 328, 330
Ballast, George, 356
Barry, Marion, 328, 362
Bennett, L. Roy, 226
Berea College, 70
Bethune, Mary McLeod, 397
Bevel, James, 329
Bidstrup, George, 92
Birdwell, Lige, 112–13, 117
Birmingham, Dave, 220
Black, Charles, 106, 327
Black, Hugo, 135
Black History Month, 391
Black History Week, 375
Blackman, L. A., 246

L

M

N

About the Editor

Eliot Wigginton, who started *Foxfire* magazine with his ninth- and tenth-grade English classes in 1966, still teaches high school in the Appalachian Mountains of North Georgia and, with his students, guides the activities of the Foxfire Fund, Inc. Mr. Wigginton was on the board of the Highlander Center for many years, and has donated the royalties from this book to its continuing work. He lives in Rabun Gap, Georgia.